Louis Blériot

FLIGHT INTO THE XXTH CENTURY

AUSTIN MACAULEY
PUBLISHERS LTD.

A CIP catalogue record for this title is available from the British Library.

ISBN
978 1 84963 517 2 (paperback)
978 1 84963 524 0 (hardback)

www.austinmacauley.com

First Published (2015)
Austin Macauley Publishers Ltd.
25 Canada Square
Canary Wharf
London
E14 5LB

Printed and bound in Great Britain

Contents

Publisher's Note

The real Louis Blériot is an unknown person. For most people he is simply the first man to fly across the Channel in 1909. For others, far less numerous, he was also an aviation industrialist, but never knew in this domain, as much success as certain of his contemporaries.

Louis Blériot was however, in 1919, the world's leading aircraft builder. But the aircraft that he built in unequalled quantities did not carry his name. The name SPAD had been saved from disappearing by Louis Blériot in 1914. The company Blériot Aéronautique designed and built Blériot and SPAD aircraft up till its nationalisation in 1936. If today the European giant EADS conserves the sign Blériot in front of its offices in the Paris suburbs, it is to show everything that the Company owes to Louis Blériot.

The principle characteristic of Blériot aircraft production is the amazing quantity of types of machines, built or simply imagined. To tell the truth, the exact number is not known, for traces of some of them have been lost. But the list of those we possess is a prodigious indication. Between 1910 and 1914 for example, the inventory stands at forty-six different types, of which forty-five were designed and built in seven years, from 1907 to 1914 ... without counting multiple versions or variations. This simple example is a witness to the enormous capacity for work that Louis Blériot possessed. Later, with six design engineers, the creativity of Blériot-Aéronautique never faltered.

Frequently, Blériot-Aéronautique brought out innovations and did much better than its French competitors. Certainly, they were not always successful. In the period in between the wars it happened sometimes that orders were passed to the aircraft companies who knew how to make themselves known to members of the relevant government departments – principle source of orders – without their design office having to show proof of much talent. Louis Blériot detested these practices. Even with an introverted character he often spoke aloud what others dared not say. It was thus that he attracted the hostility of those that in fact he should have courted. And if he pushed his design office so much to imagine new formula, it was also to compensate for the inter

service rivalry of the different Air Ministries. Between the wars France faced a cruel shortage of centralized laboratory research for the benefit for the entire aviation industry. This shortage was being made up a little late in 1939 and was only completed in 1945 with the creation of the Office National de Recherches Aéronautiques, the ONERA. The British, the Germans, the Russians and the Americans had had comparable organisations since at least 1919! Blériot Aéronautique therefore had to supply as much energy to research as it did to the design and fabrication. It was too much for one company alone, no matter how powerful it should be. For Louis Blériot had built a small empire. He was not only a flying pioneer, inventor of aeroplanes; he was also and above all a Captain of Industry. Blériot Aéronautique was his favourite company, but he had already established at the end of the XIXth century, well before his thirtieth birthday, another company Etablissements Louis Blériot. The first catalogues were the fruit of an inventive spirit and hard work. The success and the fortune – without which he would never have known success in aviation – came very rapidly, thanks to the invention and the manufacture of acetylene or electric lighting systems for cars. The headlights of our cars today, we owe them to Louis Blériot. It was he who introduced the word headlight into the vocabulary of the automobile industry. He had to sell off this prosperous activity in the middle 1920s. It was taken over by Ducellier, by one of the ex- directors of the Société des Phares Blériot, Pierre Marchal, and became the famous SEV Marchal, today Valéo.

Weakened by his efforts and by the death of his elder son, Louis Blériot died in 1936. The author, one of his grandsons, has dedicated the major part of his life to preserving the memory and to re-building as much as he can of his grandfather's industrial heritage. He has amassed hundreds of documents, photos, and objects, enough to fill a museum, which he hopes will one day attract the attention of a Town Hall or Local Authority. This book is a reminder of the past work of his grandfather, Louis Blériot. He is happy that in both the Aviation Industry and the Automobile Industry, his work goes on.

Translator's Note

Louis Blériot was a pioneer in the truest sense of the word, we owe an awful lot to the man who crossed the Channel in 1909. Louis Blériot today writes of his grandfather "The real Louis Blériot is an unknown person". This will become apparent to the reader as the story unfolds, page by page. The records, the variety, the sheer quantity of aircraft and projects, the determination to succeed. The man's foresight was amazing. The Louis Blériot Trophy offered in 1930 was not won until ... 1961.

Louis Blériot, grandson, the author of this book has become a firm friend over the past years, in the building of a replica Blériot XI as well as the work on the book. I have seen the dedication that he has for making his grandfather's story available to all. He has the same enthusiasm as his venerable ancestor, the same force of character that was needed to be at the forefront of "Flight into the XXth Century"

His style of writing is fluid, the detail is there for the dedicated historian, the story is there to be simply enjoyed. The task of translating this book was for me an occasion to learn about the history of the beginnings of aviation, to share with the reader the successes and the failures, but above all to pass on the enthusiasm and admiration that I could hear in the words written by grandson for grandfather.

Terry Froggatt
La Baule, July 2015

A portrait of Louis Blériot in his fifties, by the photographer Desgrandes. The photo shows, despite the years, the energetic character of the man, his tenacity, his quiet courage, qualities recognised unanimously by his contemporaries.

Introduction

In 1872, at the time of the birth of Louis Blériot, France was only just beginning to feel the effects of the industrial revolution. Little by little, trains were replacing stagecoaches, and steam boats replacing sailing ships. For the people of this time, Icarus's dream of rising into the air like a bird remained as utopian as it was at the time of ancient Greece. However, in a little over a quarter of a century, technical progress and the inventiveness of man would be such that the automobile, and then aviation would see the light of day, principally in France.

Louis Blériot, even at an early age, believed in science and the improvements that it would bring into daily life. He had a thirst for knowledge and even though he was capable of composing verses in Latin and in Greek, it was the science disciplines which attracted him. But progress was so rapid then that many people were "left behind", as today certain people are by computers. Gas lighting, electricity, the telephone, the phonograph, all appeared within the space of a few years.

Even in his family, Louis Blériot, having become an inventor, met with incomprehension. A little before his exploit of the 25th July 1909, his mother confided in one of her friends, "You know, Louis has become completely crazy, he wants to cross the channel on a kite".

He would know, nevertheless – in no uncertain terms – how to silence the sceptics and the worriers, in giving to France and to the world the first real *'avion'*[1] the Monoplane of the Channel Crossing. Born straight after the war of 1870 where the Army made cavalry charges as at the time of Alexander the Great, Louis Blériot died in 1936 just before the Second World War which saw, amongst other things, the birth of the jet engine and astronautics. His life, despite innumerable difficulties up to which he had to face – or perhaps because of them – is the reflection of an era that saw humanity accomplish the most surprising progress in a period of time unbelievably short.

(1) This name was used only from 1911 onwards, in order to honour Clément Ader who had used it to name one of his machines, the name was initially reserved for military aircraft.

Foreword

In 1922 when I arrived *chez Blériot* in Suresnes, Louis Blériot had been honoured worldwide for his historical success on the 25th July 1909. He later became one of the principle French aircraft builders during the First World War and his efforts allowed his country, thanks to his famous SPAD fighters, to stand victoriously against the Air Forces of Germany. It was in the fine factory of the Quay Gallieni, a model factory for the time, where, very young, I had the chance of joining the Design Office. I found Chief Engineers of great renown, and colleagues, mostly young, attracted by the newness of the specialization, and the enormous future perspectives offered by aviation, behind the leading light which was Louis Blériot. Novice for several years, it was only from 1929 onwards that, as a young manager, promoted with his agreement, I was able to approach him. I appreciated his spirit always directed towards the creation of new aircraft, before even the technical knowledge existed to allow their building. He was totally *Le Patron*, by his presence and his sober elegance, right up to the watch chain across his waistcoat (a white waistcoat in summer), by the precision of timing and the follow up of everything which was made in his factory.

Never one to let things go, he expected a lot of his managers and expected them to have constant authority over their personnel. However, he knew how to show generosity by rewarding efforts. As early as 1929 I received a bonus based on the company turnover; a small sum, but oh! how stimulating. From the factory in Suresnes, came hundreds of fighter aircraft, of all makes. In the design office, there were studies of dozens of aircraft of all categories: training, fighting/combat, public transport, flying boats and amphibians, record breaking machines, certain of these were built and gave prestigious results for France. But ... his greatest hope was to one day produce a flying boat to cross the North Atlantic, offering passengers a high degree of comfort. He left us too soon to build it. One of the last sketches that we did together was the transformation of a passenger seat into a couchette. Nothing was forgotten! If the activity of the factory knew the highs and lows of this period of uncertainty which was the "between the wars", Louis Blériot was always, even at the worst moment of the strikes of 1936, unanimously respected by his personnel.

André Paulin,
Ex Head of the Design Office of Blériot-Aéronautique

This book is dedicated to the memory of the test pilots from the House of Blériot who gave their lives so that aviation might progress. From left to right and top to bottom: Bizot, Casale, Lemartin, Massotte, Desparmets, Perreyon, Deroye.

Author's Acknowledgements

The author wishes, through this book, to render homage, as impartial as possible, to his grandfather. He does not boast of believing that he has totally reached this aim, in that the admiration that he has for his grandfather could unconsciously influence him and hopes that the reader will not hold this against him. He wishes equally to warn the reader against the possible errors in the dimensions of the aircraft, above all for the period 1910-1914, during which, in a very short time, a large number of different models were built or planned. In the absence of archives of the Blériot factory – these having been destroyed in June 1940 – it has been very difficult – even impossible, to identify certain types and above all to make a choice in the available information, often contradictory. The author has, each time, retained those figures which seemed to him to be the most likely amongst those nearest to the event, but has no pretension to infallibility.

The author thanks Mr Jean Liron for his collaboration on the second half of this book, Mr André Paulin for his preface and his precious souvenirs of the factory of Suresnes between 1922 and 1936. Messrs Jean Devaux, Michel Marani and Michel Bénichou for proof reading the manuscript, the counselling and the documentation that they supplied. The Bibliotheque Nationale and in particular Mme. Le Pavec. The Musée de l'Air, especially Messrs Jean–Yves Lorant, Stéphane Nicolaou and Joël Petit of the documentation department, Messrs Gilbert Deloisy and Roger Marvie of the photographic department. The historical department of the Armée de l'Air and its head, General Robineau. The Institut National de La Propriété Industrielle (INPI) of Paris and Rennes, in particular M. Henri Soumireu-Lartigue and Mme. Nicole Guillemot for their assistance in the research into the patents filed by Louis Blériot. Mr Andrew Renwick, the photograph curator of the Royal Air Force Museum. The Brooklands Museum and its founder Sir Peter Masefield, as well as Mr Michael Goodall. The *Daily Mail* newspaper of London. The department store, Selfridges of London, and in particular Mr David Bailey. M. Jean-Louis Ardoin Saint Amand, notably for his information about the airfield of La Croix–d'Hins. M. Bernard Cassagne for the documentation concerning the land and the factory of Tartifume. Mr James H. Rowe, Mr and Mrs David M. Barker for their help concerning the factory in Addlestone, Mr T. J. Ruffell of GEC-Marconi, current director of the factory in Addlestone. Mr Peter Richley for the research that he was happy to do in England, in particular on the Blériot Whippet. Mr J. A. Davidson and M. Roger Berthier ex-director of the Suresnes factory of Aérospatiale, for his help concerning the evolution of the ex-Blériot factory since 1945. M. Jean-Emile Cailliez, Mrs Jennifer Dean, M. Pierre Cortet, M. Michel Galand, M. René Lemaire, M. Christian–Henry Tavard and M. and Mme. Yves Deburghgraeve for their participation in the laying out of the manuscript. Messrs Benoît Boutin, Claude Ginsburger and Olivier Berger for their efforts to make the old plans of the factory readable.

Louis Blériot at home towards the end of his life, poses in front of a full size ivory eagle. We do not know if he bought it or he received this magnificent work of art as a gift. It was made in the imperial workshops of Japan; it stands on the root of a rare tree.

Origins, Childhood, Adolescence, Education

Louis Blériot was born on the 1ˢᵗ July 1872 at Cambrai, into an old family of the region. He was the descendant of a long line of Louis Blériots. His ancestors in olden times were called Blériot du Verguier, from the name of a village in the department of the Aisne, where the family had its origins. The house where he was born was the old hotel Cotteau de Simencourt, at 13b rue de L'Arbre-à-Poires, (since re-named rue Sadi–Carnot) this was the building to which King Louis XVIII came on his return from England at the time of the restoration; it was unfortunately destroyed during the First World War. Louis had two brothers, Michel and André and two sisters, Madeleine and Marthe, who all emigrated to America. Very early he felt attracted by the disciplines of science. Like many adolescents of this second half of the nineteeenth century, he was fascinated by the technical progress which finally allowed man to rise above his muscular limits (or those of the horse) On the 22ⁿᵈ November 1886, Louis Blériot wrote in a letter to his mother:

> *Oui, je vois combien la science est nécessaire à l'homme pour se créer une position quelque peu honorable. Eh bien, cette science je l'acquerrai par mon travail.*
>
> *Louis Blériot*

Yes, I see how much science is necessary to man in order to create a position of little honour. Ah well, this science, I will acquire it by my work.

The young Louis started his studies at the Institut Notre-Dame. He went then to the Lycée of Amiens, then to the Collège Sainte-Barbe in Paris, where he prepared the entrance exam to the Ecole Centrale des Arts et Manufactures. He was admitted to the class of 1895.

It seems that from this time onwards he was contaminated by the virus of what was going to become aviation, it was thus that he confided later to the journalist Jacques Mortane:

> *Already when I was at Ecole Centrale I felt myself attracted by the heavier-than-air, but it was better to keep quiet if I did not want to pass for someone crazy.*

On leaving the Ecole Centrale, Louis Blériot was twenty-three years old. He was fairly tall, brown hair, a matt complexion, brown sombre eyes, an aquiline nose and a moustache – as one wore at that time – which made him look like a chieftain of Ancient Gaul. He held himself upright and only smiled on rare occasions, which served to accentuate the impression of severity emanating from him. But the most remarkable feature in him was his regard, a piercing look, as if he had an internal fire. Raised in the respect of religious principles, Louis Blériot was a fervent Catholic, and as most of the French population at that time, profoundly patriotic.

Above: Louis Blériot age about twelve, with a confident air.

Left: The words he wrote on the 22nd November 1886 at the age of 14, showing a certain determination.

Top left: Louis Blériot at the time of receiving his diploma from the *Ecole Centrale des Arts et Manufactures* in Paris.

Bottom left: The Hotel Cotteau de Simoncourt, in Cambrai, his maternal home.

Right, from top to bottom: The Blériots who had founded a weaving company in Cambrai: Cosme Louis Joseph Blériot (1814-1882), Charlotte Sophie Blériot, née Servais (1823-1890), his grandparents. Louis Charles Pierre Alexandre Blériot (1845-1936), Clémence Marie Eugénie Blériot, née Candeliez (1850-1935), his parents.

I: Origins, Childhood, Adolescence, Education

2

Blériot Lamps

LOUIS BLÉRIOT, INDUSTRIALIST AND DESIGNER

Louis Blériot at his work table in 1902. Gifted with a prodigious capacity for work, the young *'Centrale'* would never stop imagining new inventions, at any time, day or night, in a notebook that never left his side.

After obtaining his diploma of Engineer, 'Arts et Manufactures' (class of 1895), Louis Blériot completed his military service as First Lieutenant of the 24th Artillery Regiment in Tarbes, and then joined the Baguès Company, rue des Francs-Bourgeois in Paris, an electrical factory, where the young engineer stayed only a few months, before founding a company manufacturing acetylene lamps and lanterns for automobiles, in 1897. Very quickly the Louis Blériot Company realised a rapid development, due much to the efficiency of the process – invented by Blériot – of lighting by acetylene for automobiles, and to the quality of the finish of their products. It is further to him that we owe the application of the term 'light' to the automobile; before then the term applied only to coastal lights, designed for maritime navigation. The factory was situated in Paris, 12 rue Henri–Chevreau. The repair workshops and the saleroom, initially at 41 rue Richelieu, were transferred in 1902 to 14-16, rue Duret.

Louis Blériot started being interested in automobiles being powered by a steam turbine, this was his first patent in 1897, then the following year, at a time when electricity was little known - the light bulb was only 20 years old - he invented a process for the generation of acetylene gas to feed boilers for the heating of homes. Shown above are two models of generators, the one on the left could supply enough gas for twenty five burners in the same building. His catalogue contained all sorts of heating systems - including portable heaters - and lighting systems for cinemas or public lighting, the lanterns containing their own generators. Thus when the lights on cars became obligatory, he proposed acetylene lamps where the generator could be placed in the boot of the car or even under the mud guard.

Louis Blériot's laboratory or workshop, rue Duret in 1902. On the left, the dark cylindrical object, resting on a tripod, is a Blériot acetylene generator; at the rear, a milling machine and its overhead pulley system.

Numerous luxurious cars of the time were thus equipped with Blériot lamps, Delaunay-Belleville, de Dion-Bouton, Panhard and Levassor, and Mors. At this dawn of the twentieth century, the quasi-totally of automobiles were delivered with the chassis bare. It was up to the owner to have the coachwork built on the chassis, according to his tastes, by the coachbuilder of his choice, and to purchase the accessories to be fitted.

These accessories were mounted on forks or lugs and fixed by butterfly nuts so as to make them easily removable, because in view of their price (up to 400 gold francs for a top-of-the-range lamp) it was highly imprudent to leave them on the vehicle when left stationed in the street for the night.

Progressively, the range proposed by Louis Blériot was extended, he made lanterns, acetylene generators, mechani-

cal klaxons, dashboard instruments and even heating systems, working with either the water from the engine, or with the exhaust gasses. For a long time these accessories were the only items bringing warmth to the inside of the car, other than hot water bottles and heated bricks on which passengers rested their feet, which had a relative efficiency and would be in any case only temporary.

His goods being highly appreciated on the other side of the Channel, he opened a branch in London in 1902, Blériot Limited, whose main office was initially at 54, then at 57-59 Long Acre, London, WC. The factory was also in London, in Catesby Street. The manager of Blériot Limited, Norbert Chéreau, stayed in place up to 1926, the date of the ceasing of activities of Louis Blériot in England. After the lamps, the firm produced aircraft, then light cars.

At the beginning of the XXth century, the car was a luxury item, as were the Blériot accessories (lights, heaters, klaxons). Blériot opened a shop in London as early as 1899 (on the left), which soon published its own catalogue (cover shown below).

In France, Louis Blériot published a colour catalogue which grew thicker every year. The list of clients named in there read like a *Who's Who* of the nobility: a few kings and princes, including the German Emperor. The industrial activity of Louis Blériot was very close to that of the jewellery trade - very profitable.

The Paris shop of Louis Blériot was situated in rue Duret, not far from the Avenue de la Grande Armee, in the centre of the suburbs where the 'high society' lived.

A Renault 10 hp delivery van belonging to the Blériot company, which very rapidly specialised in car lighting. The van is obviously fitted with Blériot acetylene lamps, similar to those show in one of his earliest catalogues (shown above). The lights were adapted no only to each type of vehicle, but also each type of use (town or country).

These three publicity posters, each of a different period, showed the concern of Louis Blériot to find a remarkable name for his products. At first side lights and projectors (below, 1902), then lamps (opposite, in 1905), then the word 'headlight' (below, right) in a document from 1913 for electric lights powered by the Phi magneto which he invented.

Louis Blériot, if he had a fine sense for publicity for his name, he was very discreet concerning everything that touched his private family life.

The first property acquired by Louis Blériot in 1901, Boulevard Maillot in Paris. He was also a fine manager, and knew best how to manage his interests to conserve his independence.

From its creation up to the First World War, the Louis Blériot Company occupied an important place in its domain. The first company specializing in the construction of lighting equipment for automobiles, during all this time the company maintained itself in the forefront of technical progress:

1897 Invention of acetylene generators

1898 Invention of auto generating lamps

1900 Invention of lamps with Fresnel lenses

1903 Invention of reflector lamps.

1904 Invention of multiple element batteries.

1905 Invention of insulated flame lamps.

1906 Invention of lamps oxy-petrol.

1909 Invention of Phi dynamos.

1910 Invention of Dynamo Regulator.

At the 'Salon de l'Automobile' in 1913-1914, Blériot lamps were fitted to one hundred and twenty-seven cars, of which seventy-seven were electric lamps (as against eighty-four and forty-six for his nearest competitor) After 1918, in order to adapt to the current market, production was concentrated on fewer models, of which the pear shaped Blériot lamp was the most well known. In 1926, the company, Louis Blériot S.A. was bought by the Ducellier Company.

The companies worked so well that when he got married in 1901, Louis Blériot, at twenty- nine years old, was already a prosperous industrial magnate, to whom his company brought in annually 60,000 gold francs. The wedding was held at Bagneres–de–Bigorre, from where his young wife Alicia Védère came.

She was very young, only just eighteen years old. Louis met her the previous year in the restaurant "Le Boeuf à la Mode" in Paris where she had come accompanied by her parents to visit the *Exposition Universelle.* Instantaneously seduced, as soon as he reached home he declared to his mother, *I have seen a young girl today, I am going to marry her, or I will never marry.*

The young couple moved into Boulevard Maillot in Neuilly-sur-Seine. They had six children, three boys, the eldest Louis – of course – Marcel, Jean, and three daughters, Simone, Ginette and Nelly. Alicia Blériot complemented her husband admirably, where Blériot was taciturn, spoke very little and was rather pessimistic, his wife in the enthusiasm of her youth was able to rise above her worries, to encourage him to persevere in his research. However, during this first decade of the twentieth century, which had just opened, she had plenty of occasions to worry for the life of her husband or for the household finances. But, naturally happy and full of admiration for her husband, she never doubted even in the darkest moments that he would not end up triumphing over the difficulties which he faced, or would not arrive at the goals which he fixed himself.

Husband, and father of a family, at the head of a company already prosperous, Blériot distinguished himself from the other pioneers of aviation, younger than him and still bachelors, by his image of respectability which he knew how to exploit. Excellent engineer and manager, he was conscious of the importance of publicity and public relations, but sometimes failed to be supple in his commercial negotiations. After 1909, his friend Alfred Leblanc seconded him efficiently in this domain.

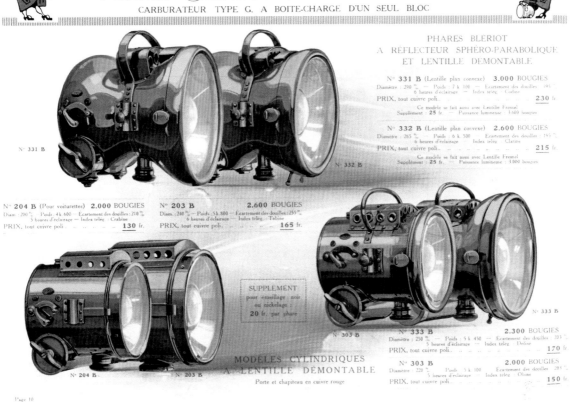

PHARES BLÉRIOT
A RÉFLECTEUR SPHÉRO-PARABOLIQUE
ET LENTILLE DÉMONTABLE

N° **331 B** (Lentille plan convexe) **3.000** BOUGIES
Diamètre : 290 ⁿⁿ — Poids : 7 k 100 — Ecartement des douilles : 195 ⁿⁿ
6 heures d'éclairage — Index télég : Codier
PRIX, tout cuivre poli . . . . **230** fr

Ce modèle se fait aussi avec Lentille Fresnel
Supplément : **25** fr . . . . Puissance lumineuse : 3.000 bougies

N° **332 B** (Lentille plan convexe) **2.600** BOUGIES
Diamètre : 265 ⁿⁿ — Poids : 6 k 500 — Ecartement des douilles : 195 ⁿⁿ
6 heures d'éclairage — Index télég : Clarine
PRIX, tout cuivre poli . . . . **215** fr

Ce modèle se fait aussi avec Lentille Fresnel
Supplément : **25** fr . . . . Puissance lumineuse : 3.000 bougies

N° **331 B**

N° **332 B**

N° **204 B** (Pour voiturettes) **2.000** BOUGIES
Diam :200 ⁿⁿ — Poids : 4 k 600 — Ecartement des douilles :210 ⁿⁿ
5 heures d'éclairage — Index télég : Crabine
PRIX, tout cuivre poli . . . . **130** fr.

N° **203 B**   **2.600** BOUGIES
Diam :240 ⁿⁿ — Poids : 5 k 800 — Ecartement des douilles :255 ⁿⁿ
6 heures d'éclairage — Index télég : Tsbine
PRIX, tout cuivre poli . . . . **165** fr.

SUPPLEMENT
pour émaillage noir
ou nickelage :
20 fr. par phare.

N° **303 B**

N° **333 B**

N° **333 B**   **2.300** BOUGIES
Diamètre : 250 ⁿⁿ — Poids : 5 k 450 — Ecartement des douilles : 203 ⁿⁿ
6 heures d'éclairage — Index télég : Doline
PRIX, tout cuivre poli . . . . **170** fr.

N° **303 B**   **2.000** BOUGIES
Diamètre : 220 ⁿⁿ — Poids : 5 k 100 — Ecartement des douilles : 201 ⁿⁿ
5 heures d'éclairage — Index télég : Oline
PRIX, tout cuivre poli . . . . **150** fr.

MODÈLES CYLINDRIQUES
A LENTILLE DÉMONTABLE
Porte et chapiteau en cuivre rouge

N° **204 B**

N° **203 B**

Page 10

Extracts from the catalogue 1914. Above for acetylene lamps, below for klaxons. The same catalogue showed similar electrical products and a large variety of small luminous accessories.

UN QUART DE TOUR DE MANIVELLE SUFFIT

*pour produire un son équivalent à celui du plus puissant
Klaxon électrique. D'un maniement facile, le parfait fonc-
tionnement de "KLAXON MÉCANIQUE BLÉRIOT"
ne dépend ni de la solidité d'une transmission, ni du
bon état des accumulateurs*

FONCTIONNE
A LA MAIN

SANS
ACCUMULATEURS

SANS
TRANSMISSION

C'EST
L'AVERTISSEUR

LE PLUS PUISSANT
LE PLUS PRATIQUE
LE PLUS FIDÈLE

DIAPHRAGMES SPÉCIAUX DE GRAND DIAMÈTRE, TRÈS SONORES ET EXTRA-RÉSISTANTS
Nouveau réglage par excentrique — *Corps en aluminium émaillé*

MODÈLE SPÉCIAL AVEC SUPPORT TOURNANT
POUR CANOT

Pavillon nickel : SUPPLEMENT **10** fr

N° **1**   AVEC GRAND PAVILLON EXTRA-PUISSANT
Dimensions extrêmes : 0ⁿ350 — Poids : 2 k 650
Index télég : Mécaniklax
PRIX, cuivre poli ou émaille noir . . . . . **130** fr

N° **2**   AVEC PETIT PAVILLON
Dimensions extrêmes : 0ⁿ260 — Poids : 2 k 300
Index télég : Petincklax
PRIX, cuivre poli ou émaille noir . . . . . **120** fr

N° **3**   AVEC GRAND PAVILLON
Dimensions extrêmes : 0ⁿ350 — Poids, avec support : 3 k 350
Index télég : Canoncklax
PRIX, cuivre poli ou émaille noir . . . . . **155** fr

Page 23

3

The Beginnings in Aviation

FROM THE BLÉRIOT I TO THE BLÉRIOT XII. FEELING HIS WAY

The Blériot I

Even before his marriage, Blériot started his research into aviation. In 1900 inspired by the flight of birds, he made a small machine with beating wings which he baptised *Ornithoptère*. It was a small machine purely experimental. It was not designed to be piloted, driven by a light-weight 2hp engine fuelled by carbonic acid, it had a wing span of 1.5m and weighed 10kg. The wings, slightly convex had a strong skeleton and a very dense array of flying wires fixed to a vertical mast in the centre of each wing. The wings were equipped with valves, which opened to let the air pass when the wings were raised and closed when the wings were lowered. This model having flown with success in January 1901, Blériot started the construction of a full size *Ornithoptère,* fitted with an engine of 100 hp. Despite the rigidity of their structure, the wings did not resist the brutal action of the carbonic acid engine.

Three of these engines exploded consecutively, Blériot stopped the trials of his "flying machine" in 1903. He recognised here a first set-back, which would be followed by many others. However, he did not give up. He believed in the notion of "aerial locomotion" and was determined to become, whatever the cost, one of the first men to fly. He believed that he had jumped stages, that before building a motor-powered flying machine he must study, amongst other things, the problems of lift and penetration through the air. Louis Blériot was part of a small group of enthusiasts of heavier-than-air, who organised themselves as early as 1905 at the Aéro-Club de France. These men were at that time a small minority in relation to those of the lighter-than-air and a certain rivalry was felt within the Aéro-Club, in as much as, that against the performance of the dirigibles, the "aéroplanists" did not have a lot to offer.

However, the lawyer and inventor Ernest Archdeacon, president of the Commission d'Aviation de l'Aéro-Club de France, built a small glider at the Military establishment of Chalais–Meudon, from plans supplied by Octave Chanute. This establishment, managed by Colonel Renard, would be the true cradle of French military aviation. Once the glider was finished, Archdeacon had to find a pilot to fly it. Colonel Renard recommended Gabriel Voisin to him, who, with his brother Charles already had a certain experience of glider flights. At first, Archdeacon employed him as chauffeur, then gaining confidence in Voisin, accepted to authorise him to fly his machine. After conclusive trials on the dunes at Berck, on Easter Day 1904, Voisin proposed to Archdeacon, the construction, from his plans, of a second glider designed to be pulled by an automobile.

I wanted, he said later, *to know with precision the power of a future engine, and only the reading of the traction coinciding with the reading of the speed on board the glider could give us an exact figure.*

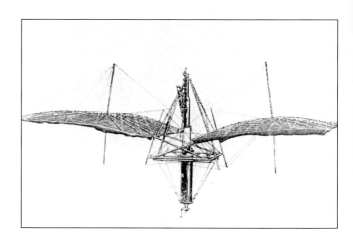

This is the only known image of the scale model Experimental Blériot Ornithoper, or the Blériot I

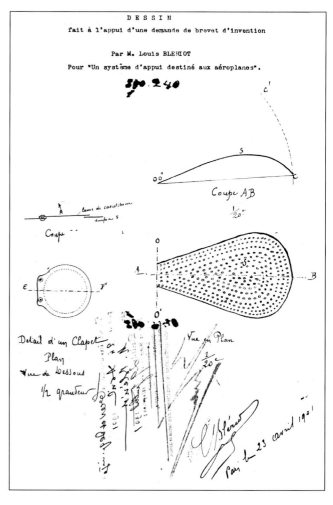

Paris, 23 April 1901, sketch by Louis Blériot for the filing of a patent for beating wings with valves which open when the wing rises and close when it descends

Archdeacon after a few days of reflection gave his agreement, and in order to cover new expenses, founded with a few friends, Messrs De Vogüé, Girardet, Turgan, Mas and Loyel, the Syndicat d'Aviation, of which he became the President.

Voisin was named engineer with a salary of 190 francs per month. He built his machine in the Turgan workshops in Levallois and then in the Etabilssements Astra, managed by Edouard Surcouf, in Billancourt. Archdeacon asked him then to equip the Berck glider to carry out traction trials. The machine was tried on the 26th March 1905 on the parade fields of Issy-les-Moulineaux, where this was their first use as an airfield. The glider, prudently loaded with a sack of 50kg of gravel in place of the pilot, took off, pulled by Archdeacon's car.

The machine would have been between eight or ten metres, wrote Voisin, *when the tail fins came away from the longerons. The glider suddenly lurched, then hit the ground ... Archdeacon who was impressed by the accident at Issy-les-Moulineaux proposed to me to think about trials on the Seine.*

Voisin therefore fitted his gilder with floats. The work was carried out at the Etabilssements Astra, then at n° 4 rue de la Ferme in Billancourt, in a workshop rented by Surcouf. The glider was only finished in June 1905. It was a double biplane – main wings and tail wings. Bulkheads joined the upper and lower wings front and rear. The glider was undoubtedly inspired by the cellular kites designed by the Australian Hargrave and which as adolescence Charles and Gabriel Voisin had built a very large example. The machine was equipped with an elevator at the front. It was ten metres long with a ten metre span. The wing area was 61m² (37.4m² for the wings, 20.6m² for the tail plane and 3m² for the elevator). It rested on two floats made of varnished cloth, seven metres long, 30cm wide and 30cm deep. Its empty weight was 220 kg.

The trials were finally held on the Seine on the 8th June 1905, between the bridge at Billancourt and the bridge at Sèvres, pulled by the *Rapière,* a racing boat powered by a Panhard engine of 150hp. The glider on floats, piloted by Voisin, rose rapidly to more than fifteen metres high, flew for about 600m and landed on the water without difficulty. The dynamometer fixed on the cable, read by Archdeacon and the anemometer read by Voisin, indicated an average power of 28hp.[1] Amongst the enthusiastic spectators were Alberto Santos-Dumont and Louis Blériot. From this day on, Santos-Dumont, who had never been interested in aviation, abandoned the lighter-than-air, to concentrate his energies on the conception of a machine which would find glory the following year, under the name of 14-bis. As for Blériot, he immediately ordered from Voisin a hydro-glider, identical to the one he had just seen tried with such success.

The Blériot II

The following day, Blériot visited Voisin in his modest office in the rue de la Ferme. He wanted a few modifications on his machine in relation to the Archdeacon glider, he asked notably for Voisin to make the lower wings shorter than the upper wings (aircraft with this characteristic would later be called Sesquiplane) and to adopt for all the surfaces (wings and tail plane) a camber of one-tenth the chord. Voisin indicated to him, from his previous experiences, that this would make the machine transversally unstable, Blériot however, maintained his position.

(1) However at the start of a second trial, the tow rope broke, the aircraft dived and burst its floats.

This publicity of 1905 shows the 'hand' of Louis Blériot

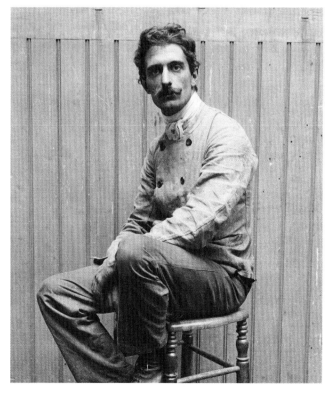

Gabriel Voisin towards 1909. Self-taught mechanic, not very methodical, 'wavering', he was the very opposite of Blériot.

The Blériot-Voisin, or Blériot on the Seine, prepared for towing by the motorboat *'La Rapière'* as its driving power. The Seine offered the advantage of a large flat surface without obstacles, and where it was thought that a crash would be less painful than on land.

The Blériot II was finished on the 18th July 1905. The wing span was 7m, the wing area was 29m². The distance between the wings was 1.5m.

After having carried out a successful trial of the machine belonging to the Syndicat d'Aviation, still on the river Seine, Voisin climbed aboard the machine belonging to Blériot. The brutal starting of the tug – the *Antoinette* belonging to Levavasseur – made him leave the water almost instantaneously. The machine started to roll from one side to the other then flipped over and dived into the water. Voisin, stuck in a tangle of debris escaped drowning by a hair's breadth and swam to one of the boats which was coming to help him. The flight had lasted thirty seconds over a distance of roughly 180m. At the end of the afternoon, the machine was put back onto his floats and taken out of the water.

The Blériot III

Louis Peyret ready to start up the engine on the Bleriot III

A few days after these harrowing trials, Blériot visited Voisin, without warning, in his bachelor flat in the Passage Dantzig, and proposed to him straight away an association for the study and construction of flying machines. Voisin accepted readily, in

that Blériot planned to take over the buildings in the rue de la Ferme in which there was a flat where he could live. He therefore abandoned Archdeacon and his Syndicat d'Aviation, and three days later the company Blériot–Voisin, the first ever Aviation Company, started its activities.

In his book, *Mes 10 000 cerfs-volants,* Gabriel Voisin wrote of this period when Louis Blériot came to rue de la Ferme as soon as he had a free moment.

The hours that we spent together were hours of happiness. After a short time of intimate collaboration, Louis Blériot said to me one day, 'My dear Voisin, it is here that I spend the best moments of my life.' I felt too foolish to reply but he saw in my eyes that I also, in his company that I too spent the best moments of my life. One evening my friend's car came to take him home as usual, but that day Mme Blériot came to fetch her husband. I had always feared this moment. In a history book that I had read when in the Lycée, a sketch condensed the life of Bernard Palissy. He could be seen on the left of the picture pushing the last debris of a piece of furniture of the Middle Ages into a furnace. On the right, Mme Palissy her feet in clogs, windswept hair, pointed nose, pointed an avenging finger towards her husband. Perhaps Mme Blériot also had a pointed nose? I was wrong, I saw entering the office a young woman so pretty, so fresh, so happy, so natural that the office lit up.

'It is therefore you, Monsieur,' she says to me, 'who is taking my husband? From now on I will come and fetch him each evening; unless I do, he will finish sleeping here!' I defended myself as best as I could and Mme Blériot accepted to be seated for an instant. How distant she was from Mme Palissy! Everything about her breathed confidence. Mme Blériot never said for example, 'My husband has a lot of confidence in his next machine.' She said, 'Louis is finishing a machine with which he will fly at one hundred kilometres per hour'.

On Lake Enghein, and in the rain, the Bleriot III fitted with two Bleriot acetylene lamps (model shown here). Bleriot bent the blades of the propellers forward, perhaps to reduce the torque effect.

But Blériot and Voisin both had a strong personality and fixed ideas. Despite their common passion many things separated them, Blériot was out-going but Voisin would not bend even though it was Blériot who was supplying the finance. Voisin was imaginative but not very audacious, Blériot was firm in his conceptions but lacked experience, Blériot was methodical and Voisin bohemian ... The climate of their association – cordial at the beginning – started to deteriorate when Blériot announced his intention to build a flying machine equipped with two cylindrical wings fitted in tandem. Voisin was totally opposed to this project which did not seem viable to him, he tried to dissuade Blériot. Finally, Blériot accepted that the circular wings should become elliptic.

The power plant of the Bleriot III, designed by Louis Bleriot with two V7 Antoinette engines of 25 hp. Before buying into the Antoinette Company, in a letter to the co-founder, Léon Levavasseur, Louis Bleriot made out a long list of faults, both in design and manufacture, that he had found on these capricious engines.

The problem of the engine was also the occasion for discussions. This time Voisin accepted Blériot's choice, it was the best performing engine of the time, an eight-cylinder Antoinette of 24hp, fitted in the centre of the front nacelle driving two, contra-rotating propellers via a complex transmission weighing 110kg (for a total weight of the machine of 400kg). Blériot also convinced his associate to replace the shell floats of the previous model by a type of skids, on which were fixed inflatable rubber sacks.

In the spring of 1906, the construction of the Blériot III was completed. Its elliptical wings had a flying surface of 60m². The framework, in ash, was covered with varnished silk. Two movable, connected flaps were installed horizontally in the front cell, as a type of elevator. A vertical panel was fitted to the centre of the rear cell. There was no rudder, simply two ailerons installed in the forward ellipse, from one side to the other of the cockpit. The machine was equipped with three pairs of floats (two at the front, one at the rear) two oval Blériot lamps were fixed to the central struts of the leading edge, to be able to carry out trials very early in the morning or very late at night, the two associates hoping thus, to benefit from atmospheric conditions more favourable than during the day.

At the end of the month of May, the flying machine was taken to the lake at Enghien for trials. Alas, these were totally unproductive, the Blériot III, too heavy, refused obstinately to leave the surface of the lake.

The Blériot IV

Making a concession to Voisin, Blériot decided to replace the forward ellipse by a structure similar to that of Archdeacon's glider, two strutted wings of equal dimensions and of slight camber, joined by two vertical panels. They were 10.5m span and 47m² wing area. As on the Blériot III, the elevator was two flaps joined together, installed well in front of the front wings. They were each 3.4m long and 0.8m wide, giving a surface of 5.0m², which, with the 26m² of the rear ellipse, the total surface of the machine was raised to 78.5m². Ailerons were fixed to the wing struts at half distance of the trailing edges, and a rudder was installed behind the vertical panel of the rear ellipse.

The failure of the Bleriot III made Bleriot give in to Voisin in adopting a rectangular wing form at the front. The floats in inflated canvas were also abandoned in favour of those similar to the Type II. The Type IV seems to be fitted with controls in three axes, pitch, yaw and roll.

Two Antoinette engines[1] of 24hp drove two contra-rotating pusher propellers, three layers of crossed Mahogany and riveted, turning at 600rpm. They had a 2m diameter with a 2m pitch, each of them driven independently by an engine. The engine group was fitted to two beams, which were in turn fixed to two consoles to the rear of the main wings. The structure in white pine was reinforced by plates in aluminium. The empty weight of the Blériot IV was 430 kg. Mounted on shell floats as on the Blériot II, it was tried on the lake at Enghein, several attempts on the 12th and 18th October 1906, the Blériot IV ran across the surface of the water reaching the speed of 30kph but would not take off. To try and increase the speed, the machine was pulled by a high-speed winch from the bank, but without any more success. Blériot and Voisin had foreseen that they may only be able to take off thanks to a strong facing wind, which did not materialise that day. Returning to Billancourt, the two associates agreed together

(1) From May 1906, Blériot was Vice President of the Board of Directors of the Antoinette Engine Company.

to fit the machine with wheels, with the view to land trials on the Bagatelle lawns.

Situated between the Bois de Boulogne and the Seine, the domain of Bagatelle belonged to a brother of Louis XVI the Comte d'Artois (future Charles X) which was built following a bet with Marie-Antoinette; it was a beautiful small château erected in a record time of sixty-six days. Below the château was a large parade field, which was placed at the disposition of the pilots. The machine was therefore fitted on three wheels, two in front very wide apart, equipped with long V shaped springs, the apex facing forward, the rear wheel under the rear ellipse, level with the leading edge. On the 12th November, the Blériot IV, thus transformed, became the IV-bis taxied on the lawn of the Bagatelle. A mechanic, Louis Peyret was in the pilot's seat. He was busy finding the best setting for the engine synchronisation when the machine hit a stone, thus out of balance the machine broke in two going over a ditch. The front wing was broken in the centre, the rear collapsed.

The Bleriot IV bis runs along in a cloud of blue smoke, on the lawn at La Bagatelle, 12th November 1906. Shortly afterwards the plane broke in two. It was on the same spot that Alberto Santos-Dumont succeeded in taking off in his 14bis.

After considering the re-building of the Blériot IV-*bis* using an Antoinette engine of 50hp in place of the two at 24hp,[2] Blériot and Voisin finally decided not to follow through their research on this model.

This new set-back led to the dissolution of their association. The same day in front of them, and in front of an electrified crowd, Santos-Dumont carried out a flight on his 14-bis, a flight of 220 metres in 21 and 1/5th seconds at an altitude of 4 or 5 metres, thus winning the 1500 franc prize from the Aéro-Club, for the first flight of more than 100 metres. This rich Brazilian of French origin, very popular in Paris, had succeeded in his first flight on the 13th September, with the same 14 bis. On the 23rd October he had cleared 50m and took the Archdeacon Cup for the first flight of more than 25m. On this 12th November he was the hero of the day. The 14-bis was a rear engine biplane, powered first by an Antoinette of 24hp, then later 50hp, it's wings were made up of large cloth boxes in an open V of 52m² of surface. At the front, a small movable unit controlled the elevator and the direction. It weighed 300kg. For Blériot it was a revelation. The fact that having seen a man fly by his own means, reinforced his determination to "raise himself into the air".

Blériot and Voisin separated, Voisin remained at rue de la Ferme. His brother Charles, returning from military service, came to help him and formed with him a new association – Les Frères Voisin – a combination which would know a much more favourable destiny. Blériot opened a new workshop, Boulevard Victor Hugo in Neuilly. The workshop was not very big, Blériot could not build more than two machines at a time. The design office was in a mansard above the workshop.

Around Louis Peyret, an ex-mechanic of Blériot-Voisin, promoted to workshop foreman, and who would later become himself a builder, Blériot, would in a very short time build up a remarkable team. As early as January 1907, he employed Louis Paragot, called "Petit Louis", who, at fourteen years old became the first ever aviation apprentice, devoted body and soul to his patron, he would never leave Blériot. Julien Mamet came next. He was a specialist in metalwork, he would be in charge of the engines. Previously a foreman in the automobile industry, Alfred Bertrand, the oldest member of the team, was started on to supervise the construction. A little later, Pelletier was started on, a carpenter, deaf and stuttering, of extraordinary skill, notably for the construction of warping wings. Later, a few other men joined the team. It is from this time on that this little group of multiple competences would give a concrete form to Blériot's conceptions.

The Blériot V

The work started on the first project of the new firm Louis Blériot Ingénieur E.C.P. Recherche Aéronautique The Blériot V was christened the *Canard*. In effect, the form of the wings and the fuselage, slightly fuller towards the rear and then streamlined towards the front, gave it a certain resemblance to this aquatic bird. It was, like the 14-bis of Santos-Dumont that Blériot saw flying at Bagatelle, a rear engined machine driving a pusher propeller, but the similarity stopped there. As much as the 14-bis had an appearance which today seems archaic, then Blériot's *Canard* already resembled a modern machine – if you make an exception of the direction of flight.

(2) *L'Aérophile* of December 1906, even announced the installation of a 50hp Antoinette on the Blériot IV

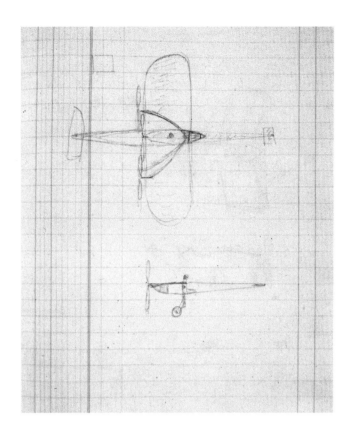

Of preliminary studies by Louis Bleriot there remain only a few rare sketches. Above, on a page from an accounts ledger, two sketches concerning the Type V, one version with two pusher propellers.

Below, 'Study of a seaplane of 100 hp', and the connecting of the two 50 hp Antoinette engines in a push-pull configuration. The power of the engines leads to thinking that the design could not be before the end of 1906.

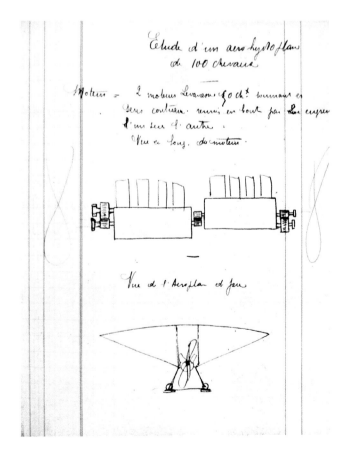

The type V under construction, Boulevard Victor-Hugo, at Neuilly. Louis Bleriot forced himself to build light and solid.

The Bleriot V at Bagatelle, a large lawn in the *bois de Boulogne*, promoted to airfield status by Alberto Santos-Dumont

Louis Bleriot climbing onboard his type V. Like preceding bi-planes, the monoplane was still inspired by that which was known of the Wright bi-plane with its pusher propeller, and its elevator and rudder to the front.

This was only the second monoplane in history. It was preceded only by the gliders of Lilienthal and Pilcher, and one aeroplane, that of Léon Levavasseur which never flew. It was equipped with an Antoinette engine of 24hp, the square section fuselage was made up of a wooden frame supported and criss-crossed by steel wires. The rear section was covered by a sheath of copper. It was 7m long, the four faces of the fuselage were covered with varnished silk in panels, which were removable thanks to press buttons. The cockpit was situated just in front of the engine, in line with the wings. Here, the fuselage was wider corresponding to the position of the pilot's seat. The wings had a very special form which would give the machine its nick-name of *Feuille d'Erable* (the Maple Leaf) they had their tips raised and re-curved towards the rear. Built of a light framework of wood, they were covered with varnished reinforced paper.

The machine had a wing span of 7.08m and a surface of 13m². The rudder and elevator were placed at the very front of the machine. The wheels – simple bicycle wheels fitted to a pneumatic suspension – were placed just below the pilot. The radiator was placed horizontally in the fuselage in front of the cockpit. The fuel tank being lower than the cylinders, it was necessary to action a rubber bulb fitted to the supply pipe to bring fuel to the engine. The propeller of 1.6m diameter, in copper and aluminium, was ground-adjustable for pitch and had an automatic clutch. The weight, with Louis Blériot on board was 236kg. Facing the pilot there were several onboard instruments fixed to a small panel.

- water pressure gauge, which would give an approximate indication of engine speed
- spherical water level, which would allow the control of longitudinal and lateral inclination
- mercury pressure gauge for the fuel pressure
- control tap, which allowed the setting of the fuel flow
- control for setting the spark advance
- electric switch

He also had two other control levers, the one between his knees controlled the warping of the wings, the other, to the side with a double universal joint controlled together – or separately – the rudder and the elevator.

By this system, Blériot could control his machine for the first time in the three axes, roll, pitch and yaw. This system, already close to the current system of control by joystick and rudder bar, would be patented by Blériot after a few modifications, the patents of 9th February and 26th April 1907, completed by three additions on the 15th October 1907 and 11th January 1908, and later on 2nd December 1909. This stabilized control would be known in it's definitive form by the name of "Cloche Blériot" (Blériot bell) because the lower part of the lever, to which the control wires were connected, had the form of a bell. This system was efficient and viable, the origins to which Blériot was much attached, but would however, be the cause of a law suit, which would only end, to his disadvantage, in 1919. The patent on the "Cloche Blériot" would be cancelled. This decision of considerable consequences on the financial side, would affect him above all in his pride as an inventor. In fact, on the 19th December 1906, fifty-two days before Blériot, Robert Esnault-Pelterie, another aviation pioneer, had taken out the patent for a simple single control lever for aeroplanes. This patent which would be completed by two others on the 19th and 22nd January 1907, covered a system which, without being as efficient as that of Blériot, presented certain similarities to the Cloche Blériot, which would lead after multiple negotiation, to the attribution of anteriority to Esnault-Pelterie.

To Jacques Mortane, a well known aviation journalist of the time, who asked him why he adopted a paper covered wing, Blériot replied:

On the 5th April 1907, the Blériot V leaves the ground helped by a strong head wind. At that time no-one had yet pierced the mystery of the forces of lift on a wing. A few rare German, British and Russian researchers were starting to make headway.

I had this idea because this paper was particularly resist-ant. The sheets were easily joined together by simple glue and we had no fear of humidity as soon as they had been varnished with copal. Paper gave me lightness as well, easy repair and allowed the covering to follow exactly the complicated forms of the frame work.

Above all the machine was conceived in a way to present as little resistance to the air as possible, by applying the theory of Pénaud, which states that the penetration through the air is a prior condi-tion to lift.

The Blériot V finished, it was necessary now to try it out; the principle difficulty for the pilot would be to avoid the rudder and elevator in front submitting too brutally to the action of the wind. On the 21ˢᵗ March 1907, the first trial was held at Bagatelle but it was very short because the wheels collapsed practically as soon as the machine started to move. Blériot fitted reinforced wheels, increased the surface of the rudder and elevator, and raised the frame work which supported them, in order to increase the angle of attack.[1]

A new trial was carried out on the 27ᵗʰ March. After a few metres the forks of the wheels bent again. The wind then caught the *Canard* on its side, causing the machine to collapse to the right. Imperturbable, Blériot repaired the machine. On the 2ⁿᵈ April, the propeller was bent during another trial. Blériot was obstinate. He was certain he was on the right path. He repaired the machine again and made further modifications, he added a third wheel under the engine, a large vertical fin on either side of the propeller, another smaller fin under the fuselage in front of the wheels. At last on the 5ᵗʰ April he succeeded in taking off!

After running for about one hundred metres against a strong breeze, the machine rose to about sixty centimetres. Feeling the wind force, Blériot cut the ignition and came back to earth abruptly, slightly bending the spacer between the wheels. His first flight was only a modest hop of 5 to 6 metres. But for Blériot it had an enormous signification, it was the finality of several years of effort and the confirmation that he was not in error.

He removed the fabric from the front fuselage sides. On the 8 and 15ᵗʰ April he carried out further flights of a few metres at 50 km/h. On the 19ᵗʰ April 1907, Blériot removed the vertical fin which he had added for the flight of the 5ᵗʰ April. He had hardly taken off when the Blériot V bounced brutally on the ground and turned over. Its fragile frame of wood was torn apart. Blériot was unhurt and not the slightest discouraged.

From fall to fall, he would he say, instead of sinking to the bottom of the abyss, I rise up – if I might express myself thus – more each day.

In his book *L'Aviation*, Captain Ferdinand Ferber, courageous aviation pioneer, who would be killed near to Boulogne–sur–Mer on the 22 September 1909 flying a Voisin biplane, remarked:

However, this campaign was not without profit... first of all Blériot sharpened up little by little to the point of becoming the most intrepid of the aviators. Then one can remark that it was better to increase the diameter even if you have to reduce the pitch to lessen the force of the propeller, then it was necessary as much as possible to let the motor run at full power. Even if you have to reduce the pitch[2] the aeroplane will not rise in effect, until after these diverse modifications.

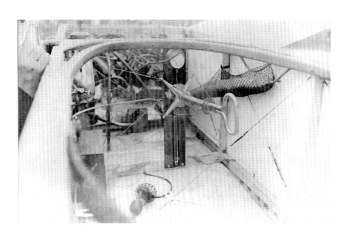

The cockpit of the Blériot V. The bulb connected to the pipe was the oil pump.

---

(1) Today we use the term "angle of incidence"; it is the angle between the wings and the horizontal. When this angle is increased, the lift – that is to say the force which allows the machine to stay in the air – increases (up to a certain point where it starts to decrease).

(2) The pitch of the propeller is the angle formed by each blade in the vertical plane, perpendicular to the shaft of the propeller.

The Blériot VI marked the abandoning of the Canard formula and the pusher propeller, and the adoption of better wing profiles. Above to the left, the tandem wing monoplane in its original form. Above on the right and below, the same in the second version, shortened, and resting on a more stable undercarriage. The robustness of this machine allowed numerous modifications as the trials progressed.

The Blériot VI

Profiting from the lessons learned from the *Canard*, Blériot built a new model in less than three months, the Blériot VI, which would be called the *Libellule* (dragonfly) because of its two pairs of wings. It was a monoplane of the type Langley, in whose conception Louis Peyret[1] participated. Its weight was 250 kg, it was only 6m long and 5.85m span. The wing surface was 18m², the two pairs of wings, fitted in tandem were practically without any flying wires, the wings had an important dihedral of 7°. The extremities of the front wings were fitted on horizontal shafts and moveable, either together, or opposed, operating thus both as ailerons and elevator. Unfortunately, as elevator, being too close to the centre of gravity, they would not be very efficient. It was this that led Blériot, after a few trials, to install a system of wheels and slides under his seat, so as to take his weight towards the front or rear of the machine, to make it climb or descend. As on the Blériot V, the fuselage was of a square section, although the dimensions were a little larger. The entire machine – wings fuselage and empennage – was covered with varnished paper. The cockpit was practically in the middle of the fuselage between the two pairs of wings. For the engine, Blériot remained faithful to the eight-cylinder Antoinette of 24 hp, which had already proved

itself. The engine drove the propeller, identical to the Blériot V, via a shaft running in the streamlined nose.

The *Libellule* rested on three wheels, two wheels in front of narrow track under the wings, with a tail wheel positioned just behind the pilot. Tried out at Bagatelle in June 1907, the Blériot VI was then much re-designed, the streamlined nose was removed, the propeller was driven by a short shaft, the radiator, initially installed under the fuselage was now placed vertically in front, the fuselage was shortened one metre by taking out one section between the two pairs of wings, the forks of the main wheels were reinforced by struts leading to the front of the fuselage, the track was increased to about three times the width of the fuselage. The Blériot VI was tried again at Bagatelle on 6th July but the field was becoming too small.

The wings and the tail were lengthened, the pitch of the propeller was reduced. The monoplane weighed 280kg and was 7m long, wingspan was 7.20m for a wing area of 20m². It was taken to Issy-les-Moulineaux on the 11th July, where the trials took place, this time on the military ground, which would in a very short time, acquire a world-wide reputation through the exploits accomplished there. On this day, Blériot flew for 25m. On the 15th he flew for 80m, in the presence of Archdeacon, Delagrange and the Voisin brothers. On the 25th he covered 120m and then 150m, at the end turning a part of a circle. On 6th August he made another flight of 143m at a height of 12m.

Blériot was exultant, he was really flying ! The hops of the *Canard* were far away.

---

(1) During the period between the wars, Louis Peyret built other tandem monoplanes, one of them, the Peyret VI was a lightweight single-seat tourer, which under the name Taupin, would be production built at Buc by the SFCA. The tandem monoplane was created by the American Samuel Pierpont Langley at the beginning of the twentieth century.

From July 1907, Louis Blériot took off several times with his type VI from the Parade Field of Issy-les-Moulineaux, 750m long to the south of Paris. The rear wingspan was reduced. Above on the right, facing the camera, from left to right: Léon Delagrange, Gabriel Voisin, Alberto Santos-Dumont, Louis Blériot and Ernest Archdeacon. Below, the take off of the Blériot VI bis with an Antoinette engine of 50hp

The problem was the longitudinal stability. It was very difficult for Blériot to control it precisely because the movements of his body towards the front or the rear had an action too brutal and the contact with the ground was severely felt, several times he damaged the undercarriage and the propeller. But this was not serious, he was beginning to get used to it. Each time he repaired the machine without losing his proverbial calm. At the end of August, the *Libellule* was fitted with a new engine, the 16 cylinder Antoinette of 50 hp and became the Blériot VI-bis. The power was twice that of the previous engine, which led Blériot to carry out a few modifications, he adopted a four bladed propeller and then increased the surface of the fin by 1m². He then reduced considerably the dihedral of the rear wings and fitted them lower. From the 5th to the 11th September, he made numerous flights with landings more or less hard, but without major damage to the machine. He then reduced the dihedral of the front wings and totally eliminated the dihedral of the rear wings. On the 17th September a new flight was being prepared ... Blériot tells the tale:

I climbed into the cockpit of my monoplane... the controls were already adjusted, I started the engine. The machine was off like an arrow. Everything went well at the beginning. Very quickly I reached 25m. I was already highly impressed by this height when suddenly the engine stopped dead. The machine started to drop as though down a chimney. I had the sensation of an unstoppable fall and for the first time in my life, I had a fear that I will always remember. Fortunately, it only lasted two or three seconds.

Seeing myself lost, the idea came to me to leave my seat, to throw myself towards the tail of the machine. This manoeuvre was almost successful, the machine returned to a flat position, lost its speed and relatively slowly crashed to the ground. I was unhurt.

Thus ended the first official flight of a monoplane. The medal that it earned was for me the most precious of all those that I received later, because it reminds me of the instant of my life where I felt nearest to my end.

In front of a crowd of spectators, at first fascinated and then worried, Blériot had just accomplished a flight of 184m at 80 kph at a height of 25m, a performance never yet reached, unheard of for the time. Unfortunately this flight even though unofficially noted by Robert Esnault-Pelterie, was not officially controlled by the Commission d'Aviation de l'Aéro-Club de France, which had not been invited. Louis Blériot could not therefore receive one of the prizes reserved for the first flight reaching 150 metres. The Aéro-Club gave him nevertheless an honorary medal for this exploit.

Despite this success, Blériot did not try to re-build his *Libellule*.

The Blériot VII

On the contrary, he had already started the construction of a new machine, it was again a monoplane; from now on he would build – with one exception – only monoplanes. The fuselage, again of square section, was tapered at each end. It was reinforced by spacers and criss-crossed with steel wires fitted with turn-buckles on all sides. The wings had a fairly strong camber. They were made rigid by means of steel wires of a type called piano wire. The upper wires tensioned above the fuselage, linked one wing to the other. The lower wires led to the extremity of a pylon placed under the fuselage.

In conserving the best of the VI bis and modifying the rest, Louis Blériot created the type VII. The silhouette is already very modern.

The Blériot type VII at Issy-les-Moulineaux at the beginning of its trials. Behind can be seen Louis Blériot's Panhard and Levassor.

The first important modification of the type VII concerned the undercarriage, now fitted with steerable wheels.

The second modification was the fittings of the wings to the top of the fuselage and the fitting of a two-bladed propeller.

The wing span was 11 metres and the wing surface 25m². The elevator was made up of the whole of the tail plane, whose two halves rotated about a shaft going though the fuselage. In order to turn, the wings, not being warpable, the Blériot VII was equipped with a mechanism allowing the movement of the two halves of the tail plane in opposition. The rudder, of very small dimensions, was fixed at the rear point of the fuselage. The engine was an 8 cylinder Antoinette of 50 hp, supplied from a pressurised fuel tank. The ignition was by magneto. The nose was made up of a cowling in the form of a pyramid, though which passed the propeller shaft. The four-bladed metal propeller was of a new type with supple blades, about which Ferber wrote:

> To streamline the front of the machines it is necessary to drive the propellers by an auxiliary shaft connected straight to the engine; it is the shaft which forms an elastic rod between two masses. As a result there can be vibrations whose amplitude when increasing in a way that something, the propeller or the shaft breaks. Blériot had the idea to make the blades flexible in the plane perpendicular to the shaft, from this day there was no more breaking of the propellers as before.

(This type of propeller would however rapidly be abandoned in favour of wooden propellers.) An article by Louis Blériot entitled "Of the resistance of aircraft propellers to high speeds" which appeared in *L'Aérophile* on the 1st of April 1908, is reproduced in Annex II of this book.

The undercarriage was made up of a chassis fixed to the fuselage by four tubes mounted on springs. The tail wheel was also fitted on a spring and was conjugated to the rudder to facilitate ground movement. The total weight of the machine was 425kg. By it's general form as well as by the disposition of its different parts (engine, wings, empennage, undercarriage and cockpit) the Blériot VII set itself apart from contemporary machines of the type "cage à poules" ("chicken cage") and can be considered as the precursor of the modern aircraft.

The trials, still at Issy-les-Moulineaux, did not start well! On two occasions, on the 5 and 6th November 1907, the undercarriage collapsed damaging the propeller before the Blériot VII could take off. He fitted a new undercarriage. Thanks to a system of triangulation, the wheels moved towards the rear in relation to the undercarriage legs, on which the springs were fitted. These springs outside the fuselage were linked to the fuselage by two large horizontal beams.

The shock due to landing was thus absorbed by the triangulation instead of being transmitted directly to the undercarriage legs as previously. These modifications would be found on practically all of later Blériot models (up to the First World War). Auguste Nicolleau, a balloon pilot with a good reputation, one of the initiators of Alfred Leblanc's airfield, future collaborator and friend of Blériot from 1909 onwards, assisted at certain flights of the aviator on his monoplane VII, which he reported thus :

> On the 16th November M. Blériot succeeded in a long flight at a speed so rapid that the observers, very familiar with high speeds, could estimate that of the machine between 80 and 90 kph, unfortunately on returning to earth the support wheels, even though steerable, and all the support legs, suffered.
>
> On the 23rd November a gust of wind threw the machine against the fence of the parade field, the propeller was broken.
>
> On the 29th November, towards 2 o'clock at Issy, a superb flight of more than 150 metres. A flight very stable and very rapid at 3 or 4 metres from the ground, stopped too soon by the fear of a collision with a platoon of cavalry. A tube of the support chariot was lightly bent at the landing.
>
> On the morning of the 6th December, Louis Blériot executed at Issy the most beautiful experiences that he had ever succeeded, on two notable occasions his flight is sustained on 400 to 500 metres, he succeeded even an aerial about face.

On the 9th December, during an engine run of the Blériot VII in the hanger, a blade of the propeller broke off, the engine, still running, unbalanced the machine which turned upside down suffering serious damage. The machine was again re-arranged, the wings were fixed higher on the fuselage. Above the cockpit was installed a 'cabane' to serve as support for the flying wires of the wings. The four-bladed propeller was replaced by a two-bladed propeller.

Auguste Nicolleau continued: -

"The aeroplane was promptly repaired and on the 18th December there was a new attempt with a view to one of the prizes of 150 metres in mechanical flight. In a first trial, Blériot missed the prize by 5 metres in clearing 145 metres of a superb flight. At five past three a new trial at 2 metres high, but on returning to earth the left support wheel collapsed, the wing of the same side scraped the ground, the machine turned over burying Mr Blériot under the debris. By a miracle the valiant sportsman had only light bruises."

Blériot started to win a reputation of "the man who always falls" (but also who always escapes!)

Auguste Nicolleau concluded: -

"This curious misadventure does not discourage M. Blériot who, in his already long career as militant aviator has hardly been saved from mischance. More reason for that he should soon have his day."

The damage was so important that Blériot did not think of repairing it, he would recreate a new type of monoplane, but time was short ... Other aviators, principally Farman and Delagrange on Voisin biplanes – built in rue de la Ferme by the ex-associate of Blériot – carried out flights of several hundreds of metres and landed without breaking. Thus Farman made a flight of 770 metres on the 26th October 1907, giving himself the world record for distance. On the 5 November Delagrange flew a semi circle of over 300 metres.

The objective that they were all seeking to achieve at the end of this year 1907, was the prize *Deutsch-Archdeacon* of 50,000 francs for the first kilometre in a closed circuit. The conditions imposed were the following: – The machine must start between two posts 25 metres apart, turn around a flag implanted at 500 metres from the two posts and return to its starting point, going through the two posts in flight.

On the 11th January 1908, Farman succeeded in making a circuit of one kilometre in the presence only of his mechanics. The performance was kept secret. The following day Farman invited the commissioners of the Aéro-Club de France to homologate his attempt. It was the first time that he had asked for their presence. Nobody had yet felt sure enough of himself to do it. But Farman had confidence. He had just discovered experimentally, that contrary to what was believed up to now to allow flight of a machine, the angle of incidence of the wings must be fairly small. But this was not all, he had got wind of the latest performances of Blériot – flight of 500 metres, turns – and thought that he was his most dangerous competitor. He knew also that Blériot had just broken his machine, but he wanted to act quickly. He felt ready. Why take the risk of being outdistanced by Louis Blériot?

On the 13th January 1908, very early in the morning in an icy fog – it had snowed the evening before – Henri Farman took off. Other than the commissioners of the Aéro-Club, a few specta-

tors were there, Blériot amongst them, who would thus witness the triumph of his competitor (but nevertheless friend). Farman carried out the programme point by point, he passed between the regulation posts, turned around the pylon on which was fixed the flag, went again between the posts and landed gently. The trial lasted 1 minute and 28 seconds. Blériot, even joining in the enthusiasm of the witnesses to this memorable performance, could not stop himself from thinking that this was the second time that he had been taken by surprise, the previous year by Santos-Dumont, today by Farman. However, far from giving in to discouragement, his determination was reinforced.

A few days later, on the initiative of the Marquis Albert de Dion, the Chambre Syndicale de l'Industrie Aéronautique was created. Lois Blériot was obviously a founder member.

The Blériot VIII

The following month in February 1908, Ferdinand Collin was started on as mechanic, thanks to his references as a military mechanic, and the engineer Raymond Saulnier came into to the design office of the Blériot company. With a Diploma of the Ecole Centrale like his new boss, he, like Collin, had just finished his military service. In 1911 he would become himself a builder in an association with Léon Morane, and would remain more than fifty years at the head of the Morane-Saulnier aircraft company.

An ex-employee with Antoinette, Robert Grandseigne was started on a little later. As a specialist in wood, he was charged with the building of the fuselage and wings. He became a pilot, he would become a celebrity on the 11th February 1911 in completing the first night flight over Paris. Later he would work as designer and test pilot with Bristol, he then moved to Clément-Bayard. A few months later the team would be reinforced, again with a fitter. His name was Rastoul and he became workshop foreman at the factory of Suresnes.

The first configuration of the type VIII. The supple propeller was also designed by Louis Blériot. The undercarriage is fitted with rubber bungees.

The completed Blériot VIII. The rudder lengthens the profiled fuselage. The elevator was very (too) small, a strong contrast with the layout of the preceding type VII.

In 1908 Blériot decided to get results whatever the cost. He abandoned the factory making lamps and lights and concentrated from now on, almost all his time to aviation. But his research cost him dearly and as he was winning no prizes, not only was he not putting money into the coffers, but above all he could not sell any machines, because buyers were interested only in those which had already proved themselves.

All changed with the Blériot VIII. The fuselage, 10 metres long and entirely covered, was very similar to that of the Blériot VII, except at the rear which finished in a triangular form in the horizontal plane. As on the Blériot VII, the forward fuselage was formed into a pyramid cowling, through which went the propeller shaft. The wings had less dihedral than on the previous models, a dihedral which was later reduced even more. The wing span was 11.8 metres and the surface 25.3m².

The Blériot VIII was equipped, as was the last version of the Blériot VII, with a cabane support for the flying wires, and the new model of undercarriage, the frame of which was slightly modified to allow the installation of a radiator between the undercarriage legs, directly under the engine, an Antoinette of 50 hp, driving a four-bladed propeller of 2.2 metres in diameter. In his first aeronautical catalogue, Blériot proposed his new undercarriage to his customers, which he described as a Chassis:

Our chassis is made up of a rigid frame formed of uprights in wood and steel tubes, assembled as two spacers and strapped by metallic blades. This frame supports the beam and the fuselage of the aeroplane and rests in an elastic fashion on two wheels coupled in parallel between them, and pivoting around vertical shafts. The liaison of the Chassis itself to each of the two wheels, is assured by a deformable triangle (patent not government approved) with an apex at the axle of the wheel. Another apex is hinged around the horizontal shaft fixed to the low point of the chassis. The third apex slides on the vertical tube taken with it in its movement, the head of a spring fixed to the chassis. Through numerous trials we have managed to fix a type of chassis remarkably light and resistant, for it is capable of absorbing on landing, a load of several hundreds of kilogram-metres under a weight of 26 kg. Further, this chassis presents the advantage that all of the organs which work under shock are fixed, which is a good working condition for metal. Our chassis offers further, a large capacity for the fitting of the wings of the aeroplane,

whatever should be their adopted disposition mono- or multi-plane because it has, on all sides, points solidly fixed onto which are possible the most rigid assemblages.

Top: Louis Blériot posing in his type VIII, his feet on the rudder bar and hands on the roll and elevator controls, the 'cloche' (bell).
Bottom: Louis Blériot, winner of the Osirs prize, in front of the type VIII, whose nose has been shortened. The supple metal propeller is of his own design.

The type VIII underwent a large number of modifications, presented here in their order. They were on the elevator and the roll control; the little fins were replaced by large panels which were lifted by the slipstream. These were then replaced by mobile wing tips and conjugated (when one is lowered the other is raised)

The rear wheel was also equipped with a triangulation system. The rudder was a square form, the same height as the fuselage. The tail plane was mobile around a shaft going through the fuselage at mid height. The weight, ready to go, was 480 kg.

The machine was unveiled to the public on the 29th February by a photo taken in the workshop, Boulevard Victor-Hugo, which appeared in *La Vie au Grand Air*.

To restrict the amount of handling, Blériot erected a hangar on the field of Issy-les-Moulineaux, of steel frame and brick, it measured 17 metres long by 17 metres wide; it had a lean-to on one side. The trials started on the 21st April 1908. Very quickly the tail plane was enlarged. The centre section became fixed. Only the tip sections remained mobile. The wings were reduced in length, the span becoming 11.2 metres, for a surface area of 22 m².

On the 19th May the propeller shaft broke. Blériot therefore removed the pyramid nose, reducing the shaft by a maximum. Further, he removed the covering of the sides of the fuselage and modified the wings, which now had a strong incidence. The machine therefore, became the Blériot VIII-*bis*.

In the month of June he carried out several satisfactory flights. On the 17th, 600 metres at a height of 4 metres. On the 18th, twelve flights of 500 to 600 metres. Triangular sails were fixed with the aid of a small mast, under the tip sections of the wings. On the 22nd, Blériot succeeded a nice flight of 500 metres. On the 23rd, he again went over 600 metres, despite a fairly fresh wind, but lightly damaged the machine on landing. He replaced the sails by non-conjugated ailerons on the trailing edge of the wing tips. On the 29th, a flight of 700 metres in the presence of the Commission d'Aviation de l'Aéro-Club de France, brought him his first official reward, the second prize of 200 metres. On the 2 July he carried out several flights in a U. On the 3rd July he completed his first two closed circuits in 2 minutes 25 seconds. On the 6th July – an excellent day – he flew for 8 minutes 24 seconds at between 18 and 20 metres high.

Blériot accumulated successes. All hopes seemed permitted. But on the 23rd July his machine was brusquely unbalanced in flight. He dived, the tail at 45° to the horizontal, the right wing leaning towards the ground. Blériot could not straighten up. A fall. The damage was important but once again the pilot was unhurt.

Blériot rebuilt his machine and made new modifications, the fuselage was shortened by 2.5 metres and the covering entirely removed. The ailerons were now made up of the tip sections of the wings fitted on shafts. It was the Blériot VIII-*ter* which made its first appearance on the 12th August. It flew then on the 19th and the 26th, when it was lightly damaged, then the 3rd and 5th September. On the 9th September he took to the air despite a wind of 40 kph and carried out several flights of 400 to 500 metres. On the 11th September, after a nice flight, Blériot received the congratulations of the Minister of Public Works who had come to witness the flights of the regulars of Issy-les-Moulineaux. On the 12th September the extremity of one of these wings touched the ground in a turn. The machine tumbled and broke up however, without damage to the Aviator!

For Blériot the moment had come to leave this field where he had taught himself to fly. He now needed wide open spaces for long distance flights. After repair and ultimate modification – he lowered the mobile tail plane below the fuselage and then added a fixed tail plane above this, with a fairly high angle of incidence – he set himself up at the Champs-Perdus, at Toury in the Département of Eure-et-Loir, on a field of fifteen hectares, placed at his disposition by the Mayor of the village, M. Lambert, whose son was one of Blériot's class mates at the Ecole Centrale. The place was well chosen, in the middle of the Beauce. The horizon was clear in all directions.

For his first flight at Toury on the 21st October, Blériot managed, despite a violent wind, to cover 7 kilometres in 6 minutes 40 seconds at a height of 20 metres, missing by a small margin the Prize for Height (2,500 francs for a height of 25 metres) The following day, the wind blew even harder. Blériot took off, nevertheless, after covering 550 metres in 30 seconds, the engine stopped suddenly. The machine dropped its nose and hit the ground fairly violently.

For once the damage was not too serious. Events suddenly accelerated on the 30th, Blériot prepared to make a new attempt to win the prize for height, after running for about 40 metres, he was on the point of taking off. Suddenly the machine pitched up and fell back to the ground. It turned out that the mechanic had simply inversed the control wires to the elevator.

The 'Voyage' from Toury to Artenay celebrated by a colour postcard (photographic composition) and by a model and flags in front of the hotel in Toury.

The propeller was bent and the undercarriage twisted, but Blériot came out of it, again, without a scratch. That evening he learned of the exploit of Henri Farman, he had just carried out the first flight from town to town, on board a Voisin biplane that he had himself modified. It was the first time that an aviator dared to leave his home field for an adventure over the countryside. Up until then records of distance were obtained in carrying out circuits around the field, without ever losing sight of it. Farman took off from Bouy where he had his hangar, he landed twenty minutes later on the Cavalry field in Reims, after a flight of 27 kilometres without problem, at an average speed of 75 kilometres an hour. Only one difficulty, clearing a copse of poplar trees, 30 metres high. Once again Blériot was left behind ! He decided that the following morning he would attack the first aerial voyage, with return to point of departure. On the morning of 31st October 1908, he made a preparatory flight, he took off from Toury, flew towards Senonville, turned around a wood and returned to land at Toury after a flight of five minutes at 15 metres above the ground. Everything went well. The same afternoon he tried his luck. He took off again in the direction of Artenay, 14 kilometres away. A line of balloons was positioned above the place where he had to turn.

Rapidly he overtook the cars which were escorting him. Eleven minutes later he reached Artenay and prepared his turn, when a fault in the magneto forced him to land a few hundred metres from the Château d'Avilliers. He had flown at almost 80 km/h. A few moments later his team joined him in the accompanying cars. The repairs took one-and-a-half hours. Blériot took off again, landed then at the Villiers Farm near to Santiloy, took off again to land at five o'clock at the Champs-Perdus; end of the circuit.

He succeeded, at the end of a flight of 28 kilometres with two stops, he had returned to his point of departure. He had at last accomplished a performance which would remain in the history of Aviation. The crowd which surrounded him re-enforced his conviction that glory was waiting for him – here, for glory, read industrial success. The press lauded Louis Blériot with praise. A sporting journalist wrote:

> One day soon perhaps, the heavier-than-air will replace the automobile. It will be the dream machine of loco-motion, bargain price, inexpensive, without bodywork, without tyres. At that time it is by the roof that one will have access to houses, the upper floors will become more popular, the most sought after and the most expensive.

But Blériot was not thinking of stopping on such a good result, his project was to go to Etampes, and even, if all went well to push on to Chartres. The plains of the Beauce were admirably suited to such an attempt. There are few villages, no high ground. Fields one after another as far as you can see, without a tree. Woods were in fact the bane of the first aviators. Other than the vertical barrier they represented, they had to be crossed, they produced eddies of air, descending currents that the frail machines at the time had a lot of difficulty in combating.

On the 4th November, Blériot prepared to leave for his voyage. But misfortune fell upon him. During a first trial he could not take off. The engine was not running smoothly and would not give full revs. After re-setting, the aviator tried to go again.

Hardly had he started to climb that the engine stopped again. One wing hit the ground. The machine "pan-caked" as was said at the time, tipped over and fell heavily onto it's back. The damage was un-repairable, but Blériot, by a miracle, was not hurt.

The Blériot IX, X and XI

On returning to Paris, the aviator speeded up the construction of the Blériots IX, X and XI that he already under construction. He wanted absolutely that the three machines be present at the first Salon de l'Aéronautique being held at the Grand Palais, in December 1908. This was in fact the first international aeronautical exhibition, which was being held as a second part of the XIth international automobile exhibition, along with cycles and sports, a section for heavy lorries, industrial machine tools and motor power boats. In the middle of the Salon was l'Avion n° 3 built by Clément Ader which, on the 14th October 1897 at Satory Camp, carried out a flight of 300 metres, unfortunately not officially recognised. The first incontestable flight of a heavier than air went back to the 9th October 1890, when on board the *Eole*, Ader flew for 50 metres in the park of the Château d'Armainvilliers, a performance which had been kept secret. Like the *Eole*, *l'Avion*

n° 3 had the general aspect of a bat. It was powered by two steam engines of 20 hp, each driving a propeller.

This plaque, shown front and rear, was for the second prize of 200m offered by the *Aéro-Club de France*. It was the first reward acquired by Louis Blériot as pilot and builder.

The lighter-than-air exhibits were suspended at mid-height under the immense glass roof. There was the dirigible *Ville de Bordeaux*, 54 metres long, 10.5 metres in diameter, along with a classical spherical balloon of 1,200 m³. At ground level the flying machines appeared a little lost in the middle of the boats, utility vehicles and machine tools.

However, the aviators and builders of the moment were practically all there. There were the biplanes, almost identical, of Dela-grange and Farman, built by the Voisin brothers. There was also the already famous machine of Wilbur and Orville Wright, one of the main attractions of the Salon. Since their arrival in France in July 1908, the two Americans out-shone the French aviators with performances that seemed inaccessible to them. On the 22nd September, Wilbur Wright flew 65 kilometres in one hour thirty minutes, on the 15th December he covered 99 kilometres and reached an altitude of 115 metres. Then, at the end of the Salon on the 31st December – to be sure that nobody would beat him in the year – he flew for more than 123 kilometres in two hours eighteen minutes. The only inconvenience of the Wright, was that it could not take off without a catapult. The Ferber was represented only by drawing and photos.

The display of aircraft increased the number of visitors to the Salon de L'Automobile, at the Grand Palais in Paris. Here is shown the Blériot IX on the ground floor. A panel invited visitors to see the bi-plane type X and the monoplane type XI displayed in the gallery.

Then came the monoplanes, the types IX, X and XI of Blériot, the red REP 2-*bis* of Esnault-Pelterie, which had only one main wheel, the Antoinette, elegant but complex and heavy, the Bard-Clément with a 7 cylinder radial engine and pusher propeller, the de Pischof et Koechlin, a curious machine with a central engine driving, via chains, two propellers one on either side of the fuselage (it was the seventh French aeroplane to have flown – 600 metres !) The two *Demoiselle* of Santos-Dumont XIX – and XX, marvels of lightness, the *Giroplane* Breguet-Richet n° *2bis* with two large flexible propellers inclined at 40°, which were both propulsive and supportive.

The exhibition was completed by a few stands of scale models – of which certain were very picturesque – and light-weight engines for aeroplanes, amongst which could be seen, other than the Antoinette, ENV, Gobron-Brillié and REP, and the Gnome rotary engine whose success would not be diminished until the beginning of the First World War.

The Salon was inaugurated in high style by President Armand Fallières on the 24th December 1908. It was straight away a success. Almost 120,000 people per day queued up to be able to contemplate close up, or even touch these famous flying machines, whose exploits had been related in the Press for months.

When the Salon closed, six days later, each one did his accounts. For the organisers it was a huge commercial success, for Blériot, on the contrary it was a disappointment. He had made considerable efforts towards the Salon, he had presented three different types of machines and hoped strongly to obtain orders for one or other of these models, thanks to his recent perfor-mances, notably his flight at Toury. Unfortunately none of them had been tried. The only one which had been proven was the Blériot VII-*ter* which had been destroyed on the 4th November. He had however on his stand a crowd of visitors keen to know the technical details of his machines, but no orders followed, whereas at the same time on Wright's stand, twenty-eight machines were ordered.

The results of 31st December 1908 were catastrophic (income = nil, outgoings = 780,000 francs since 1900) he had spent all of his fortune on his aeronautical research. He was even obliged to sell his property in Sologne, the Château Sainte-Marie, near to Vouzon in the Loire-et-Cher.

The Chateau of Sainte-Marie that Louis Blériot had to sell to finance his research.

Top, in front of the Blériot IX under construction, with its Antoinette V 16 engine of 50hp, from left to right: Louis Payret, Louis Paragot, M. Pelletier, Alfred Bertrand, Julien Mamet.

Above, Louis Blériot climbing down from his type IX.

Below, the Blériot IX shown in the Musée de l'Air, Boulevard Victor in Paris, at the end of the 1930's. After being given by Alicia Blériot to the museum, it later had its engine removed and was abandoned. It was then recovered by Charles Noetinger to be shown in his museum at Mas Palégry, near Perpignan. After the death of Charles Noetinger in 1955, the fuselage was returned to the museum, today in Le Bourget.

Even though he was fully supported by his wife, Blériot was very worried that he now had the charge of a family. From his marriage with Alicia Védère he had five children, on whose needs and future he had to concentrate. By the irony of chance, Blériot was ruined at the moment where, after ten years of effort, he had managed to resolve the principle technical problems with which he was faced, notably, a control system ensuring stability around three axes, and an undercarriage that would at last allow the absorption of a minimum of shock. Later, he would speak thus, of his memories of this black period:

> *... I must continue because I cannot do otherwise, I must continue because, like the player, I must catch up, I must continue because it is sure, because my calculations are correct, that the solution is exact, and that I must fly....*
> (*La Gloire des Ailes* (*The Glory of Wings*), Louis Blériot and A. Ramond)

At the same time, he resigned from the board of directors of the Company Moteurs Antoinette following a difference with the managers as the technical director, Léon Levavasseur, wanted to build his own aeroplanes. Blériot was opposed to this idea because he thought that this could upset the customers who usually bought these engines. Being himself a builder, he decided to resign in order to avoid being a competitor to himself. He would soon no longer purchase Antoinette engines.

The beginning of the year 1909, was for Blériot, forced labour. He had to proceed as rapidly as possible on the fine tuning of his new models.

The Blériot IX

In appearance very close to that of the Blériot VIII, the Blériot IX was put into work at almost the same time, but it remained uncompleted for a long time whilst waiting for its engine. It's fuselage, very slender, triangular at the rear section, was, at 12 metres, 2 metres longer than the VIII, the wings, in mahogany and poplar, had a surface of 26 m², for a span of 9 metres. They were covered with parchment paper. The angle of incidence was 8°. The wing tips were equipped with ailerons, moveable together, or in opposition. The cabane was replaced by a wooden longeron of a semi-elliptic form, supported by two V reinforcements on each side of the cockpit. The fuel tank, designed aerodynamically, was placed under the fuselage between the front wheels. The radiator was divided into four elements. The first two were positioned vertically in the frame of the undercarriage, on either side of the fuselage, in which was installed a 16 cylinder 50hp Antoinette engine. The two other elements were positioned behind the cockpit, they were the sides of the triangular section fuselage. The cooling system, with which the Blériot IX was equipped, was the subject of a patent filed by Louis Blériot on the 30ᵗʰ March 1908. It consisted of ... *applying the cooling to the surface of the machine itself, fuselage, empennage...*

In his aeronautical catalogue of 1909, he described this procedure in the following manner:

> *....it is thus, that we have been able to establish a surface of radiating sheet metal with the water circulating as its nerves. This surface is made up by the application of circular elements, or varied forms, on this metallic layer. No welding, each element is stapled to the metal plate and joined to the following by rubber seals. The assembly can vibrate violently without fear of leaking. The lightness of this radiator is extraordinary, its weight full of water is 2 to 3 kg per m², giving 2 m² of cooling surface. It is made manually and presents a mathematical regularity.*

The Blériot X appears to have been copied, where all else has failed, from the Wright bi-plane. Its originality was the large radiators in the two panels. They formed a network of rings in which the cooling water circulated.

Each leg of the triangular undercarriage was equipped with a double system of pulleys and rubber flanges, designed to absorb the play in the springs. The nose was equipped with a pyramid-shaped cowling, slightly rounded. The four-bladed metal propeller was 2.10 metres in diameter, with a constant pitch of 1.4 metres. The rudder and the tail wheel were conjugated. Under the fuselage there was a horizontal tailplane, whereas the elevator was situated above and further to the rear. A wind break in mica was fixed to the front of the semi-elliptical longeron. The assembled machine weighed 480 kg.

It was tried at Issy-les-Moulineaux on the 26th January, then, it seems, on the 18th February. Blériot carried out several taxi runs, but did not take off, most probably because of radiator problems, the Blériot IX was nick-named the *Arroseuse Municipale* (the Municipal water spray) by the comics, because of the continuous humid trace that it left behind. These were the only trials of this model. In fact Blériot had already started the trials of the Blériot XI, he soon became aware of the possibilities of this small monoplane. Pushed by time and financial problems, he would not follow through the fine tuning of the Blériot IX. The machine was nevertheless shown in the month of August, in Berlin and Cologne. Even though it has no wings, the fuselage still exists and will perhaps one day be the subject of a restoration.

The Blériot X

Neglecting no path in order to arrive at success, Blériot, however firmly partisan of the monoplane, again built a biplane, the first since the Blériot IV of 1906, it was the Blériot X, a large biplane whose silhouette presented a certain similarity to the machine of the Wright brothers. Perhaps he was seeking, as a last hope, to imitate them ? It was 8.2 metres long and weighted 650 kg. The rigid wings had a span of 13 metres. The wing surface was 68 m². The ribs were in mahogany covered with raw cotton. The rudder was at the front, formed by three parallel, vertical panels. To the rear of the machine were the two lateral ailerons, joined to the trailing edges of the wings by an overhanging triangular frame and a hinged support. They could act in parallel, thus, acting as elevator, or in opposition, replacing the warping system employed on the Wright. The engine was a V8 Antoinette of 50 hp driving, via reducer and chain, a wooden four-bladed pusher propeller of 3 metres in diameter. The radiators, of the same type of those installed to the rear of the Blériot IX, were made up into

large vertical panels fitted between the wings, on each side of the cockpit. These panels were formed from a metal sheet on which were affixed the elements of the radiator. These elements were made up by a circular surface into which was pressed a tubular ring in which circulated the cooling water. These tubular rings intercommunicated via rubber tubes. The elements were stapled to the metal sheet, each had two concentric circles of perforations to the inside and outside, of each circulation ring. Each panel had 18 vertical lines of 21 elements, making a total 368 elements.

The fuel tank was positioned above the engine, it was aligned longitudinally between two wing struts. The machine could carry two people, two comfortable cane chairs by Thonet, in steam-curved wood, were arranged side by side, very close to the leading edge of the lower wing, the pilot was seated to the left of the passenger.

The engine was placed to their right, longitudinally. It was even foreseen to add two further seats at the back, and to fit a 16-cylinder 100 hp Antoinette engine.

The undercarriage was made up of a very low chassis, equipped with very small wheels with large tyres, fitted on shock absorbed springs and with two castors to the rear.

Despite all the interest that it raised during the Salon de l'Aéronautique of December 1908, the Blériot X was never tried. Perhaps Blériot estimated that it was already out of date at the moment of it's completion ? It is a fact that it appeared fairly archaic by the side of the new arrival of the Blériot Company – number XI – on which the aviator would consecrate all his efforts from now on.

The only known photo showing the type XI under construction. Against the wall are leaning two very small half-wings.

The Blériot XI being pushed onto the parade field at Issy-les-Moulineaux, in January 1909 for its very first trials.

The Blériot XI

The Blériot XI with REP engine. It was towards the engineer Raymond Saulnier that Blériot turned for the responsibility to lead the construction of the Blériot XI.

It was derived directly from preceding models, particularly from the Blériot VIII, the same type of fuselage, the same form of the wings, the same cabane, the same stabilizing mechanism (the "cloche Blériot"), the same triangulated undercarriage.

In fact it only differed from its predecessor - from the flight Toury-Artenay - by three principle characteristics. An REP engine of 30 hp, replaced the 50 hp Antoinette; the control system - the ailerons were replaced by wing warping ; the Blériot XI was much smaller than the previous machines. It was 8 metres long, a span of 7.2 metres and a wing surface of only 12 m², for a weight of 310 kg, ready to fly. The wings were made up of wooden ribs supported by two longerons which were fixed to the side of the fuselage, with an angle of incidence of 7°. They were covered with rubberized cloth made by Continental. The square section fuselage was in ash and poplar. It was composed of longerons assembled by verticals and horizontals, the whole was criss-crossed by piano wire, the frames were linked by stirrups in

a U form, allowing the elimination of the turn buckles, this made an assembly without any mortise and tenon joints, which would have weakened it. The sides were covered only on the forward half.

The control lever – the "cloche Blériot" – allowed the execution of two movements which could be independent or combined; the first movement determined climb or descent, this was made by pulling or pushing the *cloche* along the central axis of the machine ; the second movement determined the warping, whose objective was to re-establish lateral balance, this was made by inclining the "cloche" to the right or to the left.

The horizontal tail plane was made up of a fixed central part of 2 m² and two mobile extremities which formed the elevator. Right at the rear of the machine the rudder was made up of a vertical fin connected by wires to the rudder bar, on which rested the two feet of the aviator. The engine a 30 hp 7-cylinder REP in a double fan configuration was air cooled. Built by Robert Esnault-Pelterie, the only builder and pilot who also built his engines, it had the particularity of having only one valve per cylinder, placed at the apex of the cylinder head. This valve, actioned by two cams, was alternately in-let and exhaust.

Left: Louis Blériot's pilot's license (inside and out), decorated with a small tricolour ribbon.

The propeller, with four wide blades, had the tips shortened to make it 2 metres in diameter, with a pitch of 1.5 metres. To improve the lateral stability, a vertical fin in the form of a tear drop was fixed above the cabane. The undercarriage was built in the classic rigid frame form of planks, wooden verticals and steel tubes. The assembly was reinforced by a steel strap. The frame rested on two wheels joined in parallel and steerable by a flexible assembly, connected to springs installed in the vertical tubes. The liaison of the chassis to each of the wheels was made by a moving triangle, made up by the two forks which carried the wheel and the tube of the chassis. The lower fork was linked by an articulation to the bottom of the tube. The upper fork slid along the upper part of the tube. The chassis with its wheels, weighed about 30 kg. The machine was also equipped with a sprung tail wheel, with moving triangle. Of his new monoplane, Blériot said to close friends:

> *I have built the number XI, probably the last. I have built it with all the passion which puts shipwrecked men to tie together the planks of their raft. It is all for me, this machine, and I shall ask all of it.*

At the beginning of January 1909, a few days before the trials of number XI started, Blériot received his Pilot's Licence from l'Aéro-Club. On the 15th December 1908, the Commission d'Aviation de l'Aéro-Club de France created the licence of pilot/aviator and wrote out the first rule. This was the obligation to carry out, on different days, three closed circuits of at least 1 km each, without contact with the ground, the candidate being the only person on board. In order to give this licence eminent godfathers, the Commission decided on the 7 January 1909, to give it automatically to eight Aviation Pioneers These were, Blériot, Delagrange, Esnault-Pelterie, H. Farman, Captain Ferber, Santos-Dumont, Orville and Wilbur Wright. Towards the end of the year, Curtiss, M. Farman, Gobron, the Comte de Lambert, Latham, Paulhan, Rougier, and P. Tissandier would be added to the preceding names, to form the glorious list of the first sixteen licences, without testing. The numbering, carried out according to alphabetical order, gave Number 1 to Louis Blériot.

The "experts" who had discovered the mono plane "extra light" at the Salon du Grand Palais, had expressed a few doubts on the capacity of the Blériot XI to stay in the air, with only $12m^2$ of wing surface. Blériot would quickly give them their answer. The first trial was held on the 18th January 1909, unfortunately the axle of the undercarriage broke. But on the 23rd January, in a piercing cold, the Blériot XI made it's first flight, without difficulty, at Issy-les-Moulineaux, a flight of 200 metres at 75 kph, in front of Esnault-Pelterie, Lamont, Fournier and a group of French and foreign officers. The machine was judged sufficiently stable, but Blériot realised that 12 m² of wing surface was really too little. On its next appearance at Issy-les-Moulineaux, on the 16 February, the Blériot XI had a wing surface of 13 m² [1] He flew 600 metres at 2 metres above the ground, then made three flights of 100 to 200 metres, in a vigorous wind. Two days later he covered the entire parade field in both directions – being twice 700 metres – despite a violent wind, however, he did not try turns, because of the lack of space in relation to the speed of his machine.

(1) The span went therefore to 7.8 metres

Above: The Blériot XI with REP engine was transported to Buc after having been dismantled.
Below: The Blériot XI in its transport frame, in front of the Blériot workshop at Neuilly-sur-Seine. The rudder has been changed.

Take-off of the Blériot XI by Louis Blériot. The rudder has been modified yet again.

The beginnings of the Blériot XII at Issy-les-Moulineaux. The V engine is off-set to the right of the fuselage.

Blériot therefore, abandoned Issy-les-Moulineaux for the field at Buc, near Versailles, where Robert Esnault-Pelterie, the builder of the engine fitted to his monoplane, carried out his own trials. On the 22nd February on the vast field at Buc, Blériot carried out several flights with turns, the rudder was now articulated on a vertical fin. The aviator from now on, had at his disposition a large enough space to evaluate the possibilities of his machine and to acquire the experience of piloting it. On the 8th March the wing surface was raised to 14 m²,² on the 9 he completed a flight of nearly 2 km, turning several times, on the 15th, in a wind of 40 kph he flew 500 and then 700 metres, and finished by a flight, with turns, of 2,500 metres in 2 minutes. On the 5th April on landing Blériot, surprised by his speed ran into the Lake *Trou-Salé*. In these beginnings of aviation the machines were not fitted with brakes³ and on landing it was necessary to cut the contact and wait until the aircraft stopped of its own accord.

The preparation for take-off of the type XII. Louis Blériot believed in the future of this machine because it could carry a heavy load.

Whilst the damaged Blériot XI was returned to the workshops in the Boulevard Victor-Hugo, the happy conclusion of a commercial negotiation with England would temporarily re-establish Louis Blériot's financial situation. For 200,000 francs he sold to British Industrialists, the patents for his electric lamps, Blériot-Phi, which were powered, as are today's cars, by an engine driven dynamo. These funds allowed him to follow through his work and notably to accelerate the construction of his new machine, the Blériot XII.

At Issy, Louis Blériot on board his type XII a few moments after the engine has been started.

The Blériot XII

As early as the 21st May, although the Blériot XI was still under repair, the trials of the Blériot XII started at Issy-les-Moulineaux. It was a high winged monoplane, considerably bigger and heavier than the type XI. It was fitted with an ENV engine of 35 hp, 8-cylinders in a V and water cooled, driving a Chauvière "Intégrale" propeller of 2.07 metres diameter, via a chain reduction gear. The propeller spun very close to the wing, and thanks to the phenomenon called "blown wing", which, at equal power considerably improved the lift, Blériot would see that he could take one and even two passengers on the number XII, initially a single seater.

The type XII, the ENV engine and the 'cloche' are clearly visible. The cloche also carries the engine controls.

---

(2) The span was now 8.4 metres

(3) The first brakes produced in series only appeared on a Voisin L in 1914

At Neuilly, the type XI fitted with a 3-cylinder Anzani engine and a Chauvière propeller in laminated wood.

Its main particularity was that the fuselage opened out towards the front, to allow the pilot (and later the passengers) to be seated inside, under the wings, behind the engine mounted off-set to the right. The wings were fixed to the upper longerons of the fuselage. They had a span of 10 metres for a surface of 22m² and they were not warping; it was the second originality of the Blériot XII. Control of lateral stability was obtained by ailerons fitted on a shaft under the fuselage and under the pilot.

The upper part of the chassis of the undercarriage, a little larger than on the Blériot XI, was fitted directly to the wings. The radiator, formed by long elliptical section tubes was placed between the upper longerons of the fuselage, behind the cockpit.

The fuel tank was also installed above the fuselage, level with the wings of which it had the same form. The fuselage was only covered on the upper surface from side to side of the radiator. The empennage was made up of two rudders around a vertical fin and two horizontal tail planes, of which the lower one was mobile (the elevator) The Blériot XII was 9.5 metres long and weighed 350 kg empty.

As often happened, this first trial led Blériot to modify his machine. On the 27th May, the XII flew at Issy-les-Moulineaux with an engine fitted on the centre line of the fuselage and with a single vertical fin.

The Blériot XI with Anzani engine. In the meantime, the Blériot XI was again available. In the following months the aviator flew alternately on these last two models. Outside of minor modifications, such as the removal of the tear drop vertical fin, which was compensated by a slight dihedral on the wings, the adoption of a new form of rudder and the fitting of two rubber extensions on each undercarriage leg to improve the absorption of shocks on landing and taxiing, the type XI underwent an important transformation, the REP engine, which over-heated too easily, was replaced by a much lighter engine, an air-cooled 3-cylinder Anzani in fan configuration (or in W).

Alessendro Anzani was an ex-cycle racer of Italian origin, who had become a leader on motor cycles and then manufacturer of bicycles and motor cycles. He was a person high in colours of exuberant temperament and a certain roughness of language. As early as 1905, he had studied the problems of light-weight engines with the engineer Buchet, who supplied the engines to Captain Ferber. Amongst the pioneers, he participated in the practical trials of traction by propeller, on the 11th September 1906, at Achères, during experiments carried out at the initiative of Archdeacon, the propeller motor cycle belonging to him, ridden by Anzani, went over 80 kph. The first Anzani engines, rustic, with un-machined steel cylinders, were initially in a V-twin configuration, directly inspired from a model conceived by Buchet shortly before his death. Following suggestions by two of his employees, Hoffman and Santarini, he added a third cylinder, thus giving birth to the 25 hp in fan configuration. The cylinders, fitted with cooling fins, had a 105 mm bore and a stroke of 120 mm. The inlet valves were automatic, the exhaust valves were operated by a push rod. The ignition was by trembler-coil. It weighed 65 kg and burned 12–15 litres of fuel per hour. Fitted with a Chauvière Intégrale wooden propeller of 2.08 metres diameter, it ran at 1,600 rpm and generated a traction force of 95 kg. Taking up little space, this engine overcame the preceding engines used by Blériot. Its first appearance could not be compared to the quality of the machining or finish of the Antoinette engines, the ENV, or even the REP.

These Anzanis, wrote Ferdinand Collin, *brutal and heavy engines, possessed only 3-cylinders in fan configuration carved by a sickle, made from rough castings, neither elaborated, nor smoothed, held their relative running regularity to the rudimentary machining of their parts and despite a formidable play in the bearings, they clattered and clanked, spitting oil by the exhaust at bottom dead centre, but they hung on easily for one hour... when they were new.*

First meetings, first competitions

And duration was precisely what Blériot now needed, because now he must win prizes, participate in the first meetings to try and straighten his vacillating finances. In the meantime, he accumulated flying hours in completing the fine tuning of his two machines.

On the 30th May he went with his wife to Toury to inaugurate a monument commemorating his first two-way aeroplane flight on the 31st October 1908. In his honour, the streets of the town were decorated with arches of foliage and garlands of flowers. A smaller copy of the Blériot VIII, built for the purpose, was placed by the side of the granite pyramid on the square of the *Marché-à-la-Chaux*, re named, *Place Blériot*. After the ceremony the model would serve as advertisement for the neighbouring café.

The natural modesty of the hero of the day was put to the test by the eloquent speeches of the orators and the ovations of the crowd. The evening ended, as it must, by a fire-work display, followed by a ball. The following morning, at five o'clock, Blériot took off from the *Champs-Perdus* with his number XI to check the setting of a new propeller. The weather was perfect and the engine was running perfectly. The aviator set the heading towards Artenay, perhaps with the intention of renewing his exploit of the previous year, but there was not enough fuel in the tank. He had to land at Château-Gaillard to take on fuel, he took off straight away, under the wide eyes of a few early risers, and flew back to the Champs-Perdus where he landed a few minutes later. During the afternoon a crowd of several thousands people gathered around the field. It was only towards seven o'clock in the evening that Blériot could satisfy the public, in carrying out a new flight; an unfavourable wind had stopped him until then. He landed to the applause of the spectators, who then escorted him for the 4km to the house of his host, M. Maurice Lambert, Mayor of Toury.

On the 2nd June, back at Issy-les-Moulineaux, he took a passenger - one of his mechanics - for the first time on board the Blériot XII. The radiator had been repositioned, it was now fitted vertically between the legs of the undercarriage, on the lower beam of the chassis. The forward sides of the fuselage were covered. The square rudder was raised on a shaft going though the tail of the machine, in front of the rear wheel.

On the 7th June at the end of the day, despite a fairly strong wind, he again took up a passenger in his number XII, André Fournier. The covering of the fuselage was reduced to a simple strip of cloth right at the front. On the 8th and 11 June he carried out several flights, alone or with a passenger, one of which he ended by a double S turn at 4 metres from the ground.

Inauguration of the Blériot monument at Toury, Place Blériot, 30th May 1909.

A first! On the 12th June 1909, Louis Blériot prepares to take off with two passengers: Santos-Dumont (less tahn 50kg) and Fournier.

On the 2nd June 1909, the second configuration of the Blériot XII whose fuselage has been partially covered at the front.

The Blériot XII on the 8th June 1909. The covering at the front has disappeared.

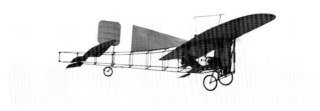

The same machine, two days later on the 10th June, with a large fin on its back.

On the 12th June, Blériot made a world premier, a flight of 250 metres with Santos-Dumont and Fournier on board. The total weight was 550 kg for 200 kg of useful load. It was the first time that a heavier than air managed to lift three people. Blériot carried out then several flights, alone or with a passenger, one of which was 5 km.

The Blériot XII in its definitive configuration at Douai.

On the 2nd July 1909 Louis Blériot beat his own record in flying for more than three-quarters of an hour. The exhaust gas was burning his foot!

The Blériot XII was then fitted with a large vertical triangular fin. On the 14th Blériot flew again, but had to land after four minutes flying; a magneto was out of timing. After being repaired, he took off straight away and while flying in all directions above the field of Issy-les-Moulineaux, several times he let go of the controls in order to test the efficiency of his new empennage. The following day, whilst taking André Fournier, as passenger, the trials were interrupted by an engine failure, a broken crank shaft.

On the 16th June he had the pleasure to learn directly from Voisin that he was co-winner with him for the Osiris prize. It was a prize worth 100 000 francs given every three years by the Institut de France, its objective was *"to serve, to reward a Frenchman who, under whatever form, had accomplished progress in science or produced the most useful work."*

The prize was unanimously attributed according to the report of Emile Picard, of the Academie des Sciences who recommended that they should crown the progress of aviation in the year of 1908, because of the two exploits that opened the way for practical use of this means of locomotion; the first flight from town to town (accomplished by Farman in a Voisin biplane) and the first two-way flight with stop (accomplished by Blériot on the Blériot VIII-ter). It was during a party given by the Association de Femmes Aeronauts Stella in the park of the Aero-Club de France that Blériot learned of the happy news. He was about to make an flight in a balloon, accompanied by his wife, Vice Présidente of the Association, and Alfred le Blanc, he spotted Voisin running towards him, arms in the air shouting from far away, *"We share the Osiris prize".* The same emotion united the two men who congratulated each other mutually.

Blériot received here his first really important reward, which, besides the financial aspect, marked the recognition of his aero-

nautical research. It was at this moment that he received his first orders. Two days later, he carried out a flight of 4 km with the number XI. On the 21ˢ June the engine caught fire on the ground but this was rapidly doused thanks to the presence of mind of the spectators, who threw sand on the flames.

Despite this incident, the type XI now seemed to be ready and Blériot had acquired control, therefore, on the 25th June at the end of the day, he flew around the parade field a dozen times, staying in the air more than 15 minutes. He landed at night fall, to the applause of the spectators. The following day Blériot flew for 36 minutes flying 20 times around the field.

The following day he went to Douai to participate in the meeting organised by Louis Breguet and a group of industrialists of the region. It was at the village called La Brayelle near to the town that Breguet had made his own field of seventy-two hectares. Ten participants were inscribed at his Concous d'Aviation, one of whom was Blériot with his number XII. The rudder was now fixed by two hinges to the horizontal tail plane, whose form had been modified. The fuselage also had been slightly shortened and the pilot's seat – a simple plank – had been moved forward.

On the 28th June, the opening day, Blériot made a flight of 2,500 metres at 50 metres height, winning therefore the first of five prizes of 2,000 francs offered by the town of Douai, for flights of more than one kilometre.

On the 2nd July he won the Prix de la Corderie, rewarding a flight in a closed circuit of 1,500 metres. The following morning he left the field, flying over woods and houses in a flight of 5 km. The machine was giving full satisfaction, he decided therefore to try that very evening to beat, at the same time, the records for distance and duration, he stayed in the air 47 minutes 17 seconds making 25 circuits of the field, a total of 47.277 km. It was a fine result which brought him close to those of the Wright brothers, but there was a price to pay:

From the first quarter of an hour, said Collin, who accompanied Manet to Douai to receive and assemble the Blériot XII, *his ankle became very hot. The exhaust pipe was covered with asbestos and the wrapping came undone and flew off, at the end of half an hour his shoe was burned and the flesh roasted, but the man, taut, fearless, imperturbable, held on. At the 47th minute when the engine stopped and Blériot came to the end of his landing, it was an injured man who came out of the aircraft.*

Louis Blériot in his type XII in June 1909. Louis Paragot stands just behind. The 'cloche' is maintained vertically by a bungee.

The first successes of the Blériot XI

Despite the burns, Blériot thought that the crossing of the Channel, which was only 38km wide, was now within his grasp. At the end of the evening he took the train to go back to Paris, because he was inscribed at the Fête de Port-Aviation which started the following day. It was all about a new field of nearly 100 hectares belonging to the Société d'Encouragement à l'Aviation, founded on the 30th July 1908 by Léon Delagrange. It was situated in the community of Viry-Chatillon, but was served by the stations of Juvisy and Savigny–sur–Orge. The aerodrome had four runways – in the form of a race course ! – of 1,000, 1,500, 1,666 and 2,000 metres in length. Its equipment was very complete, hangers, stands, pylons, restaurants and even a pavilion for the press. On the 4 July, Blériot therefore, found himself at Port-Aviation at the controls of his type XI. He carried out 24 circuits between 20 and 40 metres height, in one flight of 50 minutes and 8 seconds, thus winning the prize offered by Mme. E. Archdeacon.

> *However,* reported Collin, *there was with the Anzani engines a very important problem. It was the hot oil which escaped by the orifices at the bottom of the cylinder and invaded all the aircraft and covered the pilot with a viscous layer, meaning that the aviator needed a sort of heroism and resignation to persevere in the driving of this miserable mechanism. The eyes suffered principally and misted over …*

This was so on the Anzani engines, the lubrication was not continuous, the oil was injected into the engine and then came out again, after having lubricated the moving parts … and this until the oil tank was emptied.

Without discouragement, Blériot decided to attack the Prix du Voyage, of the total value of 14,000 francs, created by the Aéro-Club de France thanks to a Government grant. It was to reward the first straight line flight of more than 40 km in a maximum time of six hours, including stops. The flight had to take place before the 1st January 1910. Half of the prize would be attributed as soon as the first flight of more than 40 km had been completed. The other half would go to the holder of the best flight on the 1st January 1910.

The Blériot XI with Anzani engine at Juvisy, 4th July 1909.

A temporary shelter was prepared at the Mondésir farm, at Etampes, before the attempt on the Prix du Voyage.

Louis Blériot studies his route on a map with Alfred Leblanc. Alicia is behind them.

Louis Blériot in his type XI at Etampes, tensed before the departure. Alfred Leblanc is at his side.

The aviator had his type XI transported to the Mondésir Farm,[1] near to Etampes. But he could not take off because of unfavourable winds. The machine was therefore sheltered in a building and Blériot left for Douai where on the 9th July on his number XII he flew in front of the delegates of the Douma (the Russian Parliament). The following day he made several flights of which one was with his friend Alfred Leblanc.

On his return to Etampes, Blériot, wishing to be completely ready for dawn the following day, had his machine transported near to the take off field, placed in the shelter of a haystack and protected by a tarpaulin for the night. Leblanc and Fournier were the Commissaires de l'Aéro-Club de France who would control his attempt, one at the departure, the other at the arrival. The following day, on the 13th July, Blériot was on the field at half past three in the morning. The type XI was uncovered. After the usual preparations and the final tuning of the engine, Blériot took off in 50 metres, direction Orléans, followed by three automobiles, which on country roads tried not to lose sight of him. After flying over a train whose passengers waved enthusiastically, he landed sixteen minutes later at Arbouville, at a point agreed to in advance.

(1) This field has become today, the Aerodrome Etampes-Mondésir, situated alongside the RN20; the field would be home to the famous Etampes Patrol for a long time.

Eleven minutes later he took off again, passed above the hamlet of Barmainville and rejoined the route that he had taken the previous year with his number VIII, he flew over Toury then Château-Gaillard and Dambron. He touched down at last at Chevilly where the landing was made delicate by a westerly wind which came up suddenly. Blériot had covered 41.2 km in 44 minutes 30 seconds.

He took thus the first *Prix du Voyage*, winning 4,500 francs (2,500 as pilot plus 2,000 as builder) Anzani received 1,500 francs and Lucien Chauvière, the manufacturer of the propeller, 1,000 francs. The prize being open only to French nationals, Anzani of Italian nationality could not in fact receive the prize for the engine manufacturer!

This series of prizes improved momentarily the financial situation of the aviator; above all they gave him more confidence in himself for what followed.

The machine, towed by Blériot's personal car, was brought back to the workshops at Neuilly by road in pouring rain. Grandseigne had to hang the wings to the ceiling to dry them out. He also had to open certain parts to examine the interior. Mamet for his part disassembled the Anzani engine which, in fact, was in very good state, this led Blériot to pass an accord immediately with the transalpine builder, which assured him the exclusivity of the production of aviation engines with fins, from the power of 20 hp. He took then the decision to attempt the crossing of the Channel, but Latham already being in place since the 5th July, he waited until he had made his attempt in order not to appear to want to steal his lime-light. It was only in a case of Latham's failure that Blériot would try in his turn.

While waiting, he returned to Douai where the meeting was continuing and on the 18th July at the controls of the Blériot XII he took the Prix Mahieu for the semi-circular km, which he covered in 1 minute 9 seconds and the Prix du Tour de Vitesse over two kilometres which he won in 2 minutes 29 seconds.

Unfortunately the accident of the 3rd of July repeated itself during his last flight. He was this time grievously burned, his left foot, hardly healed, was burned to the third degree.

His friends had to help him climb down from the machine.

Louis Blériot in front of his monoplane type XII being re-assembled, at Douai in July 1909.

4

The Crossing of the Channel

LOUIS BLÉRIOT, WHO HAD INVESTED SO MUCH, NOW HAD TO IMPERATIVELY AND RAPIDLY FIND CUSTOMERS

The following morning, Blériot, back in Paris, learned of Latham's failure. Straight away, despite suffering and against the advice of his doctor, he telephoned to the Paris office of the *Daily Mail* to ask that they should send him a journalist as rapidly as possible. That same afternoon he gave the journalist the following letter of engagement.

> *To Monsieur the Managing Director of the* Daily Mail
> *Monsieur,*
> *I have the honour to inform you that I wish to be inscribed for the prize of £1000 offered for the crossing of the Channel. I envisage leaving Thursday or Friday next, itinerary Calais – Dover. Receive, Monsieur, my sincere salutations. Paris, 19th July.*
> *Signed. L Blériot*

The journalist from the *Daily Mail* made it clear to him that he could leave from the coast of his choice, the French or the English.

The prize, initially of £500, was created on the 5th October 1908 by Alfred Harmsworth, Lord Northcliffe, owner of the *Daily Mail,* one of the principle London newspapers. The rules appeared on page seven in a straight column in that day's edition under the title 'Cross Channel Flight';

> "*In view of the great advances which have recently been made in the domain of Aviation ... we have decided to make the following offer:*

> '*Conditions of the aerial crossing of the Channel in an aeroplane, imposed by the* Daily Mail:

> *The proprietors of the* Daily Mail *hereby undertake to pay the sum of £500 (or 12,500 F) to the first person who succeeds in flying from England to France or from France to England under the following conditions : -*

> 1 *The flight to be made between the hours of sunrise and sunset.*

> 2 *No part of the machine must touch the sea during the flight.*

> 3 *The flight to be accomplished by means of an aeroplane or machine which is heavier than air, and is not supported by gas or any other substance.*

> 4 *Entries for the competition can be made at any date by giving forty-eight hours notice to the Editor in Chief of the* Daily Mail, *either at Carmelite House, London, EC., or at the office of the* Continental Daily Mail, *36 rue du Sentier, Paris.*

> 5 *In every notification of the first attempt to be made under these conditions shall reach the Editor in Chief of the* Daily Mail *not less than forty-eight hours prior to each attempt, and in the case of all subsequent attempts not less than twenty-four hours notification shall be given.*

On Sunday the 25th July 1909 at dawn, in his monoplane type XI, Louis Blériot waits for his mechanics to finish filling the fuel tank and oil tank, and to complete their checks on the Anzani engine.

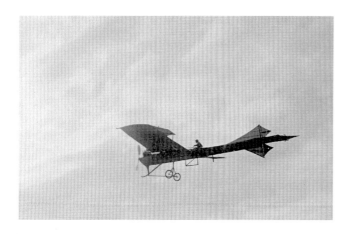

Hubert Latham in flight in his Antoinette IV monoplane.

The tug *Calaisien* brings the Antoinette IV back to port after ditching on the 19th July 1909.

Straight after leaving the train from Paris, Louis Blériot and his wife, Alicia are driven to the hangar of the type XI, at Les Baraques.

At Les Baraques, a temporary shelter of striped cloth, built against the side wall of a new milking shed at Grignon, for the Blériot monoplane.

6 *The entrants must furnish satisfactory evidence of previous flights before making any attempt under these conditions.*

7 *The entrant must supply satisfactory signed evidence of the exact points of departure and arrival.*

8 *In accordance with the rules of the F.A.I. the entrants must be a member of a club or obtain a permit from a club recognised by the Federation.*

9 *Should any questions arise at any time after the date of entry as to whether a competitor has properly fulfilled the above conditions, or should any other question arise in relation to them, the decision of the committee of the Aéro Club in conjunction with the Editor in Chief of the* Daily Mail *shall be final.*

10 *Each competitor agrees to waive all claim for injury either to himself or to his apparatus, and agrees to assume all liabilities for damages to third parties or their property, and to indemnify the proprietors of the* Daily Mail *and the Aéro Club against any such claims.*

The text of the rules had the following comment added, written by the Sports Section of the newspaper : *"The shortest distance of the English Channel is twenty one and a half miles; Messers Wright, Farman and Delagrange have all already gone over this distance at different times with their aeroplanes"*

Lord Northcliffe, warm supporter of aviation at the same time as being patriotic, was worried about the rapid development of aviation in the United States of America and in France, whereas nothing was happening in England. It was therefore, in the first place, to try and awaken the interest of his compatriots in this domain that he founded the Prix de la Traversée de la Manche, the first of a series of aviation prizes by this enterprising patron of the press, in the years before the First World War.

At the time that he established the prize, Lord Northcliffe was perfectly conscious of the fact that the Wright brothers were practically the only aviators capable of succeeding in such a performance. In trying to obtain their participation, he even offered them an extra £3,000. But faithful to their policy, Wilbur and Orville Wright refused to try this trial, (as all preceding ones) preferring to concentrate on demonstration flights.

The *Daily Mail*'s prize was not in fact the first destined to reward the crossing of the Channel by an aeroplane. As early as 4th December 1906, the Etablissements Ruinart, a very old Champagne Company in Reims, created a prize for the crossing of the Channel by a heavier-than-air machine, exclusively powered by its own means; this which excluded the Wright bi-planes, which could only take off with the aid of a catapult, in the form of a pylon and a counter-weight. This prize, a sum equivalent to that of the *Daily Mail*, carried fairly restrictive inscription conditions.

The competitors had to make their attempts either on Saturday or Sunday only, and all before 1st January 1910. Further, they had to announce their intentions in writing, at least sixty days in advance, and to pay the Aéro-Club the sum of fifty francs, valid for two days of the competition. Each attempt also had to be confirmed forty-eight hours before the foreseen date.

During nearly two years, no competitor came forward. It was only in November 1908 that a Russian aviator, Count Serge de Bolotoff, announced his participation in two trials. With this objective, he ordered from the Voisin Brothers, a tri-plane of imposing dimensions, which was to be powered by a Panhard and Levassor engine of a 110 hp, driving a Voisin metal propeller of 3 metres in diameter. The machine would be equipped with floats installed in the fuselage, which would, in principle prevent him from sinking in case of landing on the water.

Bolotoff announced in the press his intention to try his hand in the first fortnight of December. But the end of the month came and the construction of the tri-plane was still not completed.

Because of notably, the excessive weight of the machine, the Russian pilot finally had to abandon. In this situation, and after having consulted the donors, the Aéro-Club de France decided on the 31st December 1908, to relax the rules of the two trials, which was done on the 5th January 1909, by the Commission de l'Aviation.

During the months that followed, several aviators, among them, Alberto Santos-Dumont and Charles S. Rolls, were quoted as being eventual competitors, but it was Latham who was the first to send in his inscription, on the 16th June.

Hubert Latham was born in Paris on the 10th January 1883. His family – ship owners of English origin, based in Le Havre – was very rich. After law studies at Balliol College at Oxford, he returned to France to do his military service. Two years later, returning to civilian life, he did not feel disposed towards the job of ship owner, and instead of entering the family business, he took up different sports, all more or less dangerous.

It was thus in February 1905 that he crossed the Channel by night, on board a spherical balloon belong to his cousin, the *aéronaut* Jacques Faure. He participated then in power boat races, he won in Monaco on a boat fitted with an 8-cylinder Antoinette engine. He then left for Africa, and did not return to France until the end of 1908. In February 1909, his cousin Jules Gastambide,

founder of the Antoinette Company, proposed to him to become the Mark's pilot. Seduced by this new activity, Hubert Latham accepted. In a few weeks he did his apprenticeship at the Camp de Châlons, near to Mourmelon, not without breaking a bit of wood ... it must be said that his machine, the Antoinette IV, an elegant monoplane, trapezoidal wings with a triangular section fuselage, had delicate handling, it was controlled by means of three wheels arranged vertically, to the right and left of the pilot, which operated respectively, the elevator, the rudder and the ailerons, not counting the levers for the setting of the advance and the carburation. In order to pilot it in comfort, you needed three or four hands.

Nevertheless, on the 26th March, Latham made a flight of 2 km. His progress was very rapid. On the 5th June, he became an overnight celebrity, in beating the French record for duration (and the world record for monoplanes) in flying for 1 hour 7 minutes and 37 seconds. He confirmed his success the following day, by winning the Prix Ambroise-Goupy. On the 12th June, he flew for 40 km in 39 minutes, in front of the Parliamentary Group for the Locomotion Aérienne. He now felt sufficiently sure of himself to try for the Channel Crossing.

Arriving at Calais on the 5th July, he established his camp at Sangatte in the old buildings of the Channel Tunnel (the work having been abandoned in 1883). On the 13 July, despite a wind of 30 kmh, Latham made a trial flight of 10 minutes. On landing, the machine was lightly damaged.

The bad weather stopped all attempts until the 19th July. On that day a slight improvement at last allowed Latham to take off above the Channel. Both France and England followed with passion the adventure of the courageous sportsman through the reports of the journalists. A torpedo boat of the French Navy, the *Harpon*, was despatched to escort him. But after only ten minutes of flight when the Antoinette was level with the *Harpon*, its engine stopped. All that Latham could do was to glide downwards and managed to land his machine gently on the water. Fortunately the aircraft floated, and after a wait of about twenty minutes, the unlucky aviator was hoisted on board the torpedo boat, whereas the tug boat *Calaisien* collected the remains of the Antoinette.

Louis Blériot and his monoplane are pulled towards the take-off point. The time for action has arrived and the worry that the pilot suffered when he awoke has now disappeared. Even at this early hour on Sunday 25th July there were a lot of spectators.

The most precious image of the take-off for the Channel. The end of the rubber cylinder which would serve as a float in case of ditching is clearly visible in the fuselage frame.

As soon as he landed at Calais, Latham sent a telegram to the Antoinette factory demanding that the Antoinette VII, with warping wings be sent to him urgently. And urgency there was, because that afternoon he learned of the engagement of Blériot for the *Daily Mail* prize.

On the 21st July, Blériot, accompanied by his wife, arrived at the station in Calais where Leblanc and Fournier, Commissaires de Aéro-Club de France for the Channel Crossing, were waiting for them.

Blériot set up camp at the Grignon Farm, at a place called Les Braraques, between Calais and Wissant. At the end of the afternoon, Collin and Mamet, his two mechanics, completed the re-assembly of the Blériot XI, which had also arrived by train. It was equipped with a new propeller, the previous one having been slightly damaged eight days before on landing at Chevilly, in the Prix du Voyage. The new propeller, the same make and the same diameter, was only different to the previous one by its pitch, which allowed the Anzani engine to give a traction of 105 kg at 1,450 rpm (being 10 kg more for 150 rpm less). To try and improve the viability of the machine, they installed a second battery as well as a two-point switch, they wrapped the spark plug nuts in Chatterton, they doubled the control cables, lock-wired the nuts. All was carefully looked at, inspected, tightened, pinned ... The following day, the Antoinette VII was delivered to Sangatte in boxes. Its assembly would take two days and Latham, who had never piloted a machine with warping wings, could not try his new machine because of persistent bad weather.

Meanwhile, two other competitors showed up, the Comte de Lambert, with a Wright bi-plane at Wissant, and the Englishman, Seymour, at Le Touquet. But neither one nor the other were ready to try the crossing in the following days. The journalist, Charles Fontaine, of the *Matin*, arriving from Paris at the same time as Louis Blériot, went to Dover on the night of the 22nd to 23rd, to find a field ideal for the landing, where he would signal to Blériot by waving a French flag. Fontaine, who travelled from Paris in the same compartment as Blériot and his wife, had during the journey proposed to carry out a reconnaissance on the cliffs of Dover, which Blériot had accepted.

On the 23rd July, Anzani, the builder of the engine of the Blériot XI, arrived and the team was now complete. Fontaine sent a letter to Blériot, indicating that he had found a suitable place for landing, the North Foreland Meadow, a field situated between the cliffs and Dover Castle. The following day the over-cast skies

forbade all attempts. Blériot received the letter from Fontaine, but for the moment his preoccupations were turned towards the preparation for the departure. To improve the floatation of his machine, he installed a canvas cylinder full of air in the fuselage. In each camp, at Sangatte and at the *Baraques*, the tension was rising. The mechanics checked the machines one last time, the pilots scrutinized the clouds.

Blériot, whose burns still made him suffer, was however not unhappy with the respite. This would in fact be of only short duration, the long awaited improvement happened in the night 24 - 25 as recorded by Alfred Leblanc -

The wind only calmed down towards midnight, I lay down very late, having had to take all my dispositions to get Blériot off the following morning. But I was too nervous to be able to sleep for very long, so, shortly after two o'clock in the morning I was up walking along and across the terrace of the hotel. The weather was completely favourable, I decided to go and wake Blériot.

'Do you think that attempt should be possible this morning?' he says to me.

I am absolutely sure, only we must profit immediately from the calm in the atmosphere.

My friend gets dressed and has his breakfast prepared. But I must admit he is not himself ... A light emotion can be read on his face, an emotion quickly passed because, hardly had he smelt the salt air, that he recovered all of his calm and all of his energy.

My car is at the door of the hotel. M. and Mme. Blériot climb in with me. I drive firstly Mme. Blériot to the Escopette, the only anti-torpedo boat which could be put at the disposition of the friends of the aviator, to follow the flight of the aeroplane, and to be ready for all events. Blériot had to leave at sunrise, I ask the Captain Piogier to please take to sea without waiting, and I take with me one of his sailors, who will have the job of giving the departure signal to the Escopette.

In a few minutes we are at Les Baraques where the flying machine is resting. I wake Blériot's two mechanics who are fast asleep. The monoplane is rapidly brought out of its hanger. We fill her up with fuel and take a last look at the machine ... Anzani, the two mechanics Mamet and Collin and I push the machine. It is magnificent and as gracious as possible.

Blériot crossing the Riez plain, heading for the sea, turning and climbing.

On the right, Alicia Blériot on the uncomfortable bridge of the *Escopette*. To her right, Captain Piogier who pushed the speed to a maximum.

The Anzani engine of the crossing is preserved with the aircraft by the *Conservatoire National des Arts et Métiers*.

Blériot climbs into his machine. The propeller is started up, the engine roars regularly. Blériot shouts to us 'Let go!' the bird slides and rises majestically. It goes away about 3 km from us, almost as far as Sangatte. The flight lasts 11 minutes.

The trial which my friend had just completed before the supreme attempt, was over, it was 4.15 a.m., and this flight gave me the impression that Blériot is absolute master of his machine and that the engine was functioning best of all. He himself is equally very satisfied and very happy. He is like me, persuaded of success.

- 'What do you think of my flight?' he asks me. 'Can I leave?'

- 'I am entirely confident. You need to prepare yourself.' It is 4.25 a.m. The sun appears on the horizon; this is one of the conditions imposed by the rules of the Daily Mail.

Blériot can therefore leave. A last look at Sangatte with my binoculars allowed me to reassure him, telling him that Latham is not moving. At the moment where I indicated to him again the direction he must take.

'I will not leave,' he says to me again as an extra precaution, 'before being sure that the departure signal had been given to the Escopette.'

I reassured him one last time and gave him rendezvous at Dover, even as I left him.

I went up to the dunes. Arriving at my observation point I spot the counter torpedo boat. I wave my handkerchief, making a sign to Blériot that he can leave. For his part, the sailor from the Escopette, placed on the dunes gives the departure signal to the ship.

Anzani gives a last look at the engine. All goes well. The propeller is started up. The engine roars and Blériot calmly takes off. It is 4.41 a.m. The aeroplane rises rapidly, makes an arc of a circle, crosses the dunes and drives towards the high seas at 4.42 a.m. exactly. For myself I feel not the slightest emotion, so much am I convinced that Blériot must cross the Channel without difficulties. However, when I see him reach the counter torpedo boat and pass it in the wink of an eye, I cannot stop myself from a vague sentiment of apprehension, because I see now that the Escopette is not going to be able to follow him.

'What will happen to him,' I shout to myself, 'if an accident happens? the ship will not be able to bring him help quickly enough.'

During eleven minutes I can follow him with my marine binoculars and when I can no longer distinguish him, I search the horizon and I want to see him still. Oh! What a marvellous and unforgettable spectacle this big bird lost between the sky and the water, which escapes on a wing beat, followed by this warship which steams at full speed to catch him! For a long time I watch the counter torpedo boat continue its route, from which I conclude that Blériot is still flying. But in the end, the ship itself disappears completely on the horizon.

During this time, on board the *Escopette*, Robert Guérin, another journalist of the *Matin* who embarked on the counter-torpedo boat at the same time as Mme. Blériot, watched out for the passage of the aviator.

Marcel Marmier the photographer from *Le Matin* took the first photograph after the energetic arrival. The journalist Charles Fontaine poses by the side of Louis Blériot. The day before Fontaine had taken down a telephone line to clear the field.

Suddenly at a moment when we were not yet expecting, wrote Guérin, *I spot the monoplane above the dunes. I shout like crazy,*

- "There he is! There he is!"'

Everybody rushes to starboard. We raise the binoculars. Alone, Mme. Blériot, standing in a corner does not show herself.

This admirable woman who, during all the crossing, showed proof of unheard of courage, despite the anxiety which we had, who had the force to smile, to laugh even when she wanted to cry, weakened a little. But quickly overcoming this first emotion, she sees, watches, admires, as do we all. It is in fact admirable and the enthusiasm makes us dumb. The light bird runs straight towards the sea, it follows the cliffs at Sangatte, it flies with a disconcerting rapidity, with an admirable stability, with an impression of absolute security. We are running at 19 knots.

- "To 21 knots." shouts the Captain.

The Escopette leaps on the water. We are now on a line parallel to Blériot. We do not seem to be advancing.

Fontaine and Blériot were driven to the port of Dover where the pilot wanted to welcome his wife.

- "22, 24, 25 knots!"! shouts successively the Captain. The boat takes up again. It splits the breaking waves. Our match is more and more lively. But, alas our handicap is too heavy! Still gracious, still docile, lending itself faithfully to the manoeuvre of its pilot, the Blériot monoplane runs forward, no more worried about it's convoy. We hoped that he would make zigzags to keep himself alongside. But Blériot is already far away. After half an hour on the sea, he is nothing more than a small black point on the horizon and soon he disappears in the mist. It is now five o'clock in the morning and we are only half way across the strait. The minutes become long".

The moment has come to give the parole to Louis Blériot himself,

My awakening that morning there was rather grim; I do not know for which reason. My friend Alfred Leblanc, the man devoted by excellence, awoke me at 2.30 a.m. but I admit that I was nowhere near disposed to leave. I saw things rather blackly and I would have been happy to hear it said that the wind was blowing so strongly that no attempt was possible. Leblanc cheered me up a little and carried me in his car. I was saved. The lively air which whipped my face totally awakened me. I was a little ashamed of my weakened movement. This time I have courage enough for two. At the Baraques, Mamet and Collin, my two mechanics, have already opened the tent and the monoplane is coming out of the farmyard. Despite the early morning hour the village was up and about and from minute to minute the autos arrive. There are soon a few hundred people. That bothers me a little. I would have so much wished to be alone! We decide, Leblanc and myself that a preliminary trial will take place. We organise the crowd as much as we can. The machine rose easily. The extra weight of the air cylinder diminished only little the power. I have a new propeller which pulls perfectly. I stay about ten minutes in the air, agreeably surprised to notice a small fresh wind coming from the land, a tide wind which will push me towards the Channel.

On the quayside in the port of Dover, Louis Blériot waves to his wife who is being brought ashore.

CERTIFICATE OF "PRATIQUE."

The British Customs certificate handed over to *"Louis Blériot Master of a Vessel called the Monoplane"*.

The cockpit of the Blériot XI, in July 2009, after it was lowered from the ceiling of the CNAM and before being dusted. Other than the "cloche" and the rudder bar, the pilot had, on the right, a lever to set the advance and retard, a decompressor and a battery master switch.

All is ready. Faithful to the rules I wait for sunrise. Leblanc soon indicates to me that the disc is apparent by means of a flag which he waves from the dune. It is the signal. A small emotion takes me at the moment when I take my place in the machine. I say to myself,

"What will happen? Will I go as far as Dover?"

Rapid thoughts, fugitives, which happily do not last long. I now think only of my machine, of the engine, of the propeller. All is moving, all vibrates. At the signal the workers release the machine. There I am, raised.

I drive straight ahead. I rise progressively metre by metre. I clear the dune where Leblanc sends me his wishes. I am at present above the sea leaving on my right the counter torpedo boat whose opaque smoke obscures the sun. God! If suddenly one was going to object to me that Phoebe was not on the first third of its race!

I am going, I am going tranquilly, with no emotion, with no real impression. I seem to be in a balloon. The absence of any wind permits me to operate no control of rudder or warping. If I could block the controls, I could put my hands in my pockets.

It seems to me that I am not going quickly. This is because, I think, of the uniformity of the sea. Above the land, the houses, the woods, the roads appear and disappear as in a dream. Above the water, the wave, the same wave, it seems, is always in sight.

I am pleased with my machine. Its stability is perfect. And the engine, what a marvel! Ah! My brave Anzani, he does not cough but I had reached my high in the first half hour! Not wishing to retard my advance, I had said my goodbyes to the Escopette and I had no longer a guide. Never mind. Come what will! During about ten minutes I remained alone, isolated, lost in the middle of the immense sea, seeing no point on the horizon, perceiving no boat. This calm, troubled only by the roaring of the engine, was a dangerous charm of which I was well aware. Also I had my eyes fixed on the oil distributor and on the level of consummation of fuel. These ten minutes seemed long to me and truly I was happy to perceive towards the east a grey line which detached itself from the sea and grew before my eyes. No doubt, it was the English coast. I was almost saved.

I steered straight away towards this white mountain. But the wind and the mist take me. I must struggle with my hands, with my eyes. Happily, my machine obeys docilely to my thoughts. I steer it towards the cliff but however I do not see Dover? Ah! Devil! Where am I then?

Three boats come into my sight. Tug boats, packet boats! Of no importance! They appear to be steering towards a port; Dover no doubt, and I follow them tranquilly. Sailors send me enthusiastic hurrahs.

I almost wish to ask them the route to Dover. Alas! I do not speak English.

I follow, notwithstanding, the cliff from the north to the south, but the wind against which I am fighting now springs up again. Suddenly on the edge of a twist which is designed on the coast, I perceive a man desperately waving a tri-colour flag ... I remember then the letter of this good Fontaine, and I shout to myself, "Ah! the brave fellow!"

A crazy joy comes over me. I do not guide myself, I throw myself rather towards the land where he is calling me and I feel a gentle emotion. The concern now is to land, but the shaking is violent and as soon as I approach the earth a current raises me up. The struggle lasted a short time however, because I cannot rest longer in the air, I have just cleared about 43 km, in half an hour. It was enough. Also, at the risk of breaking everything, I cut the ignition at 20 metres high. And now to happiness! The chassis receives it rather badly, the propeller is damaged, but, my faith, never mind.

Charles Fontaine reported in these terms the arrival of Blériot,

The flying man has just landed ... tranquilly, Blériot climbs down from his machine and comes towards me. I embrace him ... at the same time enveloping him in the folds of my flag. But this man so hardy, so courageous, found nothing to say to me. His eyes are puffy and his eyelids blackened by the smoke of coal over the sea[1] but his forehead is cheerful.

"Ah well! that's it," I say to him simply.

"It is done!" he replied to me with the most tranquil air in the world.

Then he spoke with a calm voice,

"Over the sea, I lost my route, out from the English coast. I could not see Dover. I was going to lose my way, I do not know where, somewhere on a cliff, when I saw your flag. I understood straight away and turned immediately to my left and followed you to land then at the place that you designated. Taken however by a current of wind, I had to descend a little precipitately. My propeller is broken, but the rest of the machine is intact."

One single thing, at this moment, seems to preoccupy Blériot.

"And Latham?" he says to me

"Latham is still at Sangatte."

At this reply, his face lights up.

"I am truly happy to be the first to have succeeded the crossing of the Channel," he said.

And that was all. Blériot would not show any other joy or enthusiasm.

The aviator landed on sloping ground and the contact with the ground having been fairly brutal, the undercarriage was folded under the wings, but of no importance, the objective was achieved, Blériot had beaten the Channel and if at this minute he did not measure fully all that his exploit implied, the days and weeks to come would help him. A few instants later, several dozen soldiers ran up, soon followed by a few sailors then a knot of journalists and photographers.

Confiding the guard of his now historic monoplane, to a few police officers, still accompanied by Fontaine, he went by car to the port of Dover, where the *Escopette* had just dropped anchor. Alicia Blériot, who was uncertain of the outcome of her husband's fate since she saw him disappear on the horizon off the French coast, at last saw her anxiety dissipate. But 'her' crossing of the Channel had been perhaps more trying than that of her husband, it was thus that she told of it:

Seeing the impossibility in which the counter torpedo boat found itself to catch up the aviator ... the anxiety

tortured me. What will he become, alone, without guide, between the sky and the water? No compass on board to steer him. If he falls to the sea, no-one will be there to save him...my companions on board could themselves no longer dissimulate their worry, but by compassion no doubt, no-one wished to admit it. This long torture had to last until our arrival in Dover, that is to say more than one-and-a half hours - a century for me.

Off the English coast, M. Guérin affirmed to me to having hearing cannon fire seeming to come from Dover.

"It is the cannon of the Victory," he shouted.

But this is only a strategy, I think, done to tear me from my sorrow and to give me a little courage ... just off the bay of St. Margaret, we pass in front of Dover Castle. Nothing, still nothing. I ignore still what has become of my husband.

Broken by emotion, I struggle still ... at last the Escopette enters the English port ... everything which is said around me is indifferent to me and still this fixed idea haunts my mind: my husband, I have to have news of my husband! Ah! What joy, what deliverance when suddenly I hear a voice shout:

"He has arrived safe and sound!"!

In the wink of an eye, all of my energy came back... At last, there is little boat bringing the good news ... At the moment of climbing on board, an English steam boat came alongside the Escopette, an officer came down and came to congratulate me. I thank him as amiably as possible, but he understands my haste to leave the Escopette and withdraws discreetly. I climb rapidly into the boat followed by the passengers and we are soon on our way towards the landing quay. Half way there, Oh happiness! I spot on the jetty, my husband who is waving his handkerchief. I renounce the describing to you my joy in perceiving this little white square beaten by the wind, which announced to me that my husband is safe and sound. We tie up and I throw myself into the arms of my husband, embarrassing him with effusion. Then I look at him, I look at him again. It is really him, it is really the same man, always calm. He does not realise what he has just done and does not doubt that he has just passed into posterity.

On the evening of the 25th, proud of his exploit, Blériot poses with two trophies and the wallet containing the *Daily Mail* prize.

"Blériot you arrived too late." The cartoonist A. Roubille gives the words to Napoleon, underlining the political and strategic importance of Louis Blériot's flight. England is no longer an island.

Overnight Louis Blériot became world famous and his portrait was even on a box of cigars.

The cover (designed and made the same morning) for the menu of the dinner offered by Lord Northcliffe to Louis Blériot on 25 July, at the Savoy Hotel in London.

Above: Louis Blériot, the "new Colossus of Rhodes"! Exaggeration was the style at the time.

Below: Put back onto its wheels but resting on trestles, the Blériot XI of the Channel Crossing was first of all shown to the public by Selfridges department store in London.

Paris 29 July 1909. Today it is difficult to imagine the impact that Louis Blériot's flight across the Channel had on the French population.

The couple, driven by Fontaine then reached the hotel Lord Warden. Upon arriving, Blériot received from the French Vice Consul in Dover, the congratulations of the French Government, as well as the news of his promotion to the rank of Chevalier de la Légion d'Honneur.

But he has hardly the time to send a few telegrams to his parents and to intimate friends, that two custom officers come up to him and ask him if he had anything to declare. Upon his negative reply they hand over a Certificate of 'Pratique', a little master-piece of administrative humour (what a pity that Officer G. T. Camburn spelled his name Bléroit).

After having eaten at the hotel with the Captain of the *Escopette*, her officers and a few friends including Alfred Leblanc, Blériot and his wife that afternoon made a short trip to Calais and returned, by boat this time. The following day, receptions and official meetings started. The English, far from considering Blériot an invader, hail him. After having received the congratulations of the Mayor of Dover, Mr. W. Emden, Louis Blériot left the Lord Warden hotel to go to London, accompanied by his wife and by Fontaine, Leblanc and Fournier. On route to the station, he was acclaimed by hundreds of people. On the platform, people pressed close around him, young girls asking for his autograph. The arrival of the train allowed him to escape, but in London the occasion was magnified.

Several thousand people were waiting for the aviator at Victoria Station. The police had to force a passage to the car of Lord Northcliffe, the owner of the *Daily Mail* who had come to welcome him as he stepped off the train. In Blériot's honour

he offered a dinner at the Savoy Hotel, to which were invited amongst other personalities, Mr Haldane the British Minister of War and M. Paul Cambon the French Ambassador. At the end of the meal, Lord Northcliffe gave to the hero of the day, an engraved silver cup crowned with a Winged Victory and an envelope containing a cheque for £1,000, the much sought-after prize that he had just won.

That evening, Louis Blériot and his wife went to the Empire, a large theatre where they watched the projection of a film showing the aviator in flight above the Channel!

The following day they are invited to a private lunch at the French Embassy, then to a dinner - a real banquet of nearly two hundred guests - given in their honour by the United Kingdom Aéro-Club.

That same evening, Blériot left for Dover and spent the night in Calais. On his return to Paris on the 29 July, Blériot was welcomed at the Gare du Nord by a delegation led by Louis Barthou, the Minister of Justice (ex. Minister of Public Works with a passion for aviation) and Alexandre Millerand, the current Minister of Public Works. Outside, a crowd of more than a hundred thousand people waited for the victor of the Channel, who was coming home, mission accomplished.

On the platform, were, amongst other members of the Aéro-Club de France, Santos-Dumont and Delagrange, there were also workers from the company Phares Blériot, charged by their comrades to present to their Patron, a trophy which they had purchased by organising a collection in the factory.

Louis Blériot, Alessandro Anzani and Alicia Blériot acclaimed by Parisians.

On 13 October 1909, reception of the monoplane at the Conservatoire National des Arts et Métiers.

Surrounded by the highest personalities of politics and science, Louis Blériot reads a speech.

When the train came into the station a deafening roar rose above all; on the platform it was pandemonium. Blériot climbed down from the carriage surrounded by Leblanc, Anzani, Chauvière, Fontaine and Fournier. The crowd broke windows and doors to try to see their hero when he came out, to take his place with his wife in a horse drawn carriage. Escorted by the Garde Républican who had great difficulty in containing the enthusiasm of this crowd who wanted to touch the bird man, the carriage, under the applause and the cries of *Vive Blériot!* drove towards the Aéro-Club de France, where in an atmosphere of a family gathering, he received the congratulations of his colleagues.

The festivities would continue for the three following days, receptions were held at the Matin, at the town hall, at the Ligue Nationale Aérienne, a banquet of 500 guests was given by the Aéro-Club at the Palais d'Orsay, a party was organised at Port-Aviation on the 1st August. The following day, at last, a banquet was given by the company Phares Blériot in honour of it's President.

During these memorable days, Blériot thought of all the years of effort, of all of his falls, of financial difficulties which almost forced him to abandon his research. The wheel had turned. Now he was allowed to hope for everything. His exploit knew extraordinary repercussions. In the newspapers in France, in England, in Germany, in the United States, one could read that a new era had opened in the development of Aviation. Certain perceived already the consequences of Blériot's flight, The Préfet de Police, Lépine, during the reception at the town hall, treated the subject in a humoristic mood:

> *After William the Conquer*, he said, *you have just realised the dream of a Napoléon, the descent on England, but it was not the Entente Cordiale, that you were thinking about, the first moment of surprise passed, of the diplomatic complications? And the Customs! Have you thought about the Customs ? In a short time you are going to make their existence impossible.[1] I issue passports for overseas, no-one will any more ask me for one. There is an office to be closed and it is the only one which brings more money to the town than it costs. And the guardians of the peace! To whom we make already the reproach of making the race heavy by their boots, would you give them those of 'seven leagues' to travel through the air? I have difficulty to stop burglars breaking doors, now they will come through the windows!*

On the 15 August, invited to the House of Commons by Sir Benjamin Stone who offered a lunch in his honour, among the guests Mr Lloyd George, Chancellor of the Exchequer, Major Baden-Powell, the Honourable Charles S. Rolls, the English Aviator Cody, the Compte de Lapeyrouse, vice president and managing director of the Company Phares Blériot, the Aviator himself made allusion to the early creation of aerial transportation companies.

On the English side as well, there were clairvoyant spirits, but while saluting sportingly the performance of Louis Blériot, they had - and it was fully understandable - worried reactions, preoccupations of strategic type.

H. G. Wells, the well known writer noted,

> *'England is no longer an Island!'*

---

(1) Contrary to what the Préfet feared, the Customs Officers knew how to adapt to these new circumstances. Blériot's crossing would in fact be at the origin of a new set of Customs Regulations between France and England, known as the 'Blériot Regulations'.

Before going to the CNAM, the original Blériot XI monoplane was shown at the place of honour at the first International Aerial Transport Exposition in the *Grand Palais* in Paris. Well before the end of the exposition, the machine was transported through the streets of the capital to the CNAM.

He took up a famous phrase that Lord Northcliffe wrote at the time of the Wright bi-plane and that the Daily Mail re-printed after Blériot's victory. Captain Windham, President of the Aeroplane Club of Great Britain, said during a speech to the House of Commons, on the occasion of Blériot's visit:

...I was on board the torpedo boat when Latham tried to cross the Channel by aeroplane. The torpedo boat represents that which the human brain has been best able to make for speed on the sea for a hundred years, but the aeroplane which, however, has started it's evolutions for a little less than one year, passed above us like lightning. I do not need to bring out what precious use we could have put the aeroplanes to during the assault on Port Arthur by the Japanese. We know that thousands of the yellow soldiers perished on a hill of 307 metres, in order to learn of the Russian positions. With one single aeroplane, they would have been able to do it much earlier and probably also without any loss.[1] And the dirigibles one asks? For my part, I do not believe in the services that could give dirigibles, which have the default of offering a larger surface for firing. If we pass now to costs, let us make a comparison, M. Blériot can sell, we hear, his aeroplanes at 7,500 francs each, whereas a Dreadnought costs us 50 millions. Therefore for the price of one Dreadnought we could have a fleet of 7,000 aeroplanes and one single aeroplane could carry the dynamite in sufficient quantity to blow up a Dreadnought.

This vision, although incomplete and a little sketchy, is nevertheless prophetic on several points:

- the abandoning of dirigibles to the benefit of aircraft
- the appearance of aviation for observation and bombing
- the disappearance, eventually, of battleships.

However, whereas the foreseers of the future of the epoch give themselves to suppositions on the future of the aeroplane, the orders for the Blériot XI, from now on called 'type Calais-Dover' started to flow in. Blériot would, in a short time, become the

(1) During the recent war between Russia and Japan - 1904 to 1905- Captain Windham seemed to have ignored that France used a captive balloon to observe the battlefield as early as 1794. This was the first ever use of aeronautical military material in history.

first industrial aviation magnate. As for the glorious monoplane, repaired by Grandseigne, it was at first exhibited on-site under a tent, then in London in the department store Selfridges of Oxford Street. During all of the duration of the exhibition, numerous Londoners would queue up in the street to get a closer look at the famous Cross Channel Monoplane.

The monument laid out on the spot where Blériot landed, in Dover in the middle of what has since become a wood.

Brought back to France, it was then shown, suspended on the façade of the *Matin* who had acquired ownership, then at the *Grand Palais for the Salon de la Locomotion Aérienne* of 1909. The newspaper, having made a gift of the machine to the Conservatoire National Des Arts et Métiers the machine was solemnly welcomed on the 13th October, after having been acclaimed, once again, by a crowd during the parade through the streets of Paris.

Latham tried the crossing again on the 27th July but - accumulation of bad luck - fell into the water at less than a kilometre from the English coast. The aviator was slightly injured, but he was above all morally hurt; he abandoned and returned to France ... on the same boat as Blériot! He would never cross the Channel by plane ... After having won successes in the meetings of 1909 and 1910, he left to go hunting in Africa where, on the 7 June 1912, he was thrown into the air and killed by a buffalo that he had just shot. Thus was completed, at less than 30 years old, the adventurous career of this valorous pilot, who will remain in memory, as the unfortunate rival of Blériot, in the Crossing of the Channel.

The Blériot type XI was built in sufficient numbers for there to remain several throughout the world into the 21st century. The one shown here is one of the rare still powered by an Anzani. It still flies and belongs to Louis Blériot...grandson.

From Tradesman to Industrialist

HIS SUCCESS OVER THE CHANNEL ALLOWED LOUIS BLÉRIOT TO REACH HIS GOAL: BECOME AN AVIATION INDUSTRIALIST

The months that followed the Crossing of the Channel were a period of intense activity for Louis Blériot. In the space of one month, more than one hundred orders were recorded for the Type XI. The first customers were Leblanc, Delagrange, Molon, Aubrun, Le Blon and Balsan.[1] Several Governments were equally interested in the machine, France, of course, but also England, Russia, Austria-Hungary and Italy. At the beginning of August, Blériot trained his first student - his friend - Alfred Leblanc - who made his first flight on a Blériot XI on the 4th August, at Issy-les-Moulineaux.

Blériot then participated in the Grande Semaine d'Aviation in Champagne, organised by the Marquis de Polignac at Bétheny, near Reims, from the 22nd to the 29th August. The Marquis had planned big, a railway station was specially fitted out for the occasion. There were two giant spectator stands, press offices, parking areas for cars. There were also souvenir merchants, hair-dressers and restaurants where one could meet the most notable personalities of French society. The meeting was a great success, more than one hundred thousand people attended. Thirty-eight machines were present, the five Blériots were: -

a) three type XI, new machines equipped with Anzani engines of 25 hp which carried the numbers : 16 in the name of Delagrange, 21 in the name of Blériot, 24 in the name of Leblanc

b) two type XII, both in the name of Blériot

- 22 was also a new machine powered by an ENV engine of 60 hp. Its ailerons had been replaced by

(1) It was at this time that the distinction was made between the Type numbers and the Construction numbers, therefore the XI of Leblanc carried the construction number 13; the first XI of Delagrange carried the construction number 14.

warping wings, the cables now passed through the aileron hinges which were no longer used

- 23 was the prototype in which Louis Blériot had burned his foot twice at the meeting of Douai. It was now powered by a 40hp Anzani engine of 3 cylinders in a fan configuration

There were twenty-eight pilots. On his monoplane n° XII with the ENV engine, Blériot won the circuit prize over 10 kilometres, beating the world record at an average speed of 76.955 kmh. All hope seemed to be possible for the Gordon-Bennett cup, a speed race over 20 kilometres, with a prize of 25,000 francs. Only two competitors qualified; Curtiss on his bi-plane *Golden Flyer,* and Blériot on his type XII with the ENV engine. Curtiss had tried several times to beat Blériot's time, but in vain. The evening before the race, he visited Blériot and asked openly for his advice to improve his speed. And Blériot gave it to him, as was reported by his mechanic Collin in his book *Parmi les Précurseurs du Ciel:*

> *You must lighten your machine,* he said. *Refine your propeller, your engine turning faster will produce more power... reduce resistance to forward movement by fitting a very small fuel tank, with just the quantity of fuel necessary, you should gain thus, a few seconds...*

Blériot, from his side, had adopted a four bladed propeller and had uncovered the trailing edge of the wings over 5 m² (of a total surface of 22 m²) But, most probably thanks to Blériot's judicious advice, it was Curtiss who won the Cup, 5 and 3/5th seconds better than Blériot, at a speed of 73.637 kmh. Collin's comment was:

> *When Curtiss left the hanger, I say "That's it, we are made"... and we were.*

The Grande Semaine de Champagne, at Reims, in August 1909: the Blériot hangars.

That same evening, Blériot made a new attempt and outside the competition, reached 77 kmh. The following day, the last day of the meeting, the propeller of the Blériot XII n° 22 broke up in flight. A fragment hit the rudder. Out of balance, the machine fell and caught fire. It was completely destroyed, but Blériot, once again came out of it with no more severe injuries than burns to his hands and his face. On the 8th September, hardly recovered from his accident, Blériot took part in the meeting at Brescia, accompanied by Leblanc, Collin and Mamet, with two type XI, and a type XII.

He then participated in the meeting at Berlin-Johannistal, from the 26 to the 29th September. On this date his two machines were seized, following a difference with the organisers caused by his departure for the meeting at Cologne, which started the same day.

During his visit to Cologne, he stayed at the house of Ettore Bugatti, who was then technical director of the car firm Deutz. Every day, during the week of the meeting, Blériot went to the aviation field in a light car that Bugatti had just built for himself.[2] From the 29th September to the 5th October, Blériot carried out numerous flights with a brand new XI, type, 'Channel Crossing'. One of the flights on the 1st of October lasted 1 hour 4 minutes and 56 seconds, his longest flight at this time.

On the 8th October he went to Frankfurt where there was also a meeting. He flew the following day and won second prize for duration, a sum of 10,000 marks; the winner was the Baron de Caters a famous Belgian aviation pioneer, on a Voisin. On the 11th October he won the Krupp prize, also 10,000 marks. He then left for central Europe where he had to do a series of demonstration flights, first in Budapest then in Vienna on the 23rd, where he flew in front of the Emperor Franz-Joseph. On the 30th at Bucharest, he flew in front of Queen Elizabeth of Rumania. Every time his flights caused enormous enthusiasm in the crowds, which acclaimed him on landing. However, on the contrary, when he could not take off because of the wind or a mechanical problem, the crowd sometimes threatened to tear him to pieces.

(2) Enthusiastic about the speed and handling of this car, Blériot encouraged Bugatti to become a builder himself - Bugatti was in fact already thinking about it. Less than three months later, Bugatti founded his own company at Molsheim in Alsace, from where for thirty years would come the streamlined sports and racing cars - the 'pure-blood' Bugatti.

At Reims, Glenn Curtiss (facing the camera with cap) profiting from the advice of Louis Blériot (in flying clothes) to beat him in the speed contest for the Gordon Bennett Cup.

On the right, Louis Blériot had the honour to accompany the President of the Republic, Armand Fallières. Between them is Aristide Briand.

Whilst he was absent, it was Leblanc who represented the Blériot Company at the meeting at Blackpool, in England, which was held on the 18th to the 23rd October. Despite terrible weather, he managed to carry out a few flights, but, still short of experience, could not compete with Latham, who, on his Antoinette did not hesitate to brave the storms.

On the 26th October at the meeting at Doncaster, Delagrange, with his new Blériot XI, on which he had fitted a Gnome rotary engine of 50 hp, flew at over 80 kph, beating several world speed records. On the 30th, at Juvisy, with the same machine he covered 200 kilometres in 2 hours 32 minutes, giving himself new world records. At Issy-les-Moulineaux on the 7th November, Louis Blériot delivered a type XII with a 60 hp ENV engine, to the English aviator, Claude Grahame-White, who christened it *White Eagle*.

On the 29th during a trial flight at Pau, Blériot who accompanied Grahame-White, had to make a forced landing with the *White Eagle*. Following this incident, Blériot proposed to Grahame-White an exchange, his machine against two type XI.[1]

In December, he went to Constantinople accompanied by his mechanics. On the 12th, the day planned for the exhibition, the wind was blowing in gusts on the manoeuvring field at Taxim. In order not to disappoint the spectators, Blériot decided to take off anyway. The violence of the wind stopped him manoeuvring. He drifted towards the valley of Tatavla, a narrow ravine where his machine hit the roof of a house. The aviator was thrown to the ground and suffered fractures and multiple bruises. It was his thirty-second accident, the last and the most serious.

(1) It could be that it was the *White Eagle* that the Duke of Westminster and Colonel Laycock, Director of the ENV Company, purchased in June 1910, in order to present it to the British War Office. The fourth Type XII built was delivered at the end of February 1910 at Pau to the Dutchman Clément Van Maasdijk, who destroyed it completely in an accident on the 21st April. Christened *Flying Dutchman*, the machine was powered by a Gnome Omega of 50 hp.

GRANDE SEMAINE D'AVIATION DE CHAMPAGNE (Journée du 26 Août)
L'appareil de Blériot s'abat devant les Tribunes

In order to avoid a group of badly positioned soldiers, Blériot crashed his type XII in front of the stands.

He was at first taken care of in the French hospital in Constantinople, then a few days convalescence with his wife in Vienna, before returning to France. He recovered quickly, but the doctors informed him that his broken ribs had caused an injury to his heart, which could re-awaken later when in his 50s (this later proved, unfortunately, to be correct). Louis Blériot from now on had to live (a little) more calmly and to limit the risks to be taken. He would no longer participate as a pilot, neither at meetings nor aerial exhibitions (which did not stop him from flying again as early as 1st January in Pau). As for the wreck of the machine, only the engine and a few accessories were recovered by Collin and transported by hand to the nearest railway station, a distance of six kilometres. Upon his return to Paris, Louis Blériot became a member of the Administration Committee of the Aéro-Club de France.

At Reims, in front of the Blériot hangars. Behind two photographers, on the left Louis Blériot's father, Alicia Blériot in long coat with her husband and on the right with arm-band, Alfred Leblanc. To the rear of the hangar is a Blériot type "Channel Crossing".

In his other type XII, with wings partially uncovered for more speed, Louis Blériot attempts to beat a speed record...
but the breaking up of the propeller caused the accident from which the pilot only just escaped.

On the 23rd December, Louis Paulhan left for the United States with two pilots and four machines, of which two were Blériot monoplanes, for a tour of several months. On the programme, demonstration flights, aircraft sales and flying lessons. Paulhan appointed the Aeromotion Company of America to sell Blériots in America (the number of machines sold, alas is not known). At this end of the year 1909, the type XI was also demonstrated in Germany, in North Africa, in Argentina and in Chile.

At the same period, Miss Edith Coole became the first British Aviatrice, on a Blériot.

The following year, 1910, would be the year of the passage of Blériot's aeronautical activities from the tradesman stage to the industrial stage. Several of his first partners, Louis Peyret and Raymond Saulnier left him and Alfred Leblanc became his assistant for everything to do with aviation.

Louis Blériot's monoplane after his crash in Constantinople. On the right, a message which the Queen of Romania sent to his wife, and which shows how much the pilot was admired and appreciated by the European aristocracy: "We vibrated with terror with you! And we thank God who held his hand above your precious life! My heart rose thinking of you! Elisabeth, 15 December 1909."

The factory at Levallois

In order to face up to the constant inflow of orders, Blériot, after having made an appeal to sub-contractors such as Lioré and Régy, moved into new premises which he had built, at 39 route de la Révolte, at Levallois-Perret. Out of this factory from 1910 onwards, more than 150 engineers and operators would build, up to August 1914, almost a thousand machines, of which a great majority type XI, in different versions and extrapolations, certain of which did not have a great deal in common with the original model. During this time, the Blériot XI with all it's variants, would be the most-used machine in the world.

The success of the monoplane, type "Channel Crossing" or "Calais-Dover" was such that, other than the numerous copies, more or less conform and more or less viable which would be made, it would be built under licence in several countries.

In Great Britain, the Humber Company acquired the licence of the XI, the first example was flown by the chief pilot, George Barnes. In the United States, the Queen Aeroplane Co. of New York and the American Aeroplane Supply House, built single-seat and two-seat XI under licence, they were sold at $2,700 to $6,000 according to the type of engine. A racing version was also available. In Italy the Società Italiana Transaerea (SIT) a subsidiary of *Blériot Aéronautique*, produced several dozen type XI and XI – 2 with Gnome Omega engines. It was the same for the English subsidiary company Blériot Ltd. at Brooklands in Surrey.

The factory at Levallois was the subject of a publicity brochure from where some of these images are taken. Above, the main building, route de le Révolte. In the centre, the technical office where the ideas come from; below, the design office where the drawings and calculations are made under scale models of various aircraft. It can be seen that in the design office, the average age is lower than that in the technical office. Facing page: the assembly shop where can be seen Blériot type "Calais-Dover" with Anzani or Gnome engines, but also a type XII.

Above: The factory at Levallois. On the left, the headed note paper of the company. The heading represents, of course, a monoplane crossing the Channel. Centre: assembling fuselages. Below: covering of the wings.

Accessoires

Tendeurs Blériot n° 1
(Breveté s. g. d. g.)
Tout en acier demi-dur, — Indesserrabilité absolue.

Diamètres	Poids en grammes	Résistance à la rupture en kilos	Prix la pièce
35/10			
40/10	22	450	
50/10	45	600	2.15
	98	1400	3.25
			4.50

Tendeurs n° 2
Avec douille en cuivre.

Diamètres	Poids en grammes	Résistance à la rupture en kilos	Prix la pièce
35/10			
40/10	15	420	
50/10	20	570	?.80
70/10	40	900	1.15
	85	1300	1.50
			2. »

The catalogue of Louis Blériot Recherches Aéronautiques did not present only aircraft, but also all the parts which go to make an aircraft, many of which were designed and made by Blériot; for example, on the right, turnbuckles for piano wire which was widely used in aviation to strengthen and align the structure.

Below, an example of modern times: Military Blériot XI–2 leaving the factory in a convoy of horse-drawn carriages. The image raises a smile today, but was then very ordinary, because the horse would still be employed thirty years later and even during World War Two.

Above: Blériot monoplanes under construction in the PRTV factory in St Petersburg in Russia; machines of other makes, monoplanes and bi-planes were built in the same place.

Right: the logo of the mark SIT, Italian branch of Blériot-Aéronautique, founded in Turin on 20 July 1912 as the first industrial aviation company in Italy.

SOCIETÀ ITALIANA TRANSAEREA

Below: the British branch of a Blériot Ltd, in Brooklands. The photo is dated 1914, and the monoplanes are two-seat XI–2. On the left, the first page of the company catalogue.

The Blériot Monoplane

:: DESIGNED AND ::
MANUFACTURED BY
M. LOUIS BLERIOT,
THE HERO OF THE
GREAT CROSS CHAN-
NEL FLIGHT.

BLERIOT LIMITED,
53 & 54, LONG ACRE, LONDON, W.C.

The flying schools

Blériot had two Flying Schools, one at Issy-les-Moulineaux, where Leblanc and Delagrange trained, (the first two to acquire type XI) the second at Pau which was managed by Leblanc with Mollien as under manager, Collin (who would later be named General Manager of the schools) and Donnaud as instructor. Blériot then opened three new flying schools: at Etampes, at Mourmelon and at Hendon, near to London. The Pau school, at Caubios, was particularly well situated on the plain of Pont-Long to the north of the Gave. The mild climate of the region allowed the continuous training of the pupils through the winter. Inaugurated on the 22nd November 1909, this school had a circuit of 6 kilometres around, had workshops, garages, hangers and offices. There was even a restaurant and a few hotel rooms for the aviators blocked by bad weather.

Opened in July 1910, the school at Etampes was designed to liberate the field at Issy-les-Moulineaux. The school was installed on 60 hectares of land near to the Mondésir Farm, from where Blériot took off the previous year for his flight Etampes to Orleans.

The Blériot School at Hendon, created in October 1910, was managed by Blériot Ltd, Belfast Chambers, 156 Regent Street, in London. The Manager's name was Pierre Prier, the Chief Pilot was Henri Salmet. Each school was made up of a civil section and a military section. For those who had bought a Blériot, the lessons were free. For the others a lump sum of 2000 francs was required, any damage to the machine or breakages, were paid for by the pilot. From 1913 onwards the lump sum was reduced to 800 francs

The hangars of the Blériot School in Pau. Pupils and owners were proud to have their photo taken, often later converted to postcards.

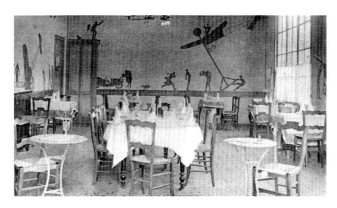

The dining room of the Blériot School in Pau. A frieze shows that machines are capricious and the apprenticeship is full of traps!

Louis Blériot dressed as "sportsman", surrounded by owners/pilots of Blériot aircraft on which they would become distinguished. From left to right, Alfred Leblanc, Emile Aubrun, Louis Blériot, Claude Grahame-White, Jacques de Lesseps.

In his catalogue of 1911 Blériot gave the following advice to would be pilots:

The greatest prudence is recommended to the student aviator. He must above all fix himself in no way to want to make progress too rapidly, which can only compromise the success of his apprenticeship. In the beginning, he must stop himself any trial if the speed of the wind goes above 3 to 4 metres per second. The ground must be carefully chosen, it must be sufficiently level to allow taxiing in all directions and to land at any point, it must present a straight line of at least 1 kilometre with a minimum width of 700 to 800 metres.

Before departure the aviator must entirely check his machine himself, he must control if all is well in order, the bolts tightened, cable fixing absolutely intact, the cables themselves without float, the controls functioning freely. One then starts up the engine to assure oneself of its good functioning. When the aviator, installed in his machine, sees that the engine obtains a regime sufficient for him to acquire the necessary speed for flight, he makes a sign to the aides who hold the machine at the rear to let go all. To do his possible that the machine be orientated facing the wind, in order to start off wind straight ahead.

The first operation that the aviator must do is to advance slightly the steering towards the front, until the tail of the machine rises in a manner to put the beam completely horizontal. The incidence of the wings is thus almost completely eliminated and does not offer any resistance to advancing; the raising of the speed is then very rapid. When the pupil will have made a certain number of straight lines in this fashion and that he will find his machine well in hand, he will then be able to attempt to raise himself a little, for that, he must have at least 1 kilometre in a straight line in front of him. When he will feel that the beam is well horizontal, he will bring slightly the steering wheel to him in a fashion to incline the elevator, and the machine will leave the ground. He must then immediately put the bell vertically in the neutral position.

If by hazard the movement of the bell was a little brusque and the machine climbs, the aviator must above all not cut the ignition to try and stop the engine, on the contrary he can give himself again a little advance, he must do this, a push slightly on the steering towards the front, up until the machine re-establishes itself horizontally in the direction of movement. To relieve the engine, he must fix himself to set the incidence of the tail plane, in a manner that the machine flies always tail up.

In order to land, the pilot must push the bell forward, very little, in a manner to come to fly at 1 metre from the ground, he reduces then the ignition advance, without cutting however, and he pulls the bell towards him in a manner that the supporting wheel or skid comes to brush the ground. He pushes then the steering forward to land completely. In full flight, it is recommended to put fairly little advance to the ignition, of a fashion not to push the engine and to have always a certain force in reserve to augment the speed if the need makes itself felt for whatever reason.

Above: At Pau, the Blériot XII *White Eagle* of the Englishman Grahame-White, future builder of aircraft in the United Kingdom.

Below: *The Flying Dutchman* at Pau in 1909. The Blériot XII of Clément Van Maasdijk, who would become the first Dutch victim of aviation in 1910 (but not on a Blériot).

One must not make use of the warping except for brusque unlevelling of the machine, for example when a gust of wind takes the monoplane on the side. In all the other cases, when the machine is inclined in a permanent manner, one must always re establish the lateral balance by the action of the rudder.[1] In the case where the engine should come to stop itself brusquely at a certain height, the aviator must not lose his cold blood and above all must not pull on the steering bell, because then the machine, losing it's speed, will fall heavily to the ground, the tail first. On the contrary, the pilot will push slightly the bell forward so that the aeroplane conserves its speed and descends, the front inclined towards the ground. At 2 metres from the earth the aviator will bring his bell to the rear and the machine will land gently, it's that which one calls the gliding flight.

The instruction, on the Blériot XI with a 25 hp Anzani engine, was divided into three parts. In the first part the aircraft was stationary, the pupil learned to operate the engine and got used to receiving both the wash of the propeller and pulverised oil in his face, he learned then to make straight runs on the ground, using only the rudder. In the second part the pupil made short hops and then straight line flights at increasing heights, from 1 metre to about 6 metres. The third part was made up of turns and figures of eight at heights up to 100 metres and finished by a glide landing into a circle of 50 metres. The time necessary to obtain a license varied from eight days for the very smart, to five or six weeks for the slower ones, also their availability, their learning capabilities, and the weather. Each lesson lasted ten to fifteen minutes and one needed, according to each person, from ten to twenty-four lessons, which means that the licence was obtained with two to six flying hours.

---

(1) This recommendation is explained by the relative inefficiency of the warping wings.

In 1912, the success of Louis Blériot was sparkling. As witness, this Palace of the Air, inaugurated at Buc, near to Paris in 1912. The Louis Blériot aerodrome, complete with restaurant, hotel, sports hall, hangars and workshops.

Entrance to the Blériot Aéroparc at Buc. The Blériot aerodrome was also a school and a meeting place for fans of aviation.

The Blériot schools knew an extraordinary success, in two years from 1910 to 1912, more than 500 pupils were trained, among them the first four military licences, Lieutenants de Rose (future creator of the French Fighter Aviation), Princeteau and de Malherbe, the Enseigne de Vaisseau Conneau (who would win several big races under the name of Beaumont). There was also Lieutenants Bellenger,[2] de Goÿs (who would in 1914-1918 be one of the leaders of the French bombing squadrons), Gouin and Bague (who would disappear in trying to cross the Mediterranean). Amongst the civil pupils, we can cite amongst others: - Emile Aubrun, chemical engineer; in 1910 he participated in several races, one of which was the Eastern Circuit where he was placed second behind Leblanc. In 1911 he became Sporting Manager of Deperdussin, then during the First World War, technical director of Dufaux-Aviation. Jacques Balsan, a personal friend of Louis Blériot, was also one of his first customers. A

Squadron Leader in 1914, then in 1941 at 73 years old he was assistant to General Cochet, in the Free French Air force.

Prince Bibesco, also tied by friendship to Louis Blériot, in 1910 created the first flying school in Rumania. In 1914 he commanded two reconnaissance squadrons. Promoted to Colonel in 1918, then in 1927 he became President of the Fédération Aéronautique Internationale.

Dieudonné Costes obtained his licence in 1912 at 20 years old. In 1914-18 he became a fighter pilot and obtained nine victories. After the war he beat several records for distance and in 1930 with Maurice Bellonte made the first crossing of the Atlantic East to West on the *Point d'Interrogation*. Claude Grahame-White, an English pilot obtained his licence on the 4th January 1910 and in that same year he won several prizes and races, one of which was the second Gordon-Bennett Cup. In 1911 he became a constructor and transport pilot. During the First World War he commanded a squadron of the RFC (Royal Flying Corps, predecessor of the Royal Air Force). Jeanne Herveu, one of the very first female pilots, participated in several competitions in 1911, before becoming instructor in a female flying school in the United States. It is said that one of her pupils was the famous aviatrice, Amelia Earhart. Jacques de Lesseps, son of Ferdinand de Lesseps, builder of the Suez Cannel, was the second aviator to succeed in the crossing of the Channel, on the 21st May 1910 in a Blériot XI fitted with a Gnome engine of 50 hp. In 1914-1918 he commanded a Bomber Squadron. When peace returned, he went to Canada and created an aerial work company. Alexis Maneyrol, pilot at 18 years old, with his savings bought a Blériot XXVIII *Populaire* with which he participated at numerous aviation meetings. He would also be, in the 1930s, one of the first glider pilots, and first aerobatic champions. Léon Morane, a few months after obtaining his licence in 1910, obtained speed and altitude records. The following year he became a aircraft builder in association with Raymond Saulnier and created an aerodrome at Villacoublay (the company Morane Saulnier would build aircraft into the 1960s).

(2) The first Military pilot to obtain his civil licence on the 5th April 1910 at Pau.

A few of Blériot's pupils: Lt Bague; André Beaumont, famous pilot before 1914; Dieudonné Costes, future conqueror of the Atlantic; Lt de Goys, future creator of the French bomber arm; Lt de Malherbe; Cne Rose, future creator of the French fighter arm; and Alexis Maynerol, future aerobatics champion.

Edmond Perreyon obtained his licence at Pau in 1911, became an instructor, then test pilot, then Chief Pilot of the House of Blériot. Senator Emile Reymond, professor of surgery learned to fly in 1912 at the age of 48. In 1914, despite his functions of Senator, his rank of Medicin-Major and above all his age, joined the air force. In the first weeks of the war he was shot in the liver when returning from an observation mission, he died while dictating his report. Jules Védrines obtained his licence in 1910. He won the race Paris-Madrid in May 1911. The following year he became the man for record speed and won the Gordon-Bennett Cup. During the First World War he was posted to N° 3 Squadron (future Escadrille des Cigognes) and it was there that he completed the training of Guynemer and carried out particularly special and perilous missions.

All of these people in their different ways would soon become celebrities.

Numerous foreigners, civilians as well as the military, also learned to fly in the Blériot schools. Americans, Italians, Russians, Belgians, Swiss, Mexicans, Serbs, Bulgarians ...

In his book *Mes Trois Grandes Courses*, Conneau tells of his first impressions of the Blériot school at Caubios, after a training course in the Gnome factory at Argenteuil :

> *It is raining again today... the exercises in the open air being impossible, they have grouped us in a hanger. My first lesson of practical aviation is reduced to a lesson in a room, I learn the terms of convention which serve the professionals, a precise slang, without metaphors, I initiate myself to the 'advance' and to the 'retard. ... At last a calm period arrives, I am placed in a machine, I am made to repeat my lesson, the engine is started up and I roll, in a straight line, under the instructions of the professor... the exercise lasts four minutes and has necessitated eight hours of presence at the aerodrome. Is this lost time? Not at all. One observes with patience, one listens to the lessons. One sees the uncertain flights, the falls, the sudden lurches, the errors of control, the stoppages of the engine, wheels which collapse; we try to research the causes. In order to learn rapidly to fly, one must commence by remaining on the ground. This series of teasing, of hopes, of deceptions, last seven days, seven wet days during which the incertitude adds to the fatigue. From time to time, a few incidents interrupt the monotony. I amuse myself in following this or that machine, they are small hops over rough ground, crazy zigzags, a sudden stop. Over there it is an inclined roll, fantastic. Here is a pupil who steps down, his face black, his clothes, soaked in oil give him a diabolical aspect, he takes off his coat, but leaves in his wake an unsupportable odour"*

Despite this week of bad weather, the Enseigne de Vaisseau Conneau obtained his pilot's licence twelve days after arriving at Pau. Earle Ovington, an American pupil noted in his personal diary the circumstances under which he accomplished his first solo:

> *The mechanics, covered in grease rolled out of the hanger one of these machines repaired and re-repaired which were conserved specially for the "taxi drivers"[1] of whom I was one, I climbed into the cockpit. The cane seat was*

(1) This name, given very early to machines reserved for ground runs, went into the pilots' jargon to denote an aircraft.

not twenty-five centimetres wide and it's back rest was made of a sheet of plywood eight centimetres wide and half a centimetre thick. To make it even lighter, it had been entirely pierced with holes. These French really undress their machines to render them lighter! I was told to steer myself towards a pylon situated at the other extremity of the field and whereas my little monoplane rolled bouncing on the ground, I must have been concentrating too much on the pylon and not enough on what I was doing. I pushed my feet so hard on the rudder bar that the back of my seat broke and I tipped backwards pulling towards me the elevator control to stop myself, I reinstall myself on the seat as quickly as I could. Instead of being on the ground as I supposed I was 100 metres high and I continue to climb.

... between the rudder, which was agitated with my feet, the wings that I manoeuvred to see the horizon there where it should be and the stick which was actioned forwards and backwards to stop the earth jumping upwards or downwards, I had a very full sixty seconds.

But the most extraordinary adventure was without doubt what happened to the pupil Jean Ors in February 1912, practising straight lines on the ground, on a machine reserved exclusively for taxiing, he arrived at the end of the runway and as normal, climbed down from the fuselage to turn the aircraft in the opposite direction. The pupil had not sufficiently closed the throttle, the machine started to roll before he had the time to climb back on board. After running alongside the aircraft hanging onto the fuselage, out of breath, he let go. Ferdinand Collin described what followed in his book *Parmi les Précurseurs du Ciel*:

The height of bad luck was that being hooked by the tail plane as it went past, Ors had the second chance in trying to hold onto the tail plane, all he did was place the elevator in the climb position ... here is the aircraft freed, left to it's own fantasy... the pupils having heard me shout in vain, brief orders, were alerted and everybody then watched, including the mechanics.

A small catalogue of several pages, destined for enthusiasts. The promenade cost 100F, a large sum in 1912.

After various attempts, the aircraft without pilot took off and rose brusquely into a chandelle. I was thinking "Oh well! the crash will not be long." I was wrong because the flight carried on with a beautiful side slip on the wing, which straightened up just at the precise moment where everything was going wrong and seemed lost. The flight continued, sometimes calmly, the engine was pulling, then upon thinking about it, the aircraft seemed to want to land but changed it's mind, climbing even better as though with an inextinguishable thirst for sky, the miracle of the side slip on the wing happened again, the aircraft just avoiding a catastrophe and going off again even better. We said to ourselves that as we were waiting for the total break up, the instinct for conservation visited this automatic machine to dictate to it the indispensable manœuvre.

It is absolutely clear that if there had been a pupil on board, all would have been broken the first time by his counter manoeuvres. Five or six times the aircraft held itself vertical at 30 metres, but then sorted itself out always in the last fifth of a second, accentuating each time the heart beats of the pupil, origin of this diversionary attraction, because it was him in the end, he knew very well, who would pay the bill of this flying school ballet. At each almost landing he started to hope again, at each new flight he tore his hair out ... but everything comes to an end, above all with Anzani engines which were happy to accumulate calories. The engine finally stopped and my most agile mechanics were already watching out the right moment to grab a wing, to fix the roaming mechanical bird and to finally stop it. Escaping again after a knowledgeable detour the aircraft was off, defying all previsions, decided suddenly to do a straight line on the ground, the tail high to turn a pilot pale and drove resolutely bang into the centre of a small wooden cabin, reserved for the most natural needs. It was a dead stop, the shock brutal in an infernal and sinister noise of the breaking of wings and propeller.

The cabin was ... occupied and out of it shot a shocked man, confused; like a crazy man he came out of the cabin howling with terror. Not taking the time to lift up his trousers, he ran with great difficulty, the banner to the wind. At every step he nearly fell, galloping to slow down his final fall which happened after racing for almost a hundred metres. When he came back to his senses and turned round he contemplated, horrified and ashamed, the laughing faces of his comrades with tears in their eyes from intense laughter.

This affair unleashed a wave of hilarity of such a size that, prudently, I had to renounce to continue the lessons.[2]

If in the Blériot schools as in the others, the breakage of wood was frequent, serious accidents were much fewer and of several hundred pupils trained from 1910 to 1914, no mortal accident ever occurred. Already Louis Blériot foresaw the future development of aerial tourism; in his catalogue of 1913 he wrote:

...there is no doubt that following the progress made recently in the security and the regularity of the machines,

(2) In his memoires, *Pilote d'Essais*, Georges Bellenger told that the linseed oil thrown out by the Anzarni engines 'dirty splutterers' sent many students to the latrines more often than normal. (Editor's note)

aviation is on the eve of entering a new phase. The period of pure demonstrations is going to close, that of applications is going to open ... already amateur sportsmen, more numerous day by day, are showing the way. They promenade, they voyage for their needs or their pleasure ... they share with their passengers the intense joys of aerial rambling. To the army of tourists of tomorrow, we must from now on prepare home bases where they will find the commodities and comfort as much for themselves as for their machines.

Rapidly putting his ideas into practice, on the 13 November 1912 Blériot inaugurated a new flying school at Buc, four kilometres from Versailles. This school, which would replace little by little all the others, was spread over a surface of 200 hectares. For Buc, Blériot had planned large: other than the hangers, he had built in one corner of the field an important building in re-inforced concrete with a tower in each corner :

> *The central building*, indicated a brochure, *shelters on its three floors and under the observation terraces which overlook it, a hall for thirty machines, a party room, a vast restaurant, rest rooms, writing rooms with a library and maps for the study of voyages, sports rooms and hydrotherapy rooms, offices and even bedrooms at the disposition of aviators wanting to leave at daybreak. Tennis courts and open air games offered distractions in the park.*

The Aéro-Parc at Buc, a visionary building which would remain a unique example, rapidly became the rendezvous of Parisian Aviation. But Blériot wanted to attract the general public. Towards this he organised every Sunday exhibitions, notably races and parachuting of models from a height of 1500 metres.

It is from this time on, that all the prototypes built by Blériot, would be tried at Buc. (except the flying boats of course). Later, the field would be the office of the Aéro-Club Rolland-Garros and the aerial branch of the Touring Club de France.

The golden age of meetings and records

As early as 1908, records and aviation meetings took place which attracted considerably crowds, with the principle means of aeronautical propaganda and the best publicity for the builders.

1910. The 4th February in Dover on the very site of Blériot's landing, saw the inauguration of the monument commemorating the Crossing of the Channel. Built thanks to the generosity of Alexander Duckham, it is a stone representation of the monoplane flat on the ground.[1] At the meeting of Heliopolis, which was held from the 6th to the 13th February, the Blériot XI of Jacques Balsan and Hubert Leblon, shared the honours with the Voisins. On the 10th March, Emile Aubrun carried out one of the first night flights at Buenos Aires. On the 29th at Biarritz, Louis Blériot carried out a demonstration in front of King Edward VII of England. In April the racing driver, Albert Guyot carried out a series of demonstration flights on his Blériot XI in Warsaw, St. Petersburg, Moscow and Nijni-Novgorod. On the 1st and 2nd of May, despite a violent wind, Blériot flew at the meeting of Barcelona. The following day Olieslagers won the altitude prize reaching 160 metres with his Blériot XI equipped with an Anzani

engine. At the Grande Semaine de St. Pétersbourg (8th to 15th May) Morane also won the altitude prize. The Russian pilot Boris de Rossinsky flew at Pau on the 16th May in front of the Grand Duke Alexander. The following day at Issy-les-Moulineaux in the presence of Blériot, Leblanc flew in front of a Chinese delegation. Ten days later still at Issy-les-Moulineaux, he flew in front of the Crown Prince Ioussouf Izzidine of Turkey. On the 21st May the Comte Jacques de Lesseps won the Ruinart Prize of 12,500 francs in carrying out the Second Crossing of the Channel.

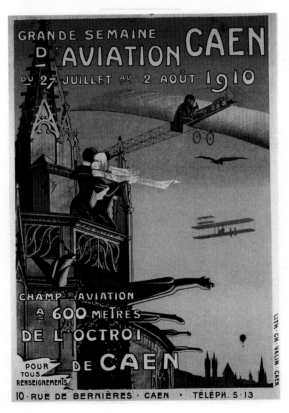

Posters for the aviation meetings of 1909–1910 at Port Aviation (Juvisy), Pau and Caen, representing Blériot aircraft.

---

(1) Carefully maintained, this monument is still visible to-day. Two other monuments still exist, one of them inaugurated on the 12th June 1910, can be found in the Municipal Park in the town of Cambrai, the second inaugurated on the 16 July 1911, was raised at Les Baraques, to-day called Blériot-Plage.

Above and below: The Chilean, Geo Chavez, flying a Blériot, was killed after being the first to cross the Alps by air. A wing broke just before landing at Domodossola. Right: the last letter from Chavez to Blériot, written on 21 November 1910, just before take off.

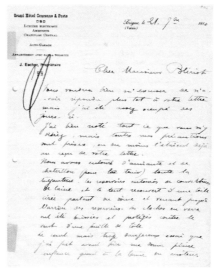

The meeting at Rouen from the 17th to the 26th June saw the victory of Morane on a Blériot XI-2*bis* for the altitude prize, and the victory of Cattaneo, on a Blériot XI with a 50hp Gnome engine for the speed prize.

The second edition of the Grande Semaine de Reims was held from the 4th to the 11th July. No less than twelve Blériots were entered: eight XI-*bis* of which six with Gnome engines, one with a Labor-Picker engine, one with an Anzani engine and four XI-2*bis* with Gnome engines. On the 10th July the Belgian Jan Olieslagers, nick-named the "Anvers Demon", covered 392 kilometres and stayed in the air more than five hours, beating both the records for distance and duration. On the same day, on a modified XI-2*bis*, equipped with a 100 hp engine and with the fuselage totally covered, Leon Morane reached 106.508 kph, winning the speed prize (over 20 kilometres) and established a new World Record.

The race, the Circuit de l'Est was held from the 7th to the 17th August, it was won by Leblanc, in front of thirteen competitors, Aubrun came second , also in a Blériot. This trial, the biggest ever organised, was made up of six stages over the route Paris-Troyes-Nancy-Mezières-Douai-Amiens-Paris, a total of 785 kilometres, which Leblanc covered in 12 hours 56 minutes and 2/5ths. On the 11th August at Lanark, (Great Britain) the American Drexel climbed to 2013 metres a World Altitude Record.

A Canadian pilot, John B. Moisant, crossed the Channel on the 17th August 1910, in a two seat Blériot with his mechanic Albert Fileux and *Paris-Londres,* his Siamese cat as passengers. Moisant with his brother, a New York Banker, founded Mosiant International Aviators Inc. with the objective of carrying out a tour of aerial presentations on the other side of the Atlantic, a tour in which several French pilots, including Garros and Barrier, participated. American citizens like Earle Ovington and C. J. Stroble bought type XI with the same intentions. During the meeting of the Baie de Seine, Leon Morane twice beat the World Altitude Record: on the 29th August at Le Havre, he climbed to 2040 metres on his XI-*bis*, then on the 3rd September at Deauville, he reached 2582 metres. This record was beaten five days later by the Peruvian, Geo Chavez with 2680 metres. A few days afterwards, another type XI was displayed at Peking in front of an astounded crowd.

Jacques Balsan and his Blériot XI with Anzani engine, at the meeting in Heliopolis, Egypt, February 1910.

Departure of a Blériot fitted with an extra fuel tank. A mechanic has just started the engine; others hold the machine back.

From the 11th to the 18th September during the Grande Semaine de Bordeaux, Morane and Aubrun won most of the trials, Aubrun became the holder of the Michelin Cup on the 16th[1] and on the 18th Morane beat several records. On the same day Blériot was attributed the prize of the Président de la République, reserved for aircraft constructors. It was a superb eagle in silver plated bronze on a red marble base. He was so proud of it that for several years it was shown on the first page of his catalogues.

The 24th September saw the opening of the meeting in Milan. In order to add a bit of spice to the spectacle, a prize was offered for the competitors to arrive in the Lombardy capital, via the Simplon Pass, whose altitude was 2009 metres. The take off had to be from the plateau of Briegenberg (900 metres) 3 kilometres from Brigue, in the Valais region. The pilots Chavez, Weymann, Cattaneo, Wiencziers and Paillette entered for this particularly perilous trial. Geo Chavez, on an all white Blériot XI, took off from Briegenberg on the 20th September at sixteen minutes past six, in the morning. Almost straight away he found himself in fog so he decided to turn back. It was only on the 23,rd, the day before the meeting, in good weather that he was again able to take off. Crossing the Alps at an altitude of 2500 metres, he descended then in the direction of Domodossola, where he planned to land. Suddenly, when he was only ten or so metres from the ground, a wing of his monoplane broke. The machine crashed leaving him mortally injured. Even though certain people supported the

idea that the accident was due to the air currents, and others to the repeated opening and closing of the throttle causing brutal shaking of the structure, the real causes appeared to come from the twisting of the wing. They did not know that in a case of high speed, notably in a slight descent or in a tight turn where the aircraft has precarious stability, there appears a torsion caused by the differential flexing of the longerons, the slightest gust therefore provoking the breaking of the wing. Less sensitive to this twisting, the bi-planes competed successfully against the monoplanes until the 1930s. Several accidents of this type (in particular those of Delagrange and Leblon) happened at the same time. On the 27th September, Chavez, the first aviator to fly over the Alps died of his injuries at the hospital of Domodossola. Blériot carried out numerous tests to try and discover the origin of the phenomena which would only be solved several decades later.

In the meantime Blériot reinforced his wings. The longerons of the XI type 'Channel Crossing' were beams of spruce, 7cm x 1.8cm for the main longerons and 5.4cm x 1.5cm for the rear longerons. To lighten the longeron the centre part was reduced to 12mm in thickness on the front longeron and to 10mm on the rear longeron. To solve the problem of wing breakages which occurred on machines fitted with the new 50hp Gnome engine, the lightening of the longerons up to the fitting of the first flying wires were removed, then the longerons themselves were increased in size and the leading edge of the wing was reinforced.

On the 29th October, the second Gordon Bennett Speed Cup, was held during the meeting of Belmont Park in the state of New York. Raced over 100 kilometres around a 5 kilometre circuit, there were three teams, the American team, an English team and a French team. Victory seemed to be coming to Leblanc in a Blériot XI with a Gnome 100 hp engine, when at 2 kilometres from the finish line his fuel tank ran dry.

Forced to land immediately he hit an electric pylon; fortunately the current had been cut for the duration of the race. The aviator got away with light facial injuries. It was the English man Claude Grahame-White, also in a Blériot with a Gnome engine of 100 hp, who won the race in one hour, one minute and four seconds (98.552 kph) beating the speed record over 100 kilometres, which had been established by Morane at Bordeaux.

On the 28th November at Pau, Louis Blériot flew with his wife on board a type XIV. On the 9th December also at Pau Georges Legagneux climbed to 3180 metres, establishing a new altitude record. On the 21st he won (temporarily) the Michelin Cup beating this time the World Distance record with 515.9km, which he completed in 5hrs 59min.

The American John Moisant and Albert Fileux, his mechanic, were the first to cross the Channel in a two-seat Blériot, August 1910.

---

(1) The Michelin Cup of 1910 was a trial of the greatest distance in a closed circuit around an aerodrome, without landing, between dawn and dusk. The Cup was won by Tabuteau on a Farman bi-plane on the 30th December. Created in 1908 by this famous firm based in Clermont Ferrand, the annual trials, after a short interruption from 1915 to 1920, were reinstated from 1921 till 1932.

1911 On the 15th January at Hendon a Japanese delegation ordered several machines. On the 17th at Pau, Blériot tried his type XX. On the 1st and 2nd February Captain Bellenger flew from Paris to Pau (approximately 720 kilometres) in four stages, with a Blériot XI with a Gnome engine of 50 hp, in 7hrs 15min flying time. On the 4th the Blériot XIII, a machine designed for four people piloted by Martin beat the record for the number of passengers on board by carrying ten people. On the 5th March, Lieutenant Bague took off from Niece to fly to Corsica. The wind blew him off course and he had to land on the small Italian Island of Gorgona, having flown 304 kilometres over the Mediterranean. On the 29th in Cuba, Barrier won the prize of the Ville de La Havane, 15,000 francs. On the 31st March and 1st April, Captain Bellenger flew the return trip from Pau to Paris, escorted this time by Lieutenants de Rose and de Malherbe,[2] he improved his outgoing time by 6 minutes. On the 12th April, Pierre Prier, Director of the Blériot Flying School at Hendon, flew with a passenger from London to Paris, in 3 hours 6 minutes. The same day Le Blanc beat the World speed record with 111.801kph.

At the beginning of the month of May, Louis Blériot went to St. Petersburg to participate in the delivery of his machines to the Russian Army, and to take part in the reception trials.

The race Paris-Madrid was organised by *Le Petit Parisian*, from the 21st to the 26th May. The race was won by Védrines and 2nd place was taken by Louis Gibert, (licence n° 92) a native of the town of Albi. The competition Paris-Rome was organised from the 28th May to the 15th June over 1465 kilometres, patronised by *Le Petit Journal.* Of the twenty-one competitors present, Beaumont was the winner followed by Garros, both on Blériot monoplanes.

In the preliminary rounds of the third Gordon Bennett Cup on the 12th June, LeBlanc won back the World speed record that he lost to Nieuport on the 11th May, with 125 kph.

André Beaumont won the European Circuit of 1,700 kilometres in nine stages, in 58 hours 34 minutes 35 seconds. There were forty finishers out of seventy-two who started. Unfortunately on the 18th June, the take off day was marked by the death of the Chief Pilot of the House of Blériot, Théodore Lemartin, on the Blériot XX, even though his engine was not giving full power, Lemartin wanted to take off at the appointed time. Shortly after the take off he stalled at a height of 25m, in turning trying to avoid a line of trees and crashed to the ground. Then the death of Lieutenant Princeteau, burned alive in his aircraft held to the ground by a gust of wind.

The same day Manissero won the principle prize of the opening day of the meeting at Turin.

On the 25th Cattaneo won the race Rosario-Buenos Aries, 400 kilometres, which he covered in 6 hours, the Prix de la Nation was worth 15,000 piasters.

The 1911 Gordon Bennett Cup was held on the 1st July over a closed circuit of 150 kilometres around the field of Eastchurch in England. Although he was ill, Leblanc on a Blériot XXI with a Gnome engine of 100 hp, came second behind the American Weymann on a Nieuport. The Englishman Hamel, who had clipped the wings of his type XXIII, in order to gain speed, destroyed his machine at the first turn. On the 7th of the same month, the Colonial Administrator, Jean Raoult flew over the town of Tananarive for the first time. Ten days later the Belgian Jan Olieslagers became the world record holder for distance over a closed circuit, covering 625.2 kilometres in 7 hours 18 minutes 26 seconds, at Kiewit-les-Hasselt.

André Beaumont won the tour of England and Scotland which ran from the 22nd to the 26th July, in 22 hours 28 minutes flying time, followed by Védrines. On the 25th Alexandra de Wassilief won the race St. Petersburg to Moscow, flying for 25 hours. On the 9th August a new altitude record was established by Captain Julien Félix with 3,450 metres, but on the 6th September Rolland Garros claimed the record climbing to 3,910 metres on a special Blériot XI, with it's structure in pine (lighter than Ash) with a lightened wing structure and simplified undercarriage. The aerial races, Valence-Alicante-Valence, Bologna-Venice-Rimini-Bologna and Salamanca-Valladolid-Salamanca were all won by Blériots, as was the Tour de Belgique which was won by Lieutenant Tyck on the 15th August.

(2) Only Bellenger and de Rose managed to get to the aerodrome Vincennes-Maison Blanche. Lieutenant Malherbe, following a breakdown caused by the rain, landed in an oak tree at Argenton, near to Chateauroux. The machine was badly damaged but the pilot was unhurt.

Extracts from the Blériot catalogue of 1911. Left: More than one hundred clients are mentioned, coming from all of Europe, Russia and the United States. Centre: In the same catalogue, the list of prizes won by Blériot aircraft is impressive. Right: Prizes won in competitions were the best publicity for the aircraft builders.

Illustration made on the occasion of the *Circuit Européen*, won by André Beaumont, followed by Roland Garros on a Blériot.

The newspaper *Le Matin* in Paris displayed the Blériot of Alfred Leblanc, winner of the Circuit de l'Est (7 to 17 August 1910).

On the 19th at Etampes, Jeanne Herveu won the Prix Femina on a Blériot XI with a 25 hp Gyp engine. In the United States, on the 5th September, Earle Ovington won the cross- country race, Boston-Nassau-Worcester-Providence (of 160 miles, 257km) in 3 hours 6 minutes 22 seconds, winning the prize of 50,000 francs on his Blériot XI with a Gnome engine of 50 hp. On the 25th Widmer, also on a type XI with a Gnome engine, crossed the Adriatic from Venice to Trieste in 1 hour 15 minutes. In Italy Blériot pilots accumulated successes, Captain Piazza at the Circuit de Haute-Italie, Widmer at Venice, Legagneux at Lugano. On the 2nd November, Manissero and Verona took the first two prizes in the race, Milan-Turin-Milan, reserved for Italian Nationals. On the 27th and the 28th. Marc Pourpe made a two-way flight France to England and back, carrying a letter from the Mayor of Boulogne to the Mayor of Folkestone.

In the last days of the year 1911, Garros accompanied by Charles Voisin, Audemars and Barrier went to South America. Representing the Queen Aeroplane Co. they presented a two-seat type XI at Rio de Janeiro.

1912. From the 7th to the 9th March, Henri Salmet, Chief Pilot of the Blériot Flying School at Hendon, flew London to Paris and back. The same month the extension to the factory at Levallois was completed. On the 2nd April a woman crossed the Channel by air for the first time, as passenger of the British aviator Gustave Hamel, Miss Davies flew London to Paris in three stages. Two weeks later the American Aviatrice, Harriet Quimby, Art Critic of the *Leslie's Weekly,* succeeded in crossing the Channel from Dover to Hardelot, on a Blériot XI fitted with a 50hp Gnome engine, the Channel had almost become a place of promenade! Wishing to create a Military Aviation School, the Ottoman Government called on the House of Blériot. At the beginning of April, Alfred Leblanc went to Constantinople, where with a military commission, he chose the sites of the future airfields. On the 16th the firm was also retained by Bulgaria to open a military school at Sofia. On the 22nd April, Corbett Wilson crossed the Irish Sea in a flight of 125 kilometres.

At the Aerial Derby, a circuit of 125 kilometres around London, Hamel on a tandem two seat type XI with a 50 hp Gnome engine, with Miss Davies as passenger, came first with Moorhouse second on a modified single seater; Sopwith, who completed the course first with a type XI with a 70 hp Gnome engine, was disqualified.

The Circuit d'Anjou, which opened on the 16th June, organised by René and Pierre Gasnier du Fresne, was held over the triangle Angers-Cholet-Saumur. Despite a very violent wind, Garros the first and only competitor to take off, won the Grand Prix de l'Aéro-Club de France as well as the Grand Prix de Vitesse. On the 4th July, at the end of the meeting in Vienna, the Blériot team alone won a quarter of the prizes, Garros won 33,500 crowns, Audemars 9,000 crowns and Barrier 2,000 crowns.

On the 18th Edmond Audemars flew from Paris to Berlin in one flight of 900 kilometres. On the 6th September at Houlgate, Garros, equipped with an oxygen mask and flying a specially built Blériot with an 80 hp Gnome engine, climbed to 5,000 metres, thus setting a new World Altitude record The engine broke at the moment he reached maximum altitude, the aviator had to make all of his descent by gliding.

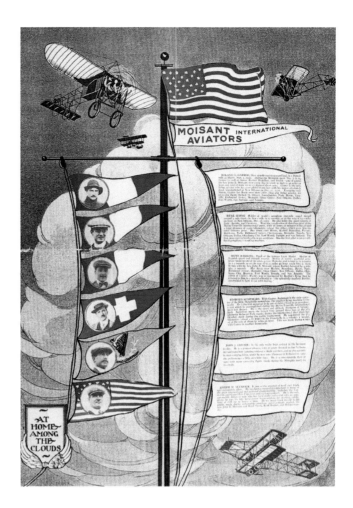

Above right: The stars of John Moisant's American Aerial circus were the Frenchmen: Audemars flying a Demoiselle and Garros flying a Blériot.

Above: A poster of the race Paris-Rome, which should have continued as far as Turin, won by Beaumont flying a Blériot.

At Houlgate, taking off from the beach on 6 September 1912 with a Blériot Spécial, Roland Garros tried – and succeeded – to beat the world altitude record by going above 5000m. The crowd was immense. An aircraft at this time was an event in itself.

At the beginning of December, Marc Pourpe and Georges Verminck participated at the first Aviation Meeting organised at Colombo, on Blériot XI with Gnome engines.

This same team Pourpe and Verminck went to Calcutta in January where they gave a flying display in front of an immense crowd. From there they went to Cochinchine then Cambodia

On the 19th January the race, Buenos Aires-Mar del Plata was won by Sergeant Fels.

On the 24th January the Swiss, Oscar Bider crossed the Pyrenees at an altitude of more than 3000 metres. Taking off from Pau on a Blériot XI with a 70hp Gnome engine, he landed at Madrid-Quatro Vientos after 7 hours 40 minutes flying time, with one stop at Guadalajara. He had earned his pilot's licence at the Blériot flying school at Pau six weeks earlier! At the beginning of February Prince Bibesco, whose aviation school in Rumania already owned several Blériots, ordered six new two-seat machines with 80 hp Gnome engines.

On the 11th March, Perreyon on a lightened Blériot XI-2 with a double Lambda Gnome engine of 160 hp reached the altitude of 5,880 metres. Perreyon had become Chief Pilot after the death of Lemartin. The second meeting of seaplanes in Monaco started on the 1st April, where a tri-plane Canard on floats, that Giraud should have piloted, was entered under the number 12. The trials for the machine were not finished and he was not allowed to participate. The *Daily Mail* created the trial for the Crossing of the Atlantic and on the 7th April they announced that Perreyon was inscribed. On the 29th May accompanied by his mechanic, Dupuis, Perreyon won the World Distance record with passenger, in flying from Turin to Rome and return (1,100 kilometres) in the same day on an XI-2 with an 80hp Gnome engine. On the 3rd June on a two-seat machine with a 160 hp Gnome engine, the same Perreyon returning to Buc reached 5,100 metres, a World Record with passenger, in fact a female passenger, Miss de Plagino a Rumanian national.

A lithograph issued in honour of Roland Garros, winner of the Circuit d'Anjou in 1912. The image is realistic because the weather was very bad, cloudy, windy and rainy; only Garros had the courage to come out and take off.

Louis Blériot, Chevalier de la Légion d'Honneur, and Lieutenant in the Artillery Reserve at Vincennes.

Blériot shows the barograph to military personnel, certifying that his pilot Perreyon had beaten the world altitude record (5100m) with passenger (Mlle de Fagino) on 3 June 1913.

At the meeting of Vienna from the 15th to the 22nd June, Perreyon, with the same machine, was the principle winner with 31,000 crowns of prize money, in front of Garros on a Morane-Saulnier who won only 18,900 crowns. Oscar Bider carried out a double crossing of the Alps from Bern to Milan and return on the 13th and 26th July.

A flight was organised from Paris to Cairo; the routing being Nancy, Prague, Vienna, Belgrade, Sofia, Constantinople, Konia, Tortosa, Beirut, Jaffa and Helipolis. Jules Védrines with his mechanic on a XI-2 with an 80 hp Gnome engine, took off from Nancy on the 20th November. He had been detained for almost a month by problems of administrative formalities. He was the first to arrive in Cairo on the 29th December having flown 5,400 kilometres, completing one of the first long distance races. Marc Bonnier on a Nieuport came second. On the 5th March 1914, Blériot became a member of the Conseil Supérieur de l'Aéronautique Militaire, as a consulting member "Charged with co-ordinating the efforts of Public Services and Private Initiatives in the search for progress of that which concerns Military Application of Aeronautics". On the 30th July 1914, the eve of the First World War, the Norwegian Trygve Gran was the first to cross the North Sea.

In 1911, before creating an aviation company with Robert and Raymond Saulnier, Léon Morane was a famous pilot with Blériot. He is shown here on a XI-2 bis at the meeting in Rouen in June 1910.

GRAND PRIX D'AVIATION DE L'Aé C.F.

CONSTRUCTEUR

CIRCUIT DE L'ANJOU 1912

An official arm-band, such as Louis Blériot or Alfred Leblanc would have worn during aviation meetings. This one is in satin, lined with violet silk.

6

Blériot Aircraft Before August 1914

THE PRODUCTION OF THE BLERIOT COMPANY FROM 1909 TO 1914

The Blériot type XI with a Gnome rotary engine of 70hp, with which Roland Garros, the only one to fly in the bad weather, won the two main prizes of the Circuit d'Anjou in 1912. His victory in the speed race between fixed points brought him 70,000 gold francs.

The Blériot XI type Channel Crossing

The first production models, called "Channel Crossing" or "Calais-Dover", came out as early as the beginning of August 1909. The three-cylinder 24 hp Anzani engine was fitted with cooling fins aligned with the direction of flight, and not perpendicular to the line of flight as on the machine of the crossing. Each wing was equipped with two extra flying wires. The rudder was now rectangular with rounded corners. The structure remained the same, in ash, a heavier wood but with excellent mechanical qualities, and spruce, much lighter.

From October 1909 a few owners of Blériot aircraft, such as Delagrange and Leblon, fitted their machines with the new Gnome rotary engine of 50 hp, in order to increase flying speed. The installation with an overhang forward of the landing wheels, it was thought (wrongly) to be at the origin of the fatal accidents that happened to these two pilots. In January 1910, the first XI with a Gnome engine, destined for Balsan, was produced. Fixed onto a cruciform mount and covered with a circular cowling in aluminium sheet, which prevented oil being thrown to the rear, the engine was installed behind the landing wheels. The flying wires were reinforced. At the end of the year the installation of an inverted 4-cylinder Gyp engine of 25 hp, was proposed by Blériot.

The price of these machines was 12,000 francs with a 25 hp Anzani, and 13,800 francs with a 25 hp GYP. However, the buyers did not stop at trying more powerful engines on the Blériot, notably before the arrival of the rotary Gnome. After 1910 the Blériot XI type 'Channel Crossing' underwent diverse improvements from year to year.

The Blériot XI of Jacques Balsan, tested with a Dutheil et Chalmers engine.

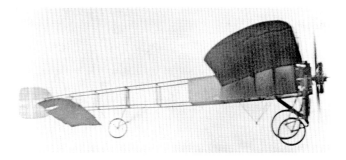

The Blériot type XI with a Gnome "Omega" engine of 50hp, placed in front of the undercarriage. On the first Omega engines the propeller was fixed to the rear of the engine, as shown here.

The Blériot XI of Guillaume Busson with a Labour Picker engine. in front of the *Château des Ducs de Rohan* at Josselin (Morbihan).

The Blériot type XI of Jacques Balsan with Gnome "Omega" engine of 50hp.

The profile of the wing of the Blériot XI, hand drawn by Gianni Caproni, a future giant of the Italian Aeronautical industry.

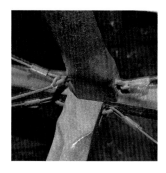 

Details of fixing of uprights and cross pieces of the fuselage to the longerons, patented by Blériot and used on production series and its derivatives. Photographs of the Channel Crossing XI before cleaning by the CNAM, in 2009.

The Blériot XI bis

The empennage of the Blériot XI bis was notably different with a large area triangular tail, more rigid than on this first example.

The prototype of the Blériot XI-*bis* appeared at the beginning of February 1910. Powered by a 25 hp Anzani engine, it was fitted with a horizontal empennage in the form of pigeon tail, the rear part, in two moving sections on a horizontal shaft, made up the elevator. The fuselage, fully covered, at 6.6 metres, was shorter than that of the type "Calais-Dover". The lower flying wires were changed to steel bands.

The examples that followed from April 1910 onwards would be equipped with "flat" wings and would most often be fitted with a Gnome engine of 50 hp. The engine had an aluminium crank case. Like the classic XI, the rear fuselage was not covered.

- *Span*: 7.20m
- *Overall length*: 6.60m
- *Wing area*: 12m^2
- *Take-off weight*: 310kg
- *Speed*: 70km/h

The Blériot XI type Circuit de l'Est

It can be difficult to identify the different versions of the type XI, especially when this concerns the wing profile which is not readily visible.

This name came after the success of Leblanc and Aubrun in this important test in August 1910. The XI, type Circuit de L'Est was fitted with a 7 cylinder Gnome Omega engine of 50 hp. It was equipped with "flat" wing" and a crossed double-skid in rattan. The propeller was a Chauvière Intégrale of 2.6 metres in diameter, with a pitch of 1.35 metres, turning at 1350 rpm. A fire-wall separated the engine from the cockpit, which was covered over the forward section.

- *Span*: 8.90m
- *Overall length*: 7.65m
- *Wing area*: 15m^2
- *Empty weight*: 250kg
- *Take-off weight*: 380kg
- *Price*: 24,000 francs

The Blériot XI type Circuit Européen

This single-seat fitted with a 50 hp Gnome engine, came out in March 1911, and had a horizontal tail plane in a trapezoidal form, with an elevator in two parts. The cowling was redesigned and the cabane became a pylon.

- *Span*: 8 m
- *Wing area*: 14m²
- *Overall length*: 7.20m
- *Empty weight*: 264kg

The Blériot XI type *Circuit Européen* showed later versions of the monoplane.

The Blériot XI for the record of Rolland Garros

In August 1911 this monoplane with a Gnome engine of 50hp was specially built for Rolland Garros in an attempt for the World Altitude record. His new record was established on the 4th September at 3910m, at Paramé. The machine was much lightened with landing gear simplified with streamlined metal tubes, but above all a structure in pine, a light wood but easily broken.

It was therefore considered fragile but Roland Garros even at this time, was already an exceptional pilot. One year later on the 6th September 1912 Garros beat this record by reaching 5000m taking off on the beach of Houlgate. The equipment was a rudimentary oxygen system: a simple tube connected to a bottle of oxygen. Garros would use other type XI specially built for him in pine.

Take-off of Roland Garros at Houlgate, at the end of the day.

The Blériot XI type Ecole Militaire

Equipped with an Anzani engine, type "Militaire", of 30 hp with 3 cylinders in a fan of 72°, it was distinguishable from the XI type Channel Crossing by its double skid in rattan, and its fire-wall. It appeared in February 1911, and was quickly ordered by the army, the first examples were put into service from the month of August onwards at the Ecole Militaire d'Etampes.

This type XI was also used in the civil schools in France and England.

The Blériot XI Taxi-Pingouin

A single-seater designed in January 1912 for the learning of straight-line ground runs, the Taxi-Pingouin fitted with an Anzani engine of 30 or 35 hp, could not leave the ground, its wings being shortened to make take-off impossible.

The wide track reinforced undercarriage was equipped with wide tyres and front-facing skids to prevent over turning.

Numerous "tired" production type XIs, were converted from August 1914 into Taxi-Pingouin (pingouin = penguin, a flightless bird, hence the name).

A *Taxi-Pingouin* with an Anzani engine of 50hp. The wings are short and it can only taxi (from whence its name). The undercarriage has been widened, reinforced and fitted with skids.

The Blériot XI type 1912

A single-seater with a 50 hp Gnome engine, it had a reinforced wing and an undercarriage with two extra legs, it appeared in March 1912. The bungees could be un-hooked. The interior of the wings had crossed support wires between the spars.

In order to improve visibility, the wing from the rear spar to the trailing edge was not covered between the fuselage and the first rib.

Initially equipped with a crossed double-skid in rattan, the machine was modified a few months later with a steerable skid.

- *Span*: 8.90m
- *Wing area*: 15m²
- *Total weight*: 370kg
- *Overall length* : 7.65m
- *Empty weight* : 240kg
- *Speed* : 90km/h

- *Price* : 21,500 francs

A Military Blériot XI type 1912, at take-off.

The Blériot XI type Artillerie

Built at the same time as the 1912, it was a version of the same model, but with a folding fuselage designed to facilitate transport by road.

At first equipped with a horizontal tailplane, type Channel Crossing, with the tips foldable, it was fitted shortly afterwards with a shorter tail plane with an elevator in one single piece, with a hollowed out centre section.

The single skid which was moved forward to allow the folding of the fuselage, replaced the double skid.

The machine was accepted by the army after the adoption of a tail plane similar to that of the XI-2 type Génie, but was abandoned after the death of Captain Echeman on the 14th May.

- *Span*: 8.9m
- *Overall length* : 8.0m

A Blériot type Artillery, dismantled and folded ready for transport.

The Blériot XI type Ecole Ordinaire

This single-seater type Channel Crossing existed in two versions. The first, designed for straight-line flights a few metres above the ground, was equipped with the old 25 hp Anzani of the Channel Crossing, the fuselage had an upper pylon which replaced the classic cabane, and with a straight, supple skid. The second, with a 35 hp Anzani, a 3 cylinder inverted Y, allowed the pupils to tune up their preparation for the tests for the Aéro-Club license. A few of these models which appeared in April 1912, were later built with the cabane, type 1909.

- *Speed* : 65km/h
- *Price* : 11,000 francs

A type XI *Ecole Ordinaire* in 1912.

- *Span* : 8.9m
- *Wing area* : 15m²
- *Overall length* : 7.65m
- *Empty weight* : 220kg

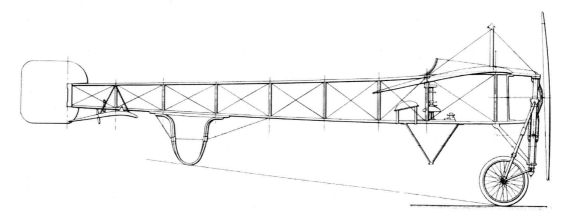

Factory drawing of the Military Blériot XI, type 1914, civil version of a type 1913 described below and recognisable by the cabane in inverted V, and the windshield cowling.

The Blériot XI type 1913

The only notable differences compared to the single-seater of 1912, appeared to be the abandoning of the two extra undercarriage legs, the return to the double skid in rattan, and the installation of more powerful engines, 60 hp Clerget, Gnome or Le Rhône.

In general the finishing was better and the machine could be delivered covered with a coloured varnish.

- *Span* : 8.90m
- *Wing area* : 16m²
- *Total weight* : 415kg
- *Overall length* : 7.75 m
- *Empty weight* : 265kg
- *Speed* : 100 km/h

The Blériot XI-2 Tandem

A tandem two-seater fitted with a 70 hp Gnome Gamma engine (1911), a Lambda of 80 hp (1913), and even a double Omega of 100 hp (1913). It was fitted with a wing and elevator of double curve. A simple pylon replaced the classic cabane. The two occupants were in the same cockpit, the observer was seated behind the trailing edge of the wing.

- *Span* : 9.70m
- *Wing area* : 18m²
- *Useful load* : 230kg
- *Oil tank capacity* : 30 litres
- *Speed* : 100km/h without passenger or 95km/h with passenger
- *Endurance* : 3 hours
- *Overall length* : 8.45m
- *Empty weight* : 300kg
- *Fuel tank capacity* : 80 litres

- *Price* : 26,800 francs (with a 70 hp Gnome)

The Blériot tandem in its first configuration, with a double skid in rattan.

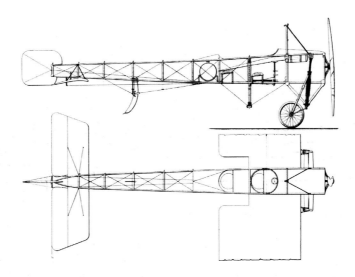

Drawings of the second configuration of the XI-2, with steerable skid, shown in a factory note.

The Blériot XI-2 bis

Side by side two-seater with an empennage in the form of a pigeon tail, and oval rudder, the XI-2 bis, extrapolation of the XI-bis appeared in April 1910, (the prototype in February) fitted first with a 50 hp Gnome engine, then with a 70 hp, it was exported to several countries, notably the Low Countries, Russia and Japan. Because of its longitudinal instability, it was progressively abandoned in favour of the XI-2 Tandem.

- *Span* : 11m
- *Wing area* : 25m^2
- *Empty weight* : 350kg
- *Overall length* : 8.50 m
- *Wing chord* : 2.30m
- *Price* : 28,000 francs

The XI-2 bis, first version: the engine is behind the undercarriage; the cabane resembles that of the Blériot XI of 1909.

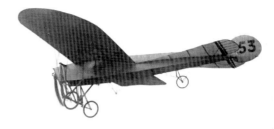

The second version of the Blériot XI-2 bis, with its lengthened nose and the engine moved forward. The cabane is replaced by an inverted V pylon.

The Blériot XI-2 type Paris-Madrid

Designed in April 1911, this was a lightweight tandem two-seater with a slightly reduced wing span and reinforced flying wires; a third flying wire, linking the wing to the fuselage was added at the front. For long distance flights, a large supplementary fuel tank replaced the passenger.

The Blériot XI-2 Militaire 1911

Military version of the XI-2, with a double skid in rattan

The Blériot XI-2 type Génie

The type XI-2, destined for the Corps of Engineers, appeared in April 1912 with a straight, steerable skid and with the trailing edge of the wings cut away near the fuselage, for ease of ground observation. The 70 hp Gnome engine was mounted on a frame in front of the undercarriage, which was reinforced by supporting legs, angled front and rear. The cabane was reduced to a simple pylon with two, and then four supports. The pilot and the observer were seated in separate cockpits. The bottom of the rudder was cut away to allow the movement of the one-piece elevator. The XI-2 type Génie was conceived to be taken apart and reassembled very rapidly. From the month of August onwards, the XI-2 had a slightly larger wing and a classic empennage, with the elevator in two parts. The 80 hp Gnome engine replaced, little by little, the 70 hp, with a modified engine mount. The double skid in rattan was replaced by a steerable skid, installed further forward.

In 1913, new modifications appeared: the two seats were moved together in the same cockpit for reasons of centre of gravity. To preserve the visibility of the observer, the cut away at the wing root was made larger. The pylon was moved forward, and the skid was moved backward, the fuel tank was installed behind the cockpit.

- *Span* : 9.70m
- *Wing area* : 18m^2
- *Total weight* : 550kg
- *Overall length* : 8.30m
- *Empty weight* : 320kg
- *Speed* : 120 km/h

Four versions of the same XI-2 existed, originally destined for the Engineers: fuselage covered (above left); bare structure which was thought to be less sensitive to gusts of wind; then new empennage (below left); finally, single cockpit for the two crew (above).

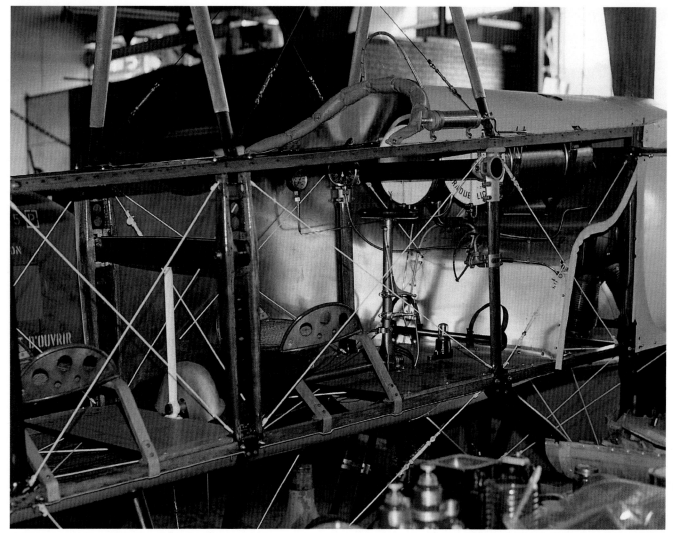

The Blériot XI-2 Tandem of Pégoud during its restoration in the workshops of the Air & Space Museum in le Bourget, before being re-covered. The two tanks, fitted with a glass tube to show the liquid level, were placed in front of the pilot. The stick is fitted with a small wheel and the engine controls are on the left. This image shows the quality of finish reached by the Blériot workshop just before the First World War.

The Blériot XI-2 Hydroaéroplane

It was in October 1913 that this machine appeared, a tandem two-seat seaplane with three floats, powered by a Gnome engine of 80 hp. It had a classical wide-track landing gear where the floats were fitted. A little later it was fitted with a slightly larger wing. The tail float was removed, the rudder was enlarged and it's water-tight lower part dropped into the water when the machine was taxiing. The floats could be removed and replaced by wheels. Several examples were built, certain of which were fitted with a Le Rhône engine of 80 hp.

The XI-2 Hyrdo, with short rudder.

XI-2 Hydro with three floats

- *Span* : 11.1m
- *Wing area* : 19.0m²
- *Total weight* : 560kg
- *Overall length* : 8.875m
- *Empty weight* : 360kg

XI-2 Hydro with rudder immersed

- *Span* : 11.05m
- *Wing area* : 21m²
- *Total weight* : 750kg
- *Overall length* : 9.0m
- *Empty weight* : 500kg

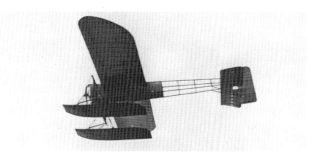

The XI-2 Hydro, with long rudder.

The Blériot XI-3

A three-seat tandem observation aircraft with the pilot in the centre, designed for the military competition of 1911. This competition,[1] the rules of which appeared to be very severe, was designed to determine the aeroplane corresponding best to military needs. It had four trials to be carried out with a load of 300kg:

- landing on various grounds (including ploughed fields)
- speed (minimum 60km/h)
- endurance (300km minimum)
- altitude (climb to 500m in less than 15 minutes)

The Blériot XI-3 was a large monoplane with warping wings, following the classic Blériot principle, rotating the rear wing spars around horizontal axes. The wings and the front of the fuselage were covered with rubberized fabric made by the Société des Téléphones. The position of the observer behind the wings permitted him to see vertically downwards. Two examples of the model were shown at the military competition. The first, entered under the number 14, was fitted with a 100 hp double Omega Gnome engine, and with wide section tyres. The second, which carried the number 26, was fitted with a 140 hp double Gamma Gnome engine, and three wheels for each undercarriage leg. Only the fuselage covering allowed the distinguishing of this machine from the second; one bay extra was covered on the n° 14. The second XI-3 which carried n° 26 in the competition was fitted with a Gnome double Gamma of 140hp and had three wheels attached to each undercarriage leg.

At the first trials on the 5th October, the N° 14 flown by Conneau, broke its tail skid whilst trying to take off from the aerodrome at Reims. The following morning at Montcornet, Conneau, who had moved over to number 26, twice failed the first test. On returning from the last test he broke the undercarriage and turned over. That evening, returning to Reims, the pilot again flew the number 14. Attempting a glide landing, the machine bounced and turned over completely. The pilot was ejected over the motor and injured by the fuselage which fell onto his leg. On the 15th October, after repairs to the badly damaged undercarriage, the number 14, flown by Le Blanc, took off with a passenger but fell back to earth almost straight away onto its left wing. The aircraft whose undercarriage this time was completely broken, could not be repaired in time and was eliminated from the competition. On the 24th, on board number 26 which had been repaired, Desparmets bounced on landing and fell in a flat position braking several fuselage cross wires. Three days later, despite a strong wind blowing in gusts, Desparmets took off with the number 26, but was victim of a breakdown near to Pontgivard. The machine crashed to the ground from 200 metres. The pilot was killed instantly. Witnesses said that they had seen the machine roll onto its right wing, climb vertically and then fall to the ground, with the engine still turning. This accident stopped the development of the XI-3, with an undercarriage too fragile and insufficient stability.

- *Span* : 11.70m
- *Wing area* : 25m²
- *Total weight* : 975kg
- *Length* : 8.70m
- *Empty weight* : 475kg
- *Speed* : 100km/h

The Blériot XI-3 with the 140 hp Gnome engine, seems to have had slightly differently dimensions.

One of the two XI-3s, which obtained pitiful results.

---

(1) Of 142 machines registered, only forty turned up, and only nine were left after the elimination trials. The winner was Weymann on a Nieuport IVM monoplane, fitted with a Gnome engine of 100hp, this was the fastest aircraft, but also the least practical, the crew, seated between the wings, could see almost nothing downwards.

The three special XI of Adolphe Pégoud

On the 8th March 1913 Adolphe-Célestin Pégoud, 24 years old, of average height and blond moustache, was started on by Blériot as pilot-instructor and tester/receptionist. Coming from the 5th Régiment de Chasseurs d'Afrique, he was accompanied by his friend John Domenjoz, a Swiss national.[2]

The aircraft carrier cable. The review, *La Vie Maritime,* in its edition of 25th June 1910, had considered that the idea of using aircraft was *"a childish idea contrary to the laws of war and inauspicious for the Navy".* Contrary to the Army, they did not consider themselves concerned by flying machines equipped with wheels and preferred to utilise dirigibles to detect and attack submarines. However, a commission presided over by Rear Admiral Le Pord, after two meetings closed its report on the 27th June 1910, proposing that efforts should be made towards both the dirigible and the aeroplane.

Conclusive trial: Pégoud succeeded in hooking on to the cable.

On the 26th August the Vice Admiral Boué de Lapeyrère, Minister of the Navy, ordered the purchase of a first machine, a Farman bi-plane. Taking account of the little autonomy of aeroplanes and poor viability of their engines, as well as the difficulties of the seaplanes handling on the sea, it was envisaged to use aircraft equipped with wheels taking off from warships. Even though Clément Ader had suggested as early as 1895 the creation of aircraft carriers, the idea was not followed through until

(2) Domenjoz, after having presented several Blériots in Europe, left for the United States in 1915, as Company Representative. His demonstration Blériot XI fitted with a Gnome Sigma engine of 60 hp, has been restored and is now on display at the National Air and Space Museum in Washington.

the end of 1913, with the transformation of the cruiser *Foudre*, as a platform to allow an aircraft to take off. The landing - on the other hand on a deck of 34.7 metres long - was particularly delicate if not impossible. Another method was considered in order that the Navy should have available aircraft capable of taking off and landing on a ship.

In 1911, the *Enseigne de Vaisseau* Lafon had tested at Châlons, an aircraft taking off from a yard arm, and hooking-on again on the return, but the experience was not followed up. During the meeting in Monaco in 1913, Louis Blériot had noted the difficulties that the seaplanes met when trying to take off in a choppy sea. He had therefore thought about a mechanism which allowed a seaplane - and obviously therefore a landplane - to fly from a cable slung along the side of a ship, and to return to hook on, thus improving the method studied by the Enseigne de Vaisseau Lafon.

Blériot modified a type XI with an Anzani engine, by adding a hook system that he had designed. He entrusted the trials to Pégoud. On the 9th August 1913, at Buc in front of the Navy Minister, Pierre Baudin and Admirals Darieu and Le Bris, Pégoud made several " take offs" from a steel cable 80 metres long and 20mm in diameter, held taut 4 metres above the ground between four pylons, as well as several suspended " landings". The hook mechanism in a V configuration was placed above the cockpit and had a manual locking system controlled by the pilot. Even though the tests were conclusive, the procedure demanded a particular skill on the part of the pilot during hooking on - plus little wind. In December 1913 the mechanism was fitted to the battleship *Jauréguiberry*, but finally, no tests at hooking-on at sea were attempted.

Abandoned after the declaration of war in 1914, the procedure would be re-examined by Herbemont in 1920 on a Blériot XI[1] and a Spad 38, then again in 1924 with a Hanriot 29 suspended from rails on the battleship *Lorraine*. Previous trials

---

(1) The trials were carried out by Second Maître Prévot, still at Buc.

in 1921 were inconclusive, from a platform fitted on the upper front turret of the battleship *Paris*, then on the despatch boat *Bapaume*. It would be seven years of reflection and studies before the coming into service of the *Béarn*, the first French operational aircraft carrier (1927).

Pégoud accomplished several take-offs and landings under the cable, thanks to this experimental hook mechanism.

The parachute. During the summer of 1913, Pégoud tried out a new experience, a parachute jump, an exceptional performance up until now. The first human experience in this domain happened on the 22nd October 1797 when Citizen Andrè Garnerin made a parachute jump at 700 metres from a balloon above the Parc Monceau. On the 1st March 1912, the first parachute jump from an aircraft had been accomplished by the American, Berry, whereas in France, Jean Ors tested a parachute of his own design from the 1st floor of the Eiffel tower on the 29th March 1913. The parachute was tested with a dead weight. Pégoud, who at first had not informed Blériot of his attempt, took off on the 16th August 1913 with a parachute designed by the engineer Bonnet, folded on the rear fuselage. The aircraft, a patched-up type XI, destined to be sacrificed, would not gather enough speed so the pilot had to put the trial off till the 19th August, when the engine had been replaced - and this time with the agreement of Louis Blériot. Diving slightly, at 100 metres high, he was torn out of his seat by the opening of the parachute, hitting the tail of the aircraft. Despite several suspension cords being broken the descent was normal and Pégoud landed safe and sound in a tree near to the field of Châteaufort, from where the aircraft had taken

off. All showmanship manoeuvring had been forbidden by the Constabulary on the field at Buc.

Looping the loop. During the descent, Pégoud had the time to observe the evolutions of the Blériot flying by itself. The aircraft carried out several aerobatic manoeuvres before hitting the ground. Because an aeroplane could manoeuvre that way without breaking up it became logically possible to make it do - with a pilot on board - identical figures and even to envisage inverted flight.

Up until that moment, builders worried only about the development of the stability and the good air-handling of their machines. Pégoud would research the limits of manoeuvrability of his machine, compatible with the security in flight. He managed to convince his employer to allow him to fly deliberately upside down. Louis Blériot was already thinking of handing this job to Perreyon, his Chief Pilot at that time.

After having carried out several very steep turns 'in order to see', Pégoud had himself strapped into an aircraft upside down inside a hanger, in order to familiarise himself with the sensations of inverted flight.

The Bonnet parachute used by Pégoud is placed on the back of the fuselage. As it opened it pulled the pilot out of his seat.

A reinforced XI-2 allocated to Pégoud.

A journalist mentioned to him the perilous side of his attempt, he replied, "*Of little importance if I die, it will only be one aviator less, but if I succeed, how many precious existences will be conserved for aviation*".[2]

On the 1st September 1913 at 8.0 o'clock in the morning, piloting a special XI-2 with doubled flying wires, he climbed to 1200 metres near to Juvisy, he turned over and flew inverted for about 400 metres. The following day at Buc, in front of a group of representatives of Civil and Military aviation, he renewed this exploit which would resound throughout the World. The fuel which came out from the fuel tank vent sprayed over the pilot. Pégoud told afterwards, "*One would have said the spray of vinegar of the barber after shaving. In spite of my bizarre position I shouted to myself: "My friend there you are at the wig makers!*" Encouraged by the good results of this operation, on Sunday the 21st September, Pégoud carried out vertical downward S turns and then carried out a complete loop, ignoring that one month earlier the Russian pilot Nesterov had carried out this same manoeuvre on a Nieuport above Kiev. On the 27th September Pégoud made two consecutive loops, and the following day three consecutive loops. On the 1st October he managed a continuous series of eight loops after 59 seconds of inverted flight. Pégoud

became therefore the loop-the-loop King, as was said at the time, in an era where the use of English was the latest "chic". Pégoud continued his capers in England (at Hendon), in Germany, in Austria, in Belgium, in Italy, in Romania, in Norway, in Holland and in Poland. In the weeks which followed Pégoud's exploit, 28 other pilots succeeded a looping, after having received his advice. The loop was at last looped.

Comical illustrations underlining the popularity of Adolphe Pégoud and his aerial looping. This was publicity for the pilot, but also for the Blériot monoplane and its Gnome engine.

(2) For the situation where the machine could not find its original position and landed inverted, Pégoud wore a helmet of his own design, made of lacquered and reinforced rattan, resting on his shoulders. Fortunately this 'anti-crash' system was never put to the test.

On the 10th December, in order that the representatives of the press should participate at his high school number, he was accompanied in turns by the journalists Guymon, Mathieu and Bruyère. At Buc on the 13th December, the aviator carried out an inverted spiral descent in front of the Commission Senatoriale de l'Aviation. The following day at Juvisy he showed the measure of his virtuosity with a demonstration flight of nearly one hour, as reported in *L'Aérophile: Pégoud climbed to 800 metres, turned over and remained 2 minutes 4 seconds head down, carrying out spirals. Regaining height, he carried out at least 15 loops, then a tail slide, straightened out and climbed again, descended again a tail slide in a spin and looped the loop upside down before landing, greeted by a formidable ovation.*

Thanks to Pégoud it was now proven that an aviator, if he conserved the necessary cold blood, could re-establish the aircraft whenever it found itself in a critical position. Pégoud had equally shown the solidity of the Blériot monoplanes, which had been called into question after several accidents in 1910[1] and 1911. In fact the use of engines much more powerful than the 25 hp Anzani of the Channel Crossing, caused axial compression and torsional forces, against which the wing spars could not resist in a dive, even a gentle one, nor in a tight turn. Blériot resolved the problem by progressively reinforcing the cables and the spars, as was shown by the pulling of a Blériot XI by a steam train up to a speed of 115 km/h. (Military flights which had been suspended for two months in May and June 1912 immediately re-started.) In January 1914, Pégoud ordered two machines with "reinforced structure", specially constructed for looping: a single-seater and a tandem two-seater, both with Gnome engines of 80 hp. With these two machines he carried out numerous exhibitions in France and abroad up until the outbreak of the First World War.

(1) The first accident of this nature proved fatal for Delagrange, the first pilot to fit a Gnome engine to his Blériot, an XI type Channel Crossing. It happened during the meeting at the Croix d'Hins near Arcachon on the 4th January 1910, on an aerodrome where Louis Blériot was committed to open a flying school. Probably because of Delagrange's accident, the school was never opened. To put an end to the judicial problems between himself and the owners of the land, Blériot bought the land in 1912 and kept it until 1920.

The Blériot XI of Perreyon's record

On the 11th March at Buc, Perreyon beat the World Altitude record 5880m on board a light weight single-seat XI-2. The fuselage was fully covered. The engine was a Gnome of 160hp. He reached 5880m in 55 minutes.

The undercarriage was simplified and built of streamlined metal tubes. The pilot's equipment included oxygen for the high altitude part of the flight which lasted a total of 67 minutes.

Mechanics hold back Perreyon's monoplane before the starting up of its large engine.

The Blériot XI Parasol or Blériot-Gouin

The XI Parasol, also called Blériot Gouin or XI type Gouin from the name of the officer who designed it appeared in February 1914 and participated in the Concours de Sécurité, in May of the same year. It was distinguished from the classical XI by a raised wing to give an excellent view of the ground, but positioned level with the pilot's eyes in a way to present a smaller dead angle as possible still preserving the view of the sky. The machine was perfect for observation, conforming to the wishes of the Military. The prototype was fitted with a high narrow windshield: the rudder (shown here) was built of two parts which could open as an airbrake either in flight or on landing, because the Military wanted to reduce the landing run.[2] However, the photos show that in flight the two rudders do not close and the drag must have been important.

(2) None of the series production models were equipped with either a windscreen or a two-part rudder.

Twenty XI type Gouin were ordered by the War Ministry on the 15th October 1914. Several dozen XI Parasol were built in England by Blériot aircraft limited and in Italy by the SIT; fifteen were delivered to the Royal Flying Corps and twelve to the Royal Naval Air Service.

The Blériot-Gouin Parasol had a certain success as a single-seater.

- *Span* : 9.20m
- *Wing Area* : 18m^2
- *Total weight* : 420kg
- *Total length* : 7.80m
- *Empty weight* : 310kg
- *Speed* : 110/115km/h

XI-2 Total Vision A two-seat tandem version of the XI-2 Total Vision designed at the beginning of the summer 1914, would in fact never be ordered. The machine was equipped either a

Le Rhône engine of 80 hp or a Gnome of 100 hp. The cockpit covering was continued rearwards into a pyramid point. As on the single-seater, the pilot was seated behind the parasol wing. The passenger, in front, was seated under the wing of which the central part between the two wing spars was uncovered, to allow the passenger's head to pass and to give him a good view upwards.

Above: A Blériot-Gouin in flight.

Opposite: The unique XI-2 "total vision".

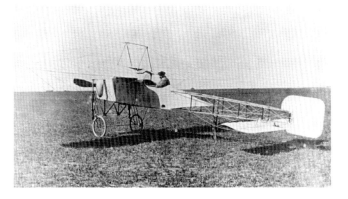

The Blériot XII

The Blériot XII is included in this list for memory because it was mentioned in the two preceding chapters. This multi-seat on which much hope was placed was found to be too unstable and was not followed through. Four examples were built.

One of the two XI-2 piloted by Louis Blériot at the meeting in Reims, in August 1909.

The Blériot XIII Aérobus

Designed for the army, this large monoplane with rigid struts and a pusher engine, a Gnome of 100 hp, was designed for the transport of four people. Its high wing was equipped with ailerons and it's elevator was placed at the front. A large fixed tail plane was situated at the rear, above it was the rudder. For ease of transport and storage, the wing and fuselage of the Blériot XIII could be disassembled. The Blériot XIII[3] appeared in December 1910.

Two days after a first trial at Pau, with eight people on board, Lemartin flew nine passengers on the 4th February 1911, thus beating the world record for the number of people carried. After modification, it remained based at Etampes.

The Blériot XIII on the ground and in flight with four passengers.

- *Span* : 13m
- *Wing Area* : 40m^2
- *Useful load* : 550kg
- *Propeller (Chauvière)* : 3,5 metres diameter
- *Total length* : 12m
- *Empty weight* : 600kg

---

(3) A first project, reference type XIII, had been designed as early as 1909. It was a three-seat monoplane with a 70 hp engine, proposed at the price of 26,000 francs. Wing area: 27 m² - Empty weight: 450 kg - Total weight: 900 kg. This model having never been built, the reference XIII was re-used later to designate the Aérobus.

The Blériot XIV

Side by side two-seater with a Gnome engine of 50 hp, it was the first machine with a "fish tail". The fuselage, whose section was reduced heavily from the cockpit rearwards, was composed of two elements which were joined at the tailing edge of the wings; the rear part could therefore be dismantled for ease of transport of the machine. The structure of the horizontal tail plane was integrated into the rear of the fuselage, allowing this entire section of the machine to be covered in one piece, but the incidence, if needed, could be modified in relation to that of the wings. The rudder was made of two semi-circular parts, above and below of the fuselage. The access to the cockpit was made through a hatch in the floor.

The prototype made its first flight in November 1910. In 1911, at least one XIV was equipped with a one-piece pointed rudder.

- *Span* : 13,38m
- *Wing area* : 30.7m²
- *Length* : 8.35m

The Blériot XIV was more compact and more aerodynamic.

The Blériot XV

A project of a tandem two-seater "face to face" with a Gnome engine of 100 hp, overall length : 8.2 m. This machine appears in the Blériot archives as a simple hand-written note, no other source confirms its existence.

Four projects with no type number

On the 29th May 1911, Louis Blériot filed two patents concerning three monoplanes.

The first two were side by side two-seaters with a "fish tail" and two-part rudder. One of these two was very similar to the Blériot XIV which differed however by a different empennage and a different tail skid. The second was equipped with a special undercarriage fitted with two short skids. The upper pylon and its flying wires were replaced by rigid masts linking the wings to the lower pylon and the bottom of the undercarriage chassis.

The third machine was a single-seater, with a rotary engine, whose fuselage of circular section was entirely covered. The empennage was in form of a "pigeon tail" and the rudder was in two parts, the shaft of the rudder was curved to form the tail skid. The elevator, as on the two models above, and on the XIV, was a single piece. In the absence of an upper pylon, the wings were rigidified by struts linking them to the lower pylon, and to the undercarriage.

At the same time, an aircraft of a total weight of one ton, with a 16 m span and a 50 m² wing area was also being designed, but the drawings have been lost. None of these four models were ever made and their type number is unknown today. On the 22nd October 1911, Blériot filed patents on a series of designs to allow vertical take off, also called "firm foot" takeoff. It seems however that no machine was ever equipped with any of these designs.

Below, side and plan views of the second project showing the type XIV.

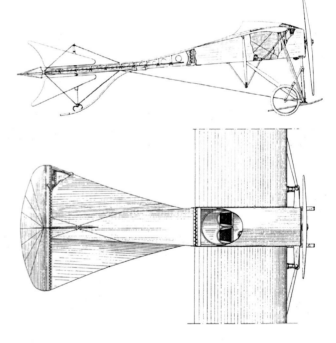

Opposite, the first project whose conception was, obviously, motivated by the search for speed. Below, the third project showed the more streamlined monocoque.

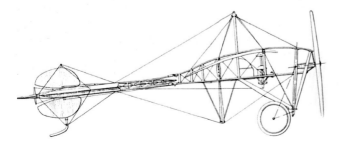

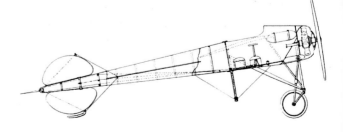

The Blériot XX

An experimental single-seater with "semi-supple" wings, the fuselage was flat, totally covered, and in the shape of a pigeon tail. The rear part of each wing rib could be taken apart. Where the front and rear parts joined, the front covering was linked to the rear covering by lacing. This separate covering from the front and the rear of the wing allowed the modification of the wing area of the machine, by changing only the rear section of the wing ribs. Fitted with a Gnome Omega engine of 50 hp, its first flight was on the 11ᵗʰ February 1911, but a first version of the XX with a double rudder nick-named "The Fish" because of its pointed tail plane appeared at Pau at the end of 1910.

- *Span* : 8.90m
- *Wing Area* : 17.5m^2
- *Propeller* (*Régy*) : 2.60 metres diameter
- *Total length* : 7.65m
- *Empty weight* : 250kg

The covering of the trailing edge was placed on the front part of the wing.

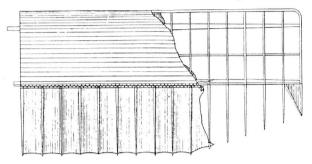

The Blériot XX with Gnome engine of 50hp. At Etamps, Lemartin climbs on board before taking off towards Toury.

The wing of the type XX and its removable trailing edge.

The Blériot XXI

Side by side two-seater with empennage in the form of a "fish tail", this elegant machine basically destined for the Army, was powered by a Gnome engine of 70 hp. It was fitted with warping wings, it included several technical refinements : the control cables were inside the fuselage, or very close to the sides; the covering of the elevator was, as was on all the "fish tail models", linked to the horizontal tail plane by lacing; a hatch in the floor of the cockpit allowed the crew to climb easily on board, the cockpit had dual controls, the bell was manoeuvrable from the passenger's side ; the flying instruments and the map table could slide on a transversal bar. Easily disassembled this model was particularly adapted to transport by road.

The Blériot XXI had a very low double skid in rattan, which, when taxing gave it a very high angle of incidence, the increase in the air resistance thus obtained, reduced the landing roll distance. Completed in February 1911, it flew at Pau as early as the following month A XXI "Taxi" with a thicker tail and a XXI B¹ flew at Hardelot in August 1911. More than a dozen examples of the Blériot XXI were built ; seven were delivered to the French Army, one to the British Army, this machine was used by Lieutenant Reginald A. Cammell, and one to the Blériot School at Etampes ; furthermore, a few Type XXI were also handed over to Russia, one to Rumania, and one to Bulgaria.

- *Span* : 11.0m
- *Wing Area* : 25m^2
- *Total Weight* : 600kg
- *Endurance* : 4.0 hours
- *Length* : 8.24m
- *Empty Weight* : 330kg
- *Speed* : 190km/h
- *Price* : 30,000 francs

The cockpit of the Blériot XXI.

At the *Salon de la Locomotion Aérienne* of 1911. The all-white Blériot XXI shown with the Blériot XXVII and XXVIII.

(1) No details are known about this machine, it could have been confused with the "Taxi"

The XXI Hydro on the Seine, in January 1913.

The Blériot XXI Hydro

A three-float seaplane without step, which appeared in January 1913, the XXI Hydro had the same dimensions as the land plane, it was mounted on a rigid chassis, and was equipped with a Gnome engine of 80 hp.

- *Empty weight* : 410kg
- *Total weight* : 660kg
- *Speed* : 90km/h

The Blériot XXII

A special side by side two-seater with a 10.25 metre span, destined for the flying school of Roger Morin. This model's existence has not been formally established, it could have been a school version of the XXI. Whatever the truth, Morin bought a Blériot XXI.

The Blériot XXIII

Powered by a Gnome Double "Omega" engine of 100 hp, the Blériot XXIII was a short-span racing monoplane which appeared in March 1911. Three examples were built.

- *Span* : 9m
- *Wing area* : 9m²
- *Speed* : 128km/h
- *Length* : 7.50m
- *Empty weight* : 315kg

The Blériot XXIII was a racing aircraft. During the Gordon Bennett Cup, in June 1911 (on the right) its wing was drastically reduced.

The Blériot XXIV Berline

A high-winged monoplane derived from the type XIII, the type XXV was ordered by Henry Deutsch de la Meurthe. Shown at the Exposition Internationale de l'Aéronautique, in December 1911, the machine was powered by a Gnome engine of 100 hp, with a pusher propeller, it was equipped with a large cabin padded with air cushions "to absorb the shocks upon landing".

Inside there were four inward facing chairs. The windows were in mica. The cockpit was outside in front of the cabin, and after the trials carried out in December, was protected by a Constantin conical transparent windscreen. To give his instructions to the pilot, the owner had a trumpet, just like the cars of the time. The aircraft was re-engined with a 140 hp Gnome in January 1912, the machine was tried again with a new wing in May.

The XXIV, flying saloon car. The "chauffeur" is in front, outside.

At the Salon of 1911, the five-seat Blériot *Berline* of 100hp was shown with Blériot acetylene lamps.

With the 100 hp Gnome.
- *Span : 14.5m*
- *Length : 12.50m*
- *Empty weight : 700kg*
- *Wing area : 40m^2*
- *Speed : 85km/h*

With the 140 hp Gnome
- *Span : 13m*
- *Length : 14.7m*
- *Empty weight : 725kg*
- *Wing area : 41m^2*
- *Speed : 85km/h*

The Blériot XXV

A very distant relative of the Canard Type V of 1907, the model XXV was fitted with a Gnome 50 hp engine, this aircraft flew for the first time in August 1911, it was a two-seater destined for Navy Observation missions. The Blériot Bell was replaced by a vertical steering wheel installed on a horizontal cross piece of the fuselage, connected by universal joints. The observer, lying face downwards had a perfect view of the ground through a window in the floor. Its wings were equipped with ailerons, the rudder initially placed under the fuselage, in front of the skid, was replaced by two vertical fins installed at the wing tips.

- *Span : 8.9m*
- *Wing area : 12m^2*
- *Total weight : 700kg*
- *Length : 5.5m*
- *Empty weight : 400kg*

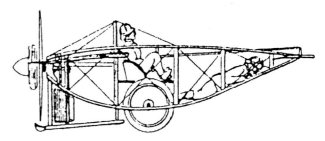

Above, the first project with wheels inside the fuselage. Opposite, the very small Blériot XXV with tiny rudders. Below, The system of flying controls of the Blériot XXV. The wheel moves laterally to control the warping, and forwards and backwards to move the elevator placed in front of the fuselage.

The undercarriage was made up of two independent wheels and a rear skid to stop the propeller from touching the ground, it had nothing in common with the classical Blériot undercarriage. Initially, an axle was to be fitted to the lower longerons on the fuselage, under the cockpit, the wheels partially running inside the fuselage on either side of the pilot. A three-seat project derived from the XXV was designed for the Military Trials of 1913.

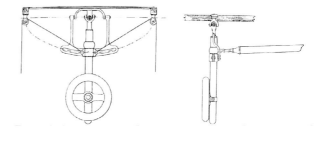

The Blériot XXVI

A tri-plane Canard with a rotary Gnome engine, filed under Belgian patent of 6th May 1911, was completed in September of the same year, but does not appear to have flown. The wing system was made up of a main central wing, and upper and lower auxiliary wings, with the lower wing very close to the ground, on landing it gave a "violent effect of compression", that is to say, ground effect. As on the XXV the propeller was fitted between the engine and the rear of the fuselage. The elevator was fitted right at the front of the fuselage.

The rudder was in two parts, above and below the fuselage pivoting around the central strut linking the leading edge of the wings. The Blériot XXVI had a nose wheel which retracted into the fuselage, the lower wing had seven supple skids.

- *Span* : 5.75m
- *Wing Area* : 19.55m^2
- *Length* : 5.64m
- *Height* : 2.62m

Three drawings of the patent of the tri-plane canard, Blériot XXVI with retractable undercarriage.

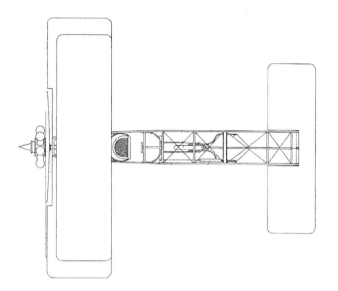

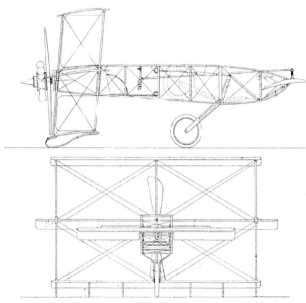

The Blériot XXVII

A racing single-seat with pigeon tail, fitted first with a Gnome 50 hp and then 70 hp engine, the engine was mounted with a large overhang It was to be equipped with an incidence corrector incorporated into the elevator. The elevator was divided into three parts, only the central part was moved by the control stick. The two extremities, joined together, were controlled by an independent lever in order to compensate the torque effect of the engine, notably the pitch-up effect when moving into gliding. This mechanism, despite being very interesting, does not appear to have finally been installed. Completed in July 1911, the machine was tried at Hardelot the following month. On the 17th September 1911, Leblanc reached 120.35km/h with this machine.

A Blériot XXVII equipped with a ground adjustable propeller and a special undercarriage with blade springs, was shown at the Salon de la Locomotion Aérienne of 1911.

An example of the first variant with a classical Blériot undercarriage, purchased by Great Britain, is still conserved today in the Royal Air Force Museum at Hendon.

- *Span* : 9.0 m
- *Wing Area* : 12m^2
- *Length* : 6.5m
- *Empty weight* : 240kg
- *Price* : 24,000 francs (with the 50 hp Gnome) or 27,000 francs (with the 70 hp Gnome)

Opposite on the left: A Blériot XXVII on the seafront at Hardelot. It has a classic undercarriage and a fixed pitch propeller.

Above: At the Salon of 1911, the fuselage of a "*Blériot 27 type Rapide*", with a lightened undercarriage, more streamlined, and a propeller whose blades are inclined forward. The pitch was ground adjustable by means of two conjugated rods on an arm through the propeller shaft.

The Blériot XXVIII Populaire

This was an XI, simplified and lightened, also shown at the Salon of 1911.

It was a single-seater, a three cylinder Anzani - an inverted Y - of 35 hp was fitted, with overhang on a narrow fuselage. It was tried by Perreyon in February 1912 at Pau, then sold in June to Alexis Maneyrol - the only known owner of a XXVIII - who took part at numerous exhibitions flying his lightweight single-seater. A two-seat version with a Gnome Gamma engine of 70 hp was proposed in 1913.

Single-seat version

- *Span* : 8.90m
- *Wing Area* : 15m^2
- *Speed* : 85km/h

- *Length* : 7.2m
- *Empty weight* : 210 kg
- *Price* : 11,800 Francs

-

Two-seat version

- *Span* ; 9.75m
- *Wing Area* : 20m^2
- *Take-off weight* : 550kg

- *Length* : 8.20m
- *Empty weight* : 300kg

The Blériot XXIX Military Special

Conceived as an application of a patent the 30th September 1912, this was a side by side two-seater observation aircraft, equipped with a Gnome engine of 70 hp with a pusher propeller. Blériot who was a specialist of monoplanes was seeking to compete with the bi-planes of Voisin or Farman whose useful load was superior, and which the crew, placed in a nacelle had a wide visibility.

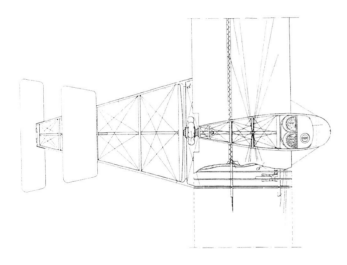

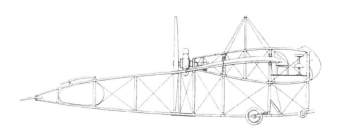

The cockpit was situated in the front section of a nacelle, to each side of which were fixed the wings. The fuselage was a triangular section, it was made up of two upper longerons starting at each wing, on either side of the propeller, and one single lower longeron forming the rigid landing skid. The wheels were mounted on steel blade springs at the ends of a horizontal axle, the small diameter auxiliary wheels were fitted on the lower longeron right at the front. The empennage was made up of two horizontal tail planes, installed one behind the other, above and at the rear of the fuselage. (The first was fixed, the second was mobile and acted as the elevator), and a rudder installed between the longerons, under the tail plane.

The XXIX bis patented on the 8th August 1913, was a version of the XXIX, in which the fuselage, still of triangular section, had two lower longerons and one single upper longeron, which was linked to the propeller shaft by a ball-bearing. A third version of the XXIX was also designed, in which the pusher propeller spun inside the fuselage longerons, which were very wide apart. None of these three models were ever built.

- *Span* : 10.6m
- *Length* : 7.6m

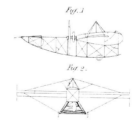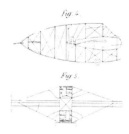

Above: Four sketches of the two versions of the Blériot XXIX, taken from the patent. The two drawings on the left represent the XXIX bis. Opposite: The Blériot XXIX (29) Military Special. The Army, tempted by the visibility of biplanes with rear engines, encouraged the builders to design monoplanes of this type, susceptible to be faster.

The Blériot XXX

This also remained a project, it was a four-seater with an 80 hp Anzani engine, designed in 1912.

The Blériot XXXII

Another project which remained without follow up, the Blériot XXXII was the subject of a patent taken out in Belgium on 25th March 1912. Equipped with an off-set flat two air cooled Blériot engine, it had a low, bellied fuselage, the undercarriage was fitted directly to the longerons, it was fitted with special controls, two pedals for the rudder instead of the classic rudder bar, and two vertical wheels fitted to a horizontal shaft, in place of the Blériot bell. The warping was obtained by turning the wheels on their shaft, the elevator was actioned by lateral displacement of the wheels. The interest of this new control system was for the pilot to be able to control the aircraft, and above all, to block the controls with his knees, thus leaving the hands free to intervene on the engine parts which were specially arranged to be accessible in flight from the pilot's seat. A pendulum weight, to be engaged or disengaged, was also written into the patent, in order to obtain an automatic stabilization of the controls without the action of the knees. This mechanism could be considered as the forerunner of the automatic pilot.

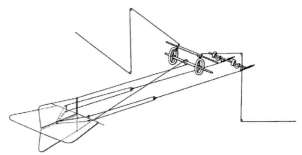

The curious but original control system of the Blériot XXXII.

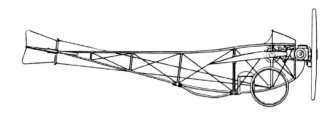

Sketch of the Blériot XXXII (32), extract from the Belgian patent.

The Blériot XXXIII

A side by side two-seater Canard, powered by Gnome engine of 70 hp, which was installed on the centre of gravity. The rear fin was made up of a tubular frame work. The elevator was situated right at the front of the fuselage, a fuselage which became smaller and smaller towards the front, until it became simply a tube.

The rudder was made up of eight small vertical surfaces positioned under the elevator. The undercarriage had two axles fitted onto a central skid. The main axle was fitted with large widely spaced wheels and was placed below the engine, whereas the auxiliary axle with small wheels and narrow track, was installed below and in front of the cockpit.

It came out in June 1912, the Blériot XXXIII christened *Canard Bleu* (blue duck) reappeared in October seriously redesigned. The undercarriage was completely transformed, the front axle had disappeared, the rear axle was replaced by the classical Blériot undercarriage of deformable triangles and steerable wheels. A large vertical rudder was installed below the fuselage.

The engine was now an 80 hp Gnome fitted in overhang on an engine mount. As for the rudder - very large dimensions, - it was fitted behind the propeller.

With 70 hp Gnome engine
- *Span* : 10.50m
- *Wing area* : 24m^2
- *Speed* : 115km/h
- *Length* : 8.0m
- *Empty weight* : 330kg

With 80 hp Gnome engine.
- *Span* 11.0m
- *Wing area* : 22m^2
- *Length* : 9.0m
- *Speed*: 120km/h

The canard Blériot XXXIII (33), modified and re-engined with a Gnome of 80hp, shown in flight (the engine is at the rear), opposite; and on the ground, below.

The Blériot XXXVI

A two-seat side by side observation aircraft, with a Gnome Lambda 80 hp engine. The fuselage was a circular monocoque made up of strips of cork rolled around a mould, between two layers of cloth, glued and shrunk. The cockpit was protected by a band of tempered steel. The wing spars had soles in ash, and a centre part made up of a beam in cork tightened into the covering. The engine was partially covered by a protective cowling

which allowed air through underneath. The undercarriage with fixed wheels had a central skid to which were fixed the lower flying wires. The tubular undercarriage had shock absorbers of compressed air and glycerine. On the ground the machine stayed horizontal, tail in the air. It was equipped with a vertical empennage in the form of a dorsal fin, symmetrical above and below the fuselage. The horizontal empennage was triangular. The machine appeared in October, the Blériot XXXVI christened the *Torpille* (torpedo) was shown at the Salon of 1912.

- *Span* : 12.25m
- *Length* : 8.9m
- *Wing area* : 25m²
- *Empty weight* : 375kg
- *Speed* : 115km/h

The Blériot XXXVI (36) *La Torpille* on an undercarriage similar to the Nieuport.

The Blériot XXXVI-bis

This was a version with three rows of flying wires (instead of two), and with the classic steerable undercarriage of the preceding model. The tail of the machine resting on the ground, the machine was equipped with a skid and a new rudder.

The Blériot XXXVI bis (36 bis) with a different one-piece rudder, and not two half-rudders.

The Blériot XXXVII

This was a two-seat side by side monoplane, with " total visibility" for the crew through their position right at the front, the 80 hp Gnome and the propeller being situated behind the wings. A design reminiscent of the Blériot XXIX *bis*, the XXXVII was also equipped with a ball bearing shaft linking the propeller to the upper longeron of the rear part of the triangular fuselage. To stop all risks of accident caused by the deterioration of the bearing, it was fitted with a special electrical contact, which, in case of abnormal overheating, rang a bell placed beside the pilot.

The undercarriage was of the classic type, but much lower and with a wider track. Access to the cockpit was made by the front of the nacelle which hinged forward and downwards. A vertical wheel situated on a lever replaced the Blériot bell. Colonel Bouttiaux Director of the Military Aeronautical experimentation centre at Chalais-Meudon, flew as passenger on the XXXVII in January 1913. On the 25th November, the machine which had been re-engined with a Gnome Delta of 100 hp, crashed on landing, the pilot, Edmond Perreyon, was crushed by the engine and died instantly.

- *Span* : 12.0m
- *Length* : 10.0m

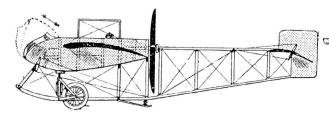 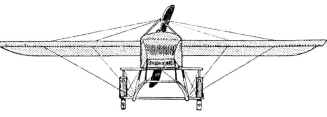

The two-seat observation Blériot XXXVII (37): the front nose lifts up for access for the crew.

The Blériot XXXIX

This was a single-seat armoured observation aircraft, designed around a new set of Military specifications. It had a shell fuselage, and was shown at the Salon of 1913. The engine, an 80 hp Gnome, ran inside an armoured cage which was in two removable parts. The cage was fitted on hinges, could pivot to the right or to the left, giving thus, immediate accessibility. To dismantle it completely it was sufficient to remove the hinge pins. The cabane, of a new shape, and the wings were also articulated. The machine which was very short, had a classical Blériot undercarriage, with deformable triangles and steerable wheels. It was

successfully tested with two different empennages. Despite its qualities (rapidity of assembly and disassembly, ease of maintenance) the Blériot XXXIX was not produced, perhaps because of the difficulties of cooling the engine due to the armour plating.

- *Span* : 10.10m
- *Length* : 6.15m
- *Wing area* : 19m²
- *Empty weight* : 440kg
- *Take-off weight* : 615 kg
- *Speed* : 120km/h

Above: The Blériot XXXIX (39) armoured two-seater at Buc.

Opposite: The same, with a modified empennage.

A "four engined" project

In 1913 Louis Blériot designed the project of a monoplane similar to a Blériot XI or one of its derivatives, but which was powered by an assembly of four rotary engines driving a single two-bladed propeller.

The layout, seen here from the front, was made up of engines whose diameter was approximately 95cm, we can estimate the inside diameter at approximately 1.50m and therefore, as a consequence the aircraft would be able to carry at least two people side by side and a load, the weight of which is not known.

In the sketch, the engines seem to be 70 hp or 80 hp Gnome engines.

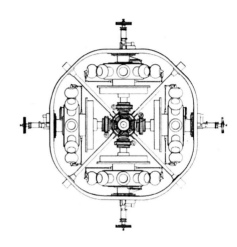

The coupling of four engines, front view, imagined in 1913.

The armoured two-seater of Jules Vedrines' La Vache

This was a tandem two-seater observation aircraft, a monocoque construction, with a Gnome engine of 160 hp. A large classical cabane covered each of the cockpits. Armed with a Hotchkiss machine gun placed on the left side of the fuselage, armoured by a sheet of special steel, the machine had a span of 12.25 metres. The machine gun fired under the wing through a hole, but because of the lower flying wires had only a limited movement. The machine made it's first flight at Buc in July 1914, in the hands of Védrines.

Shortly after the beginning of the war, Védrines gave it the name of *La Vache*, painted in large red letters on the white fuselage, René Vicaire tells on page 109 of how, aboard this aircraft, piloted by Védrines, he shot down a German Taube on the 2nd September 1914 over Suippes. The handling of the machine gun proved delicate, *La Vache* whose engine had cooling problems, only stayed in service at the front for a short time.

The number of the type of this machine cannot be positively identified as the XXXIX - bis, but it is included here in the text because it appears to be chronologically correct.

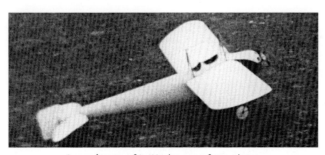

A rare image of La Vache seen from above.

This photo taken at Buc clearly shows the volume of the fuselage.

The Blériot XL

Founded in July 1912, the Società Italiana Transaerea (SIT) the Italian branch of Blériot Aéronautique, built at Corso Peschiera, near Turin, a factory of 4000 m², and rapidly employed fifty people. The Technical Director was the engineer Triaca. The factory had hardly opened when the company received an order for eighty machines from the Italian government (forty-nine Blériots and thirty-one Maurice Farmans) out of a total of one hundred and fifty machines, spread over five builders.

During the day of 28th May 1913, a Blériot XI-2 SIT with an 80 hp Gnome engine flown by Perreyon, with Dupuis as mechanic, flew Turin-Rome-Turin, in a little over ten flying hours. The same year, the engineer Triaca designed a bi-plane inspired by the Maurice Farman MF20. Fitted with an 80 hp Gnome engine with pusher propeller, this was a sesquiplane, whose framework, with the exception of the wings, was in streamline tube and pressed steel. The nacelle, which was fitted with a cowling in aluminium and a windscreen, carried from front to rear, the pilot, the passenger, the fuel tanks and the engine. The wide-track undercarriage was reminiscent of that of the Blériot IV. It was made up of two wheels mounted on steerable forks, curved and lightened, and fitted with springs. It was finished in the spring, and was shown at the Salon de Turin and then tried at the Camp de Mirafiori, but was not retained by the Italian military aviation to be produced in series. It was shown then at the Salon de Paris in December 1913 under the name of Blériot XL, where the French Army showed an interest, however, they did not order it either.

The Blériot XL (40) was a compact biplane designed by the SIT, Italian branch of Blériot-Aéronautique, seen here at Mirafiori. It was also shown in France.

- *Span* : 12.7m
- *Wing area* : 38m²
- *Empty weight* : 390 kg
- *Speed* : 90km/h
- *Length* : 9.15m
- *Height* : 3.20m
- *Take-off weight* : 665kg

At the first Italian Military Aviation Review which was held on the aerodrome of Mirafiori, twenty-five machines (thirteen Blériots and twelve Farmans) out of the thirty-two present, had been build by the SIT. At the beginning of 1914, a Blériot seaplane fitted with a Gnome engine of 80 hp, came out of the factory at Corso Peschiera. It was tried with success in April on the river Po by the pilot Manissero. In 1915 the SIT opened a flying school on the field at Mirafiori, installing its own runway by the side of the factory buildings. The company received an order of twenty Voisin bi-planes, two-seat observation aircraft with a Salmson engine of 140 hp, an order which went to forty when Italy entered the First World War (on the 26th April 1915).

The SIT also built Blériot XI Parasols, then the SP-2 and SP-3. In September 1916, Triaca left the company. At the request of the Italian Government, Blériot had to cede the branch to an Italian company, in the Autumn of 1917, the Società Italiana Transaerea was dissolved and the building purchased by the Ansaldo Company.

The Blériot XLII

This was a side by side two-seat armoured Canard, with a Gnome Lambda engine of 80 hp. It was flown for the first time by Perreyon on the 24th March 1913. On a mission, the observer lay prone and passed his head through a hole in the front face of the cockpit.

The wing was equipped with ailerons and six small vertical fins installed symmetrically on the trailing edge of each wing. The rudder, also in the form of a fin, was linked to the fuselage by a metal tube framework built around the propeller. The front of the fuselage was curved upwards towards the front. The elevator was fitted at the front of the fuselage. The machine had a classic Blériot undercarriage, and a steerable skid at the front. The skid was replaced in April by a wheel. The upper part of the tubular structure around the propeller was also modified as well as the cabane. The number of vertical fins installed on the trailing edges of the wings was reduced to four.

- *Span* : 8.30m
- *Wing area* : 18m²
- *Length* : 7.30m

A Canard on floats was to participate at the seaplane meeting at Monaco, in April 1913, piloted by Etienne Giraud. This could have been a marine derivation of the XLII, because it was described as resembling a "Terrien du Moment" (Land plane of the moment). Powered by a Gnome engine of 80 hp, it was tried by Perreyon on the Seine in March. The tests not being finished, the machine could not participate at the meeting, which appears to have put an end to its development.

The Blériot XLII (42) canard in flight (the main wing is to the rear).

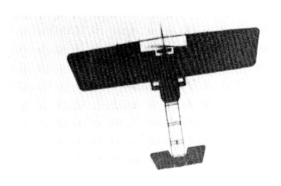

The nacelle of the Blériot XLII (42), first version.

The Blériot XLII (42) slightly modified. The cowling of the nacelle has been lowered for ease of access. An opening in the nacelle, visible in the above photo, allowed the observer, lying flat on his stomach, to pass his head through to see the ground.

The Blériot XLIII

A tandem two-seat observation aircraft of monocoque construction, it flew for the first time in November 1913, powered by a Gnome engine of 80 hp. The observer lay prone in the padded lower fuselage to examine the ground through a porthole, while remaining in contact with the pilot by means of a trumpet. The Blériot XLIII was fitted with a large pylon with four supports, and a new form of empennage. It was destroyed by fire at Buc following a collision in flight. The accident happened on the 19th April 1914. The XLIII flown by Bidot collided with a XL-2 flown by Deroye. The two machines caught fire and fell to the ground. Deroye was killed but Bidot walked unscathed from the debris of the XLIII.

- *Span* : 10.10m
- *Length* : 6.12m

- *Wing area*: 19.30m^2
- *Empty weight* : 350kg
- *Speed* : 120km/h
- *Height* : 3.10m
- *Take-off weight* : 625kg

The Blériot XLIII (43) in front of the central building on the Blériot aerodrome at Buc.

The Blériot XLIV

This was an artillery single-seater with large cut-outs at the wing roots, where the pilot/observer was seated behind the wing. It appeared in 1913 powered by a Gnome Lambda engine of 80 hp and was only 6.45 metres long. Its empennage was identical to that of the XLIII.

The Blériot XLIV (44) also designed for observation. One can consider, however, that, if the downward visibility was excellent, it was going to be much poorer sideways and to the front.

The Blériot XLV

Designed to offer as large a field of vision as possible, this was an observation single-seater which appeared in February 1914, with the Anzani engine of 60 hp fitted in the centre of the fuselage. The cylinders protruding from the fuselage, a cut-away was made in the trailing edge of each wing, the propeller shaft passed between the pilot's legs, the pilot was seated directly behind the propeller. The wing area was 17.04 m^2.

With the placing of the pilot and the engine reversed, the Blériot XLV (45) did not show any of the disadvantages of its predecessor.

But the long drive shaft to the propeller in front gave other problems.

The Blériot XLVI

Object of a simple hand written note in the Blériot archives, this single-seat with steerable skid, was to be powered with a Gnome engine of 80 hp. No other source can confirm its existence.

- *Span* : 8.85m
- *Wing area* : 17.04m^2
- *Length* : 7.4m
- *Height* : 2.94m

Blériot Military Aircraft in France and Abroad

THE ARMED BLERIOT MONOPLANES FROM 1910 TO 1915, THE TOTAL PRODUCTION AND HEAVY BOMBERS

An exceptionsal image of a French Military Bléirot XI, with the French Flag on the tail, photographed in flight from another aircraft

French Military Aviation was created by the law of the 29th March 1912. However, tests had been carried out beforehand at the Camp de Châlons, with a view to determining the models capable of being used by the army. As early as the 4th December 1909, the War Ministry ordered several aeroplanes from Farman, Wright and Blériot. The two Blériot were, an XI single-seater with an Anzani engine of 25hp for the Génie (Engineers) and an XI two-seater for the Artillery. In February 1910, four new machines of which one, an XI two-seater, were offered to the army thanks to a subscription by the newspaper *Le Temps*. On the 24th of the same month, the XI single-seat for the Génie was taken on strength at Pau. Lieutenant Bellenger was the first officer to obtain his pilot's licence on a Blériot, on the 5th April, at Pau. He was beaten by Lieutenant Félix Camerman who obtained his licence on a Farman in March. These licences were still civil. In May at Etampes, licences were obtained by Lieutenant Acquaviva (on the 2nd) and Captain Marie (on the 17th). On the 16th June it was Louis Blériot himself who, fulfilling a military obligation period, delivered to Vincennes by air, the Blériot XI-2 bis destined for the artillery. After a flight of twenty minutes from

the field at Issy-les-Moulineaux, he landed at four thirty-five in the morning, slightly damaging the undercarriage on landing.

In September 1910, two machines took part in the manoeuvres in Picardie, an XI single-seater with a Gnome engine of 50 hp, flown by Lieutenant Bellenger, and an XI two-seater flown by Lieutenant Acquaviva. This first military use gave evidence of the advantage of aircraft, notably in relation to dirigibles.

After the success of Leblanc in the Circuit de L'Est, the artillery ordered twenty Blériot, of which seventeen were two-seaters and three were single-seaters, called Type Circuit de L'Est. In 1911, Blériot brought out a new two-seater with a seven cylinder Gnome Gamma engine of 70 hp, from where came the XI-2 Military Type 1911. It was this model which would equip the first Blériot Aircraft Squadron, the BL 3, based at Pau. (the future squadron SPA3 of the Cigognes)

In 1914, in front of a surprised public, soldiers hold back a French Blériot XI whose engine is about to be started. Aircraft at that time had no brakes.

On the 22nd March 1912 there appeared a Ministerial Circular forbidding officers and military students from flying monoplanes, as long as their flying wires had not been reinforced. On the 26th, several Blériot aircraft carrying a reinforcing of the upper flying wires, were received at Reims, others were received at Pau the following day. After the accidents of Lieutenant de Ville d'Avray in April and Captain Echeman in May, resistance tests on a Blériot monoplane mounted on a railway wagon, were carried out from the 30th May to the 1st June, near to Survilliers railway station. The train ran at 110 kph, the machine, placed in all positions of flight, reacted satisfactorily on all points, which was noted by the different witnesses to the experiment. The doubts which weighed upon the solidity of the monoplanes were lifted from now on.

On the 31st March, Bellenger, recently promoted to Captain, took off from a field at Pau, accompanied by Lieutenants de Rose and de Malherbe. The following day, after having passed the night at Châteauroux, Bellenger and de Rose landed at Vincennes-Maison Blanche, having flown 720 kilometres from Pau.

Lieutenant de Malherbe, having damaged his Blériot colliding with an oak tree upon landing in a field at Chasseneuil, near to Châteauroux, would only reach Vincennes a few days later, after repairs to his machine.

On the 30th June 1912, a Commission of Engineers in Vincennes, planned several modifications to be carried out on the military XI-2, amongst them, the cutting away of the wings near the fuselage in order to improve the visibility towards the ground, a straight skid destined to slow the machine down better upon landing, and a cowling on the upper part of the fuselage to protect the crew. The machine thus modified took the name XI-2 Génie.

On the 4th July 1912, Garros offered his Blériot with a Gnome engine of 50 hp, winner of the Circuit d'Anjou, to the government. Officially accepted on the 12th September, the aircraft participated in the Western Manoeuvres which had begun three days earlier, in the presence of Grand Duke Nicolas of Russia. Allocated to Lieutenant de Rose, Garros's Blériot carried out a reconnaissance mission. In the space of fifteen minutes, the young officer, holder of military pilot's licence N° 1, took off, recognised an "enemy" cavalry division and returned to land in front of the Headquarters of the 3rd Cavalry Division. The information that he brought back allowed the commander to take the enemy by surprise and to "virtually" annihilate it.

Around the aircraft, transport trailers had to be designed, as well as workshops, hangers and temporary barracks etc, which had to be as compatible as possible with the equipment aready in service. Here a trailer designed for the transport of a Blériot.

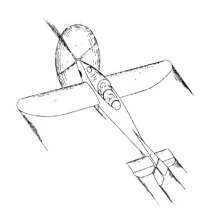

A drawing dated 1913 accompanying the patent for the installation of a machine gun firing through the hub of the propeller. The aerodynamic advantage is underlined by the presense of a cowling, and canopy, behind which the crew is sheltered. The enemy is clearly designated since 1908: The German Zeppelin, capable of transporting a larger bomb load over a long distance.

The three-coloured roundels became obligatory in France from 1912. Top, a two seat XI-2 with large roundels and painted rudder. Above a training type XI with smaller roundels.

The XI-2 Génie of 1913 had an increased wing area and the observer's cockpit moved forward by one bay. The observer was armed with a gun and grenades (after the beginning of the war, flechettes, and then bombs would be added to this range) A large cut-out was made at the rear of the wing along the fuselage side, to facilitate the dropping of projectiles. As early as 1910, Louis Blériot had designed a system for the firing of a 37 mm cannon through the propeller shaft. Ground trials, carried out in the presence of Lieutenant Bellenger, were held at the end of 1911 and the beginning of 1912, on a single-seat type XI. The weapon was a five-shot revolver, and could not be reloaded in flight. These trials even though promising, were stopped because of a break-up of the engine bearers, caused by the vibrations at each firing. At the same time, the army shelved the principle of arming aircraft, adopting the conclusions of Captain Barès, who feared that the vibrations of the machine guns would damage the aircraft, but above all that the pilots on reconnaissance flights should be tempted to go off hunting, to the detriment of their mission.

However, Blériot continued his experiments of arming aircraft, and in December 1912 installed a Hotchkiss machine gun on an XI-2 fitted with a Gnome engine of 70 hp. The gun was mounted on a tripod and operated by the passenger in the rear cockpit; it fired above the arc of the rotating propeller. The ground trials and then the flight trials were carried out by Lieutenant Bellenger, and were satisfactory. The machine was then shown at the Grand Palais at the Salon Aéronautique of 1912. On the 14th October 1913, Louis Blériot filed a patent for the installation of a machine gun firing through the propeller shaft of an aircraft. It seems that this procedure, however promising for the future, was never followed up.

Here we must mention that the first radio transmission in an aircraft was in 1910, in fact on board the Blériot XI-2 of Lt. Acquaviva.

Demostration of the loading of a Blériot XI-2, disassembled but complete, into a purpose-built trailer. The presense of a wind driven generator on one of the undercarriage legs leads to believe that it was equipped with an experimental radio.

The first Rif war

Straight from the first days of their posting to Morocco in February 1912, during the first Rif war, the Blériot of Lieutenant Clavenad, Van den Vaero, Trétarre and Do Hu Vi, carried out liaison flights from town to town, and numerous reconnaissance flights.

On the 18th August 1912, Lieutenant Do Hu Vi in his type XI, brought a message from General Gouraud to the Robillot Column, operating to the south of Fez. A few days later the treaty establishing the French Protectorate over Morocco was signed in this town. On the 21st December, Do Hu Vi informed a detachment of Zouaves who were under siege in a Kasbah near to Mogador, of the arrival of reinforcements, and brought back precious information, despite the rebel fire which hit his machine several times.

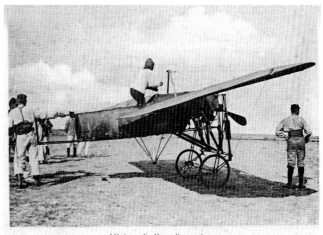

L'Aviateur Do-Hu en Reconnaissance

A Blériot XI-2 Engineers in Morocco, in 1912.

Romanian and Italian Military Blériot

The same year, 1912, Romania, at war against Bulgaria, had available a squadron of six Blériot fitted with pivoting machine guns. No aerial battle was ever fought but nevertheless, the Romanian Aviation gained the upper hand facing the Bulgarian Aviation, equipped with only unarmed Blériot. It was Italy who was the first to employ the aerial arm in a military operation. As early as 1911 the Italian army in a campaign against the Turks in Libya, used the services of eight machines, of which two Blériot XI were for reconnaissance missions. The first war flight was on the 22nd October 1911 above the Oasis of Zanzur. The pilot of the aircraft, a type XI, was Captain Carlo Piazza of the first Flottiglia di Aeroplani de Triploi.

Above, Italian Blériot XI-2, probably in June 1913. Several of them were still in service in 1915, notably with the Fourth Squadron.

An Italian Blériot XI in Libya. Under the fuselage are hanging two grenade launch tubes. The second soldier from the right is holding two Aasen grenades fitted with stabilizing fins. They were attached to a 10m cable which pulled the security pin after being dropped.

The British Military Blériot

In England the first two machines used by the Air Battalion were a Blériot XII with a 60 hp ENV engine, offered to the War Office by the Duke of Westminster and Colonel Laycock, Director of the ENV engine company, in June 1910. A Blériot XXI with a Gnome engine of 70 hp, was acquired in April 1911 by Lieutenant Reginald A. Cammell of the Royal Engineers. Lieutenant Cammell who had taken delivery of the Blériot XII[1] at Etampes on the 3rd August 1910, was also its accredited pilot. After carrying out several flights at Larkhill in October and November, the machine was sent for repair, but was never put back into flying condition. A Blériot XI with a 25 hp Anzani engine belonging to Captain Fulton, flew at Larkhill in 1911 and 1912. An XI-2 which had participated at the Military Trials of 1912, was taken on strength in September 1912, and given the number 39. On the 28th January 1913, a Blériot XI with a Gnome engine of 50 hp, was offered to the War Office by the International Correspondence Schools. In the first months of 1914, the

Royal Flying Corps took delivery of at least nine Blériot 80 hp, and four Blériot 50 hp.

Above, the XI-2 ICS of Robert Slack, offered to the War Office in 1913, after having completed a tour of England. Below, a Blériot-Gouin of which the United Kingdom was the main user.

This machine which carried constructors number 112, could have been the old *White Eagle* of Grahame-White.

The Russian Military Blériot

Blériot aircraft were imported into Russia as early as 1910. First of all, School XIs, most of them with Anzani engines; these machines, about twenty of them, were used until 1915. In the autumn of 1910, there appeared the XI-bis, with a Gnome engine of 50 hp. The building of this model started in the factories of Dux, RBBZ and Chetinine in the summer of 1911. The XI-bis remained in service as liaison and flying school aircraft up until the autumn of 1916. Several XI-2 bis with Gnome engines of 50 hp and 70 hp were used as reconnaissance and school aircraft, from 1910 to 1912. Other models supplied to Russia were as follows: An XI-3 bis with a Gnome engine of 100 hp (in the absence of all information concerning the model, unknown in France, we can suppose that it concerns an XI-2 bis in which an extra seat was installed behind the two side by side seats), a few XI-2,[2] a few XXI with Gnome engines of 70 hp, and an XXVII

with a special leaf-spring undercarriage, and an anti-roll over skid fitted with a small wheel, purchased in 1912.

During the first Semaine de l'Aviation in St. Petersburg, in August 1910, Lieutenant B. von Mathevitch successfully flew an XI-2. Lieutenant G. von Piotrovski then made the first flight across St. Petersburg at Cronstadt, also in an XI-2, but with a passenger on board.

The Turkish Military Blériot

From 1913 onwards, Turkey also owned a few type XI. These would be used notably against the allies during the battle of the Dardanelles, in 1915.

The French Blériot Squadrons during the war.

At the time of mobilization in August 1914, two cavalry squadrons equipped with Blériot single-seat fitted with Gnome "Omega" engines of 50hp, BLC 2 and BLC 4, and four artillery squadrons equipped with two-seat Blériot, BL 3, BL 9, BL 10 and BL18 were put into the line. Each squadron had six machines.

Pégoud, stationed at Belfort with the BL 3, experimented with a Type XI, with the dropping of four light bombs over Germany, the projectiles were placed vertically along the outside of the fuselage. The first night bombing of the war was carried out by Captain Max Boucher, leading Squadron BL 18, taking off from Toul for a raid on the enemy factories in Metz.

The first XI Parasols came to BLC 5 Squadron, commanded by Captain Massenet de Marancour, on the 25th November 1914. Having become too slow and vulnerable, the Types XI and XI-2 were abandoned in March 1915. Only the XI Parasols still equipped a few cavalry squadrons. These in turn were withdrawn from the front. The BLC 5 was disbanded on the 23rd August 1915. From now on, Blériot would only be employed by the flying schools based at Ambérieu, at Chartres, at Châteauroux, at Istres, at Le Crotoy and at Pau. Abroad, two Blériot X-2s were ceded to Belgium on the 2nd August 19145. The civil pilots, Jan Olieslagers and Tyck, once called up, gave their own Blériot to the Compagnie des Aviateurs, which used them in 5 Squadron.

Above, a French Military Blériot XI-2 before the beginning of the War. Below, in 1914 Pégoud is ready to take off solo in a XI-2 for an experimental bombing mission. The projectiles are shells, fixed on the fuselage side in a special rack.

The most well known photo of the armoured Blériot of Jules Védrines. The machine gunner fired through a small opening under the left wing. The armour on one side had been decided by the Military as a lesser evil, because total armouring would have been too heavy. The idea was that in a turn at low altitude, an aircraft shows only one side to the gunners who are aiming at it...

"A Blériot won the first aerial combat in aviation history". It was this which René Vicaire confirmed. He was mechanic to Jules Védrines. Called up for Military service in 1912, René Vicaire was first sent to the 45th Artillery Regiment in Orleans. Shortly afterwards he was sent to the laboratory in Chalais-Meudon. From there he was sent as machine gunner to Villacoublay, he flew with René Labouchère, Grasset and Brindejonc des Moulinais. Then came the war, and on the 2nd September 1914, at Suippes, Jules Védrines and René Vicaire, his machine gunner, shot down a Taube. René Vicaire told the tale in these terms:

We left Villacoublay on the 16th August 1914, destination Stenay passing via Champagne. After an uneventful flight we arrived at our destination the following day.

The Squadron Do 22 was made up of Captain Leclerc (Squadron Leader,) pilots Brindejonc des Moulinais, Gastinger, Robillot, Grasset and Saint–André. Grasset's aircraft had broken down and he joined the squadron by car. After Stenay-le-Chesne, I met Jules Védrines and his aircraft, a Blériot christened La Vache. A team of mechanics and helpers followed him around. The chief mechanic was a man called Ramondou, a man with an excellent reputation, a superb chap with a strong accent from the south. The Captain Leclerc introduced me to Védrines, and there I am immediately attached to this famous pilot as machine gunner. I owned a Hotchkiss machine gun, because in June 1914 I did a training course in this company, under the orders of Commandant Dorand, and we made up several fittings of the machinegun on different aircraft: Farman, Nieuport, Dorand, etc. So this gun which was still available to me was fitted to La Vache, a monocoque fuselage, with the left side armoured by a fairly thick sheet of special steel, in the middle of which an opening had been made for the barrel of the machine gun. The pilot being in front and the machine gunner behind, everything pulled by a double rotary engine of roughly 140hp. We found ourselves, my partner and myself, just behind the engine which spit out at us a fair quantity of hot linseed oil, sometimes mixed with fuel. In flight because we had to wear goggles, we carried our handkerchief between our teeth to have it ready to wipe them. As well as looking after the machinegun, I also had to use the hand pump to maintain the oil supply to the engine, and Védrines from time to time shouted "Pump!"; but the handkerchief

and the noise of the engine did not always allow me to understand what he was saying; so, impatient, he jumped up and down on his seat, so once I understood him and wiped my goggles, I pumped. I could only fire to the left and between the cables which held the wings, these wings which frightened me so much with their oscillating in flight, and I still think that if I had touched a cable with a bullet, it would be the end of our aviation career. We flew almost every day on reconnaissance or fighter missions, without seeing an enemy aircraft. Soon, the Germans arriving a little too close to us, we had to leave Le Chense for Rethel, then for Machault, Montois and Suippes. This last town appeared calm, I took advantage to clean my machine gun. But on this 2nd September 1914, busy with this task, a superb German aircraft (Taube) flew over us and penetrated fairly deeply behind our lines. Védrines jumped into his machine, yelled at me to fit my machinegun as fast as possible; the Captain Leclerc was calling me all sorts of names, I did not know where to turn, I quickly donned my flying suit and my helmet, and climbed into the aircraft with my machine gun. But the engine refused to start ... At last we took off. During this time the German had turned and was flying still in our territory towards his lines. The power of the engine and the structure of our aeroplane allowed us to very rapidly catch up to our adversary, as much in pure speed as in climbing power and there we were, very quickly at the same altitude as the Taube. However, before opening fire, I yelled at Védrines to move further to the left in order to shorten the distance which separated us, to give me a normal fire. I fired a drum of twenty five rounds, then another then a third, and we flew past the Taube which I could no longer see. So I released my belt and I stood up in the fuselage, buffeted by the air from the propeller and the speed, at last I could see our adversary smoking and at a dive angle; soon this angle was transformed into a vertical dive and he hit the ground behind our lines, brutally it seemed to me. I pressed Védrines to do the same, but he did not want to know; perhaps he was right, fear of a bad landing and turning over. However, I watched the aircraft on the ground and I saw the two crew members run into a nearby wood and disappear inside. We went home to the Squadron where a few congratulations (not from everyone) were offered to us.

The British Blériot Squadrons in the war.

In Great Britain, when war broke out, the RFC and the RNAS (Royal Naval Air Service) wishing to rapidly increase their effective strength, purchased a certain number of Blériot from their civil owners. Squadrons 3, 5, 6, 9, and 16 equipped with Blériot XI, XI-2, and XI Parasol, were sent to France, where they carried out reconnaissance missions until the spring of 1915. Then, as in the French Army, the Blériot were progressively withdrawn from active service. The last Blériot - service number 1811 - of 3 Squadron, was withdrawn on the 10th June 1915. Blériot continued however, to be used for training up until the autumn of 1918

in the Reserve Squadrons, 1, 2, 3, 4, and 13. The delivery of the last series of machines would in fact not start until mid-May 1916.

A Blériot XI-2 of the Royal Navel Air Service.

A British Blériot-Gouin with an experimental camouflage.

The total production of Blériot monoplanes.

The figure for the total production of Blériot XI is very difficult to determine.

According to the factory serial numbers, about eight hundred machines were built in France before August 1914. One hundred and eighty machines were delivered to the French army during the war. The production of Bleriot XI in England before 1914 does not appear to have exceeded a few dozen machines. During the war more than a hundred machines were delivered to the RFC, then to the RAF as well as the RNAS.

In Italy as well, several dozen XI-2 and XI Parasols were built before and during the war (as early as 1912 the Italian government ordered forty-nine two-seat Blériot XI).

To these figures it seems that one must add those of the machines built for the military flying schools during the whole of the war, the schools appear to have placed their orders directly with the Blériot factories. The total then would be over one thousand five hundred machines.

Opposite (top), little known, a Blériot carrying the German Cross.
Opposite (below), a Blériot XI-2 in Swiss colours.

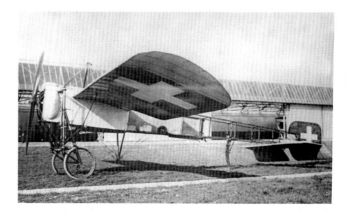

The Blériot LIII (53), with two Anzani engines. Behind the narrow cabin the fuselage which carries the empennage, is partially covered.

The Blériot LIII and other bomber projects

Blériot LIII (53) In 1915, after having produced 880 Caudron G3 and G4 under licence, and repaired one hundred and forty-seven, Louis Blériot designed the twin engined bi-plane LIII, with two 80 hp Le Rhône engines installed between the wings. The aircraft trials however, were carried out with 100 hp Anzanis. It was an army two-seater, for reconnaissance and photographic observation. No production series of this model was ever planned. Shortly afterwards, a large four engined bomber appeared, derived from the LIII, with four 100 hp Anzani engines installed between the wings. For this first "heavy lift" Blériot received no military order.

- *Span* : 13.5m
- *Wing area* : 27m²
- *Length* : 9m
- *Speed* : 95km/h.

The number of the Blériot with four Anzani engines is unknown, but the aircraft appears to be derived from the LIII

Three projects. On the 24th February 1916, Louis Blériot filed a patent on three models of four-engined bombers, a bi-plane and two quadriplanes, of which one of them had off-set wings with a bomb bay under the lower wing, it was fitted with a double elevator. None of these three projects were ever built.

On the 11th September 1915, the War Ministry, faced with a situation of an almost total absence of day bombers, had put in place a Commission des Avions Puissants. (Powerful Aircraft Commission) This Commission organised a competition in order to obtain a machine capable of stopping production of enemy industry, in particular the destruction of the industrial complex in the region of Essen. The aircraft required had to reply to the following criteria : bomb load : 200 kg, range : 600 kilometres, speed : 100 km/h minimum at an altitude of 2000 metres.

Among the aircraft presented there was the Breguet SN 3, (SN for the industrial town of Essen, which was a major objective for the Military!) and the Schmitt SBR, which finished first and

second in the competition and would be produced in series. A new competition was organised in February 1916, by the Section Technique de l'Aéronautique.[1] The new specification was for a minimum of two engines, a speed of 140 km/h and defensive armament in two turrets, the range and bomb load of the previous competition remained unchanged. From this new competition appeared a three-engined Astra, the Breguet XI, the Caudron R.5 (which had already been entered in the first competition, but was destroyed in the flight from Paris to Lyon), the Morane-Saulnier TRK and S, the Spad E, the Voisin E 50 and E 59, the Blériot LXVII (67)

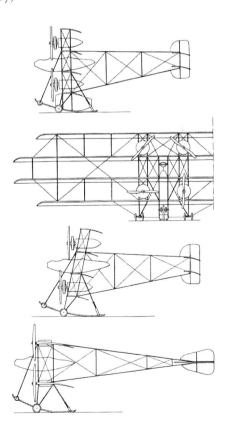

Sketches of three four-engined projects. The front view belongs to the multi-plane shown at the top in profile.

(1) Section Technique de l'Aéronautique created in February 1916, by splitting the Test Flying Section from the Aviation Manufacturing Service.

The Blériot LXV and other fighter projects

On the 8th November 1915 Louis Blériot filed the patent n° 79988 for a "monoplane with auxiliary surfaces" capable of lifting a heavy load, a pilot, a machine gunner and his machine gun.

Towards 1916 Louis Blériot proposed in vain to the Military, a project which could satisfy two needs, specified on the 31st January: that of a single-seat fighter, and that of a three-seat fighter armed with a cannon or two machine guns. This project, the Blériot LXV (65), was a two-seat tri-plane, powerfully armed with two machine guns, one firing forward the other rearward in defence. The engine was an Anzani of 200hp, a low performance engine refused by the Military, and employed here perhaps, simply to demonstrate the qualities of the prototype.

- Span : 10.0m
- Height : 3.0m
- Length : 7.845m
- Wing area : 32m^2

- Empty weight : 697kg
- All up weight : 1100kg

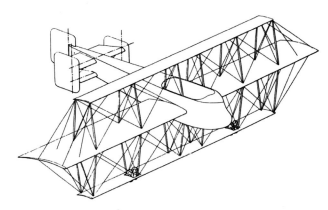

The curious project of a "monoplane with auxiliary wings" Blériot 65 of 1916.

The Blériot LXVII, 71 and 73

Blériot LXVII (67) Designed by the young engineer Touillet, this was a four engined bi-plane, fitted with four 100 hp Gnome engines. The engines fitted two-by-two in the lower wings and the upper wings were laid out in a square formation. They were linked between themselves and the fuselage by numerous struts. Each undercarriage leg had two wheels. The wing was semi-supple, with the lower wing having a marked dihedral. The empennage had three vertical fins and two horizontal tail-planes. Rudders were fitted to the two outer vertical fins, the central fin remaining fixed. The elevator was the extremities of the two horizontal tail planes.

- Span : 19.40m
- Wing area : 89 m^2
- Total weight : 3500kg
- Length : 11.80m
- Empty weight : 1800kg

Opposite top, the Blériot 67 before its trials. Opposite below, the Blériot 67 after its crash. Below, the Blériot 67 of 400hp at Buc in December 1916. The transparency of the covering reveals that the trailing edge was supple.

The Blériot 71 with Hispano-Suiza engines, under construction. The system of radiators, placed in front of the engines around the propeller shaft, as on the Blériot LXVII, was the idea of the engineer Touillet.

The Blériot 71, completed in 1918. This heavy bomber of 800hp crashed in May of the same year.

Blériot 71. Even though both machines presented complied with all conditions of the competition, no series order was ever placed. However, in November 1917, following the proposition issued in February by General Guillemin, Directeur Général de l'Aéronautique Militaire, for the putting into the front line one thousand night bombers, the STAé.[1] put out a new programme for multi-engined aircraft two-seat BN2 and three-seat BN3 concerning night bombing aircraft, a programme which would give birth to the Voisin XII, Letord 9, the Blériot 71 and 73, then the Farman 50, the CEP2 and the Caudron 23, but their coming into service would arrive too late for them to participate effectively in war operations.

The Blériot 71 at the end of construction, 1918.

(1) Section Technique Aéronautique.

The Blériot 73, an ambitious machine audacious and innovative, with, for the first time, the application of the monocoque structure (or semi monocoque) in wood to heavy aircraft.

The Blériot 73 whose curved tail was its principle weakness.

Derived from the LXVII but much bigger, the Blériot 71 was equipped with four Hispano-Suiza engines, of 200 hp then 220 hp.[2] The empennage, initially planned with three vertical fins, was modified, the central fin was removed. The doubled undercarriage had eight wheels. The wings were entirely re-designed and were rigid. This machine had an accident on the 15th May 1918 at Villacoublay, a Breguet XIV B1 flew into its path when it was coming in to land, it was obliged to try to land with engines stalled, it turned over after hitting a ditch, breaking the fuselage. A seaplane version with a hull, designated LXXI H designed in 1916, would not be followed through.

Blériot 73. The Blériot 73 was built in application of a second edition, n° 23888 of the 18th June 1918, to the same patent n° 502839. It was a night bomber powered by four Hispano-Suiza engines of 300hp.[3] It was a biplane of 27 metres span, with the rear of the fuselage very high, much like the fuselage of a seaplane. The undercarriage had eight wheels. An extra wheel fitted into the front of the fuselage, was to stop the aircraft turning over. Its empennage was, as on the LXVII, made up of two horizontal tail planes and three vertical fins. The bomb racks were fixed under the lower wing and to the front sides of the fuselage.

The type 73 was destroyed during trials at Buc on the 26th July 1918, the tail broke off at the first turn after takeoff, the aircraft crashed to the ground and caught fire.

(2) The Blériot 71 was the first addition, N° 21604 to the patent N° 502839, on the 18th June 1917. It can be seen on the first drawings that a version with a fuselage between the lower wings; this was never built.

(3) A fifth engine installed in the centre of the square of the four other engines had been planned.

During the First World War, if Louis Blériot did not succeed in imposing aircraft bearing his name, he shone elsewhere, and produced more than any other aviation industrialist. Because his principle aviation activity between 1915 and 1918, was the design and production of SPAD aircraft, the company which he acquired in taking over the aviation shares of Armand Deperdussin. The production of SPAD aircraft is covered in chapter twelve of this book.

8
The Factory at Suresnes and its Personnel

IN 1915 LOUIS BLÉRIOT BUILDS HIS LARGE FACTORY

At Suresnes, in 1915 along the Quay Gallieni, Louis Blériot had his factory built, the architect was Henri Martin.

The Blériot factory at Suresnes was built in 1915 by Henri Martin, an architect with a good reputation, notably in the area of public buildings. He built railway stations, maritime terminals, numerous hotels and thermal baths. The factory at Saint Cloud was in the form of a square of which one side gave onto the river Seine, and the three others respectively, the rue du Val-d'Or, the rue Pasteur and the rue de Longchamp. After the war, the personnel at rue des Entrepreneurs were re-grouped at Suresnes. The management of Blériot Aéronautique was comprised of a General and Commercial Manager, Alfred Leblanc (since 1912) then Jean Brun in 1925, and finally Charles Avenet, future founder of the association Les Vieilles Racines (The Old Roots), an Administrative and Financial Manager, J. B. Antelme (from 1910). The Chief Engineers were, M. Touillet and André Herbemont (from 1917) then Léon Kirste and Filippo Zappata.

Herbemont, Technical Director of the SPAD would have to his name one hundred and twenty-three flying prototypes, in 1924 he designed three types of variable pitch propeller, in 1929 he produced the first retractable undercarriage to fly in France and in 1935 was the driving force of the "Butterfly Tail". Born on a Good Friday (the 31st March 1893) Herbemont would later

say *"If it was night time, you would see my halo"* Perhaps he was alluding to his patience in his relationship with his Patron?

Started on in February 1922, Léon Kirste was an ESA Engineer with a diploma from the Technische Hochschule of Vienna. When he qualified from Sup'Aéro in 1912, this Austrian engineer had been a designer at Breguet Aeroplane Ltd, the British branch of Breguet. In fifteen years, Kirste designed around thirty Blériot projects, of which only one, the 127, would actually go into series production. In September 1937, after the nationalisation of the Blériot factories, he went back to Austria to a position of professor at the Vienna Technical School, where he had himself received his diploma.

Filippo Zappata came to Suresnes in 1927. He was an engineer from the School of Maritime Engineering in Genoa, He had presented several projects to Blériot who found them interesting. At Quai Gallieni, Zappata designed two particularly successful aircraft, the Joseph-Le-Brix in 1930, and the Santos-Dumont three years later. He designed other machines destined for the Compangnie Internationale des Taxis Aériens (CITA) a company that Blériot wanted to create but would never see the light of day. At the end of 1933 Zappata was obliged to return to Italy, the Mussolini Government deplored the fact that the talent of such a brilliant engineer should be in the service of a rival nation.

The factory at Suresnes under construction.

The design office of Blériot-Aéronautique in 1929.

Marshall Balbo, the Italian Air Minister, named him as head of the new design office of the firm CANT (ex-Cantiere Navle Triestino, which became Cantieri Riuniti dell'Adriatiaco) which was seeking new inspiration. Not even the advantageous conditions which were offered to Zappata would ever, in his eyes, compensate for his regret of having to leave Blériot. One can find in the sea plane CANT Z-501, a part of the design that the Italian engineer had given to the Santos-Dumont.

These three engineers were based in the same office, situated immediately above the main front entrance of the factory, the design office, long and narrow, was divided into three groups, Prototypes, Series and Documentation. The successive heads of departments were:- Maurice, Dagonne, Labeyrie, Louis Favre and André Paulin, previously head of the Prototype Group. Bouly was head of the Series Group, and from 1929, Ferrand was head of the Documentation Group (from 1929 onwards). Their engineers were Paul Priard, Robert Letalle, Edmond Habit, calculators of Sup'Aéro, Grillot, Siretta, (later the creator of the magazine *Aviasport*) Baudot, Bergeret, Richez, Thanat, Virmoux, Bastiou (three engineers from the Centrale) Bonnetain, Castano, Léon Anthonisson, Andretti, and Seri (two Italians who arrived at the same time as Zappata), Paul and Raymond Fouquet, Charles Favre, Robert Lacroix, Raymond Boucher, Louis Lecourtiller, Libon, Jean Ligogne, Jean Mellinger, Max Pinée, Picq, Verdier, Stratt, and finally Albert Polon who had the task of the artistic views (illustrated designs of the new projects) he was also humoristic designer and Special Policeman in Montmartre.

In 1929 the design office was reorganised and its tasks redefined according to a new directive.[1] The personnel also included

(1) The new directive reorganising the Blériot design office is shown in annex IV.

M. Bernicha, Chief Accountant, J. Caldairorn, Head of Production, M. Rastoul then L. Lerendu and C. Leplanquais Head of Manufacturing, J. Filicroft with E. Charbonnier as Head Foreman, M. Koebel, Head of the Machine Shop, L Paragot, Head of Assembly Shop, M Chassaing, Head of the Carpentry Shop, M. Lesec, Head of the Covering Work Shop, M. Lacatte, Head of the Paint Shop, M. Reynaud, Head of Maintenance, M Gardet, Head of Production Control, MM. Dureau, Olainé and Beau Head of the Personnel Department, M. Bricout, Head of the Laborty, M Gschwindt, Head of Quality Control (Director of the Suresnes factory in 1940), M Richard,Head of Aircraft Reception, G. Lauga,Director of the Aerodrome and the School at Buc, replaced in 1933 by C.Quatremare. The Flying Instructors were Antigny, Clément, Quatremare and Robin (an Aerobatic Pioneer), and Technical Instructors Dupoint and Gravier. The Comte P. De Fleurieu was Head of Public Relations.

In 1936, at the time of the Front Populaire, the personnel of the design office meeting in "Soviet" obtained a replacement of its head, Louis Favre, by André Paulin, his assistant. Even though disapproving of such procedures, André Paulin could only accept this *"nomination"*. Except during the war, he would complete his entire career at the factory in Suresnes, which he would only leave in 1970 to take a well earned retirement, at that time Head of the Main Design Office at the Société Nationale des Industries Aérospatiales(SNIAS) which came from successive amalgamation of National Aviation Instructors (today EADS). As for Louis Favre, he was offered another post, but embittered by this "treason from below" he rapidly handed in his notice.

To the pilots of the company from before 1914, Lemartin, Perreyon, (Nicknamed "Pépé"), Pégoud and Domenjoz, succeeded the old war aces, the new test pilots were Albert Deullin, Sadi-Lecointe, Jean Casale, Bernard de Romanet, Armando de Dominicis, Maurice Bizot, Raymond Villechanoux (nicknamed "Joe"), Lucian Bossoutrot (nicknamed "Bobosse"), Louis Massotte (nicknamed "le gars Louis"). The reception pilots were particularly Le Gall, Roth and R. Seitz. Among the mechanics we can mention M. Dronne, G. Boulet, the two brothers Rémy, Lousteau, E. Laversin, A. Legendre, Camuratti and Leseigneur.

The Blériot factory around 1975, integrated into the *Groupe Aérospatiale.*

A Temporary Diversification

IN 1919, THE AVIATION MARKET COLLAPSED. LOUIS BLERIOT SOUGHT TO FOLLOW UP ON A DIVERSIFICATION STARTED IN 1905

The Blériot cycle-car, of which the English version, the Blériot Whippet, was produced in series by the British branch of Blériot-Aéronautique.

The signing of the armistice on 11th November 1918 caused the cancellation without indemnity, of all current military orders. In order to face up to this difficult situation, Louis Blériot diversified his manufactured products, as would other constructors at the same time. Voisin would even definitively stop building aircraft in order to concentrate, with success, on the building of original design automobiles, calling on techniques used in aviation.

During several years, the factory in Suresnes would have a very varied production range, from furniture to light cars, sand yachts, hydroplanes, tuna fishing boats, motor cycles and even carburettors.

Hydroplanes

It was in fact as early as 1905, at the time of his association with Gabriel Voisin, that Blériot had started this diversion. It was that year that he started to construct hydroplanes, aiming for, other than private clients, the colonial market which was in full expansion. These rapid machines drawing very little water appeared to be well adapted to river navigation in Africa, in Indo China or in Guyana. Blériot, up until 1914 made several of these "sliding boats" which he called Pnydres.

The first models were single-seaters in wood and fabric, powered by an 8-cylinder Antoinette engine. He then built for a Columbian client, M. Gonzalon-Mejia, a boat with floats whose structure was very similar to the structure of a Blériot XI. Several canvas seats were installed in the centre of the machine. It's weight was 100 kg, it's length, 5.5 metres and it was 3 metres wide. It was powered by a Gnome rotary engine of 50 hp. It was equipped with a rudder positioned just behind the propeller, as in an aircraft, it was tried out on the Seine on 25th October 1912.

In 1913 Blériot made a very large hydroplane with its hull built up of three layers of mahogany, the hull in contact with the water was made up of two stepped sections, the rear section was fitted with spring loaded skates designed to absorb the shocks over the water. Steering was by two rudders installed at the extremity of the rear of the boat. The cabin was in the form of a canoe, the decking was light-weight gratings, and it had space for ten passengers. The engine was a V8 Laviator of 120 hp, connected by a chain drive to a Chauvière propeller of 2.3 metres diameter. The engine ran at 1200 rpm, the propeller at 900 rpm. The Hydroplane was 9 metres long and 2.1 metres wide, and weighed 1500 kg, of which 350 kg was the engine. It drew only 15 centimetres of water. On the 16th September Alfred Leblanc carried out successful trials on the Seine, between the bridge at

Bezons and the bridge at Argenteuil. It was then displayed at the Grand Palais during the 5th International Air Transport Exhibition. However, the Blériot hydroplane does not seem ever to have gone into series production.

Blériot hydroplanes: top left, the first Pnydre, the catamaran with an Antoinette engine of 25hp, piloted by Gabriel Voisin, in 1905. Below, the Pnydre no 3 of 1912 with a Gnome engine of 50hp. Above, the heavy hydroplane in 1913. Many other constructors would try their luck in this market.

Sand Yachts

Being the owner of a villa at Hardelot, as early as 1910 Louis Blériot tasted the pleasures of a home-made Sand Yacht, on board which he took his children along the beaches of this holiday station of the Pas-de-Calais. With an enthusiasm brought on by this rapid machine, the aviator decided to put it into production in his factories. The first production models, for which Blériot invented the name "Aéroplage", came out at the beginning of August 1911.

The very special racing sand-yacht unique in its class, designed by Louis Blériot for his friend Alfred Leblanc.

The Blériot Sand Yacht was made up of a wooden fuselage of triangular form, fitted on three aircraft wheels equipped with wide tyres. The front axle had a 3.5 metre track. The rear wheel was steerable and was connected by shafts, bearings, (a Blériot-Cazin patent) and steel cables to a steering wheel. It was equipped with a large seat able to take several passengers as well as the driver, it was equipped also with a triangular mast and a sail of 12 m². It weighed 150 kg and the ground clearance was 25 centimetres. It could reach 90 kilometres per hour. It cost 2,000 francs. One of his first customers was the coach-builder Alfred Belvalette, who spent his holidays at Berck.

Right from the start of building, the Société du Domaine d'Hardelot ordered several examples. The following year there was a Sand Yacht for Children at a reduced price.

In 1913 the sand yacht mode expanded, Blériot Aéronautique included them in their catalogue.

Two models were available :

- the "big metal Sand Yacht", made up of a rectangular steel tube chassis, with four wheels fitted on springs, and a collapsible mast with a sail of 12m². 4.8 metres long 2.35 metres wide, it's empty weight was 100 kg. Equipped with a wheel steering the rear wheels, it could carry three people at more than 60 km/h, and cost 2,500 francs.
- the Sand Yacht type "Popular", a two-seater with a wooden frame fitted either with a steering wheel or a rudder bar. The mast, of 4 metres high, was equipped

with a triangular sail of 8 m². It's weight was 60 kg and it's price 550 francs.

In 1914, Blériot proposed a racing model with two oscillating masts, two sails and a spinnaker, at a price of 1800 francs. A Blériot-Aéronautique brochure described it : -

A racing sand yacht with oscillating masts.

This special model, shown at the Salon de l'Aviation of 1913, was very carefully tried out. It was designed for the experienced enthusiast, with two masts, two sails and a spinnaker. The whole was constructed very lightly and above all very supple. With a view to avoiding the risks of capsizing in gusty wind conditions, the masts oscillated and the sails inclined proportionally to the forces acting on them. Very strong rubber bungees, with limited stretch, supported the masts allowing this temporary inclination. The sails were therefore reduced under the wind, just like those of a boat heeled over by a gust of wind.

Further, the pilot, sitting on a spring loaded seat, was given full liberty of movement, and was thus able to lean into the wind in order to load the machine on that side, to ensure stability. By these means, it was possible to use a large sail area without risk of capsizing.

The price of the Racing Sand Yacht, complete (fuselage, masts, sails, ropes, wheels with mud guard, tyres of 700 x 900) was 1,800 francs.

After the First World War, the Sand Yacht was still very popular, then little by little they were forgotten. However, for about thirty years now, we can see a re-birth of Sand Yachts, whose technical progress give them a performance much better than their ancestors at the beginning of the 20th century.

The large sand-yacht on the Blériot stand during the *Exposition de la Locomotion Aérienne* of 1913.

Motor cycles

It was at the Salon of October 1919 that the first Blériot motor cycles appeared. As soon as the war ended a motor cycle department had been set up in the factory at Suresnes. This department was headed by the engineer Brun, helped by ex-competition riders from before 1914, among them Grapperon and Pernette.

Fitted with a vertical two-cylinder four-stroke engine, and with plate steel wheels, Blériot motor cycles were available in five versions:-

• "Tourist" model, with rear suspension, at a price of 5,000 francs
• "Sport" model, with rigid rear suspension and lowered handle bars, at a price of 5,500 francs
• "Tourist" side-car, at a price of 1,500 francs (without the motor cycle)
• "Delivery" side-car, at a price of 1,625 francs (without the motor cycle)
• "Taxi" side-car with a windscreen in curved mica, and collapsible hood

With its mechanical parts of modern conception and a robust cycle frame, the Blériot motor cycle had a fairly favourable reception in the specialist press of the time.

In 1920 it had several racing successes as can be seen by the list below:-

Paris-Nice, three entrants, three gold medals. Criterium of the AMM Paris-Auxerre, six starters, six finishers. Military Transport Competition, Home Office Prize, Motocyclisme Cup. Hill climb at Ernemont, 1st in Side-Car category 600cc. Circuit of Seine et Marne, 1st overall. Circuit of Loiret, 1st in Category Side-Car 600cc. 1st Hill Climb Side-Car, 1st over 1 kilometre in Category Side-Car. Circuit of the Vosges, 1100 km without penalty, two silver medals. Paris-Orleans, 1st in Side-Car category 600cc, 3rd overall.

At the Salon of 1921, a two-stroke 750cc appeared by the side of the four-stroke 500cc.

A Blériot motorcycle, owned by the author, passes in front of a replica Blériot XI-2, built by the *Amicale Jean-Baptiste Salis.*

This new model was only distinguishable from the old model by the mechanical parts. The engine, also a vertical twin, was offset at 180°, one piston rose when the other descended, whereas on the previous model the two pistons rose and descended at the same time. The gear box, a more classical design than that of the 500cc, had three speeds and a reverse.

In 1922 the "Tourist" 500cc still cost 5,000 francs. As for the 750cc, it cost 5,400 francs. But a few months later the build was stopped, in three years the production never went over 1,000 examples.

"They do not roll they fly!" was the ideal slogan for Blériot motorcycles which despite an enviable record did not have a great commercial success. Opposite, the double centre spread of a catalogue of 1921. The side-cars were built in plywood.

Cars

Also in 1922, Blériot designed a four-wheeled cycle car (light vehicle), using the same monobloc engine with the clutch and the gear box of his new 750cc motorcycle. In order to improve the cooling, a four blade fan in aluminium was added. Driven by a belt, it ran at one-and-a-half times engine speed. The distribution was done by pre-compression in separate sumps. The manifold, common to both cylinders, was monobloc for inlet and exhaust. The fuel supply was by automatic carburettor, and the ignition by magneto with a variable advance. The central fly wheel was fitted on the crankshaft and it carried the metal disc clutch. Starting was done by pulling on a lever situated by the gear lever and the hand brake, acting as a "kick start". The gear box had three speeds and a reverse. The drive to the rear axle was by a belt. The rear axle carried a perforated aluminium pulley of 190mm in diameter. The chassis was in ash, like an aircraft fuselage, it was braced and reinforced by steel plates. The front and rear suspension was by semi-cantilever springs with push rods. The front axle was a tube and the steering wheel on the right. The two belt brakes rubbed on perforated drums. One was operated by foot, the other operated by hand. The tyres were 710 x 85.

The side-by-side two-seat coach work was made in plywood - only the wings and the false radiator (the engine was air-cooled) were in metal - the Blériot cycle-car could reach 65 km/h. However, it would know only a fleeting existence, because production ceased after a few months at the same time as the motorcycles.

The Blériot Whippet, the English version of the Blériot cycle-car had a much longer life. Built from 1920 onwards by the English branch of Blériot Aéronautique, the Air Navigation Co. Ltd (ANC) at Addlestone in Surrey, built the car with different modifications up to 1927.

The prototype was finished in 1919 by G. H. Jones and W. D. Marchant, ex- engineers of Zenith Motorcylettes. They would take the belt-drive and perfect it. The engine, initially an air-cooled V twin JAP, was replaced by a larger (1000cc) Blackburne, also an air-cooled twin. The oil circulation was drop by drop via an auxiliary hand pump, the ignition was by magneto, and the fuel mixture fed through an automatic carburettor. The chassis in ash was reinforced by steel plates and was equipped with four semi-cantilever springs. The engine was fitted on the centre line of the chassis. The rear axle was driven by a transmission belt, itself driven by a chain through a clutch taken off the crank shaft. The gear box - the great originality of the Whippet - had 18 positions. This was obtained by widening or narrowing the flanks of the belt drive pulley. This belt, of trapezoidal section, changes the drive ratio in descending more or less into the groove of the pulley. It was fitted with a three-plate dry clutch.

On this impressive photo, taken in front of the Air Navigation Company, the Blériot branch at Addlestone, women are at the wheel of most of the Whippet cars, under the eye of Norbert Chéreay, factory director (on the left in front of the railings).

To conserve the convention of appearances for the Whippet, a false radiator was installed at the front, which allowed air through for the cooling of the cylinders. The foot brake acted on the belt near the rear axle. The hand brake was fitted to the shaft of the drive pulley. Starting was done by pressing on a pedal. The access to the engine was by the upper part of the bonnet which was hinge mounted. The ignition switch and the advance and retard were fitted on the steering column. The two-seat coach work was in plywood covered with varnished simulated leather. The spoked wheels were fitted with tyres 700 x 80.

Construction started in February 1920, and the first deliveries took place a few weeks later. Production reached 50 cars per week. All assembly operations were carried out in the same building. Painting and finishing were carried out in a separate workshop, protected against dust and temperature variations. The delivery delay to the agents, London Motors, 61 Holborn Viaduct in London, was only seven days. An insurance policy by Lloyds was proposed to each buyer. The production model benefited from a few improvements, the starting pedal was replaced by a large lateral lever which was easier to use, the wheels could be taken off thanks to spring loaded lock washers. The engine was fitted with Ricardo pistons and the con-rods were fitted on roller bearings.

During the season of 1920, Marchant took part in different tests, one of which was the London to Manchester Rally, as well as races at Brooklands, where the Blériot Whippet obtained promising results. Even though the hand starter caused a few problems from the fact that there was no decompression lever - difficulties which would quickly be overcome - the first Whippets were appreciated for their suspension and for their road holding, due notably to their wide track.

At the London Motor Show in October 1920, five models were shown, a bare chassis, a standard model, a deluxe model, a Sport model and a Racing model.

The standard model, cream coloured, had wings and bonnet painted black. The deluxe model was equipped with a speedometer, a Lucas Magdyno electrical system, lights, an electric horn and even a toolbox placed behind the removable seat back. The Sport model was longer and narrower than the standard model. It had off-set seats, coach work with a pointed tail, and an engine with a higher compression ratio. The Racing model was distinguishable by its very streamlined coach work, inspired by the Peugeot Grand Prix racing car. The front axle, the steering joints - in fact all of the front suspension - were also streamlined. The engine of the standard model had side valves, the engine of the Racing model had overhead valves. The standard model and the Sport model cost £250, the deluxe model £350. The belt drive being particularly smooth, a guarantee of 10,000 miles (16,000 kms) was given for the tyres. The guarantee for the drive belt was for 4,000 miles (6,400 kms) The top speed was 75 km/h for the standard model and nearly 100 km/h for the Sport model. An export version, with a higher ground clearance was also available.

In 1921, Jones left the factory. W. S. Shackleton became the Technical Director. The Whippet, which was now priced at £210, had an option for a reverse gear for £15 extra. Shock absorbers were fitted to the rear springs, improving both the comfort and the road holding.

In October, Marchant participated in the 200 mile race at Brooklands with a Sport model, whose wings and running boards had been removed. The engine capacity was increased to 1100 cc by increasing the stroke, the oil circuit was doubled.

Above left, the chassis of the first Whippet cycle-car; right, a model photographed in the Blériot factory at Suresnes. Below, the racing Whippet with overhead valve engine, in 1920. Right, a Whippet during a competition in England.

Further, for ease of access to the magneto, the false radiator was removable. But the driver of the Whippet had to abandon after seventeen laps.

At the London Motor Show a few days later, the Air Navigation and Engineering Co. (ex-ANC now became ANEC) showed three examples of its new model, a bare chassis, a coach work in polished aluminium, and a standard coach work painted midnight blue. Externally identical to the proceeding model, this new version differed by its transmission. The belt drive system was replaced by a chain, driven by a three-speed gearbox with reverse. One of the particularities of this box was that the reverse gear remained stationary when a forward gear was engaged. The hand starting lever was retained, it reacted directly to the main shaft of the gearbox. The two brakes, (hand and foot) reacted now on the rear axle. The ground clearance was increased by 2.5 inches, and the magneto placed to the rear of the engine to improve accessibility. With the upholstery covering in Rexine (a sort of moleskin) its toolbox and it's electrical equipment, the new Whippet cost £198.

In 1922 a Blériot Whippet was again on the start line at the Brooklands 200 mile race. It was a racing model equipped with a standard 1000cc engine with overhead valves, it was fitted with a triple-choke Zenith carburettor. The ultra light coach work was in plywood over a frame work of ash, then fabric covered just like an aircraft. All of the front was open to improve the cooling of the engine. Driven by Captain L. F. Peaty, the car did not finish the race.

At the October Motor Show another new version of the Whippet appeared by the side of the chain driven model of the previous year. The engine - still a Blackburne twin of 1000cc - was fitted transversally on a U shaped chassis in steel angle iron, with horizontal reinforcing. The cone clutch was connected to a three-speed Wrigley gearbox.

The rear axle, without differential, was driven by a prop shaft fitted with a universal joint at each end. The rear wheels were fitted with drum brakes. The steering was rack and pinion. From the previous model the semi-cantilever springs and the hand starting lever - which acted now on a gear at the end of the crank shaft - were retained. For the coach work there was also innovation, a three seat version was available. The third seat, in spider was protected by a tonneau cover. The upholstery was in Karhyde for all models. The prices were respectively £170 and £175 for the two-seat and the three-seat with prop shaft, and £155 and £160 for the two-seat and three-seat with chain drive. These different models were available in cream, grey, blue or red.

The following year, Captain Peaty again raced at Brooklands in a Whippet Sport, with coach work in aluminium painted green, with the bonnet in polished metal. It was fitted with a long stroke 1100cc engine. It made a standing-start lap at 62.6mph (100.72km/h) in the eliminatory practice for the Whitsun handicap race, but was not able to qualify for the race itself. This was in fact the last appearance of a Blériot Whippet in competition.

At the Show of 1923, the model shown was equipped with a new Jukes gearbox. Its price was now only £125. The ANEC had to face up to more and more severe problems of cash flow, aggravated by the competition from the Rover Eight with a flat twin engine, which came out as early as 1920, and which was making it's presence felt more and more.

In 1924, the price of the Whippet was again reduced by £10, and for the first time it was not shown at the London Motor Show. Production however, does not seemed to have totally ceased until 1927, at the same moment that ANEC went into liquidation.

In the follow on, the factory at Addlestone, under English management this time, would build the Eric Longden light car. It would then be bought by the Weymann Co. which had been created by the Franco-American coach builder, Charles T. Weymann, who had a good reputation for his body work in simulated leather. Up until 1965 this company would principally build coach work for buses and utility vehicles. Much enlarged, the factory then belonged to the British firm, Plessey, specialists in electronics. Since 1990 the factory has belonged to the Marconi Company.

Above, one of three surviving Whippets in the author's collection. Below, the chassis of the Whippet with gear-box appeared in October 1922. Opposite, publicity photo for the Whippet.

Boats and furniture

Immediately after the war of 1914 - 1918 a series of wooden hulled tuna boats of 80 tons, equipped with an 80 hp heavy oil engine, came out of the factories of Suresnes. They were all given female Christian names. The first two examples, the *Simone* and the *Germaine*, respectively the Christian names of Louis Blériot's eldest daughter and the Christian name of his secretary. (a few years later, Germaine married one of the principle engineers of the factory, the Austrian Léon Kirste) It seems that these boats were ordered by the government as war damage, to indemnify the fishermen of the port of Boulogne. Whatever the reason for it, this order was a financial disaster for the Blériot Company.

The construction of these fishing boats (with the hydro-planes) appears to have been the only times that Blériot Aéronautique entered into the Marine world.

At the same period, wooden furniture was also made "chez Blériot" as would say the members of the personnel, many years after the death of the "Patron". There was garden furniture, tables, small cupboards, baby's cots and deck chairs, but the two most original pieces of furniture, were a chair that transformed into a step ladder, and a school desk with a lift up sliding seat and a foot rest, both adjustable for height.

Various pieces of furniture built by Blériot-Aéronautique, and a system of electric heating the *"Blériot ball in radiothermic cement"*.

Opposite: at the Government's request, Blériot-Aéronautique built tuna fishing boats. This one was launched in 1919, with the name of Louis Blériot's eldest daughter.

Carburettors

Louis Blériot was also interested in carburettors, at the beginning of the 1920s he created the Société du Carburetteur Blériot. In parallel, the Société des Phares Blériot, seeking to diversify its products, proposed to a female clientele a *"heating projector with an element in radiothermic cement"*!

During these difficult years, Louis Blériot forced himself by all possible means, to find whatever was available to give work to his personnel, but, as soon as the situation improved, he returned little by little and exclusively to the only activity that had really ever impassioned him, aviation.

Blériot Aircraft and Seaplanes (1919-1936)

BETWEEN THE WARS

An aircraft builder shows what he is capable of, from the smallest to the biggest. In 1919 the giant Blériot 71 and the tiny SPAD XV belonging to Nungesser. In the foreground, Sadi-Lecointe.

France and it's allies won the war at the price of four years of unprecedented effort and suffering. The country, drained, ravaged and decimated, wanted to believe that this was the war to end all wars. On the political side this was seen by an immediate abandoning of the armament effort. With a strength, at the Armistice of 13,000 aircraft and seaplanes, Military Aviation was for the most part, rapidly demobilised. Of the two hundred and fifty-one active squadrons in 1918, there would remain no more than one hundred and fifteen on the 1st January 1920. It would only be from the end of that year that would be the birth of a new programme, destined to replace the aircraft built during the war, the real growth not really coming until 1923. While waiting for this renewal, Louis Blériot re-grouped all of his company's activities at Suresnes, and turned towards commercial aviation.

The Blériot 74 and 75

Blériot 74. The engineer, André Herbemont, took the bomber type 71, and converted it to the type 74 Commercial Mammouth, with four, 300 hp Hispano-Suiza engines. While conserving the wing of 144 m² he reinforced it and gave it a new high lift profile,

RA 54. The fuselage of the 71, designed for bombing missions, could not be adapted to passenger transport, the 74 received a new fuselage entirely re-modelled. It had a bi-convex section capable of seating 26 people. Access to the cabin was by a retractable stairs situated under the fuselage. The undercarriage was made up of four pairs of wheels coupled two-by-two on one axle, and fitted with bungee shock absorbers.

The Blériot 74 was 15.4 metres long, 6.4 metres high and had a span of 27 metres. It could carry 1,600 litres of fuel (in 4 tanks of 400 litres each, and 120 litres of oil, in 4 tanks of 30 litres each) it's empty weight was 3,800 kg, for a useful load of 2,250 kg. With full tanks of oil and fuel the total weight was 7,550 kg, it's endurance was 6 hours 20 minutes and it could fly at 150 km/h. The machine was exposed at the Salon of 1919.

The official tests were carried out at Villacoublay and continued up to the 22nd January 1920. On this day the machine had returned from Buc for modifications requested by the Service Technique (ex-Section Technique, since August 1919). It took off with Armand Berthelot at the controls (eleven wartime victories). At the first turn oscillations started, the empennage, even though compensated, broke up. The aircraft crashed to the ground causing the death of the pilot.

Left, official presentation of the Blériot 74, Mammoth. Right, construction of the Blériot 74; passengers were seated facing each other.

Blériot 75. The Blériot 75 Aérobus or Superavion, which was finished in June 1920, only differed from the Mammouth by the sweep-back of it's wings. In the hands of Jean Casale, the 75, thanks to its excellent performance, obtained a Government grant of 150,000 francs. On the 13th August 1920, this four engined aircraft piloted by Jean Casale, climbed to 2,500 metres, reaching a speed of 155 km/h. It was the object of a successful meeting at Buc, a meeting organised by the Aéro-Club de France and inaugurated by the President of the Republic. On the 3rd November he climbed to 2,700 metres with 3,600 kg of useful load. Nevertheless, despite these performances, no commercial aviation company placed an order with Louis Blériot. Transport was still the poor relation of Military Aviation, and had only modest resources. Its budget for 1919 was only 5,000,000 francs.

The month of February 1919 saw the birth of the Compagnie des Messageries Aériennes, whose first flight was held on the 16th June, on the line Paris-Lille-Brussels. Under the management of Louis Breguet, were grouped Messrs Blériot, Caudron, Farman, Morane, Saulnier, Weiller, Renault and Leblanc. Later Blériot became part of the Board of Directors of Air-Union, a company created on the 1st January 1923 by the fusion of the Messageries Aériennes and the Grands Express Aériens.

On the 23rd April 1920, the Compagnie Franco-Roumaine de Navigation Aérienne was created, which linked Paris to the central European Capitals, and even to Constantinople. The Comte Pierre de Fleurieu, Director of Public Relations of Blériot-Aéronautique, was named Director. Blériot received several government orders, three of them (125/2, 293/2 and 20/3) for the building of twenty-nine Nieuport-Delage fighters, the order 289/3 for fifty Breguet 14 B2, and the order 773/4 for fourteen Breguet A2.

The Blériot 75 presented at Buc in front of a SPAD fighter, and by the side of a Blériot XI.

The Blériot 76

Louis Blériot also took over the study of new military machines, on the 20th October 1920, Herbemont completed the lay-out of the drawings of the Blériot 76, a night bomber with a four-man crew, based on the 75 Aérobus, but equipped with an empennage similar to that of the Cabin Spads. The engines, Hispano-Suiza 8 FB of 300 hp, were arranged in a trapezoidal form (and not in a square as on the Blériot 75), and single struts replaced the forest of struts and flying wires of the preceding models. The fuselage

was a monocoque construction and the number of landing wheels reduced to two. The undercarriage was retractable by means of a screw thread which raised the wheels into the shoulder of the lower wing, the inside legs of the undercarriage crossed each other.[1] Judged too big by the Service Technique, the aircraft was only ever made in model form.

(1)   The same year Herbemont had designed another project with a retractable undercarriage, for a racing and speed record aircraft with gull wings. The undercarriage was operated by a circuit of cables driven by a winch, which maintained the tension whatever the position of the undercarriage (see plan at the end of Annex V).

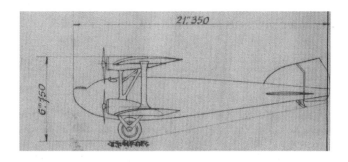

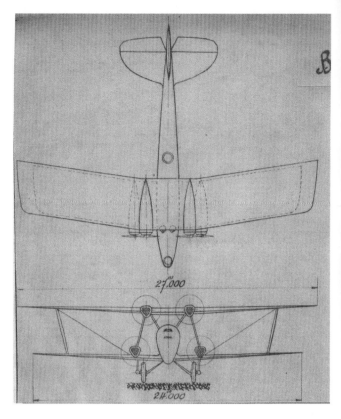

Schematic drawings of the Blério 76, such as they appear on a production summary of Blériot-Aéronautique.

The Blériot 77

The model 77 designed by Herbemont at the same time as the 76, was a four-engined monoplane of 39 metres span with two fuselages. The wheels were installed in the lower part of each fuselage. This design took up a project of a twin-fuselage monoplane aircraft that Louis Blériot had proposed to the war Ministry as early as 1916. The wing, without external struts, was made up of a wooden structure covered in fabric. Only a model of this machine was built and tried at the Eiffel laboratory in May 1921. The twin-fuselage design of ovoid section, allowed the cowling of the wheels and would be reproduced by the engineer Kirste for the Blériot 125 in 1924.

The Blériot 77. The perspective drawings gave a better idea of their projects to the enginners. This practice is continued this day, but with virtual models built in three dimensions by a computer.

THE BLERIOT PRIZES

In 1920, Blériot founded the Prix de Sécurité Blériot which was composed of two tests : -

* an eliminatory phase which consisted of a closed circuit of 300 kilometres without landing, carrying a useful load of at least 100 kg, at a minimum speed of 140 kilometres per hour. During the test the aircraft had to climb to 4,000 metres.

* a classification test which consisted of carrying out three glide landings from an altitude of 500 metres, to a given point on the ground into a circle 50 metres diameter, enclosed by a fictional fence of 5 metres high. The vertical speed had to be less than 3.5 metres per second.

The competition with it's prize, immediately attributable to the first competitor who could make a vertical speed equal to or less than 2.5 metres per second, was opened for the period from 1st June 1920 to 31st May 1925.

In 1930 Louis Blériot created the "Blériot International Speed Cup" which was won on 21st October 1923 by Lieutenant Colonel Pietro Scapinelli flying a Macchi MC72 seaplane at 619.374 km/h. The Italian pilot completed a circuit of 327 kilometres in 31 minutes 44 and 1/5 seconds The rules stipulated that the permanent holder of the cup would be the competitor who was the first to reach the speed of 1,000km/h, but it would be attributed temporarily to the competitor who reached 600km/h.

The Blériot 100

The Blériot 100 was the first project designed at Suresnes by the engineer Kirste. Designed in 1922 it was a large amphibian monoplane designed for transport. It had a span of 35 metres and an empennage with three fins. It weighed 10 tons and was fitted with five, 300 hp engines (Hispano-Suiza or Salmson). Considered too large by the airlines, to whom it was proposed on the drawing board, they estimated that the amphibian configuration was of little interest for the European lines, the machine, despite the contract 997/2 made for one example, was never built and the contract was cancelled.

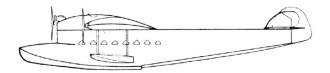

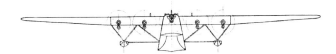

Schematic drawings of the Blériot 100, undercarriage raised. Factory drawings.

- *Span :* - 35m
- *Height :* 4.10m
- *Empty weight :* 6,900kg
- *Ceiling :* 2,500m
- *Length :* 22.60m
- *Wing area :* 202.8m^2
- *All up weight :* 10,500kg
- *Speed :* 150km/h

The Blériot 101 and 118

Blériot 101. The Blériot 101 was also an amphibian, a monoplane two-seat fighter, powered by two 180 hp Hispano-Suiza engines, carried a turret at the rear and two machine guns firing forward. Presented to a CEDANA on the 18th January 1924, it was not retained.

- *Span :* 13.0m
- *Height :* 3.70m
- *Empty weight :* 900kg
- *Ceiling :* 7000m
- *Length :* 8.40m
- *Wing area :* 25m^2
- *All up weight :* 1620kg
- *Speed :* 240km/h

Blériot 118. The design was re-worked under the type 118, and was the object of a contract for a prototype, 153/4 for a maritime aircraft. After its first flight on the 23rd January 1925, the machine flew down to Saint-Raphaël for it's official tests. It was handed over to Ernest Burri, test pilot of the F.B.A.[1] and made

available to the C.E.P.A.[2] The amphibian was refused by the Commission des Essais, the wing, following a distortion of the cabane struts which moved laterally and longitudinally with each engine power change!

- *Span :* - 12.90m
- *Height :* 2.80m
- *Empty weight :* 1,150kg
- *Max speed :* 200km/h
- *Length :* 8.815m
- *Wing area :* 25m^2
- *All up weight :* 1740kg

The Blériot 118 was to be armed with four machine guns, a pair of which were to be coupled together in a defensive turret.

---

(1) FBA: Franco-British Aviation, a company created by the engineer Schreck, before 1914, specialising in the construction of flying boats.

(2) CEPA: Commission des Etudes Pratiques d'Aviation Maritime (Commission for the Practical Design of Maritime Aviation).

This photo shows the positioning of the cockpit for the pilot and the turret for the machine gunner, one behind the other. It also shows the thickness of the wing profile, still unusual in France. Some of the flying instruments were placed in the cut-out of the trailing edge of the wing above the pilot's head.

The Blériot 102

Blériot 102 was simply the French Commercial designation of the ANEC 1, designed and built by the Air Navigation and Engineering Company, the British branch of Blériot-Aéronautique, ex Blériot Aircraft Ltd. See ANEC at the end of this chapter.

A retouched photo of the Blériot 105: extract from a presentation brochure.

The Blériot 105

The development of the Spad 45 had been abandoned following unfavourable static trials, notably those concerning the strength of the wing under load. The aircraft was taken up again in 1924 by Kirste who made it into the Blériot 105 "Maxi Saloon". It had a span of 27 metres, object of the order n°.622 of the 31st December 1921, and flew for the first time on Monday 4th August 1924.

This was a very different aircraft from the SPAD 45. It was an inverted Sesquiplane, whose four, 300 hp Hispano-Suiza engines were fitted in tandem in the lower wing, two pulling and two pushing. Its performance was insufficient, the testing of the machine was interrupted a second time, this time definitively.

- *Spans* : 24.719/26.840m
- *Length* : 15.695m
- *Height* : 5.95m
- *Empty weight* : 4815kg
- *All up weight* : 7317kg
- *Wing area* : 165m^2
- *Ceiling* : 2900m
- *Max speed* : 154 km/h; speed at 1,000: 148.50km/h Climb to 1,000m 4' 37"

The Blériot 106

This was a prototype commercial aircraft, a monoplane with a 450 hp Renault engine; it first flew on the 15th July 1924. There followed a casualty evacuation version which was designed with a 480 hp Renault engine. The cabin was 1.9 metres high and 1.6 metres wide, and could accommodate two stretchers and a seat for an accompanying nurse. The project was presented to the Third International Congress of Military Medicine and Surgery, but was never followed up. The model 106 was used as a test-bed by Kirste for trials on the Blériot wheels with internally sprung hub.

- *Span* : 18m
- *Length* : 12,20m
- *Height* : 3,5m
- *Wing area* : 59m^2
- *Empty weight (including water in the radiators)* : 1,700kg
- *All up weight* : 2,700kg
- *Ceiling* : 4,000 m
- *Maximum speed* : 180km/h

The Blériot 106 with its raised open cockpit and the radiators on the sides of the rounded nose.

The Blériot 108

This was a project of a Navy three-seat observation monoplane. It was fitted with a single Lorraine engine of 370hp and was presented at a CEDANA in 1922. Only a model was built.

- *Span* : - 6.24m
- *Height* : 1.38m
- *Length* : 4.92m

The Blériot 115, 115 bis, 133, 135 and 103

Blériot 115. A four engined transport aircraft for eight passengers, the type 115 flew for the first time on the 9th May 1923, piloted by Jean Casale.

Another design of the Austrian engineer, the 115 was a bi-plane fitted with four 180 hp Hispano-Suiza engines, without cowlings, placed two by two on the upper and lower wings. To the rear of each engine there was an individual streamlined fuel tank. With 160 m² of wing surface for a weight of 4,900 kg, the machine could take off on two engines.

The wing, of low camber, was made up by two box longerons and by criss-crossed ribs. At the front of the fuselage, a vertically glazed circular section facilitated the ground observation work of the navigator. The passenger cabin contained eight seats, a wash basin, a toilet and a baggage compartment of 2 cubic metres. Completed on the 16th April 1923, the Blériot 115, with the prototype registration F-ESBB, beat the world altitude record with 1,000 kg load, reaching 5,600 metres on the 1st June 1923, again flown by Jean Casale. The prototype was officially accepted by the Government on the 29th October (order n° 280/3).

On the 23rd of June 1923, Casale with Gaston Boulet as mechanic, transported one of Louis Blériot's sons and several passengers to Berck, where an "Aerial Week-End" was planned. He returned then towards Buc to pick up M. Pierre-Etienne Flandin, member of Parliment, and President of the Aéro-Club de France, and a few other guests. Overhead Grandvilliers (Oise) at an altitude of 600 metres, one of the control cables jumped off its pulley, stopping all movement of the ailerons. Despite the efforts of both the pilot and the mechanic, the aircraft went into a spiral dive, various combinations of the power to the four engines made no difference. Hitting the tops of the trees of the Dameraucourt forest, the aircraft was partially destroyed, fortunately without catching fire; Casale had cut the contacts at the moment of impact. Boulet, the mechanic, who had moved to the rear of the fuselage following the pilot's instructions, was only shaken, Casale was killed outright, having undone his safety belt; he was leaving the cockpit. In memory of Jean Casale, Marquis de Montferrato, a memorial was raised at Buc carrying the words "Victime de la Science". (Victim of Science).

on the left side, a door in the form of a "slice of cheese", pivoting upwards, whereas on the right side, the door pivoted downwards, the ailerons were interconnected by struts instead of wires, and the two cockpits were in tandem on the left side of the fuselage, instead of one cockpit with side by side seating. The total weight was raised to 2,150 kg.

As for the past two years, the Grand Prix Annuel des Avions de Transport, was held at Le Bourget from the 16th to the 24th September 1923, under the patronage of the Aéro-Club de France. Important prizes - a total of 500,000 francs - encouraged the French builders to present commercial aircraft adapted to the needs of the airline companies.

Eight competitors were lined up, two from Farman, a Breguet, a Potez, a Caudron, a Buscaylet-de Monge and two Blériots. On the Sunday the 16th September, the Aéro-Club learned that only one competitor, the Caudron C-83, satisfied the preliminary static tests. The rules were therefore modified, placing these tests after the flying tests. Considering themselves wronged, Caudron withdrew his aircraft from the competition. The five remaining competitors, (the Buscaylet did not turn up nor did the second Blériot) participated in the eliminatory tests, part of which consisted of, a take off at maximum load in less than 250 metres, a flight above 2,000 metres for 15 minutes with one engine stopped, and a change of spark plugs in flight. During this eliminatory phase, the Breguet had both of its engine stop, and was forced to land outside the limits of the field. The machine, which had flown for the first time five days earlier, was too badly damaged to be repaired. The three-engined Potez was disqualified by the jury. After the elimination of the Breguet and the Potez, the winner was the Farman F-3X (F-ESAR) the only monoplane in the competition. The second place went to the other Farman, a four-engined Goliath, the third and last place going to the Blériot 115. The poor visibility from the ground obliged the controllers to ask the Blériot's crew, Bizot, Villechanoux and Viguier, to carry out the tests a second time. Further, the consummation of fuel was shown to be higher than that of its competitors. The presence of chocks in front of the wheels at the moment of departure, caused it to lose several more points.

The Blériot 115 built for eight passengers, with its four Hispano-Suiza Ac engines of 180hp, at Buc in May 1923. The cockpit is positioned partially under the leading edge of the upper wing. The aircraft F-ESBB became the Blériot 135, then the 115 bis.

The Blériot 115 at the *Grand Prix des Avions de Transport*, 1923.

The second Blériot 115, leaving the factory at the end of the summer 1923, had the same registration letters as the crashed prototype. It was different from the prototype by a few details, six port holes instead of five on the right hand side of the fuselage,

The Blériot 115 mission was filmed by M. Dely.

The Blériot 115, *Jean Casale*, and its crew: from left to right, Sgt Kenchet, mechanic; Lt Colonel Vuillemin, first pilot; Captain Dagnaux, second pilot; and Sgt Vendelle, radio.

Even though the three finalists had shown good qualities, none of them appeared as the perfect commercial aircraft, which was the object of the competition. The house of Blériot had spent

700,000 francs in the construction of it's machine, but received only 77,625 francs in prize money. It would be only two years later that the winning Farman, modified, would be put into service on a commercial route, after a new victory in the Grand Prix of 1924.

At the end of 1924 several automobile missions going to Niger and the Congo were in project. The mission Haardt-Audoin Dubreuil had specifically proposed to study both climate conditions and practicable landing grounds over the route. M. André Laurant – Eynac, under Secretary of State for Aviation was planning in 1923 an aerial study trip to Madagascar. On the 9th October the principle of a mission to Lake Chad and to the Oubangui was finalised. Citroen had just completed a land route to Niamey (Niger) and could, if needs be, supply help and assistance on the ground to the aircraft flying the route. For this voyage it was decided to use powerful multi-engined aircraft, preferably rapid machines but not single engined aircraft, a breakdown of a single engine above the African forests would almost certainly end in the loss of the machine and its crew.

Captain Jean Dagnaux pioneer of the first aerial routes, had been released from the Military with a hundred percent handicap because of war wounds, had the dream of creating a "Route Impériale" France-Madagascar. He appreciated the Blériot 135 seen during the last Grand Prix des Avions de Transport. He therefore, requested two machines of this type for his African voyage. Two Blériot 115s with Hispano Suiza 8Ac engines of 180hp would finally be used. These two aircraft specifically built for this mission were fitted out with special instrument panel by Badin, called "Flight Controller", drift meter and radio, plus night flying instruments. Level with the cabin, the trailing edge of the upper wing was cut away for ease of star sights.

Contrary to the other 115 which possessed an extra cabane strut on the left hand side linking the leading edge of the upper wing to the fuselage, the two Blériots of the Chad mission were equipped with a central cabane strut just behind the cockpit. Painted in the colours of the French Military Aviation, the two machines were christened *Roland Garros* and *Jean Casale*. With 1,200 litres of fuel and 300 litres of oil, their range was 1,300km.

It was M. Laurent-Eynac who had the difficult task of choosing the Blériot crews, from amongst the numerous officers who sought the honour of participating in the voyage. The organisation and the management of the mission had been given to Colonel Louis de Mezeyrac de Goÿs, a bombing pioneer, principle assistant of the Under Secretary of State for Aviation, finally, the crews of the two machines were made up thus:

- *Roland Garros*: Colonel de Goÿs, first pilot - Captain Pelletier Doisy, second pilot - Sergeant-Major Besin, mechanic - M. Dely, camera operator (a film entitled *Vers le Tchad* (towards Chad) was made with the shots taken by M. Dely)
- *Jean Casale*: Lieutenant Colonel Vuillemin, first pilot - Captain Dagnaux second pilot and navigator - Sergeant Knecht mechanic - Sergeant Vendelle, radio operator (only the *Jean Casale* was equipped with a radio).

This study mission which had nothing of the character of a rally, was accomplished without any publicity, the voyage was to ensure a liaison with the principal French colonies in Africa, it served also to observe the reaction of future commercial aircraft under different climates, to study African meteorological conditions at altitude, and also to test long distance navigation over a continent still little known. In Dagnaux's mind, the building of an aerial network in Africa would allow France to give political and economical cohesion to its colonial empire, and to reduce the inconvenience caused by the geographical dispersion of the colonies in Africa.

This mission therefore, responded to three objectives, technical, political and economical. After having reached Fort-Archambaud (Chad) the two aircraft were to come back via Bamako, Kayes and Dakar, then through Port-Etienne, Cape Juby, Morocco and then return to Paris, a total of 13,000 kilometres.

After ten days of waiting caused by a period of intense fog over the north of France, they finally left on Sunday 18th January 1925 at 11.45 a.m. from the field at Buc. Each machine weighed 5,545 kg, for an engine power of 720 hp. At the last minute each aircraft received an extra passenger. On the *Jean Casale* the extra passenger was Captain Brulé, who had participated in the organisation of the mission, and on the *Roland Garros,* Commandant Le Prieur, who wanted to experiment with his new invention, the Navigraph, an improved drift meter, indicating the heading correction to enable the pilot to compensate for drift.

After a stop at Avord, which lengthened to 48 hours because of the return of the fog, the two Blériots reached Perpignan, completing the 480 kilometres in 4 hours 6 minutes.

On the 23rd January, after replacing one of the portholes of the *Roland Garros*, the two aircraft, without Captain Brulé who was obliged to return to Paris, flew on towards Oran. A fuel leak on the *Jean Casale* forced a landing at Los Alcazares in Spain. On the 25th after a full engine check, the two machines took off from Oran heading for Colomb-Bécher. The tyres having suffered because of the state of the rudimentary runways, the stock of spares was prematurely used up. On the 28th whilst waiting for new tyres coming from Paris, the Blériots flew to Beni-Abbès, and then on to Adrar on the 30th. They stayed there until the 2nd February 1925, when the new tyres were brought by the mechanic Edmond Laversin, who took the place of Commandant Le Prieur, who was recalled to Paris.

The following day the two 115s took off towards Ouallen and reached Tessalit the following day. On the 5th they landed at Gao, where the engines were again fully checked. Two days later, following the Niger, the two aircraft flew Gao to Niamey in 3 hours 25 minutes. At dawn on the 10th February the *Jean Casale* took off from Niamey towards Zinder and Lake Chad, followed soon afterwards by *Roland Garros*. At an altitude of 30 metres, the *Jean Casale,* too nose-high, stalled and sliding on its right wing crashed to the ground. Lieutenant Colonel Vuillemin had a skull fracture and Vendelle was mortally wounded. Knecht was unhurt. Dagnaux, had only his false left leg damaged (his left leg was amputated after a dog fight in 1916). The accident appears to have been caused by an overloading of material in the rear section of the fuselage, the incidence of the horizontal tail plane had not been set to take this into account. The authorization to follow through the mission with one single remaining Blériot, requested twice by Colonel De Goys, was refused by the Minister, the machine not being equipped with radio. The *Roland Garros* was therefore dismantled on site and the elements would be visible on the field at Niamey before falling prey to termites and ending up as dust.

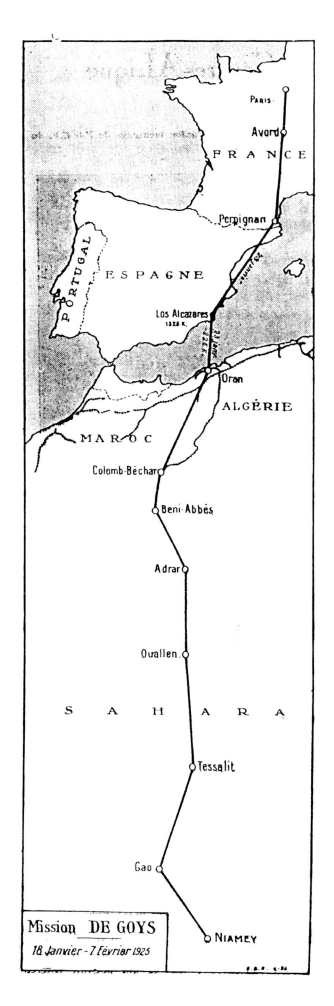

The route of the two Blériot 115 from France to Africa.

If this voyage, 4,237 kilometres, during which each landing was the occasion for a particularly warm reception from the local population, had unfortunately been shortened, it had however, opened the way to the big rallies of the following years and to future commercial lines in Africa.

- Span : 25m
- Length : 14.45m
- Height : 5.0m
- Wing area : 126m²
- Empty weight : 2,900kg
- All up weight : 4,900kg
- Ceiling with full load : 4,000m
- Speed at ground level : 180km/h (initially 170km/h)

Blériot 115 bis. The third Blériot 115 made its maiden flight in June 1924. The same year thanks to a new layout of the cockpit where the crew were again seated side by side, but further forward, a larger volume was available in the passenger cabin now fitted with twelve seats. The all up weight rose to 5,100kg. Registered F-AGEM this machine had the reference 115 bis after being fitted with Hispano-Suiza 8Ab engines of 180hp, the same power as the 8Ac of the 115 but with a different oil circulation and a fuel burn reduced by 10g per hp. On the 8th August 1924 the Blériot 115 bis was put into service by the company Air-Union on the line Paris to London where it established a speed record completing the trip in one hour forty seven minutes, easily beating the time taken by the Farman "Goliath" over the same route.

Flown by Robert Bajac the Chief Pilot, accompanied by his mechanic Laversin, the machine was joined on the route at the end of the year by F-ESBB, ex-type 135 and then 115 bis by changing of the engines.

In 1929, the Blériot 115 bis F-ESBB participated in a new form of aerial advertising; publicity by towed banner (the first showing to the public had happened at Orly on the 5th May). A cloth banner of 300 m² was rolled under the lower wing. The machine, flown by Bossoutrot, took off and then freed the banner whose cable was unrolled for 200 metres. After over flying Paris and the surrounding area, the aircraft dropped everything - cable and banner - before landing. This procedure, whose success was rapidly developed, is still used today, notably along the coasts, in the summer time.

A search light fixed to the banner was foreseen for advertising at night. A patent relating to aerial advertising had been filed by Louis Blériot as early as 11th June 1927. This followed a study by André Herbemont, undertaken in 1926, which led to numerous trials on different models on SPAD and Farman "Goliath."

Blériot 135. This variation was obtained by modification of the second 115; from May 1924 there were no orders for this machine. The four Hispano-Suiza engines in V configuration were replaced by four air-cooled Salsmon engines of 230hp. First flight of the 135 was at Buc on the 19th July 1924. The cockpit, which still had the tandem layout of the 115 n° 2, was quickly converted to side by side, as on the F-AGEM.

The 135 was shown at the Grand Prix des Avions de Transport in 1924 where only three aircraft participated! The Blériot 135, the three-engined Caudron 183 (F-ESAI) and the Farman F-3X(modified) of the previous competition (F-ESAR) The qualification tests of that year consisted of carrying out within a thirty two minute time period – with a full load (2,198kg for the Blériot) – four figures of eight without losing altitude, each manoeuvre to be completed with one motor stopped. Each engine had to be stopped and then re-started in flight. The classification tests, which started on Wednesday 20th August, had eight prizes of 100,000 francs. Each day the competitors had to fly the route Le Bourget-Bordeaux-Le Bourget, 1,030km, with a stop of a maximum of 45 minutes in Bordeaux.

For the second time it was the Farman who came out winner of the Grand Prix. The Blériot 135, flown by Bizot-Villechanoux-Dagnaux, came second and won 200,000Francs. Its average speed was 146.727km/h. A fitting out bonus of 100,000 Francs was also given to the Blériot. The 135 was transformed into a 115 bis before the end of 1924.

The Blériot 115 became the 135 with the fitting of four Salmson 9RA air-cooled radial engines of 230hp. The glazed bay window was for the navigator to allow him to observe the ground and at the same tie use his charts, sheltered from the slipstream.

The second Blériot 115 became the 115 bis when the cockpit was moved forward. See the navigator, standing in the nose, looking at the ground via the bay window, on whose shelf he could also spread his charts.

- *Span*: 25m
- *Length*: 14.450m
- *Height*: 4.222m
- *Wing area*: 126m^2
- *Empty weight*: 3,218kg *All up weight*: 5,500kg
- *Ceiling with full load*: 4,200m
- *Max speed at ground level*: 185km/h

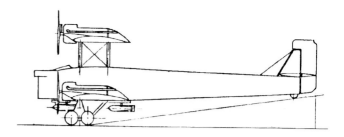

Blériot 133. Military version of the 135, this model remained at the project stage.

Blériot 103. Replying to a specification of 1923, the Blériot 103 was fitted with four Hispano-Suiza engines of 300hp; this was a larger version of the 115, destined to be a night bomber. Its competitors were the LeO 12, the Breguet 16 and the Farman 60; it was never built.

Factory drawings of the Blériot 103 project, a night-bomber.

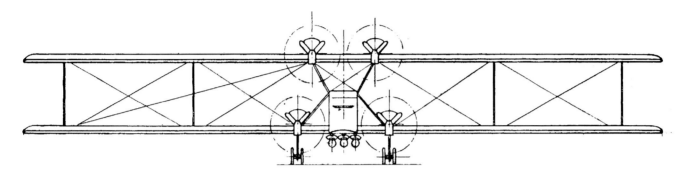

The Blériot 155 and 113

Blériot 155. The experience acquired with the models 115 and 135, had been put to use by Kirste for the design of a new four engined transport bi-plane, the type 155.

With a capacity of seventeen passengers, the Blériot 155 was powered by four 200 hp water cooled Renault engines, fitted with Blériot compressed air starters and Levasseur propellers of 2.7 metres diameter. It could reach the altitude of 2,000 metres in 15 minutes with a speed at ground level of 175 km/h, it had a range of 500 kilometres.

The cabin, ventilated by four adjustable air inlets, measured 4.6 metres long. Light was admitted by twelve port holes, and as well as a lateral entry door, it had two evacuation hatches, one to the front and one on top of the fuselage. The undercarriage, directly below the lower engines, was made up of two double wheel axles, the suspension was by bungees. The rudder had balanced compensation, but not the elevator. The four ailerons were not balanced.

The first example carried out its first flight on the 29th July 1925. It obtained its Certificate of Airworthiness (n° 1523) in May 1926, and was registered F-AICQ. It was christened *Clément Ader,* and put into service by Air-Union on the Paris to London route from the 19th May. Unfortunately the 2nd October of that year, a fire in the engines caused its loss at Penhurst, near to London, causing the death of the crew, Mallet and Royer.

The Blériot 155 no 1 at Buc, 29th July 1925.

The Blériot 155 could carry seventeen passengers.

The second Blériot 155 (registered F-AIEB, Certificate of Airworthiness n° 1559) was equipped with a larger rudder, and was christened *Wilbur Wright*. On the 26th March 1926, this machine flown by Robert Bajac, Chief Pilot of Air-Union, stayed in the air for 3 hours 46 minutes and 35 seconds with 1,500 kg of load, thus establishing new duration records for 500, 1,000 and 1,500 kg loads.

In spite of this success, its career was of short duration, a few months later at Folkestone two engines stopped suddenly during the landing phase. The aircraft descending rapidly hit the roof of a house on the edge of the aerodrome. The machine was totally destroyed, the crew (Delisle and Ducros) and four passengers perished in the accident.

- Span : 26m
- Length : 14.75m
- Height : 5.25m
- Between wings: 2.70m
- Empty weight (with water and T.S.F.) : 3,650kg
- Total weight : 6,350kg
- Wing area : 135m²
- Ceiling with full load : 3,500m
- Maximum speed : 175km/h

Blériot 113. These two tragedies led Louis Blériot to abandon the use of the Renault 8 Fg. He also immediately abandoned the

Blériot 113 Bn4, the projected military version of the 155, which was to be fitted with the same type of engine. It had already been refused by a CEDANA in March 1925.

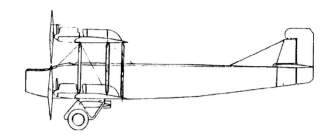

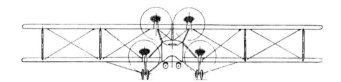

Two views of a factory drawing of the Blériot 113 project, bomber version of the 155 transport.

The Blériot 165, 175 and 123

The last bi-planes designed by Kirste were the models 165 and 175 derived from the 155. In order to replace the Farman Goliath by twin-engine aircraft with more powerful motorisation, more comfortable and carrying more passengers, there appeared in 1926 a new generation of commercial machines, presented by the Etablissements Lioré et Olivier on one hand, and Blériot on the other hand.

Blériot 165. The Blériot 165, whose fuselage was practically identical to that of the 155 was shown at the Tenth Salon de l'Aéronautique, and was powered by two Gnome and Rhône Jupiter Ab engines of 420 hp, in nacelles between the wings. The cockpit was a side by side layout, the cabin was 4.6 metres long by 1.7 metres wide, and could accommodate sixteen passengers. It was fitted with a toilet and a baggage hold. The span was slightly less than that of the type 155, 23 metres instead of 26 metres, it differed also with its vertical empennage, whose leading edge was rounded. All the inter-plane struts were vertical. The rudder had an extension of a small articulated flap on its trailing edge. (1)

This flap, independently controlled, allowed the compensation of the torque of one engine in case of break down of the other. At the rear of the fuselage the longerons were joined by verticals in duralumin tubes, strengthened by steel bracing wires. At a fully loaded weight of 5,600 kg, the Blériot 165 could reach 172 km/h at ground level, and with a thousand litres of fuel had a range of 525 kilometres. The undercarriage, initially with twined wheels, was later fitted with the Blériot internally sprung wheels. Air-Union ordered two examples for the route Paris to London.

Above, the first Blériot 165, christened Leonardo da Vinci belonging to Air Union. Below, the two Blériot 165 on the Paris-London line, painted red and gold, and christened Rayon d'Or and Golden Ray.

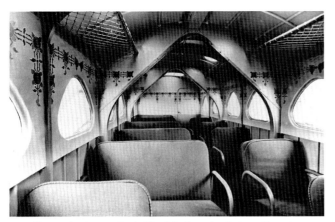

Above, the Leonardo da Vinci, below, the Octave Chanute.

- *Span* : 23m
- *Height* : 4.9m
- *Empty weight* : 2,919kg
- *Length* : 14.8m
- *Between wings* : 2.60m
- *All up weight* : 5,600kg

- *Wing area* : 119.10m² • *Maximum speed* : 180km/h
- *Service ceiling with full load* : 4,000m

The first flight of the Blériot 165 n°1 was on the 27th October 1926. It did not obtain its Certificate of Airworthiness (n° 1722), and its registration, F-AIKI until October of the following year. Christened *Léonard de Vinci*, it ended service in November 1927.

The Blériot 165 n° 1 would only be withdrawn from service in 1933 after 715 flying hours. The n° 2 had a shorter career because it was taken off the register in 1931 after 269 flying hours. A second Blériot 175 was to be used by Paul Codos and Captain Puyperon for a rally Paris to Saigon to Tokyo, with return via the USSR, but the difficulties of financing the project caused it to be abandoned.

Blériot 175. The second 165, at the request of the company, was equipped with two water cooled Renault engines of 450 hp, and equipment for night flight. After a first take off by Bossoutrot on the 22nd May 1928, this machine, thus modified, became a type 175, was handed over to Air-Union on the 20th August. Its performances were no better than those obtained with the Jupiter engines, the Blériot came back to being a model 165. As a type 165, in September it obtained its C of A n° 1932, and the registration F-AITU. As for the F-AIKI, its original name of *Octave Chanute* was replaced by *The Golden Ray*,[1] when the company decided to christen all the machines on the Paris to London route, and painted them all in a uniform colour scheme of red and gold.

- *Empty weight* : 3,347.50kg • *All up weight* : 5,600kg
- *Wing area* : 119.10m² • *Ceiling* : 4,000m

Blériot 123. The military version of the 165, with the same dimensions, the type 123, designed as early as 1926, and presented to a CEPANA[2] in the same year, was never followed up.

- *Empty weight* : 2,900kg • *All up weight* : 5,450kg
- *Wing area* : 120m² • *Ceiling* : 5,000m
- *Maximum speed at ground level* : 180km/h

---

(1) For the mechanics, it was "jaws of the ray"

(2) Commission d'Examen des Projets d'Avions Nouveaux (Commission for the Examination of New Aircraft Projects) previously CEDANA, created in 1929.

The Blériot 125, 350, 370

Blériot 125. In 1924, seeking to design a commercial aircraft offering maximum security, Léon Kirste had roughed out the first sketches of a twin fuselage machine, the Bleriot 125. For five years, different mock-up models, called 125 mI to 125 mIX, (see the table on page 139) were tried in the Eiffel tunnel, and in the aerodynamic laboratory of Saint-Cyr. Several engine layouts were looked at, but it was finally the formula, twin engine in tandem, allowing flight on one engine without compensation of the fin, which was retained. The construction of the full sized mock-up of the cabin started in 1925. At the same time an engine fitted to a wing section was tried at Buc. The full size mock-up of the entire machine was made in 1929.

Take off of the famous Blériot 125 twin-engine, with two parallel passenger cabins.

Presented to a CEPANA in September of the same year, the definitive version of the type 125-0 was the object of a prototype order n° 1204/9, on the 17th September, for a sum of 3 079 000 francs. The aircraft, built entirely of wood, except the centre part which was in steel tubes, had the form of a high wing monoplane under which there were two fuselages of oval section. This original formula allowed the insulation of the passengers from the engine noise. The wing, whose central structure was in steel tube, had a maximum thickness of one metre. The wing was covered in plywood, except the ailerons and the trailing edges which were fabric covered. The fuselage was positioned in the centre, containing the cockpit, the navigator's position, both accessible in flight from the two fuselages. Each fuselage had a cabin for six passengers with toilet and baggage hold. The front sections of the fuselages were covered in plywood, the rear sections were fabric covered. The tail plane, with a span of 8 metres, supported four vertical fins, each with a rudder. The elevator was compensated by a flettner. The undercarriage was made up of four Blériot internally sprung wheels fitted with Palmer brakes, aligned in tandem under each fuselage, in a position of semi-retraction. This layout of the fuselages, placed very close to the earth, allowed the passengers to climb on board almost directly from the ground. The two engines, situated at each end of the central fuselage, were Hispano-Suiza 12 Hbr, with a reduction gear, developing 500 hp. Firstly two-bladed metal propellers, then three-bladed metal propellers were fitted. Finally, four-bladed propellers in wood were fitted. The engines were cooled by one single frontal radiator.

The type 125 had a range of 1,000 kilometres, a ceiling of 4,500 metres, and could fly fully loaded on one engine.

After having been shown at the Salon of 1930 at the Grand Palais, between a restored Blériot XI and a Spad 91 fighter, the Blériot twin-fuselage flew for the first time at Buc on Monday 9th March 1931, piloted by Charles Quatremare. For his first take off, in order to avoid an eventual tipping over onto its nose, the aircraft was fitted with two supplementary wheels in front of the main undercarriage. The builder's trials were completed in December 1932. Handed over then to the Service Technique of Villacoublay, the machine was taken in hand by Lieutenant Viard and the Pilot/Engineer Jouy. Even though, according to the pilots of the test centre, the elevator was too small and the wing too thick in the centre, the flying qualities were satisfactory and the aircraft received the registration F-ALZD.

The Blériot 125 at Buc, and at the Salon du l'Aviation in 1930 in Paris, fitted with different propellers. The layout of the engines in tandem gave certain advantages, such as ease of piloting on one engine.

CHARACTERISTICS			DESIGN START DATE	CHARACTERISTICS OF USE AND CONSTRUCTION	WIND TUNNEL AND FLIGHT TESTS
Model I			1924	Three-engined bi-fuselage monoplane with traction propellers, sharp edged fuselage with high rectangular wing.	Airframe complete : finesse 12,48 Eiffel report n° 169/B of the 27/8/24
Model II and III			1924	Three-engined bi-fuselage monoplane with traction propellers, sharp edged fuselage with parasol rectangular wing.	Wing : finesse 17.5 - Eiffel report n° 152/B of the 18/2/24 Airframe complete : finesse 11.7 Annex 1 of the Eiffel report n° 169/B of the 1/10/24
Model IV			1924	Three-engined bi-fuselage monoplane with elliptical fuselage with high rectangular wing.	Wing : finesse 16.55 Airframe complete : finesse 13.5 Annex 2 of the report n° 169/B of the 2/10/24
Model V			1924	Two or three-engined bi-fuselage biplane with two traction propellers and one pusher, or two traction.	
Model VI			1925	Three-engined monoplane, bi-fuselage, round form, pusher propellers, high-wing trapezoidal form. Construction wood and fabric. Construction started. Full-size mock-up of cabin and cockpit, then abandoned.	Engine trials with extended propeller shaft, at Buc. Wind tunnel trials at St. Cyr. Airframe complete : finesse 13.85 St Cyr report n° 245/A of the 15/7/25
Model VII	Length : 15,35 m Height : 4,900 m Span : 28 m		1925	Three-engine transport monoplane, 3 Hispano-Suiza engines of 380hp, wing part of the cabin. Abandoned.	Wing : finesse 12.4 Eiffel report n° 236/B of the 24/2/26 Airframe complete : finesse 11.42 St Cyr report n° 300/A of the 11/6/26
BLÉRIOT 125[0] Model VIII (A & B)	Span : 28m Length : 13835m Height : 4m Empty weight : 4540kg Total weight : 7260 kg Wing area : 100 M[2] Maximum speed : 220 km/h		1928	Bi-fuselage transport monoplane, 2 Hispano-Suiza engines of 500hp, with reduction gear. Wing : plywood covered. Started on 7/1/29 Full size model. Prototype had Government Order n° 1204/9, dated 17/12/29. Presented to a CEPANA on 4/4/29	Wing : profile of centre section Cz max. 1.35 Cz min. 0.0215 Eiffel report n° 152/B of the 18/2/24 Airframe complete : A finesse 11.5 B finesse 11.8 St Cyr report n° 533/A of the 9/29. STATIC TESTS: Empennage and fuselage : factor 5.6 (5/1/30) Wing : factor 6 (20/6/30) Torsion tests : factor 1.5 (20/6/30), factor 5.3 (13/6/30) Engine mount : factor 5.31 (2/5/30) First flight 9/3/31
Model IX			1929	Tests carried out with the objective of comparing the finesse of the low wing layout of this model with the layout of the high wing of the 125[0] Construction wood and fabric	Airframe complete : finesse 10.6 Eiffel report n° 511/B of the 28/7/29
BLÉRIOT 125[1]	Empty weight : 4930 kg Total weight : 7260 kg Height : 4.3 metres		1929		

The rear engine of the Blériot 125.

The cockpit on the Blériot 125.

One of the two cabinsof the Blériot 125.

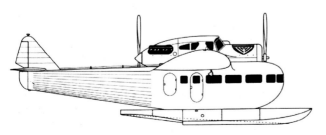

It was planned to fit the Blériot 125 onto floats.

Although an innovative machine, the Blériot 125 was not ordered by any airline, the absence of a tail skid, at that time considered the only efficient brake, discouraging the airline pilots. It was the last aircraft designed by Kirste, and built by Blériot in Suresnes. The transformation planned into a 125′, with floats replacing the undercarriage, was never carried out, even though the floats had been built and even shown at the Salon.

Blériot 350. Two models derived from the 125, the types 350 and 370 would remain at the model stage. The 350, "public transport" designed in 1934, had two fuselages, fitted with three Hispano-Suiza 18Z of 1200 hp. It was designed in 1933 with four pairs of wheels in tandem. It had a double fin.

- *Span* : 38 m
- *Length* : 18.80m
- *Height* : 4.65m
- *Empty weight* : 8,330kg
- *All up weight* : 13,000kg
- *Wing area* : 158m^2
- *Maximum speed* : 253km/h
- *Cruise speed at 1,000 m and at 7/10 power* : 220km/h
- *Ceiling* : 6,500m

Shortly after a lightened version at 12 tons was designed.

- *Span* : 34m
- *Length* : 18.25m
- *Height* : 4.65m
- *Empty weight* : 7,370kg
- *All up weight* : 12,000kg
- *Wing area* : 124 m^2
- *Maximum speed* : 275km/h
- *Cruise speed at 1,000 and 55/100 power* : 220km/h
- *Ceiling* : 6,800m

Drawing taken from the presentation dossier of the Blériot 350.

Blériot 370. The type 370 was to have been a twin engined bomber, engines to be Hispano-Suiza 18R of 1650 hp, in tandem. Four machine gun posts in front and behind the wing, three fins, four pairs of wheels, laid out two by two, in tandem.

- *Span* : 44m
- *Length* : 18m
- *Height* : 4.50m
- *Empty weight* : 15,000kg
- *Wing area* : 200m^2
- *Speed at 2,000 m with supercharger* : 260km/h

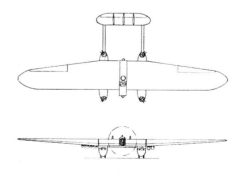

The project of the Blériot 370.

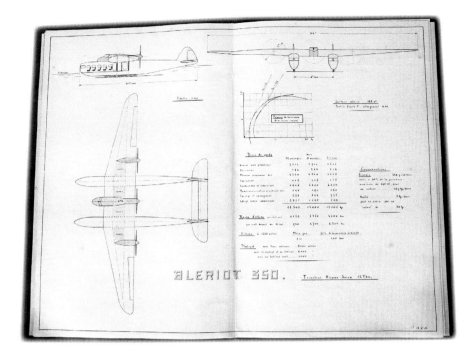

The Blériot 350 project dossier presented to the minister is a large and luxurious object, around 50cm in height and bound in a fine imitation leather.

1. Very light construction of the wing, due to the spreading of the load in the direction of the wing-span. The load spread is better than in the other forms because the different masses are of a similar nature.

2. The distribution of the commercial load on two side-by-side fuselages, allows the reduction by half of the length of the cabin, still retaining the layout of the passengers in two rows.

3. This layout ensures a maximum of comfort, each passenger having a porthole for himself and can move about the fuselage without disturbing the others.

4. Excellent visibility for the passengers, view not obstructed neither by the wing (above and to the rear of the cabin) nor by the engines nor tail surfaces.

5. Considerable volume available allowing for the use of large baggage compartments, allowing even the carrying of spare engines.

6. Undercarriage wheels hidden inside the fuselage, tandem layout, thus reducing drag to practically zero, removing the need for a retractable undercarriage, thus saving any weight supplement.

7. Possibility of adding a large number of doors for cabin access, thus each passenger could have a parachute at his disposition, through which he could pass without having to wait in line to reach the exit.

8. Easy access to the cabin, passengers could climb on board and reach their seat, without the use of stairs.

9. Possibility of a water landing without risk, the two fuselage shells are water-tight and have shock-bearing keels.

10. In-flight accessibility of the main engine accessories, magnetos, pumps etc.

11. Silence and absence of all oil and petrol smells, thanks to the positioning of the engines above and behind the cabins, at a distance of more than 7m.

12. Ease of keeping the fuselage and the cockpit clean, no oil projection cold reach them.

13. Removal of the threat of engine fire touching the cabins, the flames could not touch either wing or fuselage.

14. Better thrust from the pusher propeller than the puller.

15. Only three-engined aircraft with no engine aligned with the fuselage.

16. Ease of taxiing and take off thanks to absence of tail skid or tail-wheel.

17. Absence of fuselage stresses caused by the tailskid.

18. Fuel tanks jettisonable outside the engine bearers. No fuel lines near the cabins. The passengers could smoke without danger.

19. Finesse very close to the aircraft designed for distance records. Frontal surface reduced to the strict minimum; wing and fuselage very streamlined, engine and undercarriage producing no drag, not by cowling or other accessories, but by the very layout of the aircraft.

20. Cost of the aircraft built in wood, much less than those built in metal. The wing construction - called Type Fokker – is recognised as being virtually indestructible.

21. In case of necessity, the civil fuselages can be replaced in a few hours, by military fuselages, fitted with bomb racks and machine gun turrets, giving a field of fire with no dead arcs.

The Blériot 2222

Blériot 222. In 1926, Herbemont had designed the Blériot 2222, an amphibious double-hulled bi-plane fitted with two 450 hp Lorraine 12 Ed engines of 450 hp, in tandem in nacelles between the wings. A mechanism was designed to allow the use of both radiators on one engine in case of failure of the other one. If one radiator leaked, the remaining radiator could be used to cool both engines. The use of Blériot variable pitch propellers, allowed in case of failure, the best use of the remaining engine. After the wind tunnel trials in May 1926, the project was prepared for presentation to a CEPANA on the 10th September 1926, and was then abandoned.

- *Span* : 20.40m
- *Length* : 15.50m
- *Height* : 6.50m
- *Wing area* : 125m²
- *Empty weight* : 3,300kg
- *All up weight* : 6,200kg
- *Maximum speed* : 180km/h

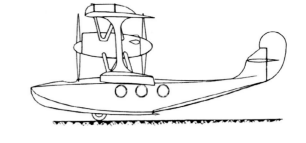

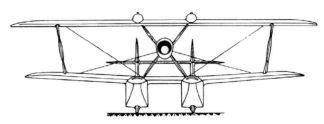

Facttory drawings of the Blériot 2222

The BZ 1 with jettissonable cabin and another varication of the BZ 1 with the cabin above the wing.

The Blériot BZ 1, BZ 3, and 250

BZ 1. In November 1928, Zappata presented to a CEDANA, a sea-plane project, the BZ 1 (Blériot – Zappata) a four-engined transatlantic machine using Hispano-Suiza - 12 Hbr engines of 550 hp, in a tandem configuration, two pushing and two pulling. It was a fabric covered metal structure. Some of the passengers were installed in the thick wing, whose leading edge was fitted with port holes. The other passengers, as well as the cockpit, were in the front section of the fuselage. This part had the shape and the water-tightness of a life boat, and could be separated in case of a forced landing at sea. It was fitted under the wing, an extension of the fuselage.

On a second version of this project, the water tight cabin was placed above the wing and was inset into the fuselage.

The CEDANA to whom the project was submitted, did not retain it.

- *Span* : 38.70m
- *Length* : 24.40m
- *Height* : 5.05m
- *Wing area* : 180m²
- *Empty weight* : 10,500kg
- *All up weight* : 17,000kg
- *Max speed* : 205km/h.

BZ 3. If the BZ 2 was a pre-project of the 5190 Santos Dumont (see later) we do not know to what the designation BZ 3 corresponds.

Blériot 250A. Zappata thought of another aircraft whose cabin could be detached in case of a forced landing. Then in March 1930 he looked again at this project and designated it Blériot 250 A. This time the aircraft was called "Transatlantic". The model was made but the wind tunnel trials gave poor results, so the project was abandoned.

- *Span* : 4.40m
- *Length* : 21.96m
- *Height* : 7.56m

The wind tunnel model of the Blériot 250A.

The Blériot 107, 117, 127, 128, 137, 195 and 227

Blériot 107. In 1922, the engineer Kirste had designed, outside of any official programme, a twin-engined monoplane, with two 370 hp Lorraine engines, the 107 M, a multi-crew combat aircraft destined to replace the Caudron R XI, produced at the end of the war. Even though the static trials were satisfactory, the fine tuning of the machine, ordered by the Government on the 31st December 1922 (Order n° 1066) was not followed through. A more powerful direct development, the type 117 M, taking over at the time of issue, in 1923, of the official programme for a multi-crew aircraft to which the 117 M replied, in the same way as did seven other machines, of which the Lioré et Olivier LeO-7, would be ordered in series.

- *Span* : 23.0m
- *Height* : 2.80m
- *Length* : 16.30m

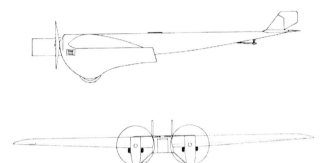

Factory drawing of the project of the Blériot 107.

Blériot 117. The principal role of these multi-crew combat aircraft was to escort day bombers, who, even though armed, were vulnerable, as when heavily loaded they were not very manoeuvrable. Fitted with a thick cantilever wing of 23 metre span and twin fins, the design of the 117 M was notable by the presence at the rear of each engine nacelle, of a gun turret, a third turret was installed in the nose of the fuselage. Thanks to the disposition of these three machine gun turrets, the defence had very few dead angles of fire.

The central part of the wing was made up of four high-tensile steel tubes, which went through the engine cowlings and the fuselage. These tubes were strengthened by steel bars, and covered in plywood and fabric, giving the profile of the wing. The outer sections of the wing, 9 metres long, were fixed by four shafts to the centre section. The rear part of these outer sections, between the inner rib and the aileron, was removable and adjustable.

The ailerons were articulated on ball bearings, a patent filed by Blériot Aéronautique. The rectangular section fuselage was made up of four longerons in spruce. The outer surfaces were covered in plywood, except at the rear where only the sides were in plywood, the upper and lower surfaces were fabric covered. In the nose, the machine gun turret had a radio installation, photographic equipment and navigation instruments.

The cockpit, two-seats side by side for the pilot and the mechanic, was positioned level with the leading edge of the wing, whose thickness - 80 centimetres for a chord of 4.6 metres - allowed access to the engine nacelles and the machine gun turrets, via lateral crawl ways. Behind the cockpit were installed the two fuel tanks, which gave the Blériot 117 a range of 800 kilometres. The two tanks were jettisonable in flight. The empennage, in spruce and plywood, had two rudders and a compensated elevator. For yaw and pitch, the controls were doubled and separated, passing along the left and right side of the fuselage. The two radiators, by Vincent André, were situated on the front legs of the undercarriage, which had an axle, each with two wheels of 900 x 165. At the end of a series of flights carried out at Villacoublay by Bizot, test pilot for Blériot (the first flight took place at Buc on the 19th June 1924) the STAé estimated that the flying qualities of the 117 M were insufficient. Despite several modification programmes, no improvement was noted. It was later admitted that its two-fin empennage, of too small dimensions, was masked by the wing at high angles of incidence.

- *Span* : 23.0m
- *Height* : 3.0m
- *Empty weight* : 3,000kg
- *Max speed* : 183km/h
- *Ceiling with full load* : 5,000m.
- *Length* : 14.50m
- *Wing area* : 86.50m^2
- *All up weight* : 4,400kg

Blériot 127 M. Abandoned, the Blériot 117 M gave birth in 1925 to the 127 M, a four-crew multi-mission aircraft: combat, night and day bomber, long range reconnaissance. 42 were ordered by the Government under the type 127-2 M, fitted with Hispano-Suiza 12 Hb engines of 550hp. Very similar to its predecessor, the Blériot 127 M differed principally by its single vertical fin, and by the rear fuselage, of a larger section than on the 117. It was also equipped with a bomb sight installed in the nose of the aircraft. For a total weight of 4,466 kg, the prototype Blériot 127 M, constructed in fabric covered wood, was equipped with two 500 hp Hispano-Suiza - 12 Gb engines in W figuration, with frontal radiators. The thick wing, as on the Blériot 117 M, allowed access to the engine nacelles from the fuselage.

The Blériot 117 M carried out its trials at Buc in 1924.

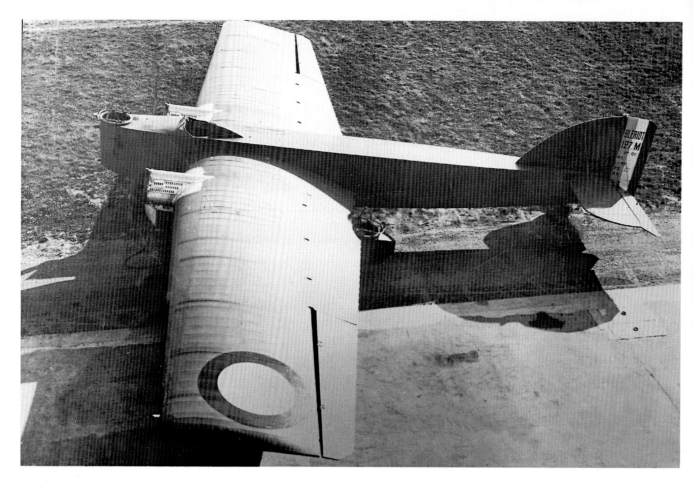

Above and below, the Blériot 127 M during its trials at Buc in May 1926.

This prototype, later christened 127-1 M, flew for the first time on the 7th May 1926.

Sent to the Service Technique at the end of the month, the machine reached 221 mph at 2,000 metres, climbed to 4,000 metres in 12 minutes 21 seconds, and reached a ceiling of 8,100 metres. These performances, for a long time kept secret, allowed the aircraft to rival the performances of the current fighters. Armed with a machine gun turret in the nose and two TO 7 turrets in the extension to the engine nacelles, all three equipped with twin Lewis guns, the 127 M could carry 250 kg of bombs.

Because of it's excellent performances, which allowed it to win the competition for multi-crew combat aircraft of 1926, the Blériot would be, with the Amiot 122, ordered in series. Three orders of eighteen, fourteen, and twelve machines spread from December 1927 to October 1930, brought the total order to thirty-four examples, at a unit price of 550,000 francs, without engines. In 1933 eight more examples were ordered, following the report on the 127 M; the order was for the equivalent number of Blériot 137 M (see later).

The prototype of the production model, was named 127-2 M, flew for the first time on the 10th January 1928. It was fitted with 550 hp Hispano-Suiza 12 Hb V engines as well as radiators under the wings. The front of the fuselage was modified, slightly higher; it had a step on its lower surface. Natural light for the cabin came through several openings, including a large one in front. The bomb sight however, was eliminated. The front gunner's turret was equipped with a protective casing. Collapsible air deflectors were fitted to the wings to protect the machine gunners installed to the rear of the engine nacelles. Also for ease of access to the cockpit, four steps were let into the right wing alongside the fuselage. Certain machines were fitted with a hand rail, others with two hand rails. It entered service on the 8th April 1929 with the 11th Aviation Regiment in Metz, 8 Squadron, then in 1930, 4 Squadron; these twin engine aircraft were in service until 1933.

- *Span*: 23.20m
- *Length*: 14.50m
- *Height*: 3.40m
- *Wing area*: 88m²
- *Empty weight*: 3,252kg
- *All up weight*: 4,466kg
- *Maximum speed*: 221km/h
- *Ceiling with full load*: 8,100m

Fuselages of Blériot 127 under construction, with a sand-yacht behind.

On the 127-2, the radiators were placed under the wings.

The Blériot 127-2 no 15.

The cockpit of a Blériot 127 M.

With the Amoit 122, the Blériot took part in numerous manoeuvres. However, several accidents, apparently unexplainable, happened to this machine, each time causing the loss of the crew and the destruction of the machine. The accidents of the 127, coming always at high speed, came from two phenomenon : - the "floating" of the wing in flexion and above all in torsion, oscillation "flutter" of the tail surfaces. In both cases the outcome was fatal, either by the break up of the wing, or by the detaching of the tail surfaces. In the absence of survivors able to explain the reason for the accidents, there was strong emotion in the Ministries, in Parliament and in the Commission of Enquiry, harassed by the press.

In order to attempt to remedy this unknown problem, the wing structure was reinforced several times, and the engine mounts in a more resistant metal were fitted. The weight of the machine rose, therefore, from 4,500 kg to 5,700 kg without notable improvement. To counter this, to lighten the aircraft, the four wheeled undercarriage was replaced by two Blériot internally sprung wheels. Despite numerous tests carried out by Captain Bogard at Villacoublay, no solution appeared. Instead of reinforcing the wing, which only served as an unnecessary increase in weight, the only remedy was to balance the control surfaces.

The solution was discovered in 1933 after the accident of René Paulhan, flying a fighter, saved by his parachute, was able to tell what he had noticed - a vibration of the control surfaces increasing until they were torn off. In consequence, the STIAé [1] recommended, and then imposed, a static balancing of all the control surfaces of all aircraft.

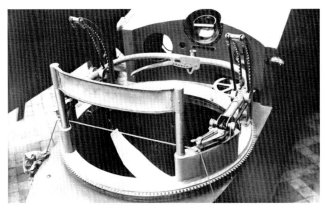

One of the two turrets of the Blériot 127.

A cylindrical corridor was fitted in the thickness of the wing of the Blériot 127 M (here, a 127-2).

(1) Created by Government decree on the 5th November 1926, the Service Technique et Industrial de l'Aéronautique, grouped together the Service Technique de l'Aéronautique and the Service des Fabrications de l'Aéronautique. (Technical and Industrial Aeronautical Service, and the Aeronautical Manufacturing Service)

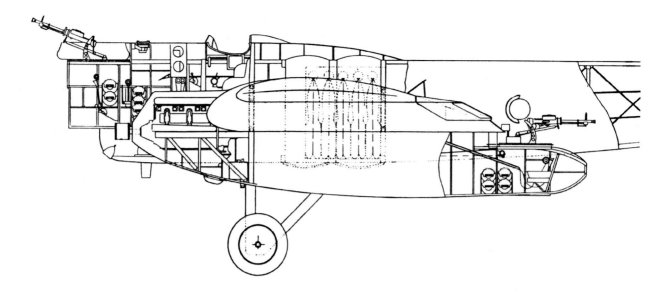

Top, schematic layout of the Blériot 127. Above, the 127-3 remained unique prototype.

The 127-2 M was the subject of an order for a prototype n° 385/7 of the 26th October 1927, then for a production series n° 994/7 of the 31st December 1927, 767/8 of the 15th November 1928, the 344/9 of the 21st August 1929, 588/0 of the 30th October 1930 for a total of forty three machines. One of them was converted to 127-4 with Government agreement.

Designed between the 2nd December 1926 and the 30th December 1927, one 127-3 M was ordered under the n° 385/7 on the 26th October 1927. This was a 127-2 with Hispano-Suiza 12Gb engines of 500hp in W configuration. First flight was on the 20th January 1928. As on the 1237-4 M it was fitted with a bomb sight, with a conical streamlining installed under the front turret.

Blériot 127-2 M

- *Span* : 23.20m
- *Length* : 14.70m
- *Height* : 3.41m
- *Wing area* : 88.0m^2
- *Empty weight* : 3,720kg
- *All up weight* : 5,200kg
- *Ceiling* : 6,850m
- *Max speed* : 189km/h
- *Climb to 4,000m* : 18'18"

Blériot 127-3 M

- *Span* : 14.65m
- *Empty weight* : 3,452kg
- *All up weight* : 4,649kg
- *Ceiling* : 7,500m
- *Max speed* : 203km/h
- *Max speed at 4,000m* : 195km/h
- *Climb to 4,000m* : 14'47"

On the 10th July 1929, the Blériot 127-2 M, n° 22 was tried with an undercarriage with enclosed internally sprung wheels, under the type n° 127-4 M. This aircraft was ordered via an annex to the second production series order. The results were not conclusive, it was returned to it's original state, and handed back to the army.

Blériot 127-4 M

- *Length* : 14.60m
- *Height* : 3.3m
- *Empty weight* : 3520kg
- *All up weight* : 4,717kg
- *Max speed* : 200km/h

The 127-4 with internally-sprung Blériot wheels.

In England, on the 20th anniversary of his Channel Crossing, Louis Blériot explains to Sir Shefton Brancker, Director of British Civil Aviation, the function of the slip-stream deflector protecting the machine gunner of a Blériot 127-2.

On the 27th July 1929, Louis Blériot went to Dover then to London on the 20th Anniversary of his Channel Crossing. Accompanied by Bossoutrot, he made the journey there and back from Buc on board the Blériot 127-4 M. The same day, Blériot became Commandeur de la Légion d'Honneur.

On the 17th October following, parachute jumps were tested at Villacoublay from a specially modified Blériot 127-2 M, the n° 15. In September 1930, five 127s led by Colonel Duseigneur flew to Bucharest for an international meeting. At the request of the Member of Parliament, Charles Delesalle, a Blériot 127 fitted with balanced control services, was tested in December 1933 at Villacoublay, which showed the necessity of balancing the control services. This balancing however, was not carried out on the Blériot 127 already in service, the Armée de l'Air (French Air Force) opposing this. It seemed abnormal at this time to put lead into aircraft. Further, the construction method of the 127 was out of date. The thirty-four examples already delivered became, as a consequence, instruction aircraft at the beginning of 1934 and were then struck-off on the 1st January 1935. Ten days after the first flight of the 127-2 M, on the 20th January 1928, the 127-3 M, fitted with larger ailerons, and like the 127-1 M, 500 hp Hispano-Suiza 12 Gb engines, took off. In October 1929 a gun turret by Saint-Chamond was tried on this machine, which was struck-off in October 1932.

The same year 1929, a study was made for the Blériot 127-5M to be fitted with two Loraine "Petrel" engines of 600hp, the U/C was to be in metal with internally sprung wheels, plus a larger wing surface. This project was not approved by the Air Ministry.

- Span : 26m
- Length : 14.65m
- Height : 3.55m
- All up weight : 4,80kg
- Ceiling : 8,000m
- Max speed at ground level : 212km/h.

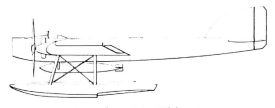

The project of the Blériot 128.

Blériot 128. Yugoslavia requested the design of the type 128, a seaplane derived from the 127, "bombing and combat" with two Jupiter engines series 6 of 500hp. A drawing shows it carrying a torpedo. It was presented without success to a CEDANA in 1928.

- Span : 29 m
- Length : 17.50m

- Height : 5.54 m
- Wing area : 136m²
- Empty weight : 4,700kg
- All up weight : 7,000kg
- Theoretical ceiling : 5,000m
- Max speed at ground level : 180km/h.

Blériot 185. Two other extrapolations of the 127, the commercial 185 of 1930, and the 227 BN4, would remain as simple pre-projects. The 185 was to be a twin engined flying laboratory destined for the adaptation of various engines to a high wing configuration inspired by the wing of the 127. Their aerodynamic influence would be studied. A model with wheels and floats went to the Eiffel wind tunnel.

- Estimated span : 8.90m
- Length : 5.25m
- Height : 1.55m

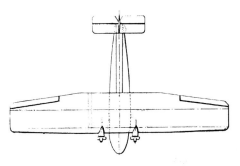

Plan sketch of the project of the Blériot 185.

Blériot 227. The 227 would have been a four-seat night bomber with rounded wing tips. It would have been fitted with two Gnome et Rhône K14 engines in October 1932.

- Span : 26.0m
- Length : 14.65m
- Height : 3.50m
- Wing area : 96.50m²
- All up weight : 5,500kg
- Ceiling : 11,200m
- Max speed at ground level : 220km/h.

Blériot 137. Derived from the high winged 127, the all-metal Blériot 137 M, was a multi-crew combat aircraft, fitted with two 500 hp Hispano-Suiza 12 Nb engines.

Its principal design point was that its lateral gun turrets were no longer in the engine nacelles, but were integrated into the sides of the fuselage, with a cut out in the trailing edge of the wing. The bomb bay, of a capacity of 500 kg, complete with a vertical camera was placed at the centre of gravity of the machine, the crew was made up of five men, two pilots and three machine gunners. The Government ordered three machines on the 12th December 1928, of which one would be for static tests.

The prototype, reference 137 M-o, flew for the first time at Buc on the 21st December 1930. It complied with the day and night bomber programme, called "Combat Multi-crew", dating from 1928. This programme would give the four following orders, for a total of 9,647,500 francs. Blériot 137:- two machines (3,400,000 F), a Breguet 411 (2,549,750 F), a Breguet 412 (2,549,750 F), a Breguet 412 modified to a 413 (1,175,000F).

Take off of the Blériot 137 at Buc.

The Blériot 137 M no 01, a multi-crew combat aircraft with Hispano-Suiza engines of 500hp, 21st December 1930.

The Blériot 137 M no 02, with Salmson radial engines of 500hp.

The second prototype, referenced 137 M-1 with two 500 hp air-cooled radial Salmson 18 Ab engines, had a larger empennage and a larger cut away on the trailing edge. The machine was equipped with a radio transceiver with a range of 600 kilometres. It was equipped for night flying, and as well as its three turrets, had an extra machine gun mounted on a swivel with a downward field of fire, through a hatch in the bottom of the fuselage. It flew for the first time shortly after the 137 M-0. In 1932 the 137 M-0 was fitted with two super-charged 650 hp Hispano-Suiza engines. Quatremare flew the second prototype in September of the following year to the S.T.I.Aé., where it was tested by Lieutenants Génin and Lecarme.

The same year (1933) General Denain Chief of the Air Staff, at the request of the Air Minister, Pierre Cot, replaced the programme of Combat Multi-crew aircraft by Multi-crew BCR (Bombing Combat Reconnaissance). This new programme was established conforming to the Government Decree of the 1st April 1933, which re-defined the needs of the *Armée de l'Air*. This caused the cancellation for an order of eight Blériot 137s, which had just been placed. This order was off-set to an equivalent number of 127s. The 137 had initially been judged unstable by the test pilots, because of its turrets integrated into the sides of the fuselage, and also because of the un-cowled engines fitted too close to the thick wing.

- *Span* : 23.0m
- *Height* : 3.25m
- *Empty weight* : 3,320kg
- *Max speed* : 220km/h
- *Length* : 14.20m
- *Wing area* : 93.44m^2
- *All up weight* : 5,380kg
- *Ceiling* : 7,000m.

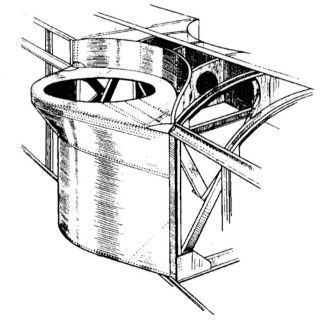

One of the two turrets inset into the Blériot 137.

The Blériot 137 M no 02. The lateral turrets were armed with twin machine guns.

The Blériot 195-2 completed on the 18th January 1929, made its maiden flight 9th March 1930.

Blériot 195. An extrapolation of the 127, the Blériot 195-1, designed by Léon Kirste, was a four-engined postal seaplane, with a 45 metres span, designed for the crossing of the Atlantic, via Iceland and Greenland. This design was never built but a model was tested in the Eiffel wind tunnel. A second design, based on a machine of more modest dimensions, referenced 195-2, was started in 1927. With this model, Blériot wanted to carry out the crossing of the Atlantic, from France to America, and gave the preparation of this flight to his elder son, also called Louis. The young man, engineer and pilot like his father, came to work in his father's factory straight after his military service. Starting from the bottom and going through all the departments, he was then named Director of the Purchasing Department.

The crossing of the Atlantic had haunted pilots' minds for several years already, but the exploit of Lindburgh, landing in triumph at Le Bourget the night of 21st to 22nd May 1927, created a great admiration for the performance of the pilot, but intensified in France the wish to return the compliment in the opposite direction. As for Lindbergh, when he arrived he was asked if he had any particular wish, he replied:

"Yes, I would like to meet Louis Blériot"! During a dinner organised a few days later in honour of the two men, Blériot complemented the American pilot:

"I admire you enormously, you remained more than thirty-three hours at the controls of your machine where as, for me, the crossing lasted hardly more than thirty-three minutes".

And Lindbergh replied with humour (but perhaps he really thought it!):

"You know M. Blériot, I admire you even more, because if I was asked to do my crossing again, I would perhaps do it, but never would I have risked myself above the Channel on board your aeroplane"!

The 195-2 was a low winged monoplane built in wood and fabric. It was equipped with a four-wheel undercarriage, identical to that of the 127. The engines were placed in tandem above the wings on either side of the fuselage. The two traction engines were 250 hp Hispano-Suiza 6 Mbr with reduction gear, and the pusher engines were 250 hp Hispano-Suiza 6 Mb, without reduction gear. It weighed 850 kg, could reach 192 km/h, and had an endurance of 20 hours. Eight fuel tanks (4 of 700 litres and 4 of 500 litres) were fitted in the thickness of the wings, suspended from beams of high resistant steel tube.

Work was started on the 29th October 1927, the machine, designed with large circular portholes, was completed on the 18th January 1929. The crew planned for the transatlantic flight was

made up of the young Louis Blériot, Lucien Bossoutrot, and the Lieutenant de Vaisseau Pierre Crespry, a giant of 100 kg engaged as pilot/navigator. Twenty years after the Channel Crossing, what beautiful symbol of continuity it would be for the house of Blériot, that this crossing of the Atlantic should be accomplished by the son of the pioneer ...

Louis Blériot and his family received Charles A. Lindbergh. On the right, Charles Fontaine, the journalist of the Channel Crossing. Below, the menu of the dinner given in the honour of Blériot and Lindbergh.

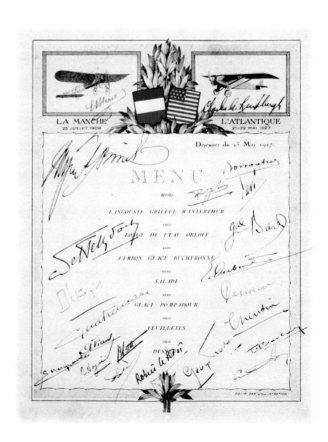

The Blériot 195-3, arriving at Caudebec, will be hoisted from the Seine by a crane whose hook can be seen in the shadow on the fuselage.

Unfortunately, on the 20th February, the young Louis, aged 24, died from a septicaemia following peritonitis. So taken up was he by the preparation of the flight, he put off several times an appendix operation, which, evolving into peritonitis was fatal for him.

This loss touched the victor of the Channel deeply. Visibly worn by the emotions and worries which had marked his life, he counted on this son, that everybody found brilliant, to second him, and later take over the management of the Company.

Immediately, this loss led Louis Blériot to renounce all attempts on the North Atlantic. On the 9th March 1929, the Blériot 195-2 took off from the aerodrome of Buc for the first time, in the hands of Bossoutrot. The four fuel tanks of 700 litres installed for the transatlantic flight were removed. A few days later, the two Hispano-Suiza engines with reduction gear were replaced by engines of the same mark and same power, but without reduction gear. Further, from information given by Bossoutrot, the horizontal tail plane was doubled, becoming a bi-plane configuration. The aircraft received a temporary registration F-AJIK. It was then transformed into a seaplane by the installation of floats designed by the engineer Blanchard, becoming the 195-3; it was still capable of receiving four supplementary tanks of 700 litres.

It was launched on the Seine in front of the factory at Suresnes on the 4th September 1929. Trials were carried out to test the floats over a two day period, and the aircraft took off for the first time at dawn on the 6th September. On board were Bossoutrot, Crespy and the engineer Kirste. Estimating that the stretch of water between the bridge at Suresnes and the bridge at Saint Cloud was too short to land the machine, Bossoutrot decided to go directly to Caudebec-en-Caux, where in any case, the tests were to be carried out. Because of fog he had to land near to Duclair, just short of Caudebec. Towards eleven o'clock after dissipation of the fog, it was impossible to re-start the engines of the 195-3, the bottles of compressed air needed for starting, were empty. It was only towards four o'clock in the afternoon, after having received new bottles from Suresnes, that the machine could take off again and finally reach Caudebec.

- Span : 23.0m
- Height : 4.31m
- Empty weight : 4,600kg
- Max speed at ground level: 192.350km/h
- Length : 14.95m
- Wing area : 90.0m²
- All up weight : 6,500kg

Louis Blériot's son indicates the transatlantic route that he will take with Bossoutrot in the Blériot 195-2. He is holding the model of the 195-2 in his hand.

Whilst "Bobosse" (Bossoutrot's nick-name) went to the hotel La Marine in Caudebec for the duration of the tests, Crespy was employed as pilot by the Amiot Works, whose factory was in the same area. After having carried out performance tests at the hydro base of Mureaux, the reconditioned 195-3, was brought back to the company to be fitted with air-cooled engines. Powered by four 230 hp Gnome and Rhône Titan engines, the seaplane, which had become the 195-4, took off again from the Seine on the 4th March 1930. Presented at the official selection, for multi-engine postal seaplanes, destined for the transport of a 1,000 kg of post between Marseille and Algiers, it would be in competition with a twin engine Villiers 32 and the three-engined Loire 60. None of these three aircraft would be produced in series.

Re-converted to a land plane and fitted with two large Blériot internally sprung wheels, the 195-4 became the 195-6. The fuselage was lengthened by 1.4 metres and painted overall in white. Under this configuration it carried out a new "first flight" on the 24th April 1931. With a useful load of nearly two tons, it was able to obtain a Letter of Intent from the Air Union Company, but the project was never finalised. From this moment on the machine would only carry out demonstration flights at meetings. Then, coming back definitively to Suresnes, it was dismantled in 1934.

The Blériot 195-4, was the 195-3 fitted with radial engines.

- *Span* : 23.20m
- *Height* : 4.0m
- *Empty weight* : 3,683kg
- *Ceiling* : 4,200m
- *Length* : 16.10m
- *Wing area* : 94.48m^2
- *All up weight* : 6,500kg
- *Max speed* : 191km/h

The Blériot 195-6, was the 195-4 lengthened and fitted with wheels.

As for the type 195-5 it was a design study carried out by Kirste in 1929, for a commercial four-engine aircraft, which was abandoned in favour of the bi-fuselage Blériot 125.

The Blériot 270

An "aerial cruiser" with four 1000 hp engines, laid out as on the 195, the Blériot 270, with a 44 metre span and 20 tons take off weight, would never leave the drawing board. The project was presented without success at a CEPANA in April 1931.

- *Span* : 44.0m
- *Height* : 5.0m
- *Empty weight* : 11,900kg
- *Ceiling* : 9,300m
- *Length* : 27.0m
- *Wing area* : 250m^2
- *All up weight* : 20,000kg
- *Max speed* : 285km/h

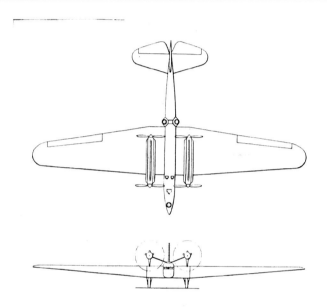

The Blériot 111, 330 and 430

Blériot 111-1. A large single-engine touring aircraft, the Blériot 111, forerunner of today's business aircraft, was designed by André Herbemont in 1927. The first 111, later called the 111-1, was a monoplane whose low wings were connected by rigid struts to the lower part of the undercarriage. The two-place cockpit had an opening roof. The four-place cabin received natural light from eleven portholes, four on the right, four on the left, and three above. Later models, equipped with an undercarriage without cross-axle, would be fitted with oblique struts linking the fuselage to the top of the wing. Fitted with a 250 hp 6-cylinder in-line Hispano-Suiza engine with reduction gear, it was shown to the public at the Salon de Berlin in 1928. It flew for the first time on the 24th January 1929, piloted by Bossoutrot, one year and a few days after the start of the construction. Blériot-Aéronautique gave out this description: -

Construction in wood and fabric. Wings fixed to the fuselage by joints allowing the wing to pivot, either in dihedral or in sweep-back, thus allowing the testing on this machine engines of different weights, the correct centre of gravity obtained by moving the wings.

The undercarriage carries two struts which support the wings, one–third distance from the wing root.

The cantilever system allows wings of medium thickness, an easy setting by means of masts, the longerons in the cabin reduced to compression tubes of low height.

The wing is built absolutely rigid in torsion between the strut attachment points, but can be slightly warped by the adjustment in the struts (...)

A section sliding out from the trailing edge served as a boarding step for the passengers of the Blériot 111-1.

The Blériot 111-1, whose port holes were converted to windows during the build.

The fuselage is in wood made up of four longerons, the cabin is made up of two halves of a monocoque, above and below. The sides are covered in thin plywood. (...) There were problems with the cooling and the reduction gear, the aircraft was converted to a 111-4 in 1930. (see later)

Blériot 111-2. In the meantime the Blériot 111-2 appeared, (at first called the 111 bis) with a 230 hp Lorraine radial engine with reduction gear. Completed on the 10th September 1929, the machine, fitted with a larger rudder and narrower ailerons lodged in the wings, and wide track undercarriage, with deep range. It had two struts reinforcing the wings from the upper surface to the top of the fuselage and a jettissonable fuel tank, *"placed squarely at the centre of gravity"*. It had its first flight on the 1st October following.

The Blériot 111-2 at Suresnes.

Blériot 111-3. Neither the engine nor it's NACA cowling were satisfactory, it was returned to the factory in order to be fitted with a Gnome and Rhône "Jupiter" engine of 420 hp. It became therefore, the type 111-3 and flew for the first time on the 12th March 1930. In April 1932, the aircraft obtained it's Certificate of Airworthiness, n° 2230, and the registration F-ALND. Weighing 2618 kg, it reached 195 km/h at ground level with pilot and five passengers. It was painted blue and silver (André Herbemont's favourite colours) as were all the 111 models, in 1933 it was part of the Blériot Patrol. This Patrol was formed of the 111-3 piloted by Quatremare, two Spad 922 flown by Massotte and Seitz, and a Blériot type Channel Crossing, piloted by Rémy Clément, and participated at numerous aerial meetings in the 1930s, guaranteeing an undeniable success. After 260 flying hours, the Blériot 111-3 was purchased by René Arrachart. On the 24th August 1936, F-ALND flown by Rémy Clément, flew off to Spain where

the Civil War had just started. The machine reached Barcelona, but its final fate remains unknown.

The 111-2 became the 111-3 after an engine change.

The modern silhouette of the Blériot 111-3.

Blériot 111-4. The model 111-4 (ex 111-1) flew on the 16th October 1930. It was fitted with a more powerful engine, a 400 hp 12-cylinder Hispano-Suiza. It had a new wing with a 17 metre span, and metal spars and wooden ribs. Lamblin radiators were fitted under the fuselage. The most important modification was the fitting of a retractable undercarriage, complete with Blériot internally sprung wheels. The undercarriage was retracted by a cable, first of it's kind in France, the undercarriage retracted laterally to the outside. Flight tested on the 27th October 1930, with the undercarriage retracted, the 111-4 reached a speed of 235 km/h. In 1931 the cable system was replaced by a screw system, the manoeuvre was still manual, and required ninety-six turns of the handle. The wheels were advanced 15cm.

For the Twelfth Salon de l'Aéronautique, the machine was shown at the Grand Palais, with the undercarriage half retracted. The 400 hp Hispano-Suiza 12 Jb was replaced in 1932 by a 12 Mbr of 500 hp, then by a 12 Mb of the same power, but without reduction gear. At the end of October, the aircraft was handed over by Quatremare to the STIAé. The registration was F-ALZE, the machine was struck off the Veritas register in 1934.

The Blériot 111-1 was extensively modified to become the 111-4.

Blériot 111-5. On the Blériot 111-5 designed in May 1932, the pilot was placed to the rear of the fuselage, completely to the left side, the passengers, a baggage hold and a wash basin being positioned at the front. Christened *Sagittaire*, this monoplane was powered by a 500 hp Hispano-Suiza 12 Mbr engine, (reduction gear 1/1.61) with an extension to a three-bladed Ratier propeller. As well as the front Chausson radiator, other heat radiating elements were lodged in the leading edge of the wing. The machine could carry 725 litres of fuel, against 515 litres for the previous 111 models. Its maximum speed was 255 km/h, and it's radius of action 1300 kilometres. Flying for the first time on the 16th October 1932, the aircraft was shown at the Salon at the end of the year. In the first days of 1933, the 500 hp Hispano-Suiza was replaced by a 670 hp Gnome and Rhône 14K radial engine; this engine allowed the removing of the radiating elements from the wing.

Blériot 111-6. The 111-5 was fitted with a four-bladed wooden Chauvière propeller and a larger rudder (to become the 111-6). It participated during the year at several meetings, including the one at Buc. In order to increase the speed even further, in 1934 the aircraft had a total re-work of its wing, the concave profile was changed to a bi-convex, the ailerons were divided and compensated by the off-set of their hinge, flaps on the lower surface were added. Re-fitted with a new Gnome et Rhône 14 Kdrs engine, whose power went up to 725 hp, the machine, which was now known as 111-6 took off for the first time in May 1934, piloted by Quatremare. The maximum speed was now 350 km/h.

Despite this high performance, the 111-6 was not ordered by the new National Air Transport Company - Air France - which re-grouped all the previous private companies.

It would however, with six other aircraft, represent France in the McRobertson Trophy, better known under the name of London to Melbourne race, which was to take place between the 20th October and the 4th November 1934. For this trial, the last model of 111 was fitted with radio equipment and supplementary tanks, bringing the fuel capacity to 1,274 litres. With a crew of three men, the machine had a range of 2,500 kilometres. Brought to Villacoublay on the 15th October, five days before the start of the race, the Blériot 111-6, in the hands of Quatremare, obtained it's certificate of Airworthiness (n° 3789) and the registration F-ANJS, in less than twenty-four hours.

Amongst sixty-four competitors entered by eleven countries, the Blériot was to be flown by the crew Massotte, Quatremare and Floret. The six other aircraft selected by France for the race, were not, for different reasons, ready in time, only F-ANJS remained on the list. The initial crew was however replaced by Corniglion, Molinier and Challe, who should have flown the Wibault 366. The reason given by the Air Ministry for the choice of this new crew, were that these were specialists of long distance voyages, and were more qualified than test pilots to lead such a race.

The Blériot 111-5 at the Salon de l'Aviation in Paris 1932, with its cockpit to the rear.

On the right, the re-tractable undercarriage of the 111-4, on the left, that of the 111-5.

The Blériot 111-5 in 1933, with its Gnome et Rhone engine of 670hp.

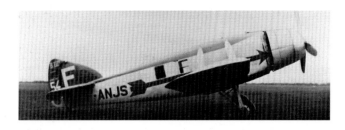

In 1934, the Blériot 111-5 Sagittaire was extensively modified to become the 111-6, with 675hp, a new wing profile and extra fuel tanks. It reached 350km/h.

On the 18th October, F-ANJS was at La Bourget, with tanks full and ready to fly to the airfield at Mildenhall, near London, the starting point for the race. The breakage of a radius arm link on the right hand undercarriage, when the aircraft was taxiing towards the runway, led to the elimination of France from the competition, the repair to the undercarriage would necessitate too long a delay for the Blériot to be ready on time.

The aircraft participated later at numerous aviation meetings until the day when, on the 17th July 1936, the Spanish Civil War started. In France it was the time of the Front Populaire. The 111-6 taken from its hanger, flew off for Spain on the 25th August, piloted by Victor Véniel, a French pilot of the Spanish Squadron, who had just trained André Malraux to come to the help of the Republican Government of Madrid. A difficult landing on a beach near to Barcelona, damaged the undercarriage and propeller. It was then taken to the Air France workshops at Prat de Llobregat to be repaired; it disappeared during the conflict without flying again.

Blériot 330 and 430. In six years, the Blériot 111 had seen its power triple, its weight increase by almost a ton and its speed almost doubled. Two aircraft derived from the Blériot 111, the 330 and the 430, designed in 1931, by the engineer Favre, chief of the design office, remained at the project stage, the Blériot 330 was to have been a transport aircraft of 1,000 hp, with retractable undercarriage, for eighteen passengers.

- *Span* : 29.0m
- *Length* : 19.20m
- *Height* : 6.65m
- *All up weight* : 11,400kg
- *Wing area* : 100m²
- *Ceiling* : 3,500m
- *Speed* : 250km/h (1)

The 430 was to have been a small day bomber with an 860 hp Hispano-Suiza 12 Ybrs engine, and retractable undercarriage.

- *Span* : 14.60m
- *Length* : 9.40m
- *Height* : 2.75m
- *All up weight* : 2,500kg
- *Wing area* : 25.0m²

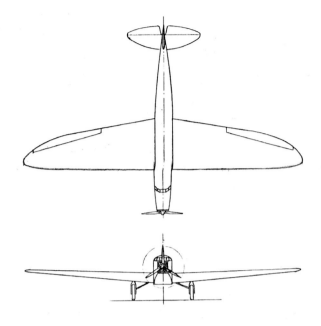

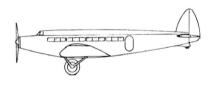

The project of the Blériot 330 transport.

- *Ceiling* : 10,000m
- *Speed at 5,000m* : 350km/h
- *Radius of action at full power* : 500km¹

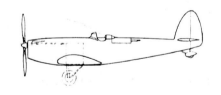

The project of the Blériot 430 bomber, the defence was a retractable turret behind the pilot.

---

(1) This data is shown on hand written notes of Blériot-Aéronautique, but some seem to have been badly copied.

The Blériot 110 newly finished in the Blériot factory in Suresnes.

The Blériot 110, 230, BZ 4 and BZ 5

Blériot 110. In 1929, the technical department of the Air Ministry, the head of which was M. Albert Caquot, wanted France to regain the distance and duration records that it had held for a long time. With the support of M. Laurent-Eynac, Air Minister, Albert Caquot issued a specification to aircraft builders, concerning a long range aircraft. A minimum range of 7,000 kilometres was specified, with a view to crossing the North Atlantic without stops. Several builders with good reputations came forward, in particular, Bernard, Blériot and Dewoitine, whose three projects were ordered by the Government, one prototype per builder. Designed by the engineer Zappata, the Blériot project presented on the 7ᵗʰ March 1929, and was accepted on the 18ᵗʰ March by the Commission d'Examen des Projets d'Avions Nouveau de l'Aéronautique.

At left and top, the construction of the rear fuselage in several layers of wooden laths (on the left the fuselage is udside down). In the centre, the fuselage and wing fuel tanks. Above, a wing, a metal structure as was the front section of the fuselage.

The undercarriage and the narrow keel of the fuselage of the Blériot 110.

BLÉRIOT
AÉRONAUTIQUE

SOCIÉTÉ ANONYME

3, Quai du Maréchal Galliéni
SURESNES (Seine)

Téléphone : WAGRAM 89-05, 89-06, 93-05

Avion BLERIOT 110, à Moteur Hispano-Suiza 500 CV à réducteur.
(Détenteur du record du Monde de distance en circuit fermé).

AVIONS BLÉRIOT
AVIONS GUILLEMIN

AVIONS SPAD ◆●◆ HYDRAVIONS

ÉCOLE DE PILOTAGE à BUC (près Versailles)

Téléphone : VERSAILLES 10-54

R. C. SEINE 192.223

Above, publicity of Blériot-Aéronautique. Below, the 110 at buc.

Without waiting for the confirmation of the order, in April, Blériot Aéronautique, without even waiting for the results of the wind tunnel model tests (which would be held in July and

October) started work on the aircraft which would carry the reference, Blériot 110, and whose build would be completed at Suresnes on the 9th May 1930. Built entirely of wood, with fabric covering for the wing and the empennage, the 110 was a large monoplane with a high, semi-elliptic wing, of 26.5 metres span. The two main spars were joined at the wing tip by an oblique false spar on which the aileron was hinged. The ribs were in three parts, each element being reinforced by a steel cable. Oil radiators with a capacity of 300 litres, were installed in the leading edge of the wing. The wing was supported by two pairs of struts down to the bottom of the fuselage, and two pairs of struts above the wing, fixed to two vertical struts in streamlined steel tube. This supple support system, with a weight of 92 kg meant that they could avoid the use of rigid lower struts (which would have weighed 240 kg). The fuselage, very narrow, with a lower surface resembling the keel of a sailing boat, it was covered in plywood, moulded on forms, made up of three layers of strips of tulip wood, 5 centimetres wide, crossed at 45°, the whole covered and varnished. The aircraft was fitted with ten fuel tanks, four in the fuselage near to the centre of gravity and six in the wing. The cockpit with dual controls in tandem, had no visibility towards the front, the cabin received natural light only from four portholes in the sides. The engine was an Hispano-Suiza 12 Lb of 600 hp with direct drive[1] driving a two bladed wooden Chauvière propeller. The undercarriage, fitted with bungees, had a track of 3.5 metres.

On Friday 16th May 1930, Lucien Bossoutrot took off in the Blériot 110, from the grass at Buc. During the flight a supply problem caused the pilot, accompanied by Zappata, to land in a field, however, without damage, neither to the machine nor to the crew. On the 1st July 1930, the aircraft was presented to the STIAé, where, twenty-one days later, it made its first official evaluation flight. The Government department insisted upon "unfavourable atmospheric conditions" being added to the list of formalities to be tested, this meant that the machine did not leave the Villacoublay until the 30th August. At a total weight of 8,900 kg fully loaded it was given the number Air 2-1955, and the registration letters F-ALCC, whilst waiting for it's Certificate of Airworthiness.

The recognised range was 8,675 kilometres. During the trials they found a maximum speed at ground level of 220 km/h, a climb to 5,000 metres with a load of 5,300 kg in 60 minutes, a ceiling, at maximum weight, of 2,000 metres and a take-off run in zero wind, in 47 seconds, over 1,200 metres. Such performance figures could be considered perfectly honourable for an aircraft reserved exclusively for distance records. Weighing only 2,700 kg empty, it was capable of lifting a load of more than 6 tons with only 600 hp. Reduced by a maximum in lightness and span, the Blériot was judged solid and very manoeuvrable. The form of the fuselage, "reversed droplet of water", gave the machine excellent lateral stability. F-ALCC with 150 flying hours, only returned to Buc on the 4th September; it was too late in the season to attempt any records in France. On the advice of his friend Georges Pitollet, Bossoutrot, fearful of being overtaken by his two rivals[2] decided to go to Algeria, to a climate better suited for the record attempts.

---

(1) The engine with reduction gear which was fitted in June 1931, was first of all refused by Blériot, who estimated that the reduction gear absorbing 2 to 4% of the power, was of no use for a long distance aircraft. He thought also that the reduction gearing would have difficulty resisting a continuous flight of 80 hours.

(2) The Bernard and the Dewoitine

Blériot 110, Joseph-Le-Brix, totalised an impressive number of kilometres flown in very few flights!

On Wednesday 5th November, the silver coloured aircraft took off for the south. Bossoutrot was accompanied by Maurice Rossi, a "pied noir" ("pied noir" is a term used for French nationals born in Algeria) as second pilot and navigator. Between the 15th November 1930 and the 26th March 1932, and after eight attempts, three World Records fell, as shown in the table below. 58,268 kilometres were flown, despite often unfavourable weather conditions, and the absence of any radio communication.

Communication between the machine and the ground were made by means of weighted messages, from the ground to the machine by cloth panels, and at night time, different coloured lamps.

Meanwhile, on the 12th September 1931, during an attempt on the straight line distance record, the Dewoitine D-33 *Trait - d'Union II*, crashed in the USSR following a mechanical problem. In homage to the navigator, the Blériot 110 was christened the *Joseph Le Brix*, at the beginning of 1932.

Despite some help - limited - from the Government, the costs arising from this series of flights, and the maintenance of the aircraft, were too high, they reached 1,000,000 francs, of which 64,562 francs, was spent simply on ground lighting during the nights flights at Oran. Blériot had to give up his records policy, even more so that all of his activities and his resources were from now on orientated towards the transatlantic sea-plane, the *Santos-Dumont*. However, thanks to a press campaign organised in favour of the *Joseph Le Brix*, it was able to continue its flights from 1933 onwards, the Air Ministry accepting the financing. Bossoutrot, retained by the trials of the *Santos-Dumont*, gave his place to Paul Codos, a confirmed long distance pilot. In a very short time, Codos had the aircraft well in hand, he wrote:

"Very quickly I became attached to this new machine whose piloting filled me with ease. A perfect glider, this aircraft gave, empty, an impression of lightness and gentleness comparable to that which one finds with a high performance sail plane".

Congratulatory letter from Laurent-Eynac, Air Minister, for the performance from the 15th to the 18th November 1930, where the World Record for the endurance was beaten by only ywo minutes, in 67h 32 min.

Photo dedicated to Louis Blériot by Boris Rossinsky, ex student of the Blériot flying schools before 1914, during the visit of the Joseph Le Brix to Moscow. Left to right M. Rossi, B. Rossinsky, P. Codos. (22nd September 1933).

The fine silhouette of the Blériot 110 in flight.

Rossi with 600 hours on the Blériot 110 became Chief Pilot. The objective of the crew Rossi-Codos, was the record for straight-line distance, currently held by the Britons, Gayford and Nicholetts, with 8,796 kilometres. The route foreseen was, departure point New York, across the North Atlantic and then overflying Europe and Asia. Dismantled, the record breaking Blériot was loaded at Le Havre on board the S/S *Champlain* in June 1933. Led by Louis Paragot, a factory team made up of Camuratti and Leseigneur as mechanics, and Paris as electrician, accompanied the machine. On arrival in New York, the American Custom service, insisted on a deposit of 500,000 francs, to allow the unloading of the machine. This incident was quickly corrected, thanks to the intervention of the French Ambassador, M. de Laboulaye. The poor weather conditions however, would delay the departure until the 5th August.

Taking off from Floyd Bennett field at 9h 41 GMT, the aircraft carrying 6300 litres of fuel, used up 1000 metres of runway (out of 1250) before taking off. After surviving a storm above the Atlantic, it was seen 30 hours later, above Cherbourg, then a low altitude pass over Le Bourget, at this, the first control point, 5,780 kilometres had already been flown. The *Joseph Le Brix* then overflew Strasbourg, Vienna, and the island of Rhodes where there was a second obligatory control point, for any flight which was supposed to pass 10,000 kilometres[1] At last they could descend over Cyprus and Beirut. Giving up the idea of reaching Baghdad, where they would have had to land at night, Codos and Rossi landed at Rayak in Syria on the 7th August, at 18h 10 GMT, after a non-stop flight of 9,104.7 kilometres, in 55 hours 29 minutes, at an average speed of 165 km/h. The Commandant Pelletier-Doisy, himself an old long-distance pilot, and numerous French pilots in the Levant, were there to welcome the two men. The World Record for straight line distance was beaten and would remain French for almost four years. (it would only be beaten on the 12th July 1937 by the USSR with a flight of 10,148 kilometres by an Antonov 25/1)

(1) At this moment the two men had all the reasons to believe that they would go over this distance.

RECORDS OF THE BLERIOT 110

Dates	Kilometres Covered	Duration of Flight (h and m)	Circuit	Comments
15 to 18/11/30	7,701	67h 32m	Oran - Oran (1)	5,900 l of fuel and 200 l of oil. Landing because of high oil consumption. French duration and distance record for closed circuit. The World duration record (67h 30m) was beaten; it had to be raised by more than one hour to be valid.
9 to 10/12/30	3,342	27h 31m	Oran - Oran (1)	Attempt interrupted by storm. On the 20th December, a mechanic cleaning the inside of the fuselage dropped an inspection lamp. This set the fuel vapours on fire. The fire was quickly put out, but it took fifteen days for the plywood to dry out from the water from the fire brigade.
27 to 29/1/31	6,739	56h 27m	Oran - Oran (1)	Attempt stopped by a storm. Weather conditions remained unfavourable till end of February.
26/2 to 1/3/31	8,822	75h 23m	Oran - Oran (1)	Take-off distance of 1,400 metres and 58 seconds at an all up weight of 7,825 kg (6,250 l of fuel). World record duration and distance in closed circuit.
29/4 to 1/5/31	7,167	57h 07m	Oran - Oran (1)	On the 4/4, Paillard and Mermoz took the record up to 8,960 kilometres. A sand storm forced the 110 to abandon after 57 hours. Whilst the crew, in view of the poor weather persisting in AFN, decide to fly to Istres, Doret and Le Brix took the distance record to 10,342 kilometres.
22 to 24/6/31	7,900	61h 45m	Istres- Bordeaux - Etampes- Istres	The storm crossed the Mediterranean, causing the 110 to interrupt its attempt (it also had a fuel leak) During the stop, the engine was changed to an Hispano-Suiza 6 Mbr of 500 hp with reduction gear, fitted with a four-bladed Chauvière propeller. The fuel capacity was raised to 7,750 l by the addition of 2 wing tanks. A Radio-Industrie AC 3 was fitted.
22 to 24/1/32	6,005	44h	Oran - Oran	Return in AFN after leaving Buc on the 9/11/31, with technical stops at Marignane and Alicante. A burnt out magneto stopped the attempt.
23 to 26/3/32	10,601	76h 34m	Oran - Oran	Torrential rains soaked the field at Oran. The wheels were replaced by others with larger diameter. The World Record for distance in closed circuit beaten, despite a leak in a fuel tank and a thick mist.

The Blériot 110 fitted with wheel spats and aileron balance tabs, in the form of a "garden seat" (beginning of 1935)

The return to France was on the 10th August. F-ALCC landed at Marignane where Louis Blériot was waiting for the day's heroes to congratulate them personally; he had thought to bring the wives of the two pilots by plane. On the 15th a triumphant arrival at Le Bourget brought this flight, crowned with success to a close.

In September 1933, the Blériot 110 was sent to the USSR, where it participated in a presentation of French goods in front of the Soviet authorities, on the occasion of an official visit of the Air Minister, M. Pierre Cot. On its return, the machine received a certain number of modifications, mostly as a result of the experience of the last flights, the ailerons were balanced, the fuel vapour[2] in the fuselage which upset the crew was eliminated and the wheels were fitted with spats, which gave an increase in speed of 15 km/h. The *Joseph Le Brix* would now attempt to improve its own record, but in the direction Europe to America. The season was not favourable for a crossing towards the coast of South America, it was the North Atlantic route which was chosen. At 5.15 a.m. on the 27th May 1934, the 110 took off from Le Bourget, destination San Francisco. The take off was touch and go, the aircraft ran the 1800 metres of the runway, the aircraft just about jumped the river Morée which crossed the end of the runway, and was climbing hard at one metre above the ground. Codos managed to avoid a line of high tension cables, but brushed the summit of a line of trees. Vibrations caused the crew, still Rossi and Codos, to land in New York on the 28th May at 18.38 p.m. It was the reinforcing of the leading edge of one of the propeller blades which, in being torn off was the cause. Furthermore, a branch was found stuck under one of the wheel spats. Even though, with 2,800 litres of fuel in it's tanks, F-ALCC could have covered another 4,000 kilometres, there was no question of records in the immediate future. After repairs to the propeller, the machine took off for Canada, fitted with modern American navigation instruments, one of them a Sperry Artificial Horizon. The *Joseph Le Brix* made stopovers at Montreal and Quebec, then returned to New York via Chicago, despite the bad weather which forced the crew to fly very low following the St. Laurence river. After dismantling, the aircraft was reloaded on the *Champlain*, then reassembled at Le Havre. It took off from here for Le Bourget, where during a military ceremony, Codos was decorated, and Rossi was promoted to Captain.

Brought back to the factory, F-ALCC was entirely checked over with a view to a new attempt, this time on the South Atlantic. At 6.36 a.m. on the 16th February 1935, the Blériot 110, weighing 8720 kg, took off from Istres for Santiago de Chile, covering 990

metres of the runway in 40 seconds. Accompanied by two Bloch bombers which should have escorted it to the Spanish frontier, the *Joseph Le Brix* rapidly left them behind!

After 31h 40m and 6,000 kilometres flown, F-ALCC was at 1,500 kilometres from Natal, when, at daybreak, Rossi noticed through a porthole, the machine was covered with large streaks of oil. Whilst Rossi sent out an SOS. giving their position, Codos turned round to try and make the field of Porto-Praia, on the island of Sao Taigo, one of the islands of the Cape-Verdi group, 800 kilometres away. At the end of four hours of worry and tension, during which the two pilots expected at any moment that the engine, emptying itself of oil, would give up the ghost, the Blériot 110 succeeded in reaching Porto-Praia and landed without difficulty. For this exploit, the crew was warmly congratulated by the French authorities. However, when Jean Mermoz proposed to fly Lesigneur and Camuratti to the site of the forced landing of the *Joseph Le Brix* - in less than 48 hours, the Air Minister would not allow this, under the pretext that there was no aircraft available, which meant that the mechanics only arrived by boat, in mid March.

The oil scavenge pump, the cause of the break down, was replaced, the engine was reassembled and run in. On the 14th March the Blériot took off again heading for Buc. The 4,700 kilometres of the route were accomplished in 24h 45m. On arrival at Buc, having flown 10,700 kilometres since leaving Istres, there still remained 535 litres of fuel in the sealed tanks.

- *Span* : 26.50m
- *Height* : 4.90m
- *Empty weight* : 2,700kg
- *Max speed* : 220 then 211km/h
- *Length* : 14.57m
- *Wing area* : 81.0m²
- *All up weight* : 6,200kg

Heavily criticised, an object of jealousy, the *Joseph Le Brix* was struck off the Veritas register, and was now condemned. Even though the CEMA[3] had judged highly satisfactory it's flying qualities, the departure of M. Caquot, Technical Director to the Air Ministry, the sponsor of the aircraft, would only precipitate its abandon. Its career thus completed, after five years of effort, crowned by a host of records, but it's possibilities had not yet been fully exploited. Its radius of action, raised to 13,000 kilometres, would have allowed the Blériot 110 to increase the series of its successes for several more years, if it had not been victim to systematic criticism.

---

(2) Anti detonation additive

(3) In 1933 the test flights section of the STIAé, the GAN, the test centre for arms and navigation in Cazaux and the CEPA in S. Raphaël were grouped together for civil and military testing within a new organisation, the CEMA.

Blériot BZ 4, BZ 5, 230 and 260. The BZ 4 was a simple pre-project of a long range postal aircraft, designed in 1929 with an Hispano-Suiza 12Nbr engine of 650 hp to show the possibilities of a commercial aircraft derived from the record breaking 110. The BZ 5 of the same time was a pre-project of a reconnaissance aircraft with an Hispano-Suiza 12Nbr engine. The Blériot 230 came later, designed in 1931 was a pre-project of a night bomber with an Hispano-Suiza 12Nb engine of 650hp. The sketches which exist lead to the belief that the military load would have been hung beneath the wings. On the back of the trianglular section of the fuselage there were three open cockpits for the crew. The rear most position was to be armed.

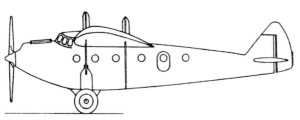

Schematic drawing of the BZ 4 project.

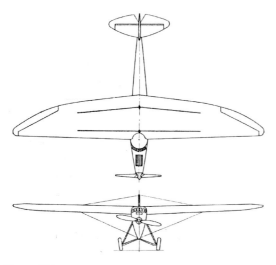

Blériot BZ 4
- *Span* : 22.80m
- *Height* : 4.81m
- *Empty weight* : 2,250kg
- *Ceiling*: 4,500m
- *Length* : 14.50m
- *Wing area* : 65.0m^2
- *All up weight* : 5,400kg

Blériot 230
- *Span* : 23.80m
- *Height* : 4.85m
- *Empty weight* : 2,763kg
- *Ceiling* : 5,000m
- *Max speed at ground level* : 242km/h
- *Length* : 13.90m
- *Wing area* : 65.0m^2
- *All up weight* : 5,600kg

Schematic drawing of the Blériot 230 project.

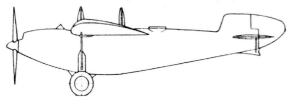

Blériot BZ 5
- *Span* : 18.70m
- *Height* : 3.97m
- *Empty weight* : 1,695kg
- *Ceiling* : 9,000m
- *Max speed at ground level* : 255km/h
- *Length* : 12.75m
- *Wing area* : 50.0m^2
- *All up weight* : 2,815kg

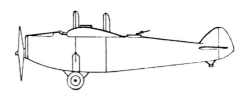

Schematic drawing of the BZ 5 project.

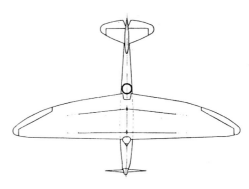

Blériot 260. Filippo Zappata opened this file in December 1931. The designation was given to a single engine high wing transport monoplane. The wing was to be swept back and the undercarriage "to be raised". The engine was to be an Hispano-Suiza 18Sbr of 1000hp. The wind tunnel model was made but the project went no further.
- *Span* : 20.0m
- *Height* : 5.125m
- *Empty weight* : 27,989kg
- *Theoretical ceiling* : 5,000m
- *Max speed at 1,000m* : 310km/h
- *Range* : 3,500km.
- *Length* : 12.775m
- *Wing area* : 51.0m^2
- *All up weight* : 6,123kg

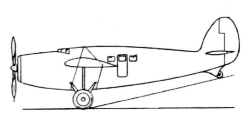

Schematic drawing of the Blériot 260 project.

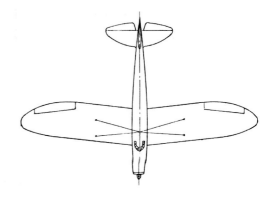

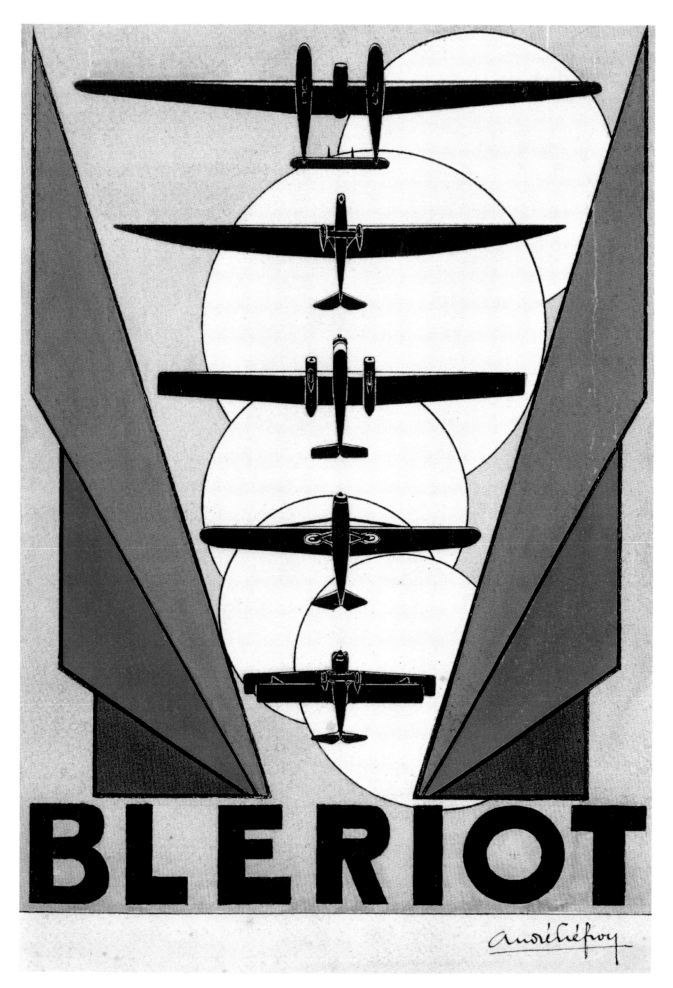

Mock-up of a publicity poster designed by André Piéfroy, representing the Blériot 125, 110, 127, 111 and a SPAD biplane.

The amphibian Blériot 290 at the meeting at Challes-les-Eaux, 15th August 1953.

The Blériot 290

In the first months of 1931, Zappata, who had a preference for seaplanes, started the drawings of a three-seat tourist amphibian. Designed with a hull in wood, with a single step, this machine, the Blériot 290 possessed a sesquiplane wing layout, whose upper wing, of a fairly complex form, was supported by a cabane of steel struts. The lateral floats where attached to the tips of the lower wing. The 230 hp air-cooled Salmson engine was fitted as a pusher. The cabin was equipped with large port holes. The undercarriage, with a track of 2.10 metres, was raised by a screw thread and fitted into hollows in the lower surface of the lower wing. The fuel tanks with a capacity of 215 litres, were also fitted in the lower wing and gave the machine a range of 650 kilometres. Its maximum speed was 215 km/h.

Bossoutrot made the maiden flight of the Blériot 290-01 in October 1931, taking off from the Seine at Suresnes. The aircraft had a Government order for the sum of 540,000 francs. Difficulties with the take off necessitated the fitting of a second step. After land trials at Villacoublay, the all white amphibian was shown at the Salon de l'Aéronautique of 1932, by the side of a Blériot 111-5.

Extract from a presentation brochure of the Blériot 290.

It was then shown at Le Bourget, at the same time as twenty-six other commercial aircraft, during the Merchant Aviation Day, on the 30th April 1933. It also took part, with the Blériot patrol, at the meeting of Challes-les-Eaux on the 15th August following.

Its price was 360,000 francs. This price would later be reduced to 212,000 francs (280,000 francs for the version with a 300 hp Lorraine engine.) The machine shown at Villacoublay in August 1934, would finally be presented to the CEMA on the 13th February 1935 by Massotte. The CEMA used the aircraft for general purposes. Lieutenant Polart appreciated the flying qualities of the aircraft to such a point, that the amphibian was used for liaison for the Chief Engineer Cambois.

Of relatively large dimensions for the engine power, but structurally perfect, the Blériot 290 remained as prototype and was struck off on the 25th April 1937. The Blériot 291 with a Lorraine engine, and the Blériot 292 with a Gnome et Rhône engine, derived directly from the 290, remained in the project stage.

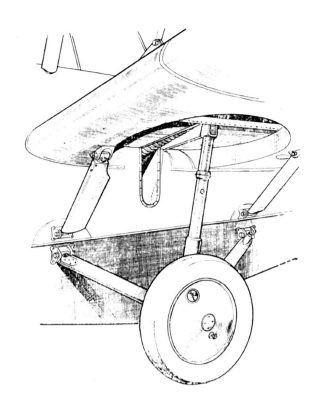

- Span : 14.60m
- Length : 9.77m
- Height : 3.50m
- Wing area : 32.0m²
- Empty weight : 1,250kg
- All up weight : 1,700kg
- Ceiling : 3,700m
- Max speed : 215km/h

Sketch of the retractable undercarriage of the Blériot 290.

The Blériot 509, 390, BZ 2, 5190, 5193, 5194

Blériot 509. On the 7th April 1928, the Air Ministry issued a special specification defining a postal sea plane, for the route Dakar-Natal. The machine had to be multi-engine (preferably four engines which could be maintained in flight) and to be able to carry a ton of post with a four man crew. Replying to this programme, Filippo Zappata did a pre-design in 1929 of a transatlantic seaplane with a 31 metres span. It was the Blériot 509 with four, 220 hp Farman 9 Eb radial engines. It was a fabric covered metal structure. In fact it was destined to experiment with the formula of the much larger BZ 2 (see later) but only a model was made because the Air Ministry had already chosen the 5190.

- Span : 31.0m
- Length : 19.0m
- Height : 4.80m
- Wing area : 115m²
- Empty weight : 4,600kg
- All up weight : 8,500kg
- Ceiling : 4,000m
- Max speed : 197km/h

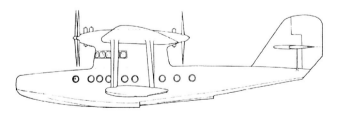

Blériot 390. The following year, within the same programme, the Italian engineer sketched out the drawings of the Blériot 390, a large four-engined seaplane. His project could not be completed; the 1000 hp Hispano-Suiza engines were not available in series production.

- Span : 52.0m
- Length : 33.250m
- Height : 9.0m
- Wing area : 335m²
- Empty weight : 17,700kg
- All up weight : 2,9450kg

- Ceiling : 4,200m
- Max speed : 210km/h

Blériot BZ 2 or 5190. In 1931 the Ministry insisted upon a range of 3,200 kilometres, because of the almost permanent presence of headwinds of 50 km/h, over the South Atlantic. The seaplane had to be able to fly with one engine stopped, and to be able to take off from a rough sea. Zappata therefore looked again at the project 509 and designed an extrapolation, the BZ 2, which became the Blériot 5190. This would later become the project 5193 for the transport of forty passengers on the line Marseilles to Algiers, and project 5194 for the transport of sixty fully equipped soldiers.

Five builders presented their projects, six prototypes were ordered for a total of more than 36,000,000 francs, a CAMS 50/0, a Latécoère 300, a Latécoère 500, a LeO H-27, an SPCA (hull only) and a Blériot 5190. The construction of the Blériot, with an order of 10,720 000 francs, started in December 1931, in the factory in Suresnes.

The hull of the Blériot 5190, launched at Suresnes, in 1932.

The wing centre section of the Blériot 5190.

Building of the hull.

The fitting of the wing of the Blériot 5190. The hull is resting on a cradle in the factory at Suresnes.

The seaplane with a span of 43 metres had a central hull 26 metres long and 3.6 metres wide and two lateral floats. The wing, which rested on a central pylon forming an upper deck, was reinforced by a network of oblique struts linked to the hull and to the floats. The wing structure was built with two main spars and angled false spars serving as supports for the ailerons, (balanced by "garden benches") with box ribs and U profile. This metallic structure made in corrugated sheet, was covered with a classic fabric. The wing area was 236 m².

After having carried out trials of models in the test tank in Rome, Zappata chose a hull design whose form resembled neither that of a ship, nor that of a conventional seaplane. From the bow until the single step, the hull had two small keels.

The completed Blériot 5190 in the factory of Blériot-Aéronautique.

View of the rear engine of the four engined Blériot 5910 Santos-Dumont.

This layout was adopted to avoid the use of a central keel which, on a machine of 20 tons, would have had to measure more than one metre, and would have reduced the manoeuvrability of the machine at low speed. On the contrary, the arch created by a double keel had the objective of making the take off easier, in concentrating the water towards the step. After the step the hull blended into a single keel. The construction of the hull with a metal skin, was based on the principal that the stressed skin would take the effort to the longitudinal ribs and the transversal frames. The engines, three pulling and one pushing, were Hispano-Suiza 12 Nbr, with reduction gear, each one developing 600 hp. They were supplied by sixteen identical capacity fuel tanks, for a total of 11,680 litres, giving the machine a zero-wind range of more than 5000 kilometres. Installed in the wing section, the engines were accessible in flight. The engine start was made with the aid of a Bristol auxiliary engine. The central radiator served for the cooling of the two central engines, fitted in tandem.

The central pylon was the crew area, the crew was two pilots, a navigator, a mechanic and a radio operator. Behind the cockpit was the navigator's position in which there were two sleeping bunks. The noise and the vibrations from the centre engines, would do little to disturb the comfort of the crew. The empennage, whose layout was the subject of a patent, was made up of two horizontal planes and three vertical fins. The elevator was the whole of the upper tail plane, it's profile was bi convex. The lower plane was fitted with a trim, working as a secondary elevator, but controlled by an independent system. The construction of the seaplane was completed in July 1933. For its first flight, it was planned to transport it by road to Buc, where it was to take off by means of a temporary undercarriage. The difficulties caused

by a road convoy of the size, were such that finally the Blériot was dismantled and transported on two barges to Caudebec-en-Caux. The lake, with an average width of 350 metres, was more than 7 kilometres long, situated in a large bend of the Seine. It was in the main central building of the Société d'Emboutissage et de Constructions Mécaniques, (Stamping and Mechanical Construction Company) that the Blériot 5190 was reassembled, following an agreement between Félix Amiot, President of the SECM, and Louis Blériot. In homage to Alberto Santos-Dumont the Franco-Brazilian pioneer, the seaplane, destined for the route France to Brazil, was quite naturally christened with the prestigious name, which was painted in large blue letters on the central pylon.

After a few high speed runs on the 1st and 2nd of August 1933, the first flight was programmed, thanks to the favourable weather forecast, for the morning of the 3rd August. Of course, the river services had been warned that no boat should pass at the moment of take off, the river traffic was normally heavy on this part of the river. The engineers Zappata and the flying mechanic Legendre, took their places by the side of Bossoutrot on board the Blériot. The aircraft rose rapidly up on the step at 160km/h, when, suddenly facing him and coming towards him at about 10 knots, was a ship flying the Swedish flag. In little more than 200 metres - about 5 seconds - Bossoutrot hauled back on the stick and pulled the plane off the water, with engines at full power, he passed just above the funnel of the Swedish ship, which did not even have the time to start to manoeuvre. In the cabin of the *Santos-Dumont*, the crew gave sighs of unbelievable relief. It was not their day!

The Blériot 5190 on the Seine without its Christened name.

Despite such eventful beginnings, the checking of the *Santos-Dumont*, followed regularly through to the month of October 1934. More than 10 km/h faster than its rival the Latécoère 300 the Blériot showed excellent flying qualities, even in turbulent weather conditions. In October 1934 the machine was fitted with new rudders, with better compensation, and its definitive wing tips. It was flown to the lake at Berre. For it's first Mediterranean flight, Bossoutrot lifted the 20 tons of aircraft and load, in only 32 seconds.

With the interior fitting out completed, the aircraft received it's Certificate of Airworthiness, n° 3825, on the 19th November. The registration, F-ANLE was painted in bright black letters on the silver grey hull and on the wing. The Government handed over the Santos-Dumont to Air France. On the 27th November it completed its first crossing, Dakar to Natal, for the new company. Bossoutrot was accompanied for this inaugural voyage, by an Air France crew made up of, Léon Givon-pilot, Paul Comet-navigator, Néri-radio operator, and the mechanics Richard and Legendre. Carrying 112 kg of post it made the 3,046 kilometres trip in 16 hours 45 minutes, at an average speed of 186 km/h, gaining 4 hours on the time taken by the Latécoère 300, whose first crossing was on the 3rd January 1934. The following year with his mission as instructor completed, Bossoutrot handed over command of the Blériot to Givon. Following the bankruptcy in March 1933, of the Compagnie Générale Aéropostale, the airlines of South America saw the disappearance of the French aircraft. By Government decree, on the 30th August 1933, the SCELA, which grouped together four large aviation companies, took the name Air France and benefitted from the status of a nationalised company. The purchase of the Aéropostale by the new company, created a difficult and complex situation for the South Atlantic. The Germans took a calculated risk with the airship *Graf Zeppelin,* and the placing in 1934, in the middle of the Atlantic, of the relay ship *Westfalen,* whose job it was to catapult seaplanes at 1,500 kilometres from the South American coast.

The Blériot 5190 Santos-Dumont was one of the most successful transatlantic airliners of its time.

Different envelopes that crossed the South Atlantic in the hold of the Blériot 5190. The one on the right is addressed to the ex President of the Aéropstale.

THE THIRTY-EIGHT TRANSATLANTIC CROSSINGS OF THE BLERIOT SANTOS DUMONT

Crossing n°	Year	Date	Direction	Crew
1	1934	27-Nov	Dakar - Natal	Bossoutrot-Givon-Richard-Legendre-Néri-Comet
2	1934	03-Dec	Natal - Dakar	"
3	1934	11-Dec	Dakar - Natal	"
4	1934	18-Dec	Natal - Dakar	"
5	1935	04-Feb	Dakar - Natal	Givon-Ponce-Néri-Comet-Richard
6	1935	11-Feb	Natal - Dakar	"
7	1935	18-Feb	Dakar - Natal	"
8	1935	25-Feb	Natal - Dakar	"
9	1935	04-Mar	Dakar - Natal	"
10	1935	11-Mar	Natal - Dakar	"
11	1935	18-Mar	Dakar - Natal	Givon-Rouchon-Néri-Comet-Richard
12	1935	24-Mar	Natal - Dakar	Givon-Ponce-Néri-Comet-Richard
13	1935	07-Apr	Dakar - Natal	"
14	1935	14-Apr	Natal - Dakar	"
15	1935	08-Jul	Dakar - Natal	Givon-Pareyre-Comet-Néri-Richard[1]
16	1935	29-Jul	Natal - Dakar	"
17	1935	05-Aug	Dakar - Natal	Mermoz-Ponce-Guillaumet-Comet-Gimié-Richard[2]
18	1935	26-Aug	Natal - Dakar	"
19	1935	02-Sep	Dakar - Natal	Ponce-Guillaumet-Comet-Néri-Richard
20	1935	13-Oct	Natal - Dakar	Ponce-Guerrero-Comet-Marret-Richard
21	1935	21-Oct	Dakar - Natal	Ponce-Pichodou-Adam-Marret-Richard
22	1935	11-Nov	Natal - Dakar	Mermoz-Ponce-Pichodou-Comet-Gimié-Richard
23	1935	27-Nov	Dakar - Natal	Ponce-Pichodou-Comet-Marret-Richard
24	1935	03-Dec	Natal - Dakar	"
25	1935	23-Dec	Dakar - Natal	Mermoz-Carriou-Comet-Gimié-Richard-Bastié[3]
26	1935	30-Dec	Natal - Dakar	"
27	1936	13-Jan	Dakar - Natal	Mermoz-Pichodou-Lhotellier-Gimié-Richard
28	1936	20-Jan	Natal - Dakar	Mermoz-Rouchon-Lhotellier-Gimié-Richard
29	1936	03-Feb	Dakar - Natal	Ponce-Pareyre-Lhotellier-Marret-Richard
30	1936	24-Feb	Natal - Dakar	Mermoz-Pichodou-Adam-Gimié-Richard[4]
31	1937	05-Apr	Dakar - Natal	Givon-Guerrero-Thomasset-Richard-Comet-Serre[5]
32	1937	12-Apr	Natal - Dakar	"
33	1937	26-Apr	Dakar - Natal	Guerrero-Leclaire-Thomasset-Courson-Comet
34	1937	04-May	Natal - Dakar	"
35	1937	25-May	Dakar - Natal	Guerrero-Leclaire-Salvat-Néri-Courson
36	1937	01-Jun	Natal - Dakar	"
37	1937	14-Jun	Dakar - Natal	Guerrero-Rémy-Salvat-Néri-Courson
38	1937	22-Jun	Natal - Dakar	"

(1)The aircraft underwent a revision from end April to the beginning of July. (2)Difficult take-off facing the land. (3)Maryse Bastié who was herself preparing a crossing of the South Atlantic in a Caudron Simoun, had to make a crossing as a passenger before she could obtain authorisation from the Air Ministry. She was passenger on the the Latécoère 301 Orion, flown by Jean Mermoz, when the aircraft had to cut short the flight to Dakar because of engine troubles. She continued the crossing in the Santos-Dumont. (4)Back in France at the beginning of May, the Blériot 5190 which had flown 100,000km in 500hrs was given a full revision. Starting on the 18th May 1936 at Marignane, the revision lasted almost a year. New engines were fitted, two Hispano-Suiza 12 Nbr and two Hispano-Suiza 12 Ner 17kg lighter than the Nbr and a lower compression ratio. Fuel capacity was raised to 12,200 litres. (5) Serre was director of equipment at Air France.

The Blériot 5190 during its trials.

The fine, balanced silhouette of the Blériot 5190.

For the Americans, they had only a coastal service New York to Buenos Aries from March 1934. In this situation, Air France judged it useful to negotiate with the German Lufthansa, allowing them to benefit from all of the organisation created by France on the South Atlantic, but following a vigorous press campaign led by Joseph Kessel, the General Denain, the Air Minister, refused to sanction the agreement of exploitation, and rejected the proposition. In order to face up to the German competition, Jean Mermoz obtained authorisation from Air France to keep up the crossings. To avoid new expenditure on the purchase of new aircraft, the Air Minister loaned to Air France the *Arc-en-Ciel*, the *Croix-du-Sud* and the *Santos-Dumont*.

At the end of 1934, le Couzinet had carried out eight crossings, six on the Latécoère and four on the Blériot. From the 4th February 1935 the crossings of the South Atlantic became regular, the first and third weeks of each month, crossing France to South America, the second and fourth weeks, crossing South America to France. On the 16th May 1935 a temporary agreement was nevertheless reached with the German Government, concerning alternating departures, uniformity of tariffs and a mutual technical assistance. On the 17th July 1937, a second and definitive agreement, coordinated the time tables for the two companies.

In March 1934, France had carried on the South Atlantic 848 kg of post and Germany 101 kg, in December 1938, these figures were respectively 1,260 kg and 2,025 kg. In four years the ratio had tipped in Germany's favour. After the 5th January 1936, the Air France Despatch boats, whose role up to now had been of major importance on the South Atlantic, were now used only in case of a breakdown of an aircraft. The route France to South America had become totally "aerial". In July 1936 Air France celebrated the 100th crossing "One hundred per cent aerial". This year however, unfortunately, two Latécoère and their crews disappeared over the South Atlantic.[1] The following year, the *Arc-en-Ciel* was sold at public auction, whereas the *Santos-Dumont*, after eight more crossings, was taken out of service. The 38th and last crossing of the Blériot was on the 22nd June 1937. The aircraft was the record holder for post carried over the South Atlantic. The table on page 167 summarises the thirty-eight crossings.

---

(1) The cause of these accidents, a) deforming of the wing, obliging the pilot to hold the "internally sprung" ailerons by violent movement, b) the engine crank shafts which were not capable of adapting to the use of reduction gear, they had to be changed every two crossings c) possible loss of propeller.

The Blériot 5190 at Dakar, waiting for its load to be carried to South America. The cockpit door is open.

As a result of the excellent results obtained by the Blériot, the Air Ministry as early as 1935, placed an order for three more seaplanes with the Blériot Company. In order to undertake such a programme, Louis Blériot had to take out loans. But the order from the Ministry was cancelled shortly after, without indemnity, whereas Blériot had already received some of the material necessary to start the work on the aircraft that had been ordered, and had started on new employees. Such practices were commonplace at the time, the Ministry being the only client of aircraft constructors.[2]

The *Santos-Dumont* had cost Blériot almost 20 million francs, the Government had paid him only the sum foreseen in the order, 10 million francs, plus a few bonuses linked to the trials and the first crossings. The true cost of the *Santos-Dumont* brought about a disagreement with the Government as early as 1935. On the 14th September 1937, the machine, after nationalisation of the Blériot factories, was immobilised at Marignane for more than two months, where it was overhauled for the last time. The aircraft at that time had a total of 1011 flying hours. Taken out of the circuit, Blériot had the Certificate of Airworthiness taken away from him in the first days of 1938. The *Santos-Dumont*, whose technical success had been recognised even by its competitors, was definitively removed from the South Atlantic route,

for reasons which had nothing to do with technical problems. Having remained for a short time on the tarmac of the aerodrome of Marignane, according to Maurice Gaillard, it was taken to the seaplane work shop at Mourillon, in Toulon to serve as a target for bombs and torpedoes. The flying instruments were recovered, the hull was stripped of its equipment, its openings were plugged by sheets of metal. It was then towed out to sea off Saint-Raphael where it was sunk.

Blériot type	5190	5193*	5194**
Span (m)	43	43	43
Length (m)	26	26	26
Height (m)	6.9	6.9	6.9
Empty weight (kg)	11,950	13,000	12,925
Useful load (kg)	10,500	6,420	8,920
All up weight (kg)	2,2000	20,200	21,845
Wing area (m²)	236	236	236
Weight per m² (kg)	93.2		
Weight pr hp (kg)	8.4		
Max speed (km/h)	230	225	214
Cruise speed (km/h)		190/195	180
Range			
With 50 km/h wind	1,200		

* Four Hispano-Suiza 12 Nbr engines of 650hp, with variable pitch propeller, forty passengers.

** Same engines, sixty fully equipped soldiers and two defensive turrets.

(2) The orders for prototypes, were from 1934 onwards, replaced by the "orders of bonuses". Only the aircraft having obtained good results according to the official services, could receive these bonuses. The Blériot 5190 had completely filled it's obligations in this respect.

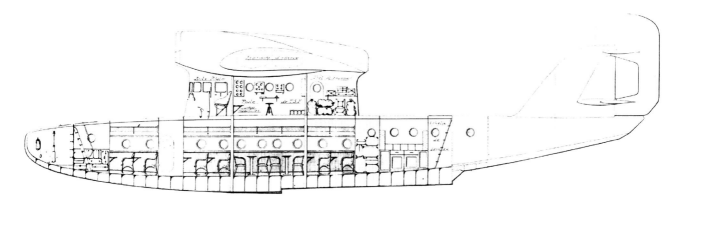

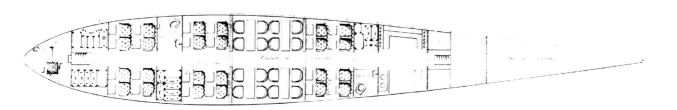

Sketch of the cabin layout of the Blériot 5193 project, a trans-Mediterranean for forty passengers.

The Blériot 280

Roughly one year later, in October 1932 Zappata designed a transport sea-plane to be fitted with four Hispano-Suiza 12 Ybrs engines of 500hp, in tandem on a series of struts above the wing. The wing was fitted to a hull with two steps, the rear one being fitted with a water rudder. The project had no follow up.

- *Span* : 63.0m
- *Height* : 6.90m
- *Empty weight* : 7,832kg
- *Ceiling* : 5,000m
- *Length* : 23.60m
- *Wing area* : 165m²
- *All up weight* : 13,100kg
- *Max speed* : 215km/h

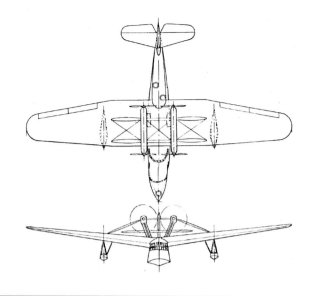

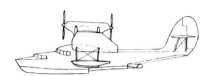

The CITA

For the Compagine Internationale des Taxis Aériens, Zappata proposed several projects in 1930. None of them was ever built. It is probable that the CITA itself remained a project.

CITA 1. Design of a two–seat touring aircraft with a Salmson 7 Ac engine of 95hp.

- *Span* : 12.0m
- *Height* : 2.59m
- *Empty weight* : 449kg
- *Max speed* : 167km/h
- *Length* : 6.87m
- *Wing area* : 18.0m²
- *All up weight* : 697kg

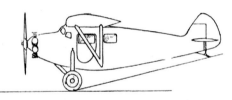

CITA 2. The previous aircraft fitted with floats and a more powerful engine and slightly larger span.

- *Span* : 13.0m
- *Wing area* : 21.0m²
- *All up weight* : 750kg
- *Height* : 3.11m
- *Empty weight* : 502kg
- *Max speed* : 185km/h

CITA 3. A three-seat aircraft derived from CITA 2 with a Salmson 9Ac engine of 120hp.

- *Span* : 13.0m
- *Height* : 2.77m
- *Empty weight* : 550kg
- *Max speed* : 168km/h
- *Length* : 7.35m
- *Wing area* : 21.0 m²
- *All up weight* : 900kg

CITA 4. The CITA 3 fitted on floats.

- *Span* : 13.0m
- *Height* : 3.81m
- *Empty weight* : 615kg
- *Max speed* : 177km/h
- *Length* : 8.18m
- *Wing area* : 21.0 m²
- *All up weight* : 965kg

CITA 5. Touring amphibian, presented as being a slightly smaller version derived from the amphibian Blériot 290.

- *Span* : 13.0m
- *Height* : 3.40m
- *Empty weight* : 763kg
- *Max speed* : 151km/h
- *Length* : 8.60m
- *Wing area* : 28.0m²
- *All up weight* : 1,138kg

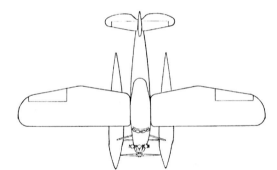

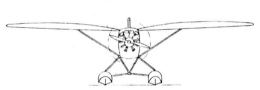

Three schematic sketches of the CITA 4, a CITA 3 on floats. Below, the sketch of the CITA 5, a smaller version of the Blériot 290 amphibian.

LOUIS BLÉRIOT AND TRANSOCEANIC FLIGHTS

The commercial crossing of the Atlantic or other large maritime surfaces occupied much of Louis Blériot's time and inspired a large number of projects. He was fully conscious of the economical and political importance of the flights, but also of the technical difficulties involved. He was not alone in these thoughts. Various ideas to counter the lack of aircraft range were proposed, floating islands were much spoken about.

In 1926, an American, of Canadian origin, Edward Robert Armstrong, founded the company, Armstrong Seadrome Development Company. He proposed floating aerodromes. Louis Blériot invested in this company and explained himself in replying to a journalist:

As you know, I have just come back from America where this company has been formed, whose objective is to build floating islands in the North and South Atlantic, they will go from dreams to reality.

I have accepted the position of Director of the company, because it seems to me to be of the greatest importance that a Frenchman be able to defend the aviation situation for our country, in order that Paris be at the head of regular European Transatlantic services.

According to the established programme, I think that in two years the project will be finalised, and that in 1937 a regular airline between Europe and America will be established. The project currently being designed, foresees three floating islands which will be built on the route between Bermuda and the Azores. This route was chosen, even though little longer, because it presents great advantages over the North Atlantic, where almost continuous fog makes the exploitation of a regular line difficult and dangerous.

The floating islands which have been designed by the American engineers, are half a kilometre long, 100m wide, and will be situated 63m below sea-level.

They have been designed with extremely comfortable fittings, and a maximum utility. The build cost of each of these islands would be about 180 or 200 millions, that is to say, to spread this out into conditions of almost perfect security over the route France to America, the total expenditure would only be 600 millions, this is less that the large modern transatlantic liners (...). The average length of each stage would be roughly 1,200km, which is a normal range for the large modern transport aircraft, and which would have an important useful load for transport of passengers, freight and post. As a consequence, the cost of freight and its transport could be considerably reduced, and the customer base would therefore be even larger (....). Let us take an example. The Santos Dumont has just crossed the South Atlantic, carrying ten tons of fuel, and only one ton of paying freight, if it had been able to cut the journey in half thanks to a floating island in the middle of its route, its freight capacity would be increased by five tons. It could therefore have carried six tons of useful load instead of just one. This would allow a reasonable cost of 200 F instead of 800 F per kilo, still taking into account the running costs of the capital expenditure.

You know that as far as maritime crossing go, two theories have been argued for a long time: land planes or sea planes. The land plane offers great advantages from the viewpoint of speed and weight, but it has a serious disadvantage that in case of a ditching, the security of the personnel and of the freight is not assured. The sea plane on the contrary, can land on the sea, carry out a repair and take off again. But the running of these machines is more expensive because of their drag resistance, and dead the weight of a large hull. This is why we have been brought to consider a third solution, which is the marine aircraft. The marine aircraft is a machine which has the form of a land plane, but whose cabin lay-out is such that it allows a ditching and a takeoff, at reduced weight if necessary. This solution maintains the advantage of land planes as far as finesse is concerned, and at the same time represents a minimum of security essential to ensure a regular service.

To resume, you see, this project which could appear utopia at first view, is on the contrary within the domain of immediate possibilities, and is by far the best solution that we can envisage. The non-stop crossing of the North Atlantic is still an exceptional, sporting exploit, and necessitates in every case enormous mastodons which are, in fact, only flying fuel tanks, which expose their pilots to the most serious dangers. The route via the far North offers no practical interest because you do not gain enough time over the liners, further, it presents also serious dangers because of the barren countries to be crossed. Whereas on the contrary, the solution that we are going to put into practice, is both economical and capable of giving an immediate financial return. It can be applied straight away with the machines that we now posses. It would place New York at less than two days from Paris, that is to say, that you would be four days quicker than the most rapid ocean liner.

France must understand the immense interest of this project, because Paris must be at the head of the line of this new aerial bridge, to conserve for our country both postal and touristic advantages, which would not be slow in coming forward as a result of the exploitation of this new line.

Model of the Armstrong floating island.

A drawing of the island in use. A Blériot 350 can be seen.

11

The ANEC Aircraft

THE AIR NAVIGATION AND ENGINEERING COMPANY, THE BRITISH BRANCH OF BLÉRIOT, BUILT ITS OWN MODELS FROM 1922 TO 1927

The ANEC I at Buc in 1924, during the Tour de France des Avionnettes.

ANEC I to IV

The British branch of Blériot Aéronautique, Blériot Aircraft Ltd., first the Air Navigation Company, then the Air Navigation and Engineering Company, was created in 1910. First of all installed on the aerodrome at Brooklands, at the same time as a Blériot flying school, the company was transferred in 1917 to Addlestone, also in Surrey, to a factory that the British Government had built for the company, as compensation for the factory at Brooklands that the Government had requisitioned. After having produced different versions of the Blériot XI, Spad VII, AVRO 504 A, and SE 5a, the company had difficulties at the end of the war because the Union of British Aircraft Builders, refused to admit Blériot, a foreigner, into their ranks. Because of this, ANEC could not obtain Government orders.

It was at that time that the firm started automobile construction, and then in 1922, under the technical management of the engineer W. S. Shackleton, three Avionnette touring aircraft were built, each fitted with an 18 hp inverted V-twin Blackburne engine of 696cc and 16 hp,[1] the ANEC 1, registered G-EBHR and G-EBIL and G-AUEQ. The access to the cockpit was by glazed hatch situated in the middle of the wing, a large rectangular high wing configuration. The wing rested on the upper part of the fuselage; from the base of the fuselage two struts supported the wing. Two small windows on either side of the fuselage helped the limited visibility of the pilot. The undercarriage axle was fixed directly to the bottom of the fuselage, which brought the total height of the aircraft to 1.36 metres. It had a 10 metre span and a length of 4.75 metres. This ANEC monoplane weighed 123 kg empty, and 207 kg at take off. Its maximum speed was 125 kph. At the competition of low powered aircraft at Lympne,

from the 8th to the 13th October 1923, the two ANECs, piloted by H. James and W. Piercey were particularly noted. James, with just one gallon of fuel (4.546 litres) covered 87.5 miles (140.787 kilometres) and Piercey reached 4,392 metres, a world altitude record for Avionette.

The Tour de France of Avionettes was held from the 24th July to the 10th August 1924, under the patronage of the Association Française Aérienne and under the Presidency of André Carlier, the Tour was a circuit of 1807 kilometres in eight stages, leaving from the Blériot aerodrome at Buc. Amongst the fifteen aircraft participating was the ANEC 1, G-EBIL, re-christened Blériot 102 now that it had crossed the Channel. It was in fact in France in 1922, that aerodynamic trials were held in the Eiffel laboratory. Report n° 67 B of November 1922 indicated a finesse of 21.3 for the wing, for an overall aerodynamic finesse of 16.7.

Flown from London to Buc by the pilot Emile Clément, G-EVIL, conserving its British registration, participated in the Tour de France, flown by Lieutenant Rabatel, carrying the n° 12. Even though the ANEC-Blériot, with only two other aircraft out of the fifteen competitors, succeeded in the eliminatory flights, it had to abandon during the first stage; in very poor weather conditions it was forced to land near to Nevers, because of engine failure. The winner of the Tour was Maurice Drouhin, on an Anzani powered Farman Moustique. Returned to England, the machine had it's wing surface reduced and it's engine replaced by an Anzani. Becoming therefore, the ANEC 1-A, it took part in the meeting in Lympne in August 1925. On the 22nd January 1926, it was transferred to the R.A.F. where it was given the serial N° J 7506. In September, the ANEC 1-A was again present at Lympne. Colonel Henderson flipped the aircraft over the evening before the eliminatory rounds. The aircraft could not take part. The G-AUEQ was built for Air Transport Ltd of Perth in Australia.

---

(1) The prototype was initially to have been fitted with a Bristol "Cherub" engine of 1070cc.

The ANEC II, a two seat tourer with an Anzani engine. This version has been modified with a cowling around the engine.

The ANEC III, Satin Bird, of Larkin Aircraft Supply Co Ltd, who also owned the ANEC III G-AUEZ Diamond Bird and G-AUGF Love Bird. This aircraft was in service in 1927 but crashed the same year. The others were re-registered in Australia VH-UEZ and VH-UGF.

ANEC 1.

- *Span* : 10.0m
- *Length* : 4.75m
- *Height* : 1.22m
- *Wing area* : 13.47m²
- *Empty weight* : 124kg
- *All up weight* : 207kg
- *Max speed* : 126km/h

ANEC II. This was a two-seater touring aircraft derived from the ANEC I, which first flew in August 1924, it was first fitted with an inverted Anzani twin, then re-engined with a Bristol "Cherub" engine, and given a very streamlined engine cowling. Only one example was produced, registered G-EBJO. It was purchased in 1937 by Richard Shuttleworth. It was recently restored and now flies with the Shuttleworth collection at Old Warden. The wing in silver, fuselage in bright red with yellow highlights.

- *Span* : 11.60m
- *Length* : 6.30m
- *Height* : 1.74m8
- *Wing area* : 17.19m²
- *Empty weight* : 175.6kg
- *All up weight* : 332kg
- *Max speed* : 126km/h

ANEC III. This was a cargo or passenger transport aircraft, of which three examples were delivered to Larkin Aircraft Supply Company Ltd. of Melbourne in Australia. It could carry six passengers. It was powered by a Rolls-Royce "Eagle" VIII engine of 375 hp. The designer was Jean Bewsher, with a prototype making its first flight in December 1922. The second aircraft crashed in 1927, and the two remaining aircraft were re-engined in 1929 with an Armstrong –Siddeley "Jaguar" S engine of 450hp. The aircraft could now carry eleven passengers. They flew on the line between Melbourne and Adelaide from 1930 to 1931.

- *Span* : 18.28m
- *Length* : 13.72m
- *Wing area* : 68.75m²
- *Empty weight* : 1,577kg
- *All up weight* : 2,545kg
- *Max speed* : 169km/h
- *Cruise speed* : 145km/h

ANEC Sky Sign Carrier. This project was never followed up but was designed for Huck's Night Flyers, a nocturnal aerial publicity company. It was to be fitted with three Siddeley "Puma" engines, six cylinders in line, giving 265hp at take-off. It was a bi-plane of 33m span but with folding wings. It could carry a crew of two side-by-side in an open cockpit behind the central engine. Four passengers could be carried in the cabin.

ANEC IV. This was built in 1926 It was a two seat bi-plane fitted with a three cylinder Blackburn, "Thrush" radial engine, of 35 hp, and was christened *Mistle Thrush*; it was registered G-EBPI. It was re-engined with an Anzani of 45hp and then an Armstrong Siddeley "Genet" engine of 80hp. It participated in the King's Cup Air Race, of 1928 flown by Guy Warwick. It was destroyed when it hit a hill in fog.

- *Span* : 8.53m
- *Length* : 6.55m
- *Height* : 2.44m
- *Wing area* : 19.50m²
- *All up weight* : 522kg
- *Max speed with 35hp* : 129km/h

The Air Navigation and Engineering Company also built three machines for George Handasyde in 1922 and 1923. The Company disappeared in 1927. The factory was sold for £16,000, whereas the construction of the factory eleven years earlier, had cost £75,000.

The ANEC IV Missel Thrush on take-off.

Aircraft and Seaplanes SPAD or Blériot-SPAD

FROM A DISORGANISED COMPANY, LOUIS BLERIOT BUILT A LEADER OF THE AVIATION INDUSTRY, AND BECAME IN 1918, THE WORLD'S LARGEST AIRCRAFT BUILDER

The build of SPAD III fighters in the Blériot factory in Suresnes in 1918. Two fuselages of the prototypes of the pre-war Blériot monocoque are suspended below the factory trusses, as well as what appears to be a Pnydre.

A businessman having made his fortune in the silk trade in Lyon, Armand Deperdussin then moved to Paris where he continued his activity of the importation of silk, then created a hot-air health care institute. In 1910, at 19 rue des Entrepreneurs in Paris he started an aviation company which carried his name. The head of his design office was an engineer from the Arts et Métiers of Angers, Louis Béchereau.[1] Thanks to this brilliant technician the company soon had success in competitions. It was Béchereau who designed the famous Deperdussin monocoque monoplane, which, piloted by Maurice Prévost, was the first aircraft to exceed 200 km/h, on the 29th of September 1913. However, in the summer of this same year Deperdussin

was accused of insider trading covering a sum of 28 million gold francs. Arrested on the 5th August, he was not judged until four years later on the 30th March 1917 and sentenced to five years imprisonment. Benefiting from a suspended sentence and taking into account time already spent in prison, Armand Deperdussin was released, becoming a representative in nuts and bolts; he disappeared from the aeronautical scene. On the 11th June 1924, the daily Parisian newspapers, in three lines, under the heading "Miscellaneous" reported that a certain A. Deperdussin had committed suicide in a small hotel in the Rue Saint-Lazare. Having no financial means, pushed aside by society, he was not able to overcome what he believed to be a come down.

After his arrest, his aviation company was placed under judicial administration, and took the name Société Provisoire des Aéroplanes Deperdussin (SPAD) and continued under the authority of a bankruptcy administrator called Michael Raynaud,

---

(1) The very first aircraft built by Deperdussin was a joint design between Defeure, a theatre decorator, and Bechereau. Originally it was destined to be window dressing, an attraction to draw the crowds to the department store the Bon Marché in Paris, owned by Deperdussin.

to produce aircraft in the offices and workshops rue des Entrepreneurs, at Puteaux, as well as at Juvisy.

In August 1914 a limited company was formed of which Louis Blériot, who was majority shareholder, was named President of the Board on the 14th November. This company which took over Deperdussin company conserved the name SPAD, which from now on stood for Société Anonyme Pour l'Aviation et ses Dérivés. It is possible that Alfred Leblanc, the Esperanto speaker[2] intervened in this decision, because the word *spad* means speed in this language. François-Max Richard became managing director of the company and Louis Béchereau conserved his position as technical director. From now on we see a sharing of tasks. Louis Blériot maintained the development of large dimension bomber aircraft, whereas he gave to Béchereau, specialist of racing aircraft, the building of fighter aircraft.

Louis Blériot, until now installed at Levallois-Perret, built in 1915 a modern factory of 40,000m² at, at Suresnes, 3 quai du Général-Gallieni (today called quai Marcel-Dassault) on the banks of the Seine. 23,500 m² were covered and the factory had an entrance door 40m wide. The plant had a laboratory to study raw materials and quality control.

(2) The lawyer Ernest Archdeacon, one of the great lobbyists of French Aviation, very active from 1903 onwards, was also a great proponent of Esperanto to which he converted several pilots such as Henry Farman who even carried on some of his aircraft, a green cross, the rallying sign of Esperanto speakers. Even before 1914 Archdeacon also gave Esperanto lessons through the weekly aeronautical magazine *L'Aéro*.

In the factory, where up to 2,500 people worked, 3,484 SPAD bi-planes were built up to the Armistice of 1918, but the total production of SPADs on the 11 November 1918, was 3,820 Spad VII, 300 SPAD XII, 8,472 SPAD XIII, 657 SPAD XI and XVI, 40 SPAD XIV, 100 SPAD XX, plus other models in smaller quantities. With such a large number of orders for fighters, and independent of the production at Rue des Entrepreneurs, of Levallois and Juvisy (which closed in 1919) several sub-contractors were employed, Bernard, Borel, Grémont, Janoir, Kellner, Levasseur, de Marçay, Nieuport, Régy, SEA (Potez and Bloch) SCAF, SCEM (Amiot), Sommer. Some of these companies had never produced aircraft.

At this period an aircraft came out of the assembly hall at the factory of Suresnes every fifty minutes. However, on the 30th November 1916 following a difference caused by the collaboration with the firm Bernard, Louis Béchereau resigned. Nevertheless, he remained in his job a few months longer to oversee the ongoing build. Béchereau continued his career in aviation for another ten years without however, creating the models as successful as the SPAD VII and XIII.

On Tuesday 15th May 1917, Max Richard called the young André Herbemont, ex-engineer with Deperdussin, for him to succeed Béchereau. At twenty-four years old Herbemont thus became the head of the technical department of the Blériot Company.

At the end of the war, Louis Blériot continued to use the mark SPAD in parallel to his own name.

The same factory ten years later, producing the SPAD 81 fighter. At the rear can be seen a Blériot-Blanchard seaplane.

The SPAD Aircraft

To design a new combat aircraft from 1914 onwards, Béchereau chose the bi-plane, which, thanks to its large wing surface, climbed better and above all carried a heavier load. He did not retain the technique of the monocoque because it presented too many disadvantages, too heavy, the load spreading had still to be invented, plus a one-off and delicate build method. The fuselages of the monocoque were built on a mould, with three layers of strips of tulip wood glued together. He adopted the classical method of the rectangular beam, but he conserved the streamlined form of the monocoque by adding forms and stringers to the frames over which was glued the fabric.

Another problem was the armament. Captain Georges Bellenger and Louis Blériot had already shown that a gun added to an aircraft was easy to point whilst piloting the aircraft. But, how to fire forwards from an aircraft without touching the propeller? Louis Blériot had thought about placing a gun in the propeller shaft, but it could not be re-loaded or un-blocked. In 1913 other builders were looking for a different answer. The most elegant, which consisted of synchronizing the firing with the passage of the blades in front of the barrel, designed by Raymond Sauliner, was not practical because of the irregular firing of the Hotchkiss machine gun then in service.

Louis Blériot had also tried with some success, a gun placed higher than the propeller disc. This layout was adopted on bi-planes, but it increased the aerodynamic drag and penalized the performance. Deperdussin tried in 1913 to place the gun on a long pivoting arm to fire above the propeller disc, the machine gunner had to stand in front of the pilot in order to use it. During a demonstration in England, the mono-plane thus equipped, crashed and Herbemont who was acting as the machine gunner, was seriously injured. In standing in the cockpit, the machine gunner blocked the view of the pilot and generated a considerable aerodynamic drag which reduced the flying capacity of the aircraft. None of this is tolerable on an aircraft that was to be fast and manoeuvrable. On the SPAD, Béchereau placed the machine gunner entirely inside a streamlined nacelle with the machine gun. The nacelle was right at the front of the aircraft, that is to say, in front of the propeller, the nacelle was fixed at the bottom to the undercarriage axle, and above to the upper main plane.

SPAD A1 to A5

SPAD A1

This was designed to reply to a request from military aviation. The bi-plane fitted with a rotary engine, the Le Rhône 9C of 80hp, was the first machine designed by Béchereau for SPAD. It was a two-seat fighter having a nacelle in front of the propeller equipped with a 7,65 mm Lewis gun. The structure was fabric covered wood with wire reinforcing stays.

The SPAD A1 made its first flight on 21st May 1915. It was seen to be much faster than contemporary two-seaters with pusher engines, but it was low on power. Only one was built.

- *Span* : - 9.55m
- *Height* : - 2.6m
- *Speed* : - 150km/h
- *Length* : - 7.3m
- *All up weight* : - 710kg
- *Endurance* : - 2hrs 45

The SPAD A1 in flight.

A SPAD A1 with the machine gunners nacelle lowered for access to the Le Rhone rotary engine.

The SPAD A1: a radical formula, but the airframe had considerable qualities.

SPAD A2

Derived from the SPAD A1, the SPAD A2 was fitted with a Le Rhône 9Ja engine of 110hp. The fixing of the nacelle was modified as was the Lewis machine gun support, which could now slide between two steel tubes in an arc. The dimensions of the SPAD A2 were identical to those of the A1 except for the length, which went to 7.85m, and its weight went to 730kg. Speed was increased to 152km/h. It appeared in November 1915 and a hundred were built, forty-three for military aviation and fifty-seven for the Russian Imperial Air Force, some of them were equipped with skis.

A SPAD A2 in the French Air Force.

SPAD A3

The SPAD A3 was a version of the SPAD A2. It had two 7.65mm Lewis guns (one firing to the front, the other to the rear). It had dual controls, each member of the crew could alternatively fly the aircraft or fire his machine gun. Only one prototype of this model, innovative but certainly complex, was built.

SPAD A4

Of the same dimensions as the SPAD A2, the SPAD A4 was fitted with an upper main plane slightly modified, only the upper wing was fitted with ailerons. twelve were built, one for the military aviation and eleven for Russia. First flight was on 22nd February 1916. It was fitted with the same engine, the Le Rhône 9c of the SPAD A1. Top speed was 152km/h and endurance was 2hrs 30m.

A Russian SPAD A4.

SPAD A5

Initially designated as the SPAD C, the SPAD A5, the final development of the SPAD A1, was a three-seat fighter with two observer/gunners. Of the same dimensions as the previous models, it was fitted with a Renault 12 Fa engine of 220hp. Its speed was 150km/h. First flight was July 1916 and it participated in the Concours Militaire of that year. Only one example was built.

SPAD B

A two-seat single engine fighter with a "double beam" fuselage came out in 1916, only one example was built.

SPAD C

Appearing in August 1915 the three-seat fighter SPAD C rapidly became the SPAD A5.

SPAD D

A two-seat bomber version of the SPAD C, the SPAD D was fitted with a V12 Panhard engine. Its dimensions were identical to those of the SPAD C, it participated in the Concours Militaire of 1915, and took part the same year in the race Villacoublay-Etampes–Orleans–Villacoublay. Only one example was built.

- *Span* : - 9.55m
- *Length* : - 7.85m
- *Height* : - 2.6m
- *Speed* : - 160km/h

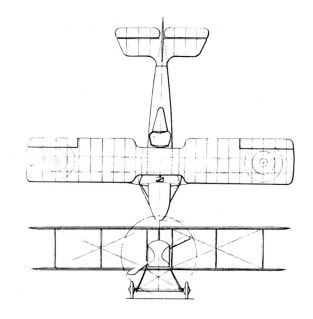

Factory schematic drawing of a SPAD D.

SPAD E

A three-seat bomber, the SPAD E was a bi-plane powered by two Renault 12FA engines of 220hp in pusher configuration, mounted in nacelles between the wings. The undercarriage had four wheels. There were two machine guns positions, one to the front and one to the rear. Coming out in 1915 this single example participated the same year at the Concours des Avions Puissants(Competition of Powerful Aircraft). Flown by Goffin it was destroyed at Villacoublay.

- *Span* : - 24.30
- *Length* : - 13m
- *Height* : - 3.45m
- *Speed* : - 140km/h

The unique SPAD E with an undercarriage which should prevent it from nosing over when taxiing. The design was obliged to couple streamlining and simplicity of build.

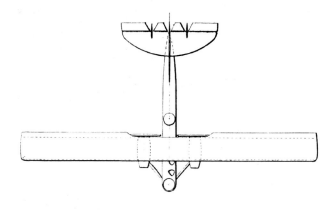

SPAD F

Designed in 1915 but never built, SPAD F was to have been a two-seat twin engine bi-plane fighter. Its control surfaces were to have been placed in front of and behind the wing and the engines and propellers were to be installed in the centre of the fuselage.

SPAD G

Of length and height identical to the SPAD A2, the SPAD G was a two- seat bi-plane fighter fitted with a Clerget 9B engine of 130hp. Its span was 9.15m and the wing area was 25m². The all-up weight was 708kg. Its speed was 140km/h. Appearing in

1915, it remained at the prototype stage. It was the first SPAD with a triangular horizon tail plane with a rounded trailing edge.

- *Span* : - 9.15m
- *Wing area* : - 25m²
- *All up weight* : - 708kg
- *Speed* : - 140km/h

SPAD H and V

First single seat fighter designed by the SPAD company, the SPAD H bi-plane was powered by the new Hispano-Suiza 8A water cooled engine of 140 hp. Re- named SPAD V, perhaps because of the engine's V8 configuration. The machine reached an exceptionally high speed for the period, 213km/h. Coming out in November 1915 it was the original of the famous SPAD VII and XIII.

- *Span* : - 7.32m
- *Length* : - 6.24m
- *Height* : - 2.3m
- *All up weight* : - 705kg
- *Speed* : - 213 km/h

SPAD I

Single-seat bi-plane fighter with a monocoque fuselage built in 1915, the SPAD I would never receive the Gnome rotary engine with which it should have been fitted. It was to be armed with a synchronized machine gun.

SPAD J

Also built in 1915, the SPAD J was a monoplane version of the SPAD I which also would never receive its engine. The SPAD I and J were almost certainly abandoned before completion to the benefit of the more promising SPAD V.

SPAD VII

The introduction of the British Vickers machine gun allowed the fine tuning of an efficient synchronization system to place the machine gun in the fuselage firing through the propeller disc. This innovation, with the arrival of the Hispano-Suiza capable of giving 140 – 150hp, incomparably more viable than all of its competitors, changed the scene and allowed the design of a truly modern fighter aircraft.

This was the first SPAD to receive a designation of Roman numerals, a single-seat bi-plane fighter fitted with an Hispano-Suiza HS 8A water- cooled V8 engine of 140hp. This fighter made its first flight at Buc in April 1916. It was armed with a 7.7mm Vickers machine gun, synchronized to fire through the propeller. Very quickly, the general staff placed great hopes in the aircraft, because the fighters then in service were outclassed by their German rivals. After a difficult fine tuning of the Hispano-Suiza engine, the SPAD VII, confirmed itself as a total success.

- *Span* : - 7.62m
- *Length* : - 6.16m
- *Height* : - 2.13
- *All up weight* : - 740kg
- *Speed* : - 150km/h
- *Endurance* : - 2hrs 45m

Top, the SPAD VII of the SPA 150 Squadron. Below, SPAD VII, perhaps belonging to the SPA 88. Opposite top, the one belonging to Warrant Officer Sardier, of the SPA 77. Opposite bottom, the cockpit of a SPAD VII.

A SPAD VII of the SPA 77, its individual number is a decorative 4.

3,820 SPAD VII were produced, in three versions; the first, fitted with an HS 8Aa engine of 150hp had the same dimensions as the prototype. Its speed was 186km/h. 813 examples of the version were built, of which 220 under licence in England, Blériot Ltd and Mann–Egerton, and 100 in Russia by Dux.

The second version was fitted with an HS 8 Ab or Ac engine of 180hp, the span was 7.82m and all up weight 755kg. Its speed was 196km/h. Out of a total of 3,004 aircraft built, 214 were exported to Italy, 189 to America, 43 to Russia, 15 to Belgium, 22 to Portugal, 20 to Brazil, 15 to Poland, 10 to Yugoslavia. Others went also to Holland, to Romania to Greece, to Czechoslovakia, to Estonia, to Finland, to Siam and to Japan.

Only three examples of the third version were built. The span went to 8.19m and the height to 2.35m. The all up weight was 790kg. Fitted with an HS 8B engine of 200hp, the speed reached 212km/h. One of these three machines became the prototype of the SPAD XIII.

Operational at the end of 1916, the SPAD VIII was in service with most of the French fighter squadrons but also with the British, American, Russian, Italian, and Belgian forces.

Besides the SPAD Company and Blériot Aéronautique, the SPAD VII was built under licence in France by Grémont, Janoir, Kellner, de Marçay, Régy, Sommer and SEA. From the autumn of 1917 it was progressively replaced by the SPAD XIII.

After the war and up to 1928, a 100 or so SPAD VII aircraft were used for advanced pilot training at the Blériot school in Buc, the aircraft were painted silver-grey with black registration letters.

A SPAD VII built in England.

SPAD VIII

Designed in 1916, the SPAD VIII was to be a two-seat artillery spotter fitted with an Hispano-Suiza HS 8Ac engine of 180hp. This project gave birth to the SPAD XI.

SPAD IX

Built in 1916, but never produced in series, the SPAD IX was fitted with an HS 8Ca engine of 200hp, with a 37mm machine gun between the banks of cylinders. A single example, it led to the SPAD XII.

SPAD X

Single seat sea-plane fighter with an HS 8Ac engine of 180hp, this aircraft was re-designed to become the SPAD XIV. Only one example was built.

- Span : - 9.10m
- Height : - 2.92m
- Length : - 7.60m
- Speed : - 160km/h

The unique SPAD IX with cowling and a streamlined vertical fin under the wing in front of the pilot's eyes.

The larger version of the SPAD VII, the SPAD XI carried a pilot and a gunner/observer.

SPAD XI

Two-seat artillery spotter with a slight sweep back to the wings, 600 SPAD XI were built, of which many were also used for trench strafing. First flight of the prototype was September 1916.

The first models were fitted with the HS 8Bc engine of 220hp, the following aircraft with the HS 8Be. In both cases maximum speed was 200km/h which was brilliant for the period.

35 SPAD XI were exported to America, to Belgium and to Japan. One SPAD XI was tested as a two seat night fighter with a searchlight fitted in front of the propeller.

- *Span* : - 11.21m
- *Height* : - 2.8m
- *Max Speed* : - 200km/h
- *Length* : - 7.84m
- *All up weight* : - 1,060kg

Above, a SPAD XI of the SPA 42. Below, the SPAD XI of the same unit leave for a ground strafing mission. Opposite, the SPAD XI equipped with a searchlight for a night fighting trial, mainly against Zeppelins.

SPAD XII

Originating from a request by Georges Guynemer to have an aircraft armed with a decisively powerful canon, the proto-type SPAD XII (that Guynemer nick-named the *"Pétadou"*) was a modified SPAD VII onto which a 37mm Hotchkiss canon fired through the propeller shaft was fitted. The fine tuning, at which Guynemer participated, was fairly long. The first operational flight only came on the 5th July 1917, three months after the SPAD XIII. Fitted with an Hispano-Suiza HS 8Bc engine of 220hp (for the prototype) and an HS 8 Bec (for the production models) 300 SPAD XII were built of which 10 were for America.

The engine was fitted with a reduction gear which allowed the placing of the hollow propeller shaft above the crankshaft. Thus, the canon could be placed between the banks of the cylinders in V configuration, so that the gun fired through the hollow propeller shaft. This 37mm cannon, derived from a trench gun designed to destroy enemy machine guns, fired either shells or bullets and had to be re-loaded after each shot by the pilot. The aircraft also had a 7.7mm Vickers machine gun.

Judged difficult to fly, the SPAZD XII was only given to the more experienced pilots such as Georges Guynemer and René Fock.

- Span : - 8.19m
- Height : - 2.33m
- Max Speed : - 212km/h
- Length : - 6.33m
- All up weight ; - 8.835kg

The prototype of the SPAD XII.

SPAD XIII

Another model derived directly from the SPAD VII, of which one modified example served as prototype for the SPAD XIII. This was a single-seat fighter fitted with an Hispano-Suiza HS 8 Ba engine of 200hp, then the 8 Bc engine of 220hp, was armed with two 7.7mm Vickers machine guns. It could reach 218km/h with the 8Ba engine of 200hp, at an all up weight of 825kg With the 8 Bc of 220hp, the speed went to 224km/h for an all up weight of 845kg and a span reduced to 8.08m by removing the rounded wing tips. Flown by René Dorne, the prototype had its first flight on the 4th April 1917.

Very similar to the SPAD VII the SPAD XIII differed notably by a larger fin and the cabane struts (between upper wing and fuselage) inclined forwards.

8472 SPAD XII were built in two years by Blériot, and numerous sub-contractors.

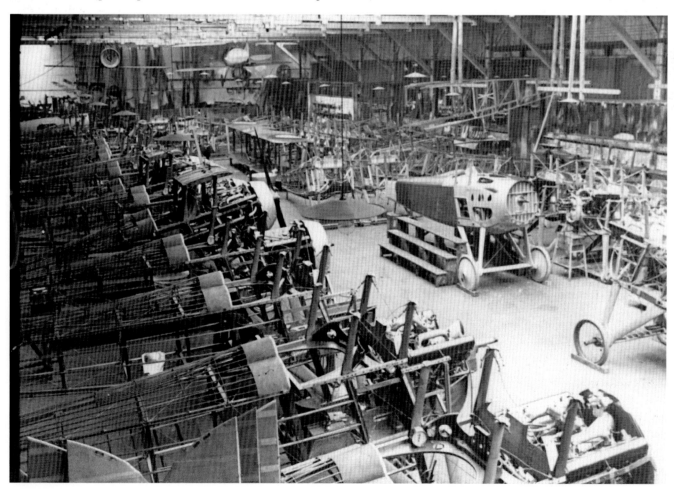

Above, a SPAD XIII in front a Bessonneu hanger. Below, a SPAD XIII of the Japanese Air Force. Bottom, one of the final SPAD XIII. The two machine guns are shielded by a modification to the upper part of the engine cowling.

Ordered in large production numbers, the majority of SPAD XIII were built at the Blériot factory at Suresnes and at the SPAD factory rue des Entrepreneurs but also by numerous sub-contractors, ACM, Bernard, Borel, Kellner, Levasseur, Nieuport, Sommer and SEA. In the space of two years, 8,472 SPAD XIII were built. At the Blériot factory in Suresnes an aircraft came off the assembly line every fifty minutes. The SPAD XIII equipped almost every French fighter squadron. They were also used by British, American, Italian and Belgian pilots. After the war they were used by Poland, Czechoslovakia, Spain, Turkey, Uruguay and Japan.

- *Span* : - 8.19m
- *Length* : - 6.2m
- *Height* : - 2.35m

SPAD XIII bis

Only one example was built, this version of the SPAD XIII with modified fuselage was fitted with an Hispano-Suiza HS 8Fa engine of 300hp, and was equipped with one machine gun and two cameras. Appearing in November 1918 the SPAD XIII bis became the SPAD XVII. The prototype broke up in flight during a trial. The builder was exonerated, the accident was caused by the poor quality of the metal fittings fixing the flying wires. Other builders complained of the same problem, the army started a general inspection.

- *Span : - 8.08m*
- *Height : - 2.39m*
- *Max Speed : - 240km/h*
- *Length : - 6.3m*
- *All up weight : - 900kg*

SPAD XIV

Fitted with an Hispano-Suiza 8Bc engine of 220hp, the SPAD XIV was designed by Herbemont under the guidance of Béchereau. It was a sea-plane fighter equipped with a 37mm cannon and a 7.65mm Vickers machine gun.

A SPAD XIV seaplane fighter.

Answering to a programme dating from the beginning of 1917, it took the fuselage of the SPAD XII with a larger wing span and tail plane. The floats, wide and short, were designed by Maurice Payonne, future head of the design office of the sea-plane builder FBA. The prototype flew for the first time on 15th November 1917, flown by Maurice Béquet. The trials were judged conclusive, and a few days later the Navy Ministry placed an order for thirty-nine examples. To speed delivery, the fuselages were taken from a series of SPAD XII under build. The floats were sub-contracted to Levasseur.

First examples of the SPAD XIV were delivered early in 1918. However, the machines had very few chances to enter the fight, and some of them did not enter service until after the Armistice.

- *Span : - 9.8m*
- *Height : - 4m*
- *Max Speed : - 205km/h*
- *Length : - 7.40m*
- *All up weight : - 1,060kg*

SPAD XV

This was the first SPAD fighter with a monocoque fuselage. As with the technique inaugurated in 1910 by Béchereau, again tulip wood was used. This aircraft in 1917 was the first SPAD designed entirely by Herbemont. It was a bi-plane with only one pair of masts on each side. The engine was a Gnome monosoupape of 160hp, a 9cylinder radial, although light (170kg) was rapidly abandoned because of its weaknesses. Five versions were tried, but none of them went into series production.

- *SPAD XV-1*, which flew for the first time on 31st August 1917 had a wing span of 7.10m. It was handed over to Charles Nungesser. It's all up weight was 590kg.

- *SPAD XV-2*, had a larger wing span (7.7m). It made its first flight the following month before being delivered to Georges Madon.

- *SPAD XV-3*, had its first flight in January 1918. It only differed from the XV2 by a reduced wing cord.

- *SPAD XV-4*, was fitted with a Le Rhône 9R engine of 170hp and had a larger fin.

- *SPAD XV-5*, was a sport aircraft built after the war. The engine was a Le Rhône 80hp, it had an enormous spinner fitted to the propeller. It had a maximum speed of 170km/h.

Joseph Sadi-Lecointe made the first flight in this aircraft on the 18th May 1919. Fonck and Nungesser received the first two - and probably the only - examples of this fighter disguised as a touring aircraft. Fonck's aircraft carried his (RF) on its fin, and then later F-ONCK in large letters on its fuselage. Nungesser's aircraft carried the insignia which he carried on each of his aircraft during the war which had just finished (see photo page 128).

- *Span : - 7.10m*
- *Height : - 2.3m*
- *All up weight : - 500kg*
- *Length : - 5.51m*
- *Wing area : - 16m²*
- *Empty weight : - 350kg.*

The SPAD XV was the first of a new generation of SPAD.

SPAD XVI and XVI bis

An observation bi-plane coming out in 1918, the SPAD XVI was a variant of the SPAD XI with a Lorraine engine. 657 were built in three versions.
- Lorraine 8 Bc of 265hp
- Lorraine 8 Bd of 275hp
- Lorraine 8 Bd of 240hp, this last version being named XVI bis.

In 1919, 11 SPAD XVI were converted to two-seat touring aircraft with the Lorraine Bc engine. SPAD XVI and XVI bis were supplied to America and to Belgium.

- *Span :- 11.21m*
- *Height : - 2.79m*
- *Max Speed : - 150km/h (158km/h for the civil version)*
- *Length : - 7.89m*
- *All up weight : - 1,280kg*

The SPAD XVI was a SPAD XI with a Lorraine engine.

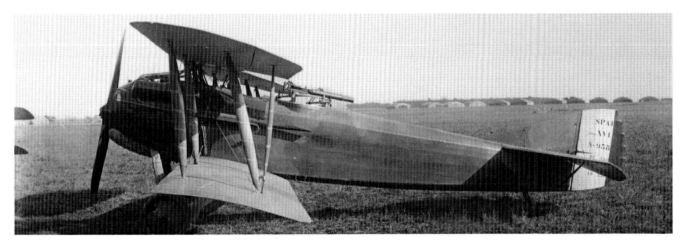

SPAD XVII

The SPAD XVII was the series version of the SPAD XIII bis. It was fitted with an Hispano-Suiza 8Fb engine of 300hp. Twenty examples of this single seat fighter were built in 1918.

- *Span :- 8.08m*
- *Height :- 2.39m*
- *Max Speed :- 240km/h*
- *Length :- 6.3m*
- *All up weight :- 900kg*

The SPAD XVII entered service shortly before the end of hostilities. Here is the prototype.

SPAD XVIII

At the beginning of 1918, the aviation section of army head-quarters decided to replace the 220hp SPAD XIII by single-seat and two-seat combat aircraft of 300hp, at a ratio of two C.2 two-seaters for one C1 single-seater. Replying to this program the SPAD XVIII was a "protected single seat fighter", this meant in fact, a two-seater in tandem with a machine gunner facing backwards armed with a Vickers machine gun. A single stream-lined inter-plane strut linked the upper and lower wings. The upper wing of larger area had a slight sweep back. The Hispano-Suiza 8Fbc engine was abandoned because of heavy vibrations, and was replaced by a 300hp engine of the same mark; this caused a change in the designation, becoming the SPAD XX.

- *Span : - 9.70m*
- *Height : - 2.8m*
- *Length : - 7.3m*
- *Wing area : - 30m².*

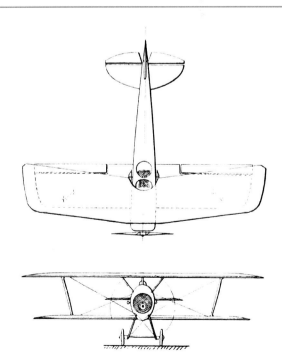

Schematic drawing of the unique SPAD XVIII. The fuselage is wooden monocoque.

SPAD XIX

Another two-seat fighter which was to be fitted with the HS 8Fbc engine of 300hp, the SPAD XIX was abandoned for the same reasons as the SPAD XVIII.

SPAD XX C.1 and C.2

Given the name of its designer "SPAD Herbemont" the prototype of the SPAD XX flown by Sadi Lecointe made its first flight at Buc on the 7th August 1918. The fuselage was a wooden monocoque structure. Blériot Aéronautique presented two versions, the first called C.1 was a "single-seat fighter with lookout". Armed with two Vickers machine guns and 1000 rounds, and a supplementary pivoting Lewis machine gun with 200 rounds operated by a "lookout" in the rear cockpit. The second version, which came out later, was the C.2 "combat two-seater" with the same armament firing forward, and two Lewis machine guns in a rear turret with 800 rounds. Both versions were fitted with the Hispano-Suiza 8 Fb engine of 300hp.

SPAD XX C.1 Tested at Villacoublay in September1918, the SPAD XX C.1 (1) had several modifications requested by the Aviation Technical Section, notably to the tanks and armament. Louis Blériot took an order of 300 examples per month for this machine (or 200 according to other company archives) without time limit. Production was started immediately but the signing of the Armistice on the 11th November led to the cancelation of this unlimited order, it was replaced by another of 100 machines, which corresponded to the number of aircraft built up to that date.

Before being sent to the squadrons, the first SPAD XX were given to four fighter pilots of the 1st and 2nd Aviation Regiments for comparative trials at La Bourget, with other production series aircraft.

The SPAD XX C.1 was recognized as having the best manoeuvrability and the highest ceiling.

The production series aircraft were sent first to the 2nd Aviation Regiment in Strasbourg, and then from 1923 onwards, to the bases at Châteauroux and Dijon. A few were exported, three to Japan delivered to the Mitsubishi Company, and one to Bolivia, a government order.

In parallel to it's military use, the SPAD XX C. participated in aerial competitions and gained several world records :
- World speed record with passenger in 1918, at 230km/h
- World altitude record in July 1919, at 8,900m established by Joseph Sadi-Lecointe.
- World altitude record with two passengers in February 1920, at 7,300m established by Jean Casale.

It also won :
- The Prix du Grand Ecart offered by the newspaper *L'Auto*, flown by Casale and Dronne, with a speed varying between 240km/h and 60km/h
- The altitude prize at the meeting at Le Bourget, in1922
- The Dubonnet Cup in the hands of Lieutenant Schmitter.

- Span : - 9.72m
- Length : - 7.3m
- Height : - 2.75m
- Wing area : - 30m^2
- All up weight : - 1,310kg
- Empty weight : - 850kg
- Max Speed : - 240km/h
- Endurance :- 2h 30m at full power with 170kg of fuel.

SPAD XX C.2 This aircraft made it's first flight on the 7th July 1921. Two examples were built without government order, one was delivered to the "French government" the other was sold to Japan.

- Span : - 10.41m
- Length : - 7.385m
- Height : - 2.75m
- Wing area : - 33m^2
- All up weight : - 1,370kg
- Empty weight : - 887kg
- Max Speed : - 230km/h
- Endurance : - three hours at full power with 193kg of fuel.

Above and below, the SPAD XX "single-seat fighter with look-out".

Above, one of the three SPAD XX delivered to Japan. Below, one of the two SPAD XX C.2, two-seat fighters.

SPAD XX bis and 20 bis

Built from the SPAD XX bis this was a prototype fighter with an Hispano-Suiza HS8Fb engine of 300hp, the SPAD 20 bis was a racing aircraft also called upon to beat speed records. There were six variants numbered 20 bis1 to 20 bis6, each only having one example built except 20 bis5, which had two examples. All had the HS 8Fb engine with the exception of the 20 bis6.

These racing SPAD had their span progressively reduced for an increase in speed.

SPAD 20 bis1 made its first flight at Buc on the 1st September 1919.

- *Span :* - 10.02m
- *Length :* - 7.3m
- *Height :* - 2.9m
- *Wing area :* - 25m²
- *Max Speed :* - 250km/h

The SPAD 20-bis-1.

SPAD 20 bis2 Its span was reduced to 9.47m, and the wing area dropped to 23m². It could reach 252km/H. First flight was the 10th September 1919.

SPAD 20 bis3 This aircraft had a span of only 8.10m, with a wing area of 21.5m². It flew at 270km/h. First flight was on 25th September 1919.

These three aircraft, piloted by Sadi-Lecointe, participated at the Coupe de Vitesse Deutsch de la Meurthe.

SPAD 20 bis4 With only 6.60m span, it had a maximum speed of 290km/h. First flight was 2nd January 1920. Sadi-Lecointe moved to Nieuport and he was replaced by Jean Casale. The aircraft beat the world speed record on the 26th February, reaching 283.864km/h during the Coupe Deutsch de la Meurthe.

SPAD 20 bis5. Two machines were built for the Gordon Bennett Cup, the span was again reduced and was much lower than the previous models. The upper wing had no cabane struts and was fitted directly to the fuselage. The all up weight of the aircraft was 1050kg and it reached 300km/h. The first SPAD 20 bis5 flew for the first time on the 22nd September 1920 piloted by Jean Casale and the second aircraft flew the following day. The Gordon Bennett Cup was held on 28th September following, where the aircraft were flown by Jean Casale and Bernard de Romanet. The first was disqualified for a track error caused by the poor visibility. The second lost all chance of winning when an oil leak kept it on the ground for thirty-five minutes. At the meeting at Buc which opened on the 9th October, Romanet reached 292.682km/h. Two days later the pilot had to land in a field when the propeller became detached.

The SPAD 20 bis-5 is the one which differs most from the other SPAD 20-bis.

SPAD 20 bis6 This was the final evolution of the family of single seat racers, it was fitted with an engine even more powerful than that of its predecessors, an Hispano-Suiza 8Fe of 330hp. The machine was once again fitted with cabane struts. Romanet made the first flight at Buc on the 7th October 1920. He was obliged to land immediately because of cooling problems caused by the large spinner.

- *Span :* - 6.84m
- *Length :* - 6.48m
- *Height :* - 2.9m
- *All up weight :* - 1,200kg
- *Max Speed :* - 322km/h

The SPAD 20 bis-6 and its pilot Bernard Barny de Romanet.

Taken back to Suresnes, the 20 bis6 lost its spinner and its head-rest, the windscreen was reduced in size and the wing area was reduced from 15.2m² to 14m². The tail surfaces however, were increased in size. The aircraft flew again on the 3rd November 1920. The following day Bernard de Romanet took to the air again to attack the world speed record won by Sadi-Lecointe with a Nieuport the previous 20th October at 302.529km/h. Despite a thick fog which obliged him to fly at 2m above the ground, he beat the Sadi-Lecointe record with a speed of 309.012km/h.

The SPAD 20 bis-6 in its original state.

SPAD XXI

Derived from the large wing of the SPAD XVII, the SPAD XXI was also a single seat bi-plane fighter fitted with the same engine, an HS 8 F6 of 300hp. Only two machines were built.

Its flying tests were completed in October 1918, but the signing of the Armistice the following month led to the abandoning of series construction of this model.

- *Span* : - 8.54m
- *Height* : - 2.39m
- *Length* : - 6.3m
- *Max Speed* : - 220km/h

One of the two examples of the SPAD XXI during trials.

SPAD XXII

Another single seat bi-plane fighter designed at the end of 1918, the SPAD XXII was fitted, as was the SPAD XXI, with an HS 8F6 engine of 300hp and two 7.7mm Vickers machine guns.

It had the particularities of having the upper wing swept back and the lower wing swept forward. The SPAD XXI was named "high visibility" because of the shape of its lower wing allowing the pilot to see the ground better. It was only completed after the Armistice.

Tested at Buc at the beginning of 1919, but because of the end of the war, only the prototype was built.

- *Span* : - 7.95m
- *Height* : - 2.50m
- *Length* : - 6.20m
- *Max Speed* : - 228km/h

The strange and unique SPAD XXII with wings in sweep back and sweep forward.

SPAD XXIII

A two-seat bi-plane project with a Salmson RA9 engine of 240hp, was designed in 1919 for Japan.

SPAD XXIV

Land version of the sea-plane fighter SPAD XIV, the SPAD XXIV was a single seat fighter designed for the Navy's aircraft carrier. As on the SPAD XIV, it was fitted with an Hispano-Suiza HS 8Bec engine of 220hp. The aircraft flew for the first time on the 5th November 1918. Because of the signing of the Armistice, its test flying was not followed up, only the prototype was built.

- *Span* : - 9.80m
- *Height* : - 2.56m
- *All up weight* : - 950kg
- *Length* : - 6.48m
- *Wing area* : - 26.20m^2

The unique SPAD XXIV.

The SPAD 25 belonging to Robert Bajac, entered the Coupe Michelin. The two spare wheels were of no help.

SPAD 25

Work on this aircraft started in 1919 for the Danish pilot Leith-Jensen, who volunteered for the French army during World War I. The SPAD 25 was a single-seat bi-plane designed to cross the Atlantic non-stop, from Newfoundland to Ireland; an attempt for the Daily Mail prize. The fuselage was a lengthened SPAD 15, made watertight in order to float after emptying its tanks. The engine was Le Rhône 9Cda up-rated to 95hp.

The build was slowed by a strike, then abandoned when the prize was won by Alcock and Brown on the 14th June 1919.

In 1921 the SPAD 25 was re-engined with a Le Rhône 9 C of 80hp, and handed over to Robert Bajac for the Michelin Cup. After having been obliged to land at Miélan, in the Gers, Bajac took off again the following day the 30th August at dawn, but the engine stopped again near Tarbes, the aircraft fell into a sunken road and was too damaged to be repaired.

- *Span* : - 8.10m
- *Length* : - 16.50m
- *Wing Area* : - 19.90m^2
- *All up weight* : - 981kg
- *Empty weight* : - 267kg
- *Range* : - above 3,000km

SPAD 26 and 26 bis

SPAD 26 A racing sea-plane fitted with an Hispano-Suiza 8 Fe engine of 330hp, the SPAD 26 was a single-seat bi-plane. First flight was from the river Seine on the 28th August 1919. The following month it was transferred to England to participate in the Schneider Trophy races which were held at Bournemouth that year. The upper wing was reduced in span by 1.50m in order to increase its speed. The sea plane received racing number 6, but was eliminated from the competition, the pilot, Sadi-Lecointe, seriously damaged a float striking a hidden object during a take-off.

- *Span* : - 8.69m
- *Length* : - 8.10m
- *Height* : - 3.16m
- *Wing area* : - 26m^2
- *All up weight* : - 1,100kg
- *Empty weight* : - 850kg
- *Speed* : - 250km/h

SPAD 26 bis. The aircraft was entered for the Aviation Meeting in Monaco in April 1920, the SPAD 26 which had been fitted with new flat floats took part in the altitude competition, with an extended wing span (10.42m instead of 8.69m) and fitted with compensated ailerons. All up weight was 1,210kg, empty weight 925kg, and speed 214km/h. Carrying the race number 35, the SPAD 26 - with the new wing becoming the 26 bis - reached 6,350m on the 23rd April flown by Jean Casale. Two days later,

having been re-converted to the SPAD 26, it participated in the speed trial with the number 34. Flown by Bernard Romanet, it won the prize at an average speed of 211.395km/h. The circuit for the Guynemer prize was 80.5k with 6 turns.

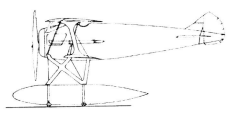

Above, the SPAD 26 and its cylindrical floats. Below, the same at Monaco, becoming the 26 bis with its larger wing.

The SPAD, again as a 26, takes off at Monaco, flown by Bernard de Romanet.

On the 27th April it again became the 26 bis. The aircraft flown by Jean Casale climbed to 6,500m in 1h 16m 10sec., winning the Rolland Garros prize, the sum of 2,500 francs; the prize was for the sea-plane which, between the 18th April and the 2nd May 1920, reached the greatest altitude.

SPAD 27

A three-seat public transport aircraft with an Hispano-Suiza 8Fa engine of 275hp, a "limousine" bi-plane, the SPAD 27 came out in November 1919, and was a cabin version of the SPAD XX fighter. Its dimensions were identical. Four examples were built and this model, of which the prototype was registered F-CMAV, was the first aircraft put into service on the line Paris to London.

Jean Casale flying a SPAD 27 beat the world altitude record with two passengers, reaching 6,800m on the 26th December 1919. A SPAD 27 flown by Bourdon won the race Paris to London in 4hrs 16min, and beat the speed record for the journey at an average 242km/h

- *Span :* - 9.72m
- *Height :* - 2.80m
- *Speed :* - 250km/h
- *Length :* - 7.30m
- *All up weight :* - 1,260kg

The SPAD 27 (the designation is written on the fuselage above the short mention "Blériot, constructeur"). The two passengers entered the cabin via the top of the fuselage. Below, an illustration by H. Gazan, taken from a catalogue of Blériot-Aéronautique... the aircraft brushes the peaks that it could fly over, at least in Europe.

SPAD 28 and 28 bis

SPAD 28 another development of the SPAD XX with the same fuselage, undercarriage and engine, the SPAD 28 was a single seat bi-plane with an Hispano-Suiza 8Fb engine of 300hp. Two examples were ordered by the Aeronautical Technical Service. The first SPAD 28 flew for the first time at Buc on the 26th September 1919. Handed over to Lieutenant Bajac it was destroyed the following year in an accident at Toussus-le-Noble.

The second example, handed over to Lieutenant Charles Nungesser to establish distance records. First flight was on the 10th November 1921. Nungesser was in total disagreement with management over the conditions imposed upon him and the project was abandoned.

- *Span* : - 10.50m
- *Height* : - 2.80m
- *Speed* : - 210km/h
- *Length* : - 7.30m
- *All up weight* : - 1,506kg

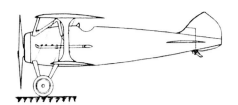

Factory schematic drawing of the SPAD 28.

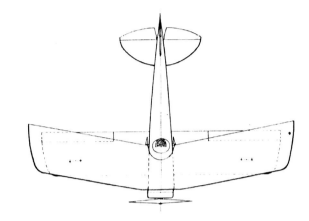

SPAD 28 *bis* The aircraft was transformed to a two-seater. Re-named therefore, 28 bis, it was entered in the Michelin Cup of 1921, with the crew Lieutenants Largeau and Daurelaincour. The aircraft crashed near Noyon and was destroyed.

SPAD 29 and 52

SPAD 29. Developed from the SPAD XV, the SPAD 29 was a two-seat tandem bi-plane touring aircraft fitted with a Le Rhône 9C engine of 80hp. After being exhibited at the Salon de l'Aéronautique in December 1919, the prototype SPAD 29 flew for the first time at Buc in January 1920, it was registered F-ABDK. Three examples of the SPAD 29 were built. The prototype was bought by André Dubonnet and the two others were acquired, one by Argentina and the other by Ecuador.

- *Span* : - 7.70m
- *Height* : - 2.35m
- *All up weight* : - 627kg
- *Speed* : - 160km/h
- *Length* : - 5.19m
- *Wing area* : - 18m^2
- *Empty weight* : - 397kg

SPAD 52 Two SPAD 29 were modified being fitted with the Le Rhône engine of 120hp, to become SPAD 52. The tail planes were enlarged and four ailerons were fitted instead of two. They were registered F-AEED and F-AEDD. They were handed over to Maurice Becquet and Jean Casale. Becquet was due to compete at the Grand Prix de l'Aéro-Club de l'Ouest in 1922, but weather prevented him from participating. After the death of Jean Casale F-AEDD was handed over to Pierre de Vizcaya who in turn gave it to the Musée de l'Air de Paris.

- *Length* : - 5.21m
- *Speed* : - 190km/h

The SPAD 29, future SPAD 52 belonging to Casale, behind is the SPAD XV belonging to Fonck.

SPAD 30 and 30 bis

SPAD 30 This single-seat touring bi-plane was fitted with an Anzani 6A engine of 45hp. Also shown at the Salon of 1919, the SPAD 30 made its first flight at Buc in January 1920.

- *Span* : - 7.14m
- *Length* : - 5.94m
- *Height* : - 2.24m
- *All up Weight* : - 460kg
- *Empty weight* :- 333kg
- *Speed* : - 170km/h

SPAD 30 *bis* The aircraft was re-engined the same year with a Le Rhône 9C of 80hp. It made a new first flight, this time as a

30 bis, and became a single seat aerobatic aircraft. All up weight went up to 480kg and its speed to 172km/h.

The unique SPAD 30, which became the 30 bis.

The new SPAD numbering system, from SPAD 31 onwards.

It is necessary to draw the reader's attention here to the numbering system of SPAD aircraft from 31 onwards, designed in 1920.

SPAD production is presented in this book in numerical order of the types, but this does not reflect the chonological order of designs, according to which, we would need for example, to place three fighters in the order : - SPAD 81, SPAD 61, SPAD 60 ... The first digit is not a chonological order. It designates a family. The second digit – or the last digit in the designation of three digits – is a function. In the numbering of Blériot aircraft, the numbering is simple and respected. With SPAD aircraft, it appears evident that the 6 of the SPAD 46, 56, 66, 86, 116

and 126, designates public transport aircraft ... except for the 36 (combat aircraft) and the 33, also a transport aircraft. In principle, because there are numerous exceptions, the 0 designated a two-seat fighter (for example SPAD 60), the 1 was reserved for single seat fighters (SPAD 61, 81, 91) the 2 for the two-seat tandem training aircraft (SPAD 42), the 4 for training aircraft (SPAD 34, 44), the 3, the 6 and the 7 for transport aircraft (SPAD 33, 37, 66) the figure 5 appears once (type 45) leads us to believe that this figure was reserved for multi-engine aircraft. The attribution of figures 8 and 9 is not clear. This logic, although far from perfect, explains that several numbers are not attributed, as shown by the production listing established by Blériot-Aéronautique. Also some designations carrying the suffix "bis" are not of an original version, but a totally different machine.

SPAD 31 and 31 bis

SPAD 31 This was a single-seat racing sea-plane designed for the circuit Monaco-Bizerte-Monaco, and was fitted with an Hispano-Suiza 8Fb engine of 300hp. It flew from the River Seine for the first time on the 10th April 1920. It had insufficient endurance to participate in the circuit.

The SPAD 31 was however, selected to represent France in the Schneider Trophy races to be held in Venice from the 20th September onwards. It did not take part in this competition, for reasons unknown.

- *Span* : - 10.43m
- *Length* : - 8.20m
- *Height* : - 3.32m
- *Wing area* : - 31.45m^2

- *All up weight* : - 1,510kg
- *Empty weight* : - 1,075kg
- *Speed* : - 210km/h

SPAD 31 *bis* This was a SPAD 31 fitted with wings from a SPAD XX and with Tellier floats. It was fitted with two machine guns and became a sea-plane fighter. Only one was built, it went to Japan in 1921.

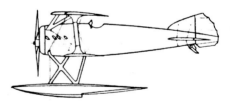
Factory schematic drawing of the SPAD 31.

SPAD 32

This single-seat bi-plane was designed for an attempt on the altitude record, with a Damblanc Mutti engine of 165hp, fitted with a variable compression to compensate for power loss at altitude. The speed trials at full power were cancelled because of a fault in the balancing of the engine. At the end of its first flight on the 10th May 1920, the engine of the SPAD 32 was sent back to the factory from where it returned seven months later. A new trial flight on the 30th December led to the definitive abandoning of the project.

- *Span* : - 8.59m
- *Length* : - 5.91m

- *Height* : - 1.51m
- *Wing area* : - 20.50m^2
- *All up weight* : - 675kg
- *Empty weight* : - 510kg
- *Estimated max speed* : - 200km/h.

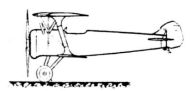
Factory schematic drawing of the SPAD 32.

Two Blériot-SPAD 33 on the aerodrome at Le Bourget.

SPAD 33, SPAD 33 bis, SPAD 47, SPAD 48, SPAD 49 and SPAD 50

SPAD 33 This single engine bi-plane was a four-seat public transport aircraft. The construction was a "shell fuselage" three thicknesses of tulip wood formed and glued around a mould. The prototype was fitted with a Salmson Z9 engine of 250 hp. This was a 9 cylinder water cooled engine; the aircraft flew for the first time at Buc on the 12th December 1920, the pilot was Albert Deullin. Registration was F-CMAZ. One afternoon Deullin flew the aircraft Paris to Strasbourg and back at an average speed of 180km/h. Forty examples of the SPAD 33 were built which were equipped, as was the prototype, with the Salmson Z9. From 1921 onwards, the aircraft was fitted with a Salmson CM9 engine of 260hp.

At the front, the cabin was fitted with four basket work seats and six port holes. Behind the cabin, the open cockpit was fitted with a head rest and protected by a windscreen. Two aerodynamic fuel tanks, each of a capacity of 400 litres were installed on the upper wing.

The Compagnie des Messageries Aériennes created in 1919 by a group of aircraft builders, among whom, Louis Blériot, bought fifteen SPAD 33 for the line Paris-London, Paris–Lille–Brussels and Paris-Brussels–Amsterdam. The Belgian Company SNETA (Sydicat National d'Etude du Transport Aériennes) bought five of them, putting them into service on the same destinations. The Compagnie Franco–Roumaine de Navigation Aérienne was founded on the 23rd April 1920 in Paris by Aristide Blanck, who was president of the Marmorosch Blanck Bank. The Bank bought twenty SPAD 33 for the lines from Paris to Prague, to Warsaw, to Budapest and later, Constantinople. Between times the Franco–Roumaine became the Compagnie Internationale de Navigation Aérienne (CIDNA) on the 1st January 1925.

The Company Air Union started on the 1st January 1923 as a result of the fusion between Messageries Aériennes and Grands Express Aériens, used several SPAD 33 on the line Paris to Marseilles from 25th May 1926.

Revision and repair of SPAD 33 fuselages. On the one in the centre an important repair shows how these fuselages were built, in several thicknesses of strips of tulip wood rolled around a mould. Here, the horizontal laths serve only to maintain the bands during bonding.

Manoeuvering a SPAD 33.

In order to train its pilots in blind flying, the CIDNA modified SPAD 33 N°3062, F-AICC, at the beginning of 1927, by fitting it with a larger wing with a profile RA 54 called "High Lift", and installed a second cockpit in the cabin without any forward visibility. Three SPAD 33 became type 50 (See SPAD 50), nine others became type 56 (see SPAD 56), one SPAD 33 became the prototype of the SPAD 46 (see SPAD 46)

- *Span* : - 11.66m
- *Length* : - 9.06m
- *Height* :- 3.20m
- *Wing area* : - 43m²
- *All up weight* : - 1,797kg
- *Empty weight* : - 1,050kg
- *Speed* : - 160km/h

SPAD 33 bis The SPAD 33 registered F-ADAS was modified in 1921 for engine trials requested by the STAé. With a Salmson A29 engine of 300hp it became the SPAD 33 bis, and could carry six people at 180km/h. It had a wing span of 11.66m and a length of 8.76m. Its height was 3.20m, its all up weight was 1,780kg. Speed was 162km/h. In 1922 the 33 bis became the 47 with the fitting of a Salmon AZ9 engine of 300hp.

- *Span* : - 11,66m.
- *Length* : - 8,76m.

SPAD 47 A SPAD 33 bis with a Salmson AZ 9 engine.

SPAD 48 At the end of 1921, the SPAD 33 F-FRAU of the Franco-Roumaine, was tested with a Lorraine 8bd engine of 275hp, and designated SPAD 48. It first flew on the 4ᵗʰ October 1921 but the combination was not a success and was not followed through.

The nose of the SPAD 48 and its Lamblin radiators.

SPAD 49 The SPAD 49 was designed at the request of the Belgian Company SNETA. It was a SPAD 33 with a Rolls-Royce Eagle VIII engine of 350hp. Only a mock-up of the engine was made in the SPAD works before the project was abandoned.

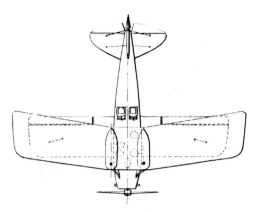

Plan view of the SPAD 49, a SPAD 33 with a Rolls Royce engine. Note the two open cockpits of the cabin SPAD, one for the pilot and the other for a passenger.

SPAD 50 The SPAD 50 was another version of the SPAD 33, the only difference being the engine, an Hispano-Suiza 8Fb or Fd engine of 300hp. The prototype was registered F-ESAX and then F-ADAR. First flight was on the 23ʳᵈ December 1921. The dimensions and performances are those of the SPAD 33 with the exception of the ceiling, 1,000m higher.

Another SPAD 50 was built with a larger wing span for Pierre–Etienne Flandin, Pilot and Under Secretary of State for Aviation up to 1921, a lawyer linked to several aviation companies and future Minister. The aircraft was registered F-AECH .

In 1923 three SPAD 33 of the Compagnie Messargies Aérinnes, numbers 7, 10 and 16 were transformed into SPAD 50.

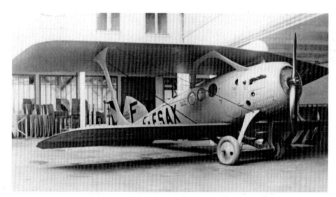

Above, the first completed SPAD 50. Below, the same SPAD 50 in service. The inscription reads "Charge utile: 660kg" (Useful load: 660kg).

SPAD 34, SPAD 34 bis, SPAD 52

SPAD 34-1. This was a single engine side by side two–seat bi-plane trainer, it was fitted with a Le Rhône 9C engine of 80hp. First flight was on the 16th July 1920.

- *Span* : - 6.45m
- *Height* : - 2.36m
- *Wing area* : - 18m²
- *Speed* : - 155hm/h

SPAD 34–2. The SPAD 34–1 was judged too fast and too delicate to be a basic trainer aircraft, and was abandoned to be replaced by the SPAD 34–2 with the same engine. It appeared in September 1920 and one hundred and fifty were built, of which one hundred and nineteen for military aviation, six for the Navy, six for Argentina, one for Bolivia and two for Finland. They were equipped with wheels or with floats which made the aircraft 5cm longer and 12cm higher. The SPAD 34–2 flown by Bourdon took off easily from the airfield of La Paz, even though the airfield was at 4000m above sea level. A SPAD 34–2 flown by Deullin, flew from Paris to Strasbourg to Prague. Another flown by Béquet won the Henry Roget Cup.

Easy to fly with a cruising speed of 110km/h the SPAD 34–2 remained in service until 1936.

- *Wing area* : - 21m²
- *All up weight* : - 719kg
- *Empty weight* : - 470kg
- *Max speed* : - 145km/h

SPAD 34–3 A single example of this machine was built for experiments with a mobile leading edge. First flight was on 30th April 1923. See also SPAD 54.

Opposite, two views taken at Buc of the SPAD 34-1 side by side two-seater. Below, one of the three 34 bis aquired by the French Navy.

SPAD 34 bis This touring version of the SPAD 34–2 kept the same dimensions, only the tail surfaces were enlarged. It was fitted with a Clerget 9B engine of 130hp, It was a little heavier (all up weight 740kg, empty weight 482kg) but a little faster (160km/h) First flight was on the 1st December 1920. Three examples were ordered for the Navy, contract N° 906, dated 24th October 1922. Two SPAD 34 bis were based at Marignane, the third one, at Saint–Raphaël was registered S–41. Seven further machines were built for the civil market, of which three were handed over to Bajac, Béquet and Janoir. A modified SPAD 34 bis became the SPAD 54 bis.

SPAD 35

The SPAD 35 was never built. It was designed in 1920 as a variant of the SPAD 20, with an Hispano-Suiza 8Ab engine of 180hp, for the Chilean Air Force.

- *Span* : - 9.72m
- *Length* :- 7.30m
- *Height* : - 2.80m

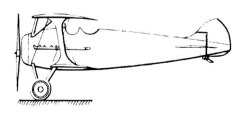

Schematic drawing of the SPAD 35 project.

SPAD 36 P2

Designed in 1920, the SPAD 36 P2 was a two-seat Army aircraft designed for high altitude reconnaissance. It corresponded to a new programme established after the first World War, stipulating a ceiling of 8,500m and a speed around 200km/h. Five machines were ordered in 1921 of which one was to be a static test frame, it made its first flight on 17th January 1923. The construction was typical SPAD for the period with monocoque fuselage and wing of fabric covered metal structure. The fuselage had the particularity of being deep but narrow in order to facilitate vertical view of the ground by the crew.

It was fitted with an Hispano-Suiza 8Fbr engine of 300hp. The engine was fitted with a Rateau super charger, to establish nominal power at 6000m. The fine tuning of the super charger was made impossible because of the lack of suitable metal alloys. The project was abandoned.

- Span : - 11.469m
- Length : - 9.024m
- Height : - 3.25m
- Wing area ; - 39m^2
- All up weight : - 1,725kg
- Empty weight : - 1017kg
- Ceiling : - 7000m
- Max speed : - 200km/h

The SPAD 36, characterized by its high, narrow fuselage.

SPAD 37

Only one SPAD 37 was built and was flown by the *Compagnie Messageries Aériennes* with the registration F-CMAW. Its first flight was on the 9th September 1920. It was a four place development of the SPAD 27. The pilot's open cockpit was at the rear, passengers sat in two open cockpits positioned close to the centre of gravity. Right at the front, two passengers were seated side by side deep inside the fuselage, as can be seen by the presence of a porthole either side. The third passenger is behind them, also in an open cockpit just in front of the pilot. It was fitted with an Hispano-Suiza 8Fg engine of 275hp.

- Span : - 9.72m
- Length : - 7.30m
- Height : - 2.80m
- Wing area : - 31.50m^2
- All up weight : - 1,716kg
- Empty weight : - 1,066kg
- Ceiling : - 6000m
- Max speed : - 190km/h

The unique four-seat SPAD 37, a pilot and three passengers. The inter-plane strut hides the small fuselage porthole.

SPAD 38 and 38 bis

The Navy, studying various means of transporting aircraft, carried out trials with a system designed before the First World War. This was a cable stretched the length of the ship, where aircraft would hook on. SPAD developed the type 38 under its own initiative, by modifying two SPAD XV, with a hook system above the upper wing. The aircraft was fitted with a Le Rhône engine of 80hp. The first aircraft, which made its first flight on 25th October 1920, was destroyed following a stall accident. The second aircraft with a different hook system was designated 38 bis. The formula would be taken up again for aircraft attached to American Airships.

- Span : - 7.10m
- Length : - 5.51m
- Total height : - 4.0m
- Wing area : - 16m^2
- All up weight : - 500kg
- Empty weight : - 320kg

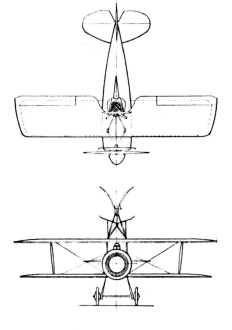

Schematic plan view drawn at the factory of the SPAD 38.

Conclusive ditching trials of the unique SPAD 39 at Saint-Raphael.

SPAD 39

At the beginning of the 1920s, the Navy requested the aircraft industry to design a land aircraft capable of ditching in the sea without danger, and to float until such time as it could be recovered by a crane. SPAD proposed a "Marine SPAD". The wing had a hollow profile to improve take off performance. But the principle feature was the undercarriage fitted with wheels that could be jettisoned, and in front of the axle, a large rectangular float with a tear drop profile. The fuselage and the lower wing were made watertight. The wing struts in inverted V were reinforced to absorb the shock of contact with the water. The float, the two struts which held it in place and other miscellaneous reinforcing increased the overall weight of the two-seater by about 100kg, bringing the all up weight to 1,520kg. However, fitted with an Hispano-Suiza 8Fg engine of 275hp, the SPAD 39 exceeded the Specification Performance, flying at 211km/h where 150km/h was stipulated, and climbing fully loaded to 2,000m in less than

14 minutes, when the Specification stipulated a maximum of a quarter of an hour.

On the 27th July 1921, Bernard de Romanet tried the first ditching on the Seine, but the aircraft turned over and disappeared under the water. Romanet escaped unharmed, the machine was recovered and repaired. Another trial at Saint-Raphël was conclusive. Nevertheless the Navy chose the Levasseur aircraft whose lower fuselage was in the shape of a boat.

The SPAD 39 with its "float" between the wheels.

SPAD 40

After the failure of the Rateau supercharger, the Army modified its two-seat recognisance bi-plane programme, and Herbemont converted the SPAD 36 with the V 12 Lorraine Dietrich 12Da engine of 370hp. He kept the fuselage and the wings and the engine was fully enclosed. The static tests were carried out on a SPAD 36.

The SPAD 40 was equipped with the new cylindrical Lamblin radiators under the nose. First flight was on 22nd August 1922. The following year the Government who had ordered the prototype, had it modified by fitting a Lorraine 12Db engine of 400hp. The aircraft flew for the first time on 17th January 1924, but no series production contract was forthcoming.

- *Span* : - 12.47m for the upper wing, 11.425m for the lower wing

- *Length* : - 9.024m
- *Height* : - 3.25m
- *Wing area* : - 43m²
- *All up weight* : - 1,982kg
- *Empty weight* : - 1,288kg
- *Max speed* : - about 220km/h

The unique SPAD 40, a modified SPAD 36.

SPAD 41 and SPAD 41 bis

SPAD 41 This was a single-seat fighter, another version of the SPAD 20. The fuselage was shorter and the wing structure was in metal. It was armed with two 7.5mm Vickers machine guns in the fuselage synchronised to fire through the propeller arc, and two Darne of the same calibre in the upper wing.

Ordered by the Government, this aircraft flew for the first time on the 17th July 1922. It was fitted with an Hispano-Suiza 8Fb engine of 300hp and Lamblin radiators. It reached 243.5km/h but its ceiling of 6,500m was judged insufficient.

SPAD 41 bis This same aircraft was modified to 41 bis in 1924 to beat the speed record over a 1,000km. It was fitted with extra fuel tanks which formed two humps above the upper wing. It was flown by Adjutant Discours of the STAé. After 300km when the aircraft was well in front of the time to beat, the motor broke. Discours who was flying very low landed immediately but the aircraft nosed over. He escaped unharmed but the aircraft was destroyed by fire.

- Span : -8.68m
- Height : - 2.76m
- All up weight (41) 1307kg
- Empty weight : - (41) 887kg
- Length : - 6.65m
- Wing area : - 26.40m
- Ceiling : - 6250m

The unique SPAD 41 as it came out of the factory, unarmed.

The unarmed SPAD 41. The traditional front radiator is replaced by two Lamblin radiators.

SPAD 42

This aircraft flew for the first time on the 6th August 1921 and was presented by the builder as a two-seat trainer aircraft, directly derived from the SPAD VII. The fuselage was lengthened to accommodate a second cockpit, but the wing layout was more modern with a single strut on either side and a greater span. As on many SPAD aircraft in the years after the war, the upper wing was advanced to improve the upward visibility from the front cockpit, and built with sweep back to re-establish the centre of gravity. The aircraft was ordered by the Government at the end of 1921. In 1923 André Bernard, pilot of the STAé presented the aircraft at the Concours des Avions de Tourisme, the aircraft was well noted for its speed.

Nineteen SPAD 42 were built. Thirteen were bought by the Navy in 1923, and one of them landed on the new aircraft carrier *Béarn*, two were sent by Blériot-Aeronautique to the flying

school at Buc, they were registered F-AEGB and F-AFCE, two were exported to Persia and two to Japan.

- Span : - 8.65m / 74.70m
- Height : - 2.65m
- All up weight : - 1,004kg
- Ceiling : - 4,800m
- Length : - 6.77m
- Wing area : - 22.12m^2
- Empty weight : - 684kg
- Max speed : - 180km/h

A SPAD 42. The name Blériot is on the fuselage and the fin.

SPAD 43

The only trace of the SPAD 43 that the author has found, is a note on the bottom of the commercial brochure of the SPAD

34. It is possible that this three-seat aircraft was not built. It was presented as a SPAD 34 fitted with a Clerget engine of 130hp, with a *special wing and rear passenger*.

SPAD 44

At the Nieuport factory where the type 29 was modified as a record beating monoplane, in 1920 Herbemont had a project to transform the SPAD 20 bis5 into a monoplane. It was to be

flown by Bernard de Romanet at the 1920 Gordon Bennett Cup. The design was started the day after the race. The wing was to be fitted directly to the fuselage in front of the cockpit, and reinforced by two struts. The work was started and then abandoned.

The "Super Aircraft" shown half completed in the Grand Palais, in Paris. It would be finished as the Blériot 105.

SPAD 45 "Super aircraft"

Herbemont tried to extend the success of his airliners, in developing the design of the Blériot 76 bomber into a four engined transport aircraft, the SPAD 45.

The 15m long fuselage was built as a circular section monocoque, large enough to carry twelve passengers and three crew. Four Hispano-Suiza 8F engines of 275hp were fitted in pairs on the lower wing, two pushing, two pulling. The upper wing with a slight sweep back had a shorter span than the lower wing. The struts were reduced to the simplest possible. The undercarriage was two 2 wheel axles fully enclosed.

The aircraft, which was capable of being re-roled as a night bomber, was ordered by the Government. Unfortunately the static tests were not conclusive and the SPAD 45 was abandoned. In fact it became the Blériot 105 in August 1924 after being modified by Léon Kirste.

- *Span : - 23.90m*
- *Height : - 6.18m*
- *All up weight : - 5,430kg*
- *Projected max speed : - 175km/h*
- *Length : - 15.30m*
- *Wing area : - 130m²*
- *Empty weight : - 3,226kg*

The SPAD 45 is shown with temporary cabin layout.

The cockpit of the SPAD 45.

A SPAD 46 before departure.

SPAD 46, SPAD 66, SPAD 86, SPAD 116, SPAD 126

SPAD 46 The SPAD 46 was a modified SPAD 33 transport aircraft for three to five passengers, four of whom were in an enclosed cabin. It was fitted with a Lorraine 12Da engine of 370hp. The fuel tanks contained 500l. The wing span was 12.60m in order to lift an all up weight of more than 2.10 tons. The first example, registered F-AGFD, flew for the first time on the 16th June 1921. It confirmed the designers expectations through various flights in the regions served by the Compagnie Franco-Roumaine, and won the Circuit d'Anjou in covering 315km in a little under two hours in very poor weather conditions.

The Compangie Franco-Roumaine ordered thirty-eight machines for a total 2.28million francs; altogether forty were built.

- *Span : - 12.60m*
- *Length : - 9.0m*
- *Height : - 3.20m*
- *Wing area : - 47m²*
- *All up weight : - 2,105kg*
- *Empty weight : - 1,417kg*
- *Projected max speed : - 180km/h*
- *Radius of action with 36km/h head wind : - 400km*

SPAD 66 In 1925 when the Franco-Roumaine became CIDNA, Compgaine Internationale De Navigation Aérienne, the thirty four SPAD 36 which remained, were slightly modified with a headrest behind each of the open cockpits. They were designated SPAD 66. The Company also modified eight of it's SPAD 33 to SPAD 66.

SPAD 86 The SPAD 86 was certified in 1925. In fact it was the first production SPAD 46, registered F-AHDI, but re-engined with a Lorrain 12EW engine of 450hp. The engine configuration was in a W. The empty weight dropped to 1,3502kg and the all up weight increased to 2,360kg. This aircraft was in service until 1929.

SPAD 116 The SPAD 116 was the SPAD 46 (modified to SPAD 66) N° 32, F-AEHH, re-engined by the CIDNA, via André Herbemont, with a Renault 12Ja engine of 450hp. It was taken out of service in 1930 with 1,296 flying hours.

SPAD 126 In 1929, the CIDNA again modified F-AHDI to carry out in-service tests with the Hispano-Suiza 12Ha engine of 450hp. Herbemont was in charge of the tests. The aircraft became thus, the SPAD 126. The all up weight was 2,430kg and its empty weight was 1,623kg.

The aircraft was taken out of service in 1931 with 685 flying hours.

Above, a SPAD 66: a SPAD 46 with head rests. Below, the unique SPAD 86, the first modified SPAD 46.

SPAD 47 to SPAD 50

See SPAD 33

The prototype SPAD 51 fighter, with Gnome and Rhone Jupiter engine.

SPAD 51, SPAD 251

SPAD 51 The SPAD 51 was designed following the 1924 specification for a single-seat fighter; it was destined to find a successor to the famous Nieuport 29. The specification imposed four machine guns and a power of 380 to 500hp. The fuselage of the SPAD 51 was shorter and less bulky than the preceding SPAD monocoque fighters. However, the aircraft was very close to the SPAD 41 fighter which was only ever used for attempts on speed records. The wings and undercarriage were of metal structure. The engine was the new Gnome et Rhône Jupiter 9cylinder air-cooled radial. Several variants were fitted to several versions of the SPAD 51. The prototype, SPAD 51-1, with a Jupiter 9Aa engine of 380hp flew on the 16th June 1924.

SPAD 51-2 A version with a Jupiter 9Ab engine of 420hp, flew on the 18th August 1925. At the Concours des Chasseurs Monoplaces of the same year, it was noted by climbing to 8,000m in 38 minutes. One example was reserved for the STAé, fifty others were bought by Poland.

SPAD 51-3 This aircraft was used for trials on a Blériot variable pitch propeller, which allowed a gain of 12km/h at 2,000rpm. First flight was on the 7th September 1926.

SPAD 51-4. This aircraft was fitted with a super charged Jupiter 9Ac engine of 600hp. First flight was on the 30th August 1928. One machine was sold to the USSR, another to Turkey and a third to Spain.

SPAD 251 A fourth SPAD 51-4 with a Jupiter 9Ab engine was registered F-AIVS to serve as overseas demonstrator. Re-engined with a Jupiter 9Aa and re-designated 251, it was sold in 1933 to a private owner M. Tournier, as an aerobatic aircraft.

Above, the SPAD 51 no 2. Below, the prototype of the variable pitch propeller on the SPAD 51-3.

- *Span* : - 9.47m/8.47m
- *Length* : - 6.45m
- *Height* : - 3.10m
- *Wing area* : - 23.95m^2
- *All up weight* : - 1,311kg
- *Empty weight* : - 886 kg
- *Useful load* : - 475 kg, of which 165 for armament
- *Ceiling* : - 8,650m
- *Max speed of the 51-2* : - 219.2km/h at 2000m

SPAD 52

See SPAD 29

SPAD 53

The SPAD 53 was a derivative of the SPAD 34, with a longer fuselage, and a larger wing area with the objective of reducing the landing speed. It was fitted with a Clerget 9Bc engine of 110hp. Four machines were built, registered F-ADBT, F-ADBV, F-ADDQ and F-ADDR. They made very few flights before going into storage and then being re-assembled in 1924. Three were re-converted to SPAD 54-3 in 1928.

- *Span :* - 8.98m
- *Height :* - 2.57m
- *Max speed :* - 140km/h
- *Length :* - 7.14m
- *All up weight :* - 709kg

SPAD 54

The SPAD 54 was very similar to the SPAD 53, but was fitted with a Le Rhône engine of 80hp. Fourteen versions are known.

This SPAD 53 became a 54 bis with a new engine.

SPAD 54-1 The first one was fitted with a Blériot undercarriage, designed in 1908. It made its first flight on the 23rd February 1922. The Blériot undercarriage was rapidly abandoned for a more classic design. Twenty five production machines were ordered by the Government in February 1922, for the training of future military pilots.

SPAD 54-2 This was the first SPAD 54-1 re-engined with an Anzani of 90hp. It made its first flight on the 18th April 1925.

SPAD 54-2bis The SPAD 54-2 was re-fitted with the rotary Le Rhône engine in 1929. It was also fitted with new shock absorbers. It therefore became the SPAD 54-2bis. Eight machines were purchased by Brazil and one by Japan.

Above, a SPAD 54-1 with a Le Rhone rotary engine. Below, the unique SPAD 54-5 with Salmson engine.

SPAD 54-3 or SPAD 54bis This was a series of nine SPAD 34, 34bis, 53 and 54-1, re-engined with a rotary Clerget 9B of 130hp.

SPAD 54-4 This was a SPAD 54-1 re-engined with a Salmson 9Ac of 120hp, and fitted with a new higher undercarriage to improve the ground clearance of the propeller. First flight was on the 14th April 1926. On the 30th July this aircraft was the very first to tow a publicity banner.

SPAD 54-5 In 1927 Herbemont started the design of the "all engine" SPAD 54-5. This meant a system to adapt the SPAD 54 to be capable of accepting all sorts of engines from 80 to 150hp. The aircraft F-AHBE served as guinea pig. The first trials were carried out on the 4th June 1928 with a Lorraine 5Pc engine of 120hp, the aircraft was designated SPAD 54-5a. On the 28th August it became SPAD 54-5b with a Salmson 7Ac engine of 95hp. Apparently the maximum speed did not change (115km/h)! On the 6th October, F-AHBE was fitted with a Le Rhône 9C rotary engine of 80hp, and was designated SPAD 54-5c. In 1946 it was fitted with an in-line Hirth engine, then later, returned to an original configuration with a Salmson engine. It was offered to the Musée de l'Air where it is currently on show.

F-AHBA was modified by its owner in 1935 with a Renault 4Pgi Bengali engine of 100hp, which gave it a maximum of 125km/h.

- *Spans :* - 8.97m/8.27m
- *Height :* - 2.57m
- *All up weight :* - 757kg
- *Max speed :* - 112 to 120km/h
- *Endurance :* - 3hrs at full power
- *Length :* - 7.24m
- *Wing Area :* - 23.52m²
- *Empty weight :* - 520kg

Above, the SPAD 54-3. Below, the SPAD 54-5 F-AHBA with Renault Bengali engine.

The cabin of a SPAD 56.

SPAD 56

The SPAD 56 was the ultimate of the now famous *Blériot-SPAD Berlines, 33 and 46 logical conclusion of never ending improvements brought to these aircraft during their long service over the most diverse routes and climates.*

This time it was a case of using the excellent Gnome and Rhône Jupiter engine. The fuselage remained wooden monocoque, with fabric covered metal for the wings.

The SPAD 56, registered F-AGEO, took off for the first time at Buc on the 3rd February 1923. The engine was a Jupiter 9Aa of 380hp. Flown by Jean Casale, it beat two World Altitude records the same month, 4,790m with 500kg and 7,338m with 250kg.

Belonging to the Government, F-AGEO was loaned to the CIDNA for service trials with an extra fuel tank of 110litres. Maurice Noguès pioneered the lines towards the Middle East, but on the return flight on 24th December 1925, he was forced to ditch off Naples. He was saved unharmed but the aircraft was lost.

- *Span* : - 13.08m
- *Height* : - 3.51m
- *All up weight* : - 2,045kg
- *Useful load* : - 500kg
- *Length* : - 9.0m
- *Wing area* : - 46.28m²
- *Empty weight* : - 1,470kg
- *Max speed* : - 180km/h

SPAD 56-2 This was initially built as a personal aircraft for Louis Blériot. It was registered F-AIDC and made it's first flight on 28th September 1925. Similar overall to its predecessor, it was fitted with four ailerons linked two-by-two by a streamlined strut.

In 1928 it was modified for banner towing for the company Air Publictié. The wings were different, built in wood with a profile giving a better lift. Dimensions and performance were those of

the SPAD 56; it was fitted with a Gnome and Rhône Jupiter 9Ab engine of 420hp.

- *All up weight* : - 2244kg (2,310 with *Air Publicité*)

The SPAD 56-2 painted blue and silver when it belonged to L. Blériot.

SPAD 56-3 Six machines of this version were built for the CIDNA, and two for Air Union. It was comparable to the SPAD 56 but easily recognisable by it's four port-holes per side. It carried more fuel, but above all, six passengers instead of four. Air Union fitted it's SPAD 56-3 with the Jupiter 9Ab engine. The first flight was on the 14th June 1926. On the 9th August the same year Robert Bajac, with the first production model, F-AIEE made an exceptional flight, Paris to Marseilles and return in the same day, a total of almost eleven flying hours. They were fitted with either a Jupiter 9Aa or 9Ab engine of 380 or 420hp.

- *All up weight* : - 2449kg

The first SPAD 56.

A SPAD 56-3 modified to 56-4.

SPAD 56-4 At the request of the Aviation Companies, the SPAD 56 was modified in moving the open cockpit to the front, and the cabin fitted out for six passengers. The upper wing was raised to improve the pilot's visibility. The wing profile was increased to reply to new standards, which imposed higher coefficients of resistance. The axle between the wheels was removed. It was fitted with a Jupiter 9Ab or 9Ady engine, both of the same power. First flight was on the 25th October 1926. Twelve machines were built, two of them being modified SPAD 56-3, four of them being used by Air Union.

- *Span* : - 13.15m
- *Height* : - 4.10m
- *All up weight* : - 2,712kg
- *Useful load* : - 739kg
- *Ceiling* : - 4,000m
- *Length* : - 9.0m
- *Wing area* : - 48.60m²
- *Empty weight* : - 1471kg
- *Max speed* : - 192km/h

SPAD 56-5 Six SPAD 56-3 were modified to become the SPAD 56-5. Registrations were consecutive F-AIEM to F-AIER. The pilot's cockpit was in the front. It was fitted with a Jupiter 9Aa engine. The passenger cabin was divided into two compartments, one for four passengers, the second for two passengers or freight. The all up weight was 2,657kg, and the maximum speed was 172km/h

SPAD 56-6 Two machines were built, F-AJTN and F-AJVA, for Air Publicité. The pilot's cockpit was to the rear. The high-lift wing had no dihedral on the lower main plane. The four-place passenger cabin also had a winch for banner towing. The tail unit was enlarged and fitted with a new trim mechanism to facilitate the pilot's task with the different centres of gravity. It was fitted with a Jupiter 9Ab engine.

See also the SPAD 76

One of the SPAD 56-4 with a cockpit at the front.

The second SPAD 56-6, for banner towing.

SPAD 57

Unused designation

SPAD 58

This was a racing aircraft derived from the SPAD 41 fighter with a wing structure in duralumin, and was destined to participate in the Coupe Deutsch de la Meurthe of 1922; it was to be flown by Jean Casale. It was christened *Louis Blériot*. It was painted in blue and white and carried the racing number 3. It was fitted with a Lorraine 12Eb engine of 450hp. The engine was in a W configuration. On the 30th September it was the first to take off ... after a takeoff run of only 45m. Flying at over 246km/h it suffered an important leak on one of its radiators, Lamblin had to abandon the race.

- *Span* : - 8.68m
- *Height* : - 2.80m
- *Length* : - 6.59m
- *All up weight* : - 1,250kg
- *Max speed* : - 250km/h

The unique racing SPAD 58 at the time of the Coupe Deutsch de la Meurthe.

SPAD 59

Unused designation

SPAD 60 C.2

Three examples of this two-seat fighter with a Jupiter 9Ab engine of 420hp were ordered by the Government in 1925. They were to be armed with four machine guns firing forward, plus a turret for defence. First flight was on 26th June 1926. It reached a maximum speed of 201km/h and climbed to 4000m in 15 mins. 39s. One of the three machines became the SPAD 70.

- *Spans* : - 11.30m / 10.40m
- *Length* : - 6.88m
- *Height* : - 3.215m
- *Wing area* : - 36.60m^2
- *All up weight* : - 1,803kg
- *Empty weight* : - 1,224kg

- *Max speed:* - 209km/h
- *Theoretical ceiling* : - 6,800m

The first SPAD 60 in 1926.

The first SPAD 61 shortly after completion photographed in the factory in Suresnes.

SPAD 61, SPAD 61 bis

This family of single seat fighters with two synchronized machine guns was well thought of; there were fourteen variants.

SPAD 61-1 Only one example was built following a contract of 1922, making its first flight on the 6th November 1923, and taking part in the Concours des Avions de Chasse of 1924. The Lorraine 12Ew engine of 430hp gave it an aggressive but flowing silhouette. The fuselage was wooden monocoque and the wing structure was metal. A retractable radiator by Vincent André was positioned beneath the engine.

- *Span* : - 9.40m
- *Length* : - 6.48m
- *Height* : - 2.80m
- *Wing area* : - 29.50m^2
- *All up weight* : - 1,503kg
- *Empty weight* : - 1,005kg
- *Max speed* : - 250km/h
- *Theoretical ceiling* : - 6,400m

SPAD 61-2 This aircraft followed in 1924 with a wing structure in wood and its cabin struts spread wider to improve forward visibility. It reached 237km/h and climbed better thanks to a slight increase of wing span. 381 machines were built, 280 - of which 30 under licence - were for Poland, a further 100 went

to Romania. One last example was modified to SPAD 61-bis. Numerous accidents showed that the resistance co-efficient calculated by the builder was over optimistic. The aircraft was not very manoeuvrable and recovery from a spin was difficult. Four machines F-AHBJ, F-AHDG, F-AHDH and F-AIRN, destined for Poland were retained at Buc and gradually improved with each with each problem being identified. The main wing spar was reinforced.

- *Span* : - 9.53m
- *All up weight* : - 1,531kg
- *Max speed* : - 237km/h

The SPAD 61-2, a great commercial succss.

The unique SPAD 61 bis.

SPAD 61 bis The sixth SPAD 61-2, F-AHDJ once reinforced, was modified to take a Lorraine 12Eb engine of 450hp, and was registered F-AIKU to act as overseas demonstrator.

SPAD 61-3 Identical to the 61-2 but with a metal wing structure containing a supplementary fuel tank. It was fitted with two extra Darne machine guns in the upper wing, this aircraft corresponded to the new programme. First flight was on the 9th May 1925. The speed was 212.60km/h at 4,000m; altitude reached in 10 mins. 46 ses.

- *All up weight* : - 1,565kg • *Empty weight* : - 1,075kg
- *Max speed* : - 215.7km/h
- *Theoretical ceiling* : -7400m

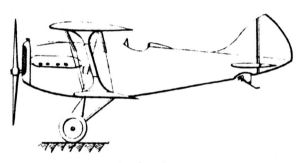

Factory drawing of a SPAD 61-3.

SPAD 61-4 Also destined for the Concours des Chasseurs of 1925, this aircraft resembled the SPAD 61-3, but was equipped with a Lorraine 12Ee engine of 480hp. It was slightly faster but did not climb as well.

The unique 61-4 similar to the 61-3, except for the engine and radiator.

SPAD 61-5 Resembling the SPAD 61-3, this variant was built on Blériot's initiative during the first quarter of 1925, with an Hispano-Suiza 12Gb engine of 450hp. The engine was in a W configuration. First flight was on the 19th May 1923. It reached 233km/h but was seriously damaged during a trial by Capitaine de Slade, at the GEPA. It was re-built to be presented at the Concours des Avions de Chasse in 1925, but was not able to participate because it was damaged again by a fall of a beam inside its hanger. It was repaired and used as a test stand for the Zenith carburettor, beating a climb to ceiling record, 6,000m in

14min 38secs. It was flown by Capitaine Stadion. It was then modified to a SPAD 61-8.

Another SPAD 61-5 was sold to Turkey, and a third with wing structure in wood was included in the Polish production series.

- *All up weight* : - 1,631kg • *Empty weight* : - 1,093kg
- *Max speed* : - 240km/h
- *Theoretical ceiling* : - 7,750m

The SPAD 61-5, an elegant silhouette.

SPAD 61-6 This version had four sub-variants.

The SPAD 61-6a was the old SPAD 81 bis converted to a flying test stand for the Lorraine 12Eb engine of 450hp. First flight was on the 31st March 1925.

Top, two photos of the SPAD 61-6c carrying the logo of Pelletier d'Oisy. Above, the same becoming 61-6d.

The same machine became SPAD 61-6b, F-ESAU, with the same engine but a larger fuel tank, to be flown by Capitaine Pelletier d'Oisy (nick-named Pivolo) for the Coupe Michelin of 1925. This modified version flew for the first time on the 25th June 1925. Pelletier d'Oisy won the 1925 Cup, completing the course of 2,835km, with stops, at an average speed of 187.129km/h.

The same aircraft was again modified to become SPAD 61-6c, to try for the World speed record over 1,000km. First flight was on the 10th November 1925, but was destroyed seventeen days later during an attempt by Lieutenant Maurice Bizot.

The SPAD 61-6d was a modified SPAD 61-2 with a Lorraine 12Ew engine. It was registered F-AIIU for the Coupe Michelin of 1927. Flown by Léon Challe, it won the Cup at an average speed of 215km/h. Several months later it became a SPAD 61-9.

- *All up weight : - 1,600kg*   • *Empty weight : - 1,150kg*
- *Theoretical ceiling : - 6,000m*

SPAD 61-7 This variant was designed to beat the World Altitude record. It was fitted with a Lorraine 12Eb engine of 480hp, the supercharger was a Rateau. The wing span was 11.72m giving a wing area of 37.7m². Jean Gallizo, who already held an impressive World Altitude record, was engaged by Blériot, and improved upon his previous performance by reaching 12,440m on the 23rd August 1926. The following year an out-raged Louis Blériot discovered that Gallizo had cheated in manipulating the barograph ... he had never reached the altitude recorded. The wings of the SPAD 61-7 were then modified and fitted with a new engine at the request of the Services Techniques, who bought the aircraft. It flew again in January 1928 before being withdrawn from service.

- *Spans : - 11.72m/10.64m*   • *Length : - 7.185m*
- *Height : - 3.22m*   • *Wing area : - 37.70m²*
- *All up weight 1,500kg*
- *Empty weight : - 1,202kg*

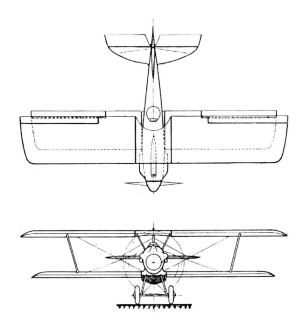

Factory plan view of the SPAD 61-7 aircraft for World Altitude Record attempt.

SPAD 61-8 This was a fighter aircraft, a modification to the second SPAD 61-5. It was fitted with an Hispano-Suiza 12Hb engine of 500hp.

- *Span : - 9.40m*   • *Length : - 6.78m*
- *Height : - 2.8m*   • *Wing area : - 30m²*
- *All up weight : - 1,631kg*   • *Empty weight : - 1,093kg*
- *Max speed : - 240km/h*

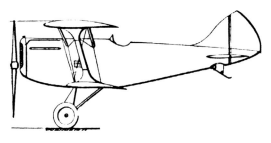

Schematic profile of the SPAD 61-8.

SPAD 61-9 This variant was obtained by fitting a SPAD 61-6d with a Lorraine 7ma radial engine of 230hp. This was to conform to the new rules of the Coupe Michelin of 1929. The wing area was also reduced.

It was registered F-AJCR. Even though the aircraft was seriously under- powered, the pilot, Léon Challe, finished only a few minutes behind the winner, Michael Détroyat, flying at an average of 183km/h. It was then used for public demonstration flights.

- *Span : - 8.20m*   • *Length : - 6.90m*
- *Height : - 3.08m*   • *Wing area : - 20.50m²*
- *All up weight : - 1,326kg*   • *Empty weight : - 845kg*
- *Max speed : - 200km/h*
- *Theoretical ceiling : - 3,750m*

The SPAD 61-9 during the Coupe Michelin of 1929.

SPAD 61 "ses" This ultimate variation of the SPAD 61 was built at the request of Poland. It was a Sesquiplane whose upper wing was advanced to improve the pilot's visibility. The wing tips had a sweep back in order to re-establish the centre of gravity. There was no improvement in performance, and the aircraft which made its first flight on the 1st May 1926, was abandoned.

- *Max Span : - 10.40m*   • *Length : - 6.78m*
- *Height : - 2.80m*   • *Wing area : - 30m²*
- *All up weight : - 1,590kg*   • *Empty weight : - 1,100kg.*

SPAD 62

One SPAD 62 was built in 1923 to be shown at *the* Concours des Avions–Ecoles which was held that year from the 28th May to the 7thJuly. First flight was on the 18th April 1923, and it was purchased by the Government in October, at the same time as the SPAD 64 and SPAD 72.

Derived from the SPAD 42 it was a two-seat tandem biplane fitted with an Hispano-Suiza 8Ab engine of 180hp. It was designed for second stage training.

- *Spans* : - 8.65m and 7.70m
- *Length* : - 6.77m
- *Height* : - 2.80m
- *Wing area* : - 23.70m^2
- *All up weight* : - 1,025kg
- *Empty weight* : - 717kg

- *Max speed* : - 180km/h

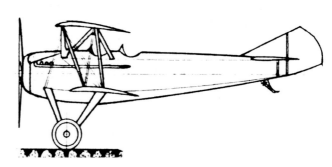

The similarities of the SPAD 62 with the SPAD of 14-18 are evident.

SPAD 63

Unused designation

SPAD 64

Two-seat side by side basic trainer, the SPAD 64 made it's first flight on the 5th April 1923, to be shown at the Concours des Avions-Ecoles. It was derived from a lightened SPAD 54, fitted with a steerable undercarriage - of a 1908 design – and fitted with a Le Rhône rotary engine of 180hp. It had no better success than the SPAD 62; it was however purchased by the Government.

- *Span* : - 8.96m
- *Length* : - 7.25m
- *Height* : - 2.84m
- *Wing area* : - 23.52m^2
- *All up weight* : - 761kg
- *Empty weight* : - 511kg

- *Max speed* : - 130mm/h

The SPAD 64 with its undercarriage designed in 1908.

SPAD 65

Unused designation

SPAD 66

See SPAD 46

SPAD 67 to SPAD 69

Unused designations

SPAD 70 C.2

Even though it had the designation C.2 - a two-seat fighter - this single aircraft resulted from a Government order that appears to have no other destination except experimental. It was a SPAD 60 C.2 modified by removing the armament and by adapting a Lorraine 12Eb engine of 450hp. The supercharger was a Rateau. First flight was on the 21st April 1927 and it was delivered to the STAé.

- *Length* : - 7.5m
- *Height* : - 3.20m
- *All up weight* : - 1,393kg
- *Max speed* : - 210km/h
- *Empty weight* : - 1,331kg

All other characteristics identical to the SPAD 60 C.2

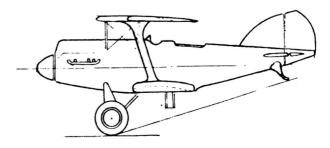

The SPAD 70 C.2 was a re-engineered SPAD 60 C.2.

SPAD 71

The SPAD 71 was a single seat fighter derived from the SPAD XX. The cockpit was insulated from the Hispano-Suiza 8Fb engine of 300hp by a metal fire wall which did not exist on the previous model. The tail surface area was increased. The wings were fitted with four ailerons. Leaving the factory in January 1923 the aircraft was shown at the Spanish Concours de Chasseur Monoplace, and was purchased by Spain.

- *Max span* : - 9.72m
- *Length* : - 7.30m
- *Height* : - 2.80m
- *Wing area* : - 30m^2
- *All up weight* : - 1,360kg
- *Empty weight* : - 867kg

- *Max speed* : - 237km/h

The SPAD 71 could be considered as a modernised SPAD XX.

SPAD 72

The silhouette of the SPAD 72 which flew for the first time on the 15th April 1923, was remarkably similar to that of the SPAD VII which appeared six years earlier. It was in fact a SPAD VII with an Hispano-Suiza engine of 180hp, and modified according to new standards with a longer undercarriage. The flying wires were simplified and the structure re-enforced. Without armament it was destined for pilot progression, conforming to the rules of the 1923 Concours des Avions-Ecoles. It had no more success than the SPAD 62 and SPAD 64, but was paid for by the Government.

- *Spans* : - 7.822m/7.572m
- *Length* : - 6.35m
- *Height* : - 2.60m
- *Wing area* : - 18m^2

- *All up weight* : - 874kg
- *Empty weight* : - 634kg
- *Max speed at ground level* : - 188.9km/h

The SPAD 72, second-cycle trainer.

SPAD 73 to SPAD 75

Unused designation

SPAD 76

This single engine bi-plane project was started in 1926 to replace the famous cabin aircraft. A wind tunnel model was made but the airlines did not want this old generation aircraft. The Fokker VII monoplane attracted all the attention, and it is this that the transport companies wanted. As a result, the project was abandoned. See the SPAD 86 bis.

- *Max span* : - 16m
- *Length* : - 11m
- *Height* : - 4.50m
- *Wing area* : - 66m^2
- *All up weight* : - 2350kg
- *Empty weight* : - 1,800kg

- *Max speed* : - 190km/h

The SPAD 76 exists only as drawings and in model.

SPAD 77 to SPAD 80

Unused designations

SPAD 81

Despite its high designation number, the single-seat fighter SPAD 81, was a contemporary of the SPAD 61, with which it shared many attributes, in fact, one SPAD 81 became a SPAD 61-6. One can suppose therefore, that this aircraft was a development of the SPAD 61. However, the facts show that the SPAD 81 was older than the 51, 61 and 71. The SPAD 81 was designed in 1922, and the prototype flew on the 13th March 1923, nine months before the end of the build of the first SPAD 61. It corresponded to the 1922 specification for a single-seat fighter of 300hp. The specification stated two machine guns, at least 242km/h at 5,000m and a ceiling of 9,000m. The SPAD 81 was a bi-plane with wings of metal structure and a wooden monocoque fuselage. The upper wing was carried above the fuselage by a single pylon in front of the pilot. First flights showed that this disposition was not good, and the pylon had to be replaced by short, oblique struts. The machine was found to be unstable in flight, the fuselage had to be lengthened and the tail unit increased in area.

SPAD 81-1 The modified prototype 81, was designated 81-1 in production. First flight was on 5th September 1924. This same year, even if performances were judged to be slightly inferior to its only competitor, the Dewoitine D.1 metal monoplane, eighty machines were ordered for the Aviation Militaire. The last production SPAD 81-1 was delivered with a frontal radiator without the designation being modified.

SPAD 81-2 This was a prototype tried as early as May 1924, with a retractable radiator in place of the two Lamblin radiators fixed under the cowling of the Hispano-Suiza 8F engine.

SPAD 81-3 This was a SPAD 81-1, number 79, modified in August 1924 with a radiator called "Pile of plates". It was destroyed in an accident.

SPAD 81-4 This was a SPAD 81-1 modified with a wing structure in wood.

- *Spans* : - 9.612m/8.80m
- *Length* : - 6.40m
- *Height* : - 2.90m
- *Wing Area* : - 30m²
- *All up weight* : - 1,266kg
- *Empty weight* : - 846kg
- *Max speed* : - 235km/h

A SPAD 81 carrying the insignia of the SPA 65, shown by Villechanoux at Vincennes. The SPAD 81 was the "big brother" of the SPAD 51, 61 and 71.

The SPAD 81-1 photographed from all angles in the factory in Suresnes, for a brochure.

The SPAD 81-1 no 3: the engine is more closely cowled.

The SPAD 81-2 with retractable radiator.

SPAD 81bis

This "rapid single-seat tourer" derived from the 81 under the initiative of the Company, had a wing area of 20m². First flight was on the 3ʳᵈ August 1923, but attracted no customers and was modified to SPAD 61-6.

- Max span : - 8.20m
- Length : - 6.40m
- Height : - 2.90m
- Wing area : - 20m²
- All up weight : - 1091kg
- Empty weight : - 760kg
- Max speed : - 250km/h

SPAD 82

This sesquiplane with large wing span was built in fabric covered wood, for the towing of publicity banners; it allowed experiments into low speed flight. The very long fuselage had a horizontal tail plane larger than normal, in order to ensure manoeuvrability at low speed. Although it had two open cockpits, it was a single-seater. The cable and the winch in the front cockpit was operable by the single pilot. It was fitted with an Hispano-Suiza 8Ad engine of 180hp, "type dirigible" fitted with a reduction gear driving a large diameter propeller, turning at 700rpm. The aircraft flew for the first time on the 18ᵗʰ November 1926. The aircraft was flown the following year with the wing span greater than 19.20m. The wing profile had a double curve designed by Henri Coanda. The abandoning of this wing so soon after its first flight of the 27ᵗʰ April 1927, leaves no doubt as to it's inefficiency. After the conclusion of a series of experiments, the SPAD 82 was abandoned for further trials with a two-seater carrying an operator for the winch.

- Spans : - 13.10m/12.60m
- Length : - 7.80m
- Height : - 3.02m

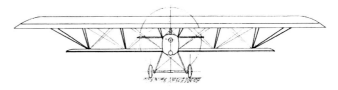

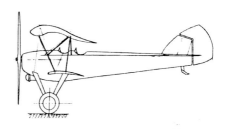

Schematic drawing of the SPAD 82 with the Coanda wing.

SPAD 83 to SPAD 85

Unused designations.

SPAD 86

See SPAD 46.

SPAD 86 bis

Despite its designation, the SPAD 86 bis had no relation to the cabin aircraft SPAD 86, excepting that this was also a transport aircraft. It was a high wing monoplane with an in-line engine and the cockpit at the front, the profile was similar to that of the Fokker VII. Designed by Herbemont at the request of the CIDNA, the 86 bis was never built. Only a wind tunnel model was ever made.

At this time Blériot decided to turn towards the more modern formula of the low wing monoplane, and built the Blériot 111.

- Span : - 15.50m
- Length : - 10.30m
- Height : - 3.70m

SPAD 87 to SPAD 90

Unused designations.

SPAD 91

The single-seat fighter SPAD 91 conformed to the illusory specification of "Jockey Fighters" of 1926 and 1928, destined to adapt needs to reduced budgets.

Armament was limited to two machine guns and a radius of action of 400km. Herbemont therefore designed an aircraft qualified as "SPAD 91 light". The structure was all metal, the fuselage was mainly rectangular tubes with lightening holes.

It was fitted with an Hispano-Suiza 12Hb engine of 500hp. First flight was on the 23ʳᵈ August 1927 and was registered F-AKBP. It was a subject of many tests with such a new structure.

It exceeded 270km/h and could fly easily at an altitude of 7,000m. After 200 flying hours it was dismantled and revealed *no appreciable deterioration nor apparent wear*. The fighter was then modified to SPAD 91-4.

- Span : - 8.65m
- Length : - 6.52m
- Height : - 3.04m
- Wing area : - 22.20m²
- All up weight : - 1439kg
- Empty weight : - 1,088kg
- Max speed : - 278km/h
- Ceiling : - 8,000m

SPAD 91-1 On this second SPAD 91, the honeycomb radiators, which had been placed against the landing gear, were moved to a frontal position.

- *Span* : - 8.50m
- *Height* : - 3.04m
- *All up weight* : - 1,465kg
- *Max speed* : - at 4,000m 270km/h
- *Ceiling* : - 8,500m
- *Length* : - 6.20m
- *Wing area* : - 20m²
- *Empty weight* : - 1,161kg
- *Climb to 4000m* : - 7' 48"

SPAD 91-2 This was the only SPAD 91 which was not financed by the Government order for four SPAD 91, passed in 1930. First flight was on the 31st August 1928, fitted with an Hispano-Suiza 12Gb engine in W configuration. It was equipped with the Blériot "elastic wheels", the spring and shock absorber being contained inside the wheel rim. It was then registered F-AIVT for a tour of Greece and Romania. Upon its return it was modified to SPAD 91-3.

- *Span* : - 8.65m
- *Height* : - 3.04m
- *All up weight* : - 1,439kg
- *Max speed* : - 265km/h
- *Length* : - 6.22m
- *Wing area* : - 22.20m²
- *Empty weight* : - 1,088kg
- *Ceiling* : - 8,000m

Three images of the SPAD 91 called "Light Fighter" and its narrow cockpit before the fitting for the fuselage covering.

SPAD 91-3 This was a SPAD 91-2 re-engined with a Gnome and Rhône 9As Jupiter VII, supercharged to 420hp. It flew on the 6th June 1930. In the spring of 1931 it became a SPAD 91-5.

- *Length* : - 6.35m
- *Empty weight* : - 970kg
- *All up weight* : - 1270kg

SPAD 91-4 The prototype SPAD 91 registered F-AKBP, was re-engined with an Hispano-Suiza 12Mb of 450hp, and fitted with a thinner wing, becoming therefore the SPAD 91-4. First flight was on the 4th July 1930. The following year it was subject to major modifications and became a SPAD 91-6.

- *Length* : - 6.30m
- *Empty weight* : - 1110kg
- *All up weight* : - 1,440kg
- *Max speed* : - 285km/h

The SPAD 91-4.

SPAD 91-5 The SPAD 91-2 - then SPAD 91-3 - F-AIVT, was re-engined with a Gnome and Rhône 9AE Jupiter VI of 420hp, to become the aerobatic aircraft of Raymond Villechanoux, one of the SPAD company pilots. A few days after its first flight it crashed, on the 10th May 1931 during a public demonstration at Niort, Villechanoux was killed.

- *Length* : - 6.36m
- *Wing area* : - 22m²
- *Empty weight* : - 945kg
- *Ceiling* : - 8,000m
- *Height* : - 3.04m
- *All up weight* : - 1,260kg
- *Max speed* : - 265km/h

SPAD 91-6 The prototype, F-AKBP, became SPAD 91-6 having been heavily converted, the inter-plane height increased by 15cm, rounded wingtips, a cut-out in the upper wing centre section, and the tail plane lowered. First flight was on the 10th November 1931. In May 1932 the tail plane was returned to its original position. The aircraft was used by the pilots of the STAé, and then abandoned.

- *Span* : - 8.80m
- *Height* : - 3.10m
- *All up weight* : - 1,439kg
- *Max speed* : - 294km/h
- *Length* : - 6.84m
- *Wing area* : - 22m²
- *Empty weight* : - 1,160kg
- *Ceiling* : - 8,700m

The SPAD 91-6.

SPAD 91-7 The same F-AKBP was designated SPAD 91-7 and re-registered F-ALXC, after being re-engined with an Hispano-Suiza 12Mc of 500hp. The span of the upper wing was considerably reduced. In this form, flown by Louis Massotte, it beat the World Speed Record over 500km, at an average speed of 308.779km/h, on the 2nd June 1932.

- Length : - 6.5m
- Height : - 2.87m
- Wing area : - 17.80m²
- All up weight : - 1,458kg
- Empty weight : - 1,093kg
- Speed at 4000m : - 295km/h
- Ceiling : - 8,000m

The SPAD 91-7 World Speed record holder, flown by Louis Massotte, emplyed by Blériot the previous year.

SPAD 91-8 This was the same F-ALXC re-engined with an Hispano-Suiza 12Xbrs supercharged to 500hp.The fuselage

had a head rest for the pilot, the engine cowling was pierced to improve cooling, the propeller was a ground-adjustable Ratier.

- Spans : - 7m/8.65m
- Length : - 6.03m
- Height : - 2.87m
- Wing area : - 17.80m²
- All up weight : - 1,458kg
- Empty weight : - 1,093kg
- Speed at 3500m : - 360km/h

The SPAD 91-8, ex 91-7.

SPAD 91-9 F-ALXC was used for flight tests with a cannon firing through the Hispano-Suiza 12Xcrs engine. It was fitted with a Levasseur metal propeller. It participated in the 1933 Coupe Michelin, without being placed.

SPAD 92, SPAD 922, SPAD 923, SPAD 924

SPAD 92-0 The SPAD 92-0 was designed as a basic single-seater, inexpensive and easy to repair, designed to be a "transformation" aircraft for pilots, that is to say up to navigation exercises and flight tests. Fifteen production machines were built for the Blériot school at Buc, just after November 1928.

The fuselage was fabric covered wood with piano wire cross bracing. The bi-plane configuration had metal longerons and wooden ribs "for ease of repair". For the same reasons the wing tips were detachable if anything was hit. It had a wide undercarriage track to reduce the risk of ground loops, the fuel tank could be jettisoned. It was fitted with an Hispano-Suiza 8Ab or Ad engine of 180hp. It had a large wing area with a low speed. It was in fact, a safe aircraft.

- Span : - 10m
- Length : - 7.10m
- Height : - 3m
- Wing area : - 26.15m²
- All up weight : - 1,077kg
- Empty weight : - 854kg
- Max speed at ground level : - 161km/h

The SPAD 92-0 no 5.

SPAD 92-1 An aerobatic aircraft fitted with a Salmson 9Ne engine of 175hp

The SPAD 92-0 no 8, modified in 1922.

SPAD 922 These were eight SPAD 92-0 modified as two-seaters, with a cut out in the wing centre section, and re-engined with a Salmson 9Ab of 230hp.

- Length : - 7.196m
- Height : - 3.05m
- Wing area : - 24.40m²
- All up weight : - 1232kg
- Empty weight : - 922kg
- Max speed : - 200km/h
- Ceiling : - 6,200m

SPAD 922 V One of the 922 was modified with a V tail to evaluate the flight characteristics, as a result of work done by the STAé, and to prepare the adaptation of this tail - which would later be called "butterfly" - to high speed aircraft. Two controls which work at the same time as rudder and elevator, were actioned via an "oscillating rudder bar", patented by Blériot. First flight of the aircraft with a V tail was 12th October 1935. Louis Massotte carried out all the elementary aerobatic figures, including spins, and estimated that the aircraft was more stable than with its old tail plane. (See SPAD 710)

- *Length* : - 7.20m other characteristics unchanged.

The SPAD 92-0 no 1, became the 922 no 2, then the 922 V with a butterfly tail which was expected to give a reduction in drag.

SPAD 923 The SPAD 922 n° 8, F-AJHK was modified to an aerobatic aircraft for Louis Massotte, and with a Lorraine 9Na Algol engine of 300hp. It was painted white and blue.

SPAD 924 The SPAD 923 F-AJHK became SPAD 924 after several improvements, NACA cowling around the engine, wheels spats, wind profile bi-convex, inverted systems, and a smoke system. Flown by Louis Massotte, it was christened *Raymond Villechanoux*.

- *Length* : - 7.10m
- *Height* : - 3m
- *Wing area* : - 25.30m^2
- *All up weight* : - 1,233kg

The SPAD 92-4.

SPAD 116

See SPAD 46

SPAD 126

See SPAD 46

SPAD 210

The project of the SPAD 210 was presented to the STAé in reply to an eventual programme of a "Jockey Fighter" of 230hp. A model went to the Eiffel wind tunnel on the 5th November 1929, but the programme was not published. The machine was presented as a small version of the SPAD 91. The undercarriage had no cross axle and the two legs had a common shock absorber in the fuselage. It was fitted with a Gnome and Rhône 5Bc Titan engine of 230hp.

- *Span* : - 7.84m
- *Length* : - 6.20m

- *Height* : - 3.24m
- *Wing area* : - 16.45m^2
- *All up weight* : - 1,100kg
- *Ceiling* : - 8,200m

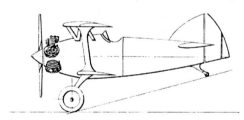

The SPAD 210 project.

SPAD 310

This aircraft was also a project in preparation for the improbable "Jockey Fighter" programme. The design was a mid-wing layout with the wing in plan form almost elliptic. The wing root was very narrow to improve the downward visibility. The undercarriage was without cross axle and with its legs in pressed steel presented as a "type PZL" the name of the largest Polish Aviation company. It was fitted with a Gnome and Rhône 7Kb Titan engine of 280hp.

- *Span* : - 10.0m
- *Length* : - 6.5m
- *Height* : - 3.0m
- *Wing area* : - 15.0m^2
- *All up weight* : - 1,020kg

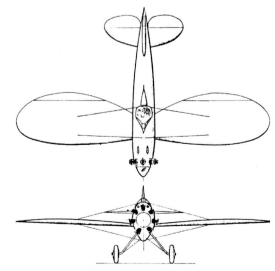

The SPAD 310 project with a radical vision of the elliptic wing, recently invented in Germany.

SPAD 510 and SPAD 511

This was the last fighter aircraft built in series to carry the famous SPAD name. This SPAD 510 had a direct link to the SPAD 91. The dossier was opened in 1930. A scale model went to the wind tunnel in 1931, and the project submitted to the Ministry, which ordered a prototype in 1932. The all-metal aircraft was built at Suresnes. The fuselage centre section was in duralumin and steel, it was in the form of a cage, for the cockpit and two synchronised machine guns. The rear of the fuselage was a metal shell made of duralumin sheets, following the Kellner-Béchereau method. It was fitted with an Hispano-Suiza 12Xbrs engine of 500hp, then 690hp. Cooling was by a frontal radiator. The air going through the radiator was evacuated by lateral openings in the cowling. First flight was on the 6th January 1933. Louis Massotte flew the tests flights, reaching 10,600m in 29min, and 360km/h at 4,000m. Registered as F-AKGW, the aircraft was then sent to the STAé who tested it with different propellers, and then requested several modifications, the fitting of an Hispano-Suiza 12Xirs or 12 Xcrs (cannon mounting), four machine guns, an improvement to the stability by lengthening the fuselage. SPAD replied that the frame was strong enough to accommodate all types of engine, up to 1,000hp, but lengthened the centre section of the fuselage by 40cm "without appreciable reduction performance", according to the words of André Herbemont..

The very first SPAD 510 in 1933, an all-metal fighter with an excellent climb rate.

The SPAD 510 no 18 at the Fighter Group 11/7 in 1937.

The SPAD 510 no 56. These aircraft were painted dark green and grey with the French Air Force.

The definitive engine was a Hispano-Suiza 12Xbrs of 690hp. The four MAC34 machine guns were arranged under the lower wing below the struts. The addition of a radio, TSF (Télégraphie Sans Fil), and instruments for blind flying, completed the definition of the production version. This was then evaluated by the Military. One of them judged the flying qualities severely, which made Louis Blériot request a public demonstration.

Louis Massotte carried out a series of six times thirteen spins without difficulty, to eliminate the alarming report from the Military. Nevertheless, the army considered that the SPAD 510 was out dated. Louis Blériot complained to the Minister, denouncing the manoeuvres of bad publicity of which he was the subject, and obtained a confrontation at Reims with the all new Dewoitine 510 monoplane. Both aircraft had an open cockpit and a fixed undercarriage. The D.510 was fitted with an engine capable of accepting a cannon - whose use was denied on the SPAD 510. It was not surprising that the SPAD 510, a bi-plane, was shown to be more manoeuvrable, and much better in the climb. It climbed better even than the first modern French monoplane, the Morane-Saulnier 405, with a closed cockpit and tractable undercarriage. It is to be noted that the British Gloster Gladiator, bi-plane with fixed undercarriage and an engine of 650hp, obtained similar results when compared to the Hawker Hurricane, monoplane, with retractable undercarriage and an engine of 1000hp.

Finally 80 SPAD 510 were ordered on the 13th August 1935, more than two years after the first flight!

Of the eighty SPAD 510 built, twenty were delivered to the Spanish Republic and sixty to the French Air Force, where they went into service in April 1937 with the 7th Escadre de Chasse. The leader, René Weiser, head of the fighter group II/7 transformed his famous demonstration patrol onto the SPAD 510, and gave twenty-one demonstrations over the whole of France. The aircraft was manoeuvrable, but the engine cut out during the chandelles, but above all the undercarriage was fragile.

When the more modern machines entered service, the SPAD 510 was sent to schools and instruction centres. In May 1940 around forty remained, of which a good half were in an Air Force depot; seven or eight were in flying condition.

- *Span* : - 8.84m
- *Height* : - 3.418m
- *All up weight* : - 1,677kg
- *Max speed at 4100 m* : - 372km/h
- *Radius of action* : - 875km
- *Length* : - 7.465m
- *Wing area* : - 22m^2
- *Empty weight* : - 1,250kg

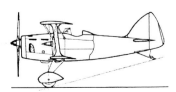

Factory drawing of a long SPAD 510.

SPAD 511 In between times, in 1933, André Herbemont designed the SPAD 511, a SPAD 510 with a Lorraine 12Hars "Petrel" engine of 600hp. This version remained at the project stage.

SPAD 510 J In 1934, Herbemont developed two other projects, the SPAD 510 J2, with a Gnome and Rhône 9Kers radial engine of 600hp, with a reduced span on the upper wing, as on the SPAD 91-7. He also developed the SPAD 510 J3. This was a SPAD 510 with a Gnome and Rhône 14drs engine of 760hp. He was hoping for 400km/h. The aircraft was particularly interesting to the Navy because the landing speed was less than 100km/h. For them he designed a version equipped with flotation chambers and a landing hook. A version with larger wing span was also designed for night flying. None of these projects were ever made.

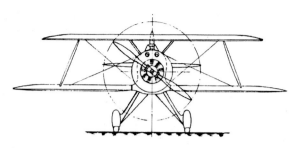
The SPAD 511 project.

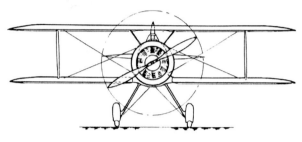
The SPAD 510 J2 project.

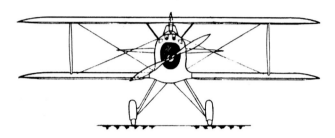

The SPAD 510 J3 project.

SPAD 610

The SPAD 610 was a pre-project of a sea-plane, derived from the SPAD 510 but fitted with a larger tail and a wing lay-out called "night flying". The STAé did not follow up.

- *All up weight : - 1850kg* • *Wing area : - 28m²*
- *Max speed at 3,500m ; - 288km/h*

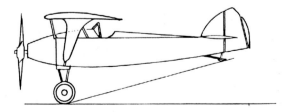
The SPAD 610 project.

SPAD 540, 541, 542

Replying to the specification from 1929, the SPAD 540 was designed to replace the SPAD 54. Side by side two-seater with fuselage a little shorter, it was above all the first SPAD monoplane (if we exclude the projects of the SPAD 86bis and SPAD 310). First flight, a few months after the order of a prototype, was on the 4th October 1930, with a Salmson 7Ac engine of 95hp. The main undercarriage legs were linked to a shock absorber in the fuselage.

- *Span : - 10.90m* • *Length : - 7.08m*
- *Height : - 2.80m* • *Wing area : - 19m²*
- *All up weight : - 862kg* • *Empty weight : - 630kg*
- *Max speed : - 145km/h*

SPAD 541, SPAD 542 The SPAD 541 was fitted with a Salmson 9Ac engine of 135hp, it became SPAD 542 with a Salmson 7Aq engine of 135hp, and a slightly larger wing.

SPAD 541

- *Span : - 12.30m* • *Length : - 7.15m*
- *Height : - 3.09m* • *Wing area :- 22.10m²*
- *All up weight : - 950kg* • *Empty weight : - 683kg*
- *Max speed : - 150km/h*

The SPAD 540 no 1, the first monoplane SPAD, built in 1930.

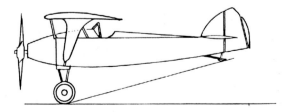
Factory schematic profile of the SPAD 541.

The Martinet

This racing monoplane was originally a Caudron. If it is to be mentioned in this chapter about SPAD aircraft, it is because it was the product of a modification by SPAD. André Herbemont was to adapt a super-charged 200hp Régnier engine to the fuselage, replacing the fixed undercarriage by retractable undercarriage (Blériot patent n° 793494 of the 23rd November 1935) and to modify the wing as a result of this. He had to lower the cockpit to eliminate all turbulence on the rear of the fuselage (a solution adopted by Caudron the following year).

All of this work was so that Louis Massotte could fly the aircraft in the Coupe Deutsch of 1935, but he had to abandon because of the unreliability of the engine. This problem caused the abandoning of several later record attempts. The system of retractable undercarriage on the Martinet, was later used on the SPAD 710.

The Régnier Martinet at the beginning of the Coupe Deutsch of 1935.

SPAD 710

Another derivative of the SPAD 510, the SPAD 710 was a two-seat fighter with closed cockpit. The fuselage was a fabric covered metal structure. The upper centre section of the wing was very thin to improve visibility. The pilot had an in-line 20mm cannon and four light machine guns. The machine gunner, sitting behind the pilot, facing rearwards, had one or two machine guns.

The Blériot undercarriage was retractable, the tail plane was in a V configuration, but without compensation. Flaps fitted to the under surface of the upper wing made the compensator unnecessary. Calculations from the study from the wind tunnel model, showed a maximum speed of 470km/h, with an Hispano-Suiza 12Ycrs engine of 860hp.

- *Span* : - 8.84m
- *Height* : - 3.06m
- *Length* : - 7.60m

First flight of the SPAD 710 was in April 1937. After the first trials the gyroscopic effects of the propeller with its 860hp, were judged too strong, and Herbemont doubled the offset angle of the engine. At Buc on the 17th June 1937, during a trial carried out in high winds (a test that Herbemont wished to delay), Louis Massotte was victim of tail plane flutter. The aircraft fell from a height of 150m, slid along a ditch and caught fire. The mechanics tried in vain to extract the pilot from the flames.

The saga of SPAD aircraft thus came to an end by a double tragedy – a fatal accident and the disappearance of the name under Nationalisation – after having started in the most glorious manner possible.

Even though derived from the 510, the SPAD 710 was a two-seat fighter.

13

The Blériot-Blanchard and Guillemin

THE BLERIOT FACTORIES WERE ALSO THE SCENE OF OTHER BUILDERS: GOUPY, BLANCHARD, GUILLEMIN, LIGNEL, ETC.

The Goupy n°2

The Goupy n° 2 was built at the beginning of 1909 in the workshop at Neuilly, it looked like a Blériot XI bi-plane. It followed on from the Goupy n° 1, which was a tri-plane built the previous year, by the Voisin brothers. Built according to the wishes of Ambroise Goupy, helped by Lieutenant Calderara of the Italian Navy, it was fitted, like the first Blériot XI, with a 30 hp REP engine, and a wooden four-bladed propeller. Its fuselage, its control bell, its undercarriage, its tail wheel and its rudder were all very similar, if not identical, to those of a Blériot XI. However, the wings and the horizontal tail plane were both bi-plane, the upper surface in both cases, staggered forwards.

Also, in both cases, the upper and lower wings were linked to each other by removable vertical panels. The elevator was in front of the propeller.

- *Span* : 6.0m
- *Length* : 7.0m
- *Wing area* : 20m²
- *Max speed* : 75km/h
- *All up weight* : 290kg with 35 litres of fuel and 10 litres of oil

Successful trials were carried out at Buc on the 9th March 1909, flown by Goupy it made a flight of 200 metres, at 7 or 8 metres of altitude, then another of 100 or so metres flown by Lieutenant Calderara. The machine was then re-worked, initially a single-seat, and then later fitted out as a two-seat. The eleva-tor was replaced by a moving section of the horizontal tail plane, the ailerons were re-positioned and the wing area increased by 2m². The REP engine was replaced by a 25 hp three-cylinder Anzani, and the four-bladed propeller was replaced by a two-bladed *Chauvière Intégrale*. In 1910 the aircraft was fitted with a Gnome engine of 50hp. The undercarriage was modified. At the second Champagne meeting, Ladougne beat the World Speed record with a passenger, over 10 kilometres, in 8 minutes 14 2/5 seconds. The wing span was increased by 1.0m and the wing area by 5m². Described as "Double monoplane" the Goupy was shown at the third Salon in December. The Goupy Company would make a sea-plane and a military three-seater before disappearing in 1914.

The Goupy no 2 with REP engine.

THE BLANCHARD SEAPLANES

Blanchard HB 3, Blériot-Blanchard HB 3 four engines, Blanchard HB 3 T2, Blanchard HB C1 and Blanchard HB 3 T

Blanchard HB 3. On the 30th December 1922, the engineer Maurice Blanchard was given an order for a prototype (n° 990/2) for a twin-engined three-seat surveillance seaplane. On the recommendation of Léon Bathait, Blanchard obtained the agreement of Louis Blériot, that the construction of his machine could be carried out at Suresnes.

It was a bi-plane with a hull in birch and mahogany, it was equipped with two, 260 hp Hispano-Suiza 8 Fd Marine engines in pusher configuration, and fitted in nacelles between the wings. Only the upper wing was fitted with ailerons. It flew for the first time in August 1923. The machine had two individual side-by-side cockpits, and two machine gun positions, one in the front, The other behind the wings. It took part in the cruise/race in the Mediterranean, which was held from the 1st to the 5th September 1923.

The prototype of the Blanchard HB 3.

Out of ten machines entered, eight, including the two Blanchard aircraft, got through the eliminatory trials. The race itself was run over the route Saint-Raphaël-Ajaccio-Bizerte-Ajaccio-Berre. The HB 3 with 548kg of useful load was flown by Maréchallat carried the n° 6. On the first stage he broke down at fifteen miles to the west of Calvi. The crew was saved by a boat, but the seaplane sank whilst being towed to the coast. It had cost 350,000F.

The HB 3, accepted by the STAé, 24 were ordered in two contracts in January and December 1923. They were built by Blériot who had acquired the production rights. On the 14th April 1924, Pelletier-Doisy reached an altitude of 2130m, world records for altitude with 250, 500, 1,000 and 1,500kg of useful load. In practice it could carry 150kg of bombs or a fourth crew member, and two small calibre machine guns.

- *Spans* : 19.0m/17.0m
- *Length* : 13.60m
- *Height* : 4.20m
- *Wing area* : 85m²
- *Empty weight* : 2,500kg
- *All up weight* : 3,915kg
- *Ceiling* : 4,000m
- *Max speed* : 170km/h

A Blanchard HB 3 of the 5R1 Squadron of the French Navy.

Blériot-Blanchard HB 3 four engines. One example of the HB 3, this time associating the name of Blériot with the name of the designer, was modified in June 1923 with four Hispano-Suiza 8A engines of 180hp fitted two by two in tandem also took part in the cruise/race, carrying the n° 9. It also completed the preliminary rounds with 785kg of useful load, a record for the competition. Slowed down because of a problem in a fuel tank, it reached Ajaccio without a problem. On the following stage, Ajaccio-Bizerte, the aircraft broke down and had to land within sight of the Tunisian coast. It was also taken in tow, but the cable broke after dark, and this machine was also lost. The total cost was 400,000F.

- *Empty weight* : 2300kg
- *All up weight* : 3665kg
- *Max speed* : 180km/h.

The four engined Blériot-Blanchard, derived from the HB 3.

Blanchard HB 3 T2. The T2 was the commercial variation of the HB 3. It was ordered on the 22nd November 1922 before the official order of the Military version. The T2 flew in August 1923. It was fitted with two Hispano-Suiza 8F engines of 300hp.

- *Spans* : 18.50m/16.50m
- *Length* : 13.70m
- *Height* : 4.20m
- *Wing area* : 85m²
- *Empty weight* : 2,500kg
- *All up weight* : 3,800kg
- *Max speed* : 170km/h

Blanchard HB C1. This was a single-seat single engine seaplane, two examples were ordered on the 17th February 1923 and made its first flight in September. It was fitted with a Gnome and Rhône 9Aa engine of 380hp.

The two Blanchard C1 were candidates for the Schneider Trophy of 1923. The French preparation, a decision taken very late, was rushed. The Blanchard belonging to Maréchalat, the most powerful (550hp) hit a jetty during a trial and was eliminated. The other Blanchard, flown by the Commandant Teste, was judged much too slow with its engine of 380hp.

- *Span* : 12.20m
- *Length* : 9.715m
- *Height* : 3.72m
- *Wing area* : 21m²
- *Empty weight* : 930kg
- *All up weight* : 1,280kg
- *Max speed* ; 220km/h

Above, a Blanchard C1 at Saint-Raphael.

Blanchard HB 3 T. This single example was one of the production series HB3, created by an order of the 30th March 1935 to convert it to puller engines. Characteristics and overall performance were unchanged.

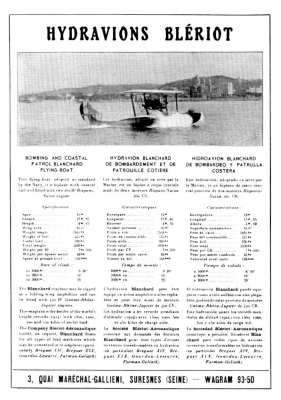

Publicity by Blériot Aeronautic for Blanchard seaplanes.

THE GUILLEMIN AIRCRAFT

The engineer, Jean Guillemin, having left the design office of the Hanriot Company, founded his own company in 1929.

Having no work shops, he signed an agreement with Louis Blériot to produce several models in the Blériot factory.

THE JG 40, 41, 42 and 43

JG 40. Replying to the light weight Medical Evacuation aircraft programme launched in 1929 by the Air Ministry, the JG 40 received an order n° 12/0 on the 2nd June 1930, for the building of two prototypes, for a sum of 717,200 francs. It was powered by a 120 hp, air-cooled 9-cylinder Salmson 9c engine, fitted with a ring cowling. The propeller was a two bladed fixed pitch Ratier in metal. The high cantilever wing in wood, which contained two jettisonable fuel tanks, was covered with a fabric with a special treatment, allowing prolonged use in a hot and humid climate. The fuselage was a structure in square section duralumin tubes, metal skinned except for the sides from the cockpit to the empennage, which were covered in removable panels in simulated leather. The cabin, installed exactly on the machine's centre of gravity, was designed to accommodate the regulation stretcher, 2.25 metres long by 0.58 metres wide. The cabin had a forced air circulation and power points for heated blankets. The cabin was accessible by a large lateral opening, natural light came from three triangular windows, and was separated from the cockpit by a transparent bulk head. The build of the first prototype, the JG 40-01, started at Suresnes on the 1st May 1930, and was completed at the end of the month of September. The machine was straight away transported to the field at Buc where it carried out its first flight on the 2nd October 1930. The JG 40-02, underwent a certain number of modifications as a result of the trials of the first prototype, the fin was increased in surface and the windscreen modified to improve the pilot's visibility of the ground. At the end of the month of July, during the "Aviation Medical Evacuation Days" which were being held in Paris, nine machines made their presentation on the aerodrome at Orly, at the end of which the JG 40-01 was classed first. At the same time the second prototype was delivered to the Government. It was fitted with a five-cylinder radial Lorraine 5 Pc engine, without cowling. The much lighter exhaust pipe allowed a gain of 20 kg on the weight of the machine. At the beginning of December, the JG 40-01, flown by Captain Weiser and Adjutant Terrade, went to Morocco, where it took part in the pacification operations in the Atlas Mountains, in the beginning of 1932.

The Guillemin 41 no 01, with right hand side of the fuselage open.

A stretcher in the Guillemin 42 no 01.

JG 41. The appearance in October 1931 of a new competitor, the BM 80, lighter by 180 kg with a ceiling better by 1,800 metres, than that of the JG 40 and clearly faster, led M. Guillemin, to modify his machine in December of the same year. In January 1932, the tests were continued at Villacoublay under the name JG 41 n°01. At the beginning of February it crashed. The JG 41 was returned to the Blériot factory where the restoration work, and the modifications, to JG 42, would immobilise it for almost ten months.

JG 42. This was the modified JG 41. The wing having been raised, the roof of the cabin was now entirely glassed, thus improving the visibility for the pilot. The front spar was reinforced where the undercarriage was fixed, the wheels were fitted with balloon tyres. The machine, now called the JG 42-01 was flown to Villacoublay by Massotte, in the second week of December. After various trials for fuel consumption, for speed and landing on stony fields, it flew to Madrid at the beginning of June 1933, to be shown at the Congress of Medical Evacuation Aviation (for this occasion it was allocated the temporary registration F-AKCY) The JG 42-01 participated in the third Tour de France for prototypes, flown by Adjudant-Chef Reste, with Sergeant Moog as passenger. On the 13th September 1933, the machine was forced to land, caused by an engine stoppage.

JG 43. Despite this accident, the Air Force Procurement Service placed an order for five Blériot-Guillemin machines, in January 1934. The building of the production machines, named JG 43, would in fact be done by the Union Corporative Aéronautique (UCA)[1] in its factory at Tartifume at Bègles, near to Bordeaux, under the management of Jean Guillemin. The wing span was increased by 1.20 m was equipped with a nine-cylinder radial Salmson 9 Nd engine, of 175 hp, which gave a maximum speed of 200 kph, at an altitude of 2,500 metres, a range of 600 kilometres and a ceiling of 7,000 metres.

(1) The Union Corporative Aéronautique was a grouping of the companies, Blériot, Farman and ANF-Les Murcaux. Albert Caquot, Technical Director of the Air Ministry, tried to impose a voluntary regrouping of the industry, but it was too diverse and the end result was only a façade.

The first JG 43 came out of the factory at Bègles in mid-April 1936. The production series was hardly completed, when, on the 16th June 1937, the two-seat tourer, the Guillemin JG 10-01, used for a year by the test centre at Villacoublay, lost a wing in flight and crashed. The enquiry raised the question of premature aging of the fuselage. The JG 43 had the same construction principles as the Guillemin tourer so every JG 43 was grounded. The JG 40-01, still in service in Morocco, had however, not known the slightest problem. The same year (1937) a JG 43 used by the army would serve as a flying test bed to check a system of flaps - flaps invented by the engineer Poriet. These tests, even though conclusive, did not give rise to any definite applications.

The JG 10

The JG 10 was a two-seat tourer aircraft with wings pivoting through 90° on a shaft, then folding to the rear. The centre section in duralumin, contained two jettisonable fuel tanks. The wings were made of wood covered with plywood and then covered with fabric. It was fitted with a 95 hp Renault 4Pb engine. The cockpit had dual controls side by side and the canopy was removable, allowing the aircraft to be flown as an open cockpit. Two bunks could be installed in the cockpit after removing the seats and controls. The fuselage structure was in square section duralumin tube. The outer dimensions of the tubes were constant, but the wall thickness varied according to the structural loads. The fuselage was metal skinned except for the rear side surfaces, which were covered in laced moleskin. The JG 10 was also fitted with two Salone and Lucas parachutes, let into the sides of the fuselage.

- *Span* : 13.0m
- *Length* : 7.10m
- *Wing area* : 23m²
- *Max speed* : 160km/h
- *Range* : 500km
- *Ceiling* : 4,500m
- *Empty weight* : 554kg *ll up weight* : 850kg

Completed at Suresnes in July 1931, the JG 10 was given the registration F-ALPE, and in September of the same year took part in the National Technical Competition for touring aircraft, flown by Quatremare. A leak in the fuel circuit caused the elimination of the machine. Later, the machine was transferred to the test flight services at Villacoublay, where it underwent several modifications to the fuselage and empennage. It was a short time after a pilot of the test centre had noted vibrations in the wing, that the accident happened as related in the previous chapter. Jean Guillemin designed other touring aircraft outside Blériot Aeronautic and the UCA : the JG 11, JG 50 and JG 60. Other aircraft were built in the Blériot factories by the Blériot personnel but after Nationalisation these became SFCA. Contrary to the Blanchard sea-planes and the Guillemin aircraft built under the responsibility of Blériot Aeronautic, and presented and sold under the name Blériot, they were proposed for sale to the Government and to the public by the SFCA itself. This Société Française de Constructions Aéronautique, was created by Jean Lignel whose head office and design office were installed on the Champs-Elysées in

Paris. It had taken up the licence of the Maillet-Nennig MN-A and would develop up to the Second World War a series of rapid single-engined monoplanes, as well as monoplanes with tandem wings – The Taupin. A part of this production was made in the Blériot factory at Suresnes and at Buc: Maillet 20, 21, Maillet-Lignel 20, 22, 201, Taupin and Taupin 5/2, Lignel 10, 16, 161, 20, 201, 30/31.

The Guillemin 10.

The cockpit of the JG 10, with small luggage compartment open.

The JG 10 with engine cowling open.

The UCA, Nationalisation, after Blériot

BLERIOT-AERONAUTIQUE FORMED A BASE ON WHICH FRENCH AVIATION SURVIVES

On the 25th July 1934, the 25th anniversary of the Channel Crossing - the last one where Louis Blériot participated - was marked by important celebrations at Buc, in the presence of the President of the Republic, Albert Lebrun and Lord Londonderry, the British Air Minister, as well as other celebrations in Dover. November of the same year saw the conclusion of an agreement between the Companies, Blériot-Aéronautique, the ANF-Les Mureaux and the Avions Farman, which gave birth to the Union Corporative Aéronautique. With a capital of 600,000 francs, the UCA named Charles Pélabon as Chairman of the Board. It had a head office at 54, Avenue Marceau, in Paris, a joint factory at Tartifume, near Bègles in the southern district of Bordeaux, which was the contribution of Blériot-Aéronautique. In principle, any order coming from the Government to any one of the three companies, was to be shared between them. The grouping, inside of which each company conserved its independence, had only a short life, the UCA disappeared during the nationalisations of 1936/1937.

If the activity had been good at the end of the 1920s (between 1920 and 1928, the Company income was 39,7 million francs), in the middle of the 1930s, very few production orders were being placed with Blériot-Aéronautique. Others had hardly been passed when they were cancelled, which led to the factories being closed several times, with the design offices reduced to a strict minimum. Blériot therefore, had to accept sub-contract work. Henry Potez sub-contracted to Blériot, the building of two hundred Potez 25 A2. In 1935, he then placed a further order, 922/5, for the build by Bleriot Aéronautique, of thirty, Potez 540. Thanks also to an order, 894/5 of the 30/8/35, for SPAD 510, the factory could be opened up again.

Despite a powerful production line, this activity was particularly difficult to manage, as much from the diversity of the machines ordered, as from the shortness of delivery delays and the indecision of the end user concerning the equipment. Further, the banks refused any long term loan. The social and political events of 1936, would lead to the nationalisation of a large majority of the industries working for the national defence, or "making material with a military objective", according to the terminology of the time.[1]

---

(1) The Nationalisation was adopted by the members of Parliament on the 25th July - an anniversary of the Channel Crossing! - and by the Upper House on the 11th August. The inheritors of Louis Blériot, who died between these two dates, received as a Nationalisation indemnity, the sum of 12 million francs.

The imposing Aéroparc created at Buc, near to Paris, by Louis Blériot. Today, the only remains are the stones of one of the entry gates.

The Société Nationale de Constructions Aéronautiques du Sud-Ouest (SNCASO) was one of the seven national companies created in the domain of aviation. Between January and March 1937 the group would be formed of, Bloch aircraft (factories at Courbevoie, Châteauroux-Déols and Villacoublay) The Société Aéronautique du Sud-Ouest (Bordeau-Bacalan), the UCA (Bègles), the factories Lioré de Rochefort, and Blériot at Suresnes. As for the other national companies "Air", the General Manager was M. Caquot and the Under Manager M. de l'Escaille. The Delegated Administrator was M. Bloch (future Marcel Dassault) and the administrators Messrs Nordmann, representing the Air Ministry, Devaux, the Financial Inspector, and Charriére the CGT Union representative. The Head Office was at n° 41, Quai Paul-Doumer in Courbevoie.[2] This nationalisation, had for an objective, to produce a production tool adapted to the circumstances of the moment, and to allow the country to have rapidly available aviation material of quality and in sufficient numbers. Hardly one year before the Munich agreement, the organisation of the aviation industries, carried out in a climate of social disorder, did not allow the attaining the hoped for results. Voted, despite the warnings of the head-quarters of the Air Force, the Nationalisation Law, was above all, political.

A short time beforehand, when these movements were already foreseeable, the health of Louis Blériot, worn out by overwork and the worries of a difficult existence, suddenly deteriorated. On Saturday the 1st August 1936, ten days before the passing of the law nationalising his factories, Louis Blériot, in his apartment at 288 Boulevard Saint-Germain, fell victim to an embolism.

Member of the Governing Board of the Aéro-Club de France, Vice President of the Fédération Aéronautique Internationale, he had just turned sixty-four.

On the 5th August, the Government as well as all French Aviation rendered an ultimate homage to the pioneer, in the church of Saint Louis des Invalides.

A few weeks later, the new twin engined Caudron-Renault 640-05 *Typhon*, a record breaking aircraft, had painted on its fuselage in gold letters, the name of the man who conquered the Channel.[3] The following year, the factory at Suresnes, which maintained the name Blériot on the façade of the building until its demolition in December 1991, made 200 of the 405 Salmson "Cricri", ordered in the name of the Aviation Populaire.[4] The factory also built elements for several Bloch aircraft, and built the prototypes Bloch 500 and 700. The airfield at Buc, whose principle occupant was the SFA, was now used only for the flying school and the reception of machines built by the SNCASO.

From 1940 to 1944 the factory at Suresnes had to work for the Germans. The SNCASO was obliged, at Suresnes and at Courbevoie, to build wings and engine mounts for the Junkers 52. When, in 1941 the SNCAO was incorporated into the SNCASO, they built the Heinkel 111, the Arado 196 and elements of the Focke-Wulf 189. After the total occupation of France in November 1942, other models were produced for the Luftwaffe. At the liberation of France and up to 1948, Suresnes continued its activities in the field of aviation, with the building of the small twin-engined SO 90, the wings of the SO 30, and the first French jet aircraft, the SO 6000 "Triton". After 1945, the youngest of the Blériot sons, Jean, living in Suresnes, 29 Rue Pasteur, for a short time gave a new industrial activity to the company Blériot Aéronautique. Under his management, the company produced variable speed units and different models of transmission drives, but the company's life was only a short lived. Blériot Aéronautique which had conserved a private status, became Buc-Aviation in 1959, with a head office at n° 4, Rue Meissonnier, in Paris. This company, with the capital of six million francs, ceased to exist when the airfield at Buc was converted to an industrial zone. Hired out on the 23rd August 1949 to the service of American Surplus, the factory at Suresnes was taken over in June 1956 by Ouest-Aviation (ex-SNCASO), a company which with the SNCASE formed Sud-Aviation on the 1st March 1957. Sud-Aviation and Nord-Aviation, combined with SEREB, in turn gave birth to SNIAS on the 1st January 1970, future Aérospatiale, today EADS.

The UCA, as with all the other amalgamations, did not last long.

(2) Main office of Marcel Bloch aircraft.

(3) The machine, piloted by Maurice Rossi, beat the World Speed record over 5,000 kilometres in closed circuit, on the 24th April 1936, at an average speed of 311 kph.

(4) The *Aviation* Populaire was created under the Ministry of Pierre Cot. It had as an objective, aviation training of young people, paid for by the Government, and was destined to face up to the impressive German organisation the National Sozialistisher Flieger Korps.

THE DOMAIN OF TARTIFUME

The Domain of Tartifume, situated on the banks of the Garonne, was made up of sixty-five hectares of land and an eighteenth century Chateau. Louis Blériot bought it for 450,000 francs in June - July 1918. A factory was straight away installed

and started to produce SPAD VII and SPAD XIII when the armistice of 11th November intervened. After different attempts at reconversion, notably the creation of a mechanical barrel making line, all activity ceased in the 1920s.

An aerodrome was immediately laid out at Tartifume. The inauguration was held on the 18th October 1924 in the presence of Pierre-Etienne Flandin, with an aviation meeting organised by Charles Robin, founder of an aerial propaganda company. In 1926, the premises were rented to the Etablissements Voulton who made plywood panels until the spring of 1935. The factory was recovered by Louis Blériot and put back into service within the UCA, under the management of the Engineer Guillemin, with Paul Boutiron as Chief Engineer for the manufacturing of aviation items. The number of employees went from fifty in October 1935 to three hundred and eighty (of which twenty were women) in June 1936. The covered surface was 10,300 m². The five JG 43 medical evacuation aircraft and a series of Potez 540 were built here.

The factory was nationalised on the 13th March 1937, but the rest of the domain, fifty hectares, was conserved by the Blériot family. The city of Bordeaux bought six hectares in 1946, and in April 1948 the rest was sold to the CENPA (a paper manufacturing company). The factory belonged to the SNCASO, then

to the car manufacturer Georges Irat who built the DOG diesel engines, before being razed to the ground in 1968 at the same time as the chateau which had been badly damaged during the Second World War. An Industrial Zone now covers the site of Tartifume, where there is one road named Louis Blériot.

Part of the industrial building at Tartifume around 1950.

After having built honeycomb metallic structures, stratified units and specialising in metal-to-metal bonding, the factory contributed to the building of elements for several types of aircraft, such as the Breguet Atlantic and the vertical take-off Dassault Balzac. At the same time it carried out different designs and builds in the nuclear sector, as much as for the "Force de Frappe", as for civil applications (notably EDF), as well as in the missiles sector. Becoming independent once again on the 1st January 1966, the factory at Suresnes, having a design office and work shops charged with the building of structures in both the aeronautical and nuclear sectors, started an in-depth period of restructuring.

This restructuration had as an objective, the creation of a research centre capable of replying to the common needs of the four Aerospatiale Divisions, aircraft, helicopters, missiles and space. It caused, of course, the transfer of production activities which did not conform to this objective, which necessitated an important adaptation of human resources and on-site materials, as much as in the quality as in the quantity. The extreme difficulty of resolving such problems, notably at the social level, were further aggravated by important and brutal fluctuations in work load.

It is this which explains the delay, which was necessary, to arrive on the 1st September 1987, at the creation of the common research centre, Louis Blériot, placed under management of M. Jean Jamet. This new centre participated in several large projects in cooperation with French and European Industrialists. Complete renovation work of the old Blériot factory has been started. Its original conception, completely rational for the time, had been overtaken by numerous changes in activity. It no longer corresponded to the demands of new technologies such as computers or electronics, which impose themselves on the design of modern industrial buildings. The first stone of the new building was laid on the 17th June 1990, by the research Minister M. Hubert Curien.

The work was completed in 1998. Today the only parts of the old factory that are still visible, are the ceramic frontispieces, which were on top of the brick façade, and which have now been re-installed at ground level in front of the new buildings, occupied by EADS, the Headquarters of Airbus.

This modern building was built on the site of the old Blériot factory at Suresnes, by the group EADS, proud of its origins.

Conclusion

When Louis Blériot started his research in aviation, towards 1900, just about all of aviation was still to be discovered. George Cayley had, as early as 1809, announced the basic principles of heavier than air flight, and Clément Ader had left the ground on the 9th October 1890, but it was the Wright brothers, who, on 17th December 1903, made the first real heavier than air flight, even though their machine could not take off alone. If, in France, Blériot had been beaten by Santos-Dumont for the first autonomous flight in September 1906, and by Farman for the first kilometre in a closed circuit as well as for the first flight town-to-town in 1908, it was to Blériot that came the glory of the exploit marking the beginning of aviation. In thirty-seven minutes of flight above the Channel, the aeroplane ceased to be considered as an experimental machine, or even a toy of rich sportsmen, to become a real means of transport and communication, even a strategic tool.

Another merit is due to Blériot, that of having designed the first machine which was a real aircraft, and the layout of which most of its successors would copy.

During the First World War, builder of the famous fighters Spad VII and Spad XIII, he allowed France to gain aerial supremacy from the Germans in 1916 and 1918. Between the wars, despite difficult economical conditions, he was amongst the first to build aircraft for passenger transport; he was also one of the forerunners in aerial publicity.

Amongst many others, two superb machines came out of his factory in the 1930s, the record breaking *Joseph Le Brix*, and the transatlantic seaplane, the *Santos-Dumont*. Too often, alas, these aircraft gave rise to no production orders, putting in danger the very existence of the company Blériot-Aéronautique.

Pioneer of aviation, Blériot always believed in future development. He had foreseen, as early as 1928, the expansion of transport aviation on the North Atlantic. In order to exploit this line, with an American company, he formed a project to install five floating islands over a route to the North of the Azores and Bermuda, which would have allowed the reduction in the distance between stops to 1,000 kilometres. Further, he foresaw the use of maritime aircraft: *"which has the forms of a land aircraft, but whose layout of the cabins is such that it allows a landing and take off with a reduced load in case of necessity"*. This formula allowed the reaching of a finesse comparable to that of land aircraft, whilst still offering a *"minimum of security indispensable to ensure a regular service"*. It was only after the Second World War that transatlantic aerial transport would be developed, to the detriment of ocean liners. The autonomy of airline aircraft at the time, as well as the reliability of the engines, would lead to the abandoning of the formula of floating islands, and maritime aircraft.

Louis Blériot, in his office in the middle of the 1920s. A large part of the furniture seen here has been conserved by the author.

Louis Blériot also foresaw an important and rapid increase in the speed of future aircraft, as well as the development of commercial flights at high altitude. At the beginning of the 1930s, he created a prize, the Louis Blériot Trophy, destined to reward a flight in a closed circuit at a speed above 2,000 kph for a duration of half an hour. (The maximum speed at that time was around 400 kph.) The prize was won on the 10ᵗʰ May 1961 by Major Elmer B. Murphy and his crew, of the US Air Force, flying a four engined strategic bomber, a Convair B 58 Hustler, christened *Firefly*;2,095 kph during 30 minutes and 43 seconds. It was Alicia Blériot, twenty-five years after the death of her husband, who handed over the trophy.

Seeing, as early as 1923, the blocking and the problems of credit of which French Aviation was a victim, he warned the politicians of the time by this prophetic warning:

And already it is time to react! The English and the Americans are at our heels, and what would become of us, if tomorrow the Germans went ahead of us? That this single thought should make tremble those who have in their hands the destiny of our industry! That they should think of the day, unfortunately soon, when Germany, our implacable, our eternal enemy, will at last be able, after having repaired its wounds and gathered its forces, to throw itself with joy upon us, realising at last that they had never ceased to hate us. The idea of revenge that they are cultivating with care since the Armistice. With what would we oppose him then, if our industry was not prosperous?

Let us work and let us stay watchful ... because that is what will be tomorrow!

A striking portrait of Louis Blériot in the blue flying clothes that he wore when he crossed the Channel on his monoplane, 25th July 1909.

Louis Blériot and King Edward VII of England, at Pau in 1910.

Louis Blériot, explaining to the Austro-Hungarian Emperor Franz-Joseph 1, the workings of his machine, at Simmeringer Heide, 23rd October 1910.

In 1909, engineer, builder, and pilot, Blériot was, of all the aviation pioneers, the only one who possessed the experience of the managing of a company. Passionate by his research, supported morally by his admirable wife in the difficult moments, he saw his courage and his tenacity finally crowned with success, after ten years of effort, by the historic Channel Crossing. Having become a captain of industry, at the head of a factory employing up to two thousand five hundred people, he showed proof of real qualities of an organiser. However, the success carried by Louis Blériot as an aircraft builder, before and above all during the First World War, where from 1916 onwards he held the quasi-monopoly of the building of fighter aircraft, either directly, or under licence, brought to him solid scorn in the aeronautical world. This scorn, once the peace had returned, had dire consequences for the running of Blériot Aéronautique, even more so because its President was sometimes lacking in "flexibility" in his dealings with Ministries and Official Services, without whose agreement no order could be obtained. He brought upon himself a long lasting hostility of the Service Technique de l'Aéronautique in issuing in 1924 a paper, widely defused in the aviation world, in which he questioned the work methods of this organisation, an annoying state of mind with regard to the builders, as well as it's incomprehension of industrial reality. Even though these criticisms were not without foundation, the least one can say is, that from this moment on, each time a Blériot aircraft was presented to the Service Technique, it did not benefit from a prior favourable impression! We can even confirm that the project of reform of the STAé, foreseen by Louis Blériot, was the origin of the decline of Blériot Aéronautique in the 1920s and 1930s.

attempted to loosen the administrive iron collar which suffocated French aeronautical building. Louis Blériot also suffered, for more than fifteen years, the attacks of tax officers concerning profits made during the 1914 - 1918 war, even going as far as blocking monies paid by the Government for new orders, which strangled the treasury of the company. Up until his death, just before the nationalisation of his Company in 1936, he nevertheless continued, despite many difficulties, to be part of a small number of great French aircraft builders.

More than seventy-five years after his disappearance, his memory remains alive even outside France, and outside the aviation world. Constantly honing new ideas which he noted, at any hour of the day or night, in a small note book which never left him, Blériot was, for Gabriel Voisin, a "mutant", an opinion which in his colourful language he confided, towards the end of the 1950s, to the author of this book, who had asked him what he thought of his grandfather. It is a fact that, in his domain, Louis Blériot revolutionised his era and that the pilot of today still follows the traces that he left in the sky with his fragile monoplane.

Louis Blériot received a delegation from the Chinese Government, at Issy-les-Moulineaux in 1913.

Louis Blériot and the King of Spain, Alphonse XIII, also at Issy in 1913.

The few orders obtained by Blériot Aéronautique during this period can be explained, to a large measure, by the resentment felt by the Service Technique towards the man who had

Annex

THE PROPELLERS WHICH BREAK: THE RESISTANCE OF AIRCRAFT PROPELLERS AT HIGH SPEED

ARTICLE BY LOUIS BLÉRIOT WHICH APPEARED IN L'AÉROPHILE OF 1ST APRIL 1908

All those who have up till now tried the construction of aerial propellers at high speed have found numerous disappointments. One after another, the propellers broke and the paddles were projected at considerable distances. However, the calculations of resistance seemed to assure them of a prolonged life. Even though the centrifugal force was considerable, the sections of arms of steel allowed still, a coefficient of security of 2 or 3, at 1,200 rpm and even at 1,500, and however each propeller had a short lived life, resisting fairly well in static tests, but breaking up almost straight away on the field.

I have myself, broken on the field four propellers successively. The conditions in which ruptured the last one awoke my attention: my engine turned at only 700 rpm (I had my counter in front of my eyes). My rear wheel met a stone which broke it: at the same instant my propeller flew in pieces. Assisting at numerous tests, I saw one day, Santos-Dumont break his propeller in the full centre of the arm, at the place which seemed the most resistant to traction, and this, in rolling on the prairie of Bagatelle at a place a little jolting. This propeller of small diameter could not have broken by centrifugal force, not even following the explosions of the engine, because what ever one thinks, these explosions are always of little nuisance for the propeller. Their effects are easily calculated, their force of shearing on the arms is of an order much inferior to that which gives for example an error of a few centimetres in the de-axing of a paddle.

I have been therefore, sensitively brought to asking myself if it was not the vibrations of the shaft of the propeller and the sudden variations of orientation of this shaft, veritable axis of gyroscope, which produced on these arms and the paddle unknown forces, and I have the formal conviction that almost all the accidents which happened and which will happen, came from and will come from, this gyroscopic resistance of the shaft of the propeller, resistance opposite to all vibration, to all brusque change of orientation and which produces efforts such that nothing can resist them. I wanted therefore, to calculate what order could be this couple of torsion, and I have made the following calculation which applies fairly well to my aeroplane n° 7.

Let us consider an aeroplane equipped with a propeller of 2m 20 in diameter weighing 15 kg, turning at the speed of 1,300 rpm, running on the ground at the speed of 20m per second and which, for example, the rear wheel of 0m 40 in diameter has just encountered a bump in the ground of 0m 10. Note that these conditions could be increased, the ground could be very rough and the speed of landing considerable. I suppose the wheels with a distance of 3 m (in the aeroplane of Santos-Dumont, the wheels were much more closer). (V. fig. 1 and fig. 2)

What is the resistance which will oppose the gyroscopic action of the propeller to the angular displacement of the axis resulting from the shock of the rear wheel on the little bump?

Jouffret, in his theory of the gyroscope, gives us the means to carry out the calculation. When a body of revolution, he says, whose moment of inertia is A and which turns around its axis with a constant speed $\mathbf{w}$, is submitted to an exterior couple making an effort to change the direction of this axis, if at what ever instant $\boldsymbol{\theta}$ is the angular speed of this, the forces of inertia would have for result, at the same instant, a couple whose axis would be perpendicular at the time to the axis of the figure of the body and to the axis around which is accomplished the instantaneous rotation $\boldsymbol{\theta}$ and whose moment will be equal to the product A.

Let us apply this theorem to the case which occupies us and let us determine successively, A, $\mathbf{w}$, $\boldsymbol{\theta}$.

1.-Value of A: the moment of inertia of a blade of a propeller of variable thickness, in relation to an axis perpendicular to it's plan and passing by it's centre of rotation, could hardly be determined except by experience. In order to find it approximately, I cut a paddle into ten slices which I weighed, and I was thus able to make the sum of the moments of each element, giving me with sufficient approximation the $S m R^2$ of the entire arm

	Weight	Distribution of Centre of Gravity	P/g V²
1st element	0.237	1.040	0.02592
2nd element	0.435	1.934	0.03828
3rd element	0.452	0.825	0.03128
4th element	0.438	0.715	0.02244
5th element	0.430	0.606	0.01615
6th element	0.380	0.498	0.00967
7th element	0.370	0.388	0.00570
8th element	0.330	0.275	0.00225
9th element	0.330	0.165	0.00092
10th element	0.345	0.055	0.00010
	3.717		0.15271

$\Sigma m R^2 = 0.15271$ and for four palettes (constant torque of two palettes) $A = 2 \times 0.15271 = 0.30542$

2. - *Value of w* :

The propeller turning at 1300 rpm = $2 \times 1300/60 = 136$

3. - *Value of* $\boldsymbol{\theta}$:

Let us consider the rear wheel (diameter of 0,40m) with it's centre at O, at the moment where it arrived at the stop T of the obstacle (distance from the ground 0,10m). (V.fig.2.)

In the instant which follows the contact, the point O starts to describe a circular trajectory having the point T as centre. The tangent with O at this trajectory makes with the horizon an angle

α. We understand what follows, if v is the horizontal speed of the assembly, that the speed of point O will be v/cos α and the vertical component of this speed will be vtg α.

Now, the vertical component is justly equal to θ/distance between the wheels.

Therefore, θ = vtg α/distance between the wheels = 20 tg α/3

We see by the graph that the value of α is equal to 60° (exactly).

From where tg α = 1.732 and o = 11.55.

The product $Aw\theta$ = 0.30542 x 136 x 11.55 = 480 kg, represents the value of the couple at one metre from the point of oscillation; in other words, if we consider the propeller as having the ends of it's wings figuratively concreted into a cylinder of 2 metres of diameter, we must be able to suspend on the axis of this propeller and at one metre from the point of attachment of the arms, the formidable weight of 480 kg. I do not know of a propeller capable of resisting to a similar test. I believe that few of my colleagues are aware of these efforts which are not easily perceivable. Note that I have exaggerated nothing, it is probable that one will encounter sometimes obstacles of more that 10 centimetres. Further, many propellers have only two arms instead of four for the same weight of 15 kg. The couple is therefore variable and can reach the double, being 960 kg at one metre from the point of oscillation. Finally, the vibrations of the shaft of the engine, which for an engine of 8 cylinders turning at 1,400 rpm are of the order of 200° per 2nd, giving again to the arm of the propeller a continuous considerable flexing. Note, further, the alternating of the effort on the arm which changes direction two times per turn, and you will understand the vibratory work which comes to disrupt the most solid propellers, and which disrupts them even more that they are more rigid. The tests that I am carrying out for a long time on rapid propellers have allowed me to put my finger on these phenomena and many others whose existence I ignored ; I have assisted sometimes at the curious facts such as the apparent immobilisation, at speed, of the propeller, when it is seen under the lighting of electric arcs in alternating current (a procedure which I mention in passing for the study of deformation under load ; and controlled by an alternator serving the lighting of a local a propeller conveniently and invariably connected to the shaft of the alternator, the propeller seems immobile at all speeds) I continue these studies each day, and I can say that the problem of the propeller flying at 1,800 or 2,000 rpm at 2 metres in diameter is perfectly solvable and that the solution is in the flexibility. But this flexibility makes appear several new phenomena of which I will explain the nature later. No one will ask me why I am not content with propellers turning at 800 or 900 rpm; it is that I estimate that the future is towards high speed propellers and I think that when I have made the propeller of 2 metres in diameter, 2 metres pitch, turning at 2000 rpm, I will still only have an aeroplane capable of making (with a slip of 20%) 53 metres per second, being 190 kph, a speed lower than that obtained by certain automobiles.

L. Blériot

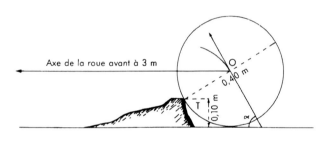

SUMMARY OF FRENCH PATENTS FILED BY LOUIS BLERIOT

1897

Application of hot air turbines to automobiles
Blériot represented by Chassevent, bd Magenta, 11, Paris
262.8807th January 1897

1898

Portable acetylene lamp
Blériot and Candeliez, rue de Richelieu, 43, Paris
276.6875th April 1898

Apparatus for producing acetylene gas
Blériot and Candeliez rue de Richelieu, 43, Paris
276.6885th April 1898

1899

Apparatus for automatic distribution of calcium carbonate for producing acetylene gas
Blériot represented by Boramé and Julien, av. de la République, 8, Paris
288.16024th April 1899

Apparatus for producing acetylene gas
Blériot, rue de Richelieu, 41, Paris
290.79613th July 1899

Improvements of acetylene generators, special application to automobiles, tramways and other vehicles
Bleriot, represented by Bert, bd St. Dennis, 7, Paris
295.74530th December 1899

1902

Apparatus for raising water or other liquids
318.8377th July 1902II2 1st addition n° 37525th August 1902

1903

Lantern for vehicles, cycles and other applications
329.04318th May 1903XVI

1904

Heating for automobile vehicles

341.1762nd June 1904X4
Use of lost heat in a mechanical vehicle
341.60314th June 1904X4
Remote air horn
342.00425th June 1904X1
Lantern holder for automobiles
347.91321st January 1905X4
Acetylene generator for automobile lanterns and other applications
349.13710th March 1905X4
Procedure and apparatus for removing the inconvenience in over production in acetylene generators
350.07222nd July 1905XV3
Apparatus for eliminating the flame and gas action on the acetylene lamp reflectors or other applications
350.07322nd July 1905XV1
1st addition n° 4.2643rd August 1905

Apparatus and machine for lighting of automobiles
351.11130th January 1905X4
Apparatus for lighting of automobiles and other applications
353.1658th April 1905XV1
1st addition n° 5.1978th September 1905
Lantern holder for automobiles
1st addition n° 4.475/347.91318th February 1905X4
Acetylene generator for automobile lanterns and other applications
1st addition n° 4.689/349.1378th April 1905X4

Tensioning device
365.06410th April 1906V3

Control by universal joint
374.4949th February 1907V3
Aeroplane
374.73711th February 1907VI4
System of tensioning of wires, cables and similar products
375.1861st March 1907V3
Control system
377.17426th April 1907V3 1st addition n° 8.32315th October 1907
Assembly
377.17526th April 1907V3
System for balancing of aircraft
380.09820th July 1907VI4
Beam for aeroplanes and similar machines
380.09920th July 1907VI4
Process and mechanism to allow the vertical ascension of aeroplanes and similar machines
382.5304th October 1907VI4
System for landing of aeroplanes and similar machines
384.25331st October 1907VI4

System of assembly of support wheels of aeroplanes and similar machines
386.25715th January 1908VI4
Procedure for the fitting of aircraft propellers, and systems for its application

386.48923rd January 1908VI4
Improvements concerning the cooling of water of the engines of aircraft, aeroplanes and similar machines
388.68230th March 1908V8
Procedure allowing the offset of the flywheel on internal combustion engines, onto a shaft other than the crankshaft of the engine, and articles relative to the application
389.63627th April 1908V8
Control system
2nd addition n° 8.770/377.17411th January 1908V3

Improvements to aeroplanes and to similar machines
400.57811th June 1908VI4

Improvements to the parts which are needed in the building of aeroplanes, and the aeroplanes carrying the application
414.96722nd February 1910VI4
Improvements to aeroplanes and similar machines
415.2146th July 1909VI4
Procedure and mechanism to modify the curve of active surfaces such as for example the flying surfaces of aeroplanes and similar machines
418.56030th September 1909VI4
Improvements to aeroplane landing skids and similar machines
418.8673rd August 1910VI4
Control system
3rd addition n° 11.850/377.174December 1909V3

Improvements to internal combustion engines for machines of aerial navigation
42354617th February 1910V8
Rotary engine and application of this to the rotary propulsion system of automobiles
423.59019th February 1910V8
Rotary propulsion automobile
423.59119th February 1910VI2
Improvements of aeroplanes and similar machines
430.23429th May 1911VI4
Improvements of aeroplanes and similar machines
430.27629th May 1911VI4
Improvements to aeroplane landing skids and similar machines
1st addition n° 13.489/418.86726th November 1910VI4

Improvements to aeroplanes and similar machines
452.05830th September 1912VI4
1st addition n° 18.0818th August 1913
Improvements to the means of transport of aeroplanes and similar machines
452.64120 the December 1912VI4
Improvements to the means of transport of aeroplanes and similar machines
458.8856th June 1913VI4
Improvements to pilots' harnesses and similar articles
458.8866th June 1913VI4
Improvements to floats notably and above all for hydroplanes and floatplanes
460.1418th July 1913VI4

Improvements to fire arms, notably and above all, machine guns for machines of aerial locomotion
463.601 14th October 1913 XI2

1914
Improvements to the means to be used to allow aeroplanes and similar machines to take off and land in specific points especially on ships
468.639 19th February VI4

1917
Improvements to distributors of liquid under pressure notably for the mechanisms of starting of internal combustion engines
484.874 28th February 1917 V8

1919
Improvements to assemblies notably for aerial navigation machines
492.342 26th June 1916 VI4

1920
Improvements to aeroplanes and similar machines
502.839 24th February 1916 VI4
1st addition n° 21.604 18th June 1917
Improvements to the installation for the distribution of liquid under pressure, notably the fuel supply for internal combustion engines
503.859 16th November 1917 V8

1921
Improvements to aeroplanes and similar machines
1st addition n° 23.309/400.578 28th April 1915 VI4
Improvements to aeroplanes and similar machines
2nd addition n° 23.888/502.839 18th June 1918 VI4

1922
Improvements to internal combustion engines notably those for aeroplanes
546.988 10th November 1915 V8

1928
Improvements to a means of aerial signalling, notably that used for publicity
635.872 11th June 1927 XVIII3

1929
Improvements to aeroplanes notably to transport aeroplanes to be used for sea crossings
656.864 30th June 1928 VI4

PATENTS HELD BY WELDHEN and BLERIOT Ltd

1907
Shade for powerful vehicle lanterns on the road, to improve the effective range of these, and to stop them being a danger for pedestrians
374.973 23rd February 1907 XVI1

PATENTS HELD BY TONNET (M) and BLERIOT (L)

1908

Process enabling the building of level indicators unaffected by effects that might induce false readings and level indicators making use of this process
390.069 8th May 1908 XII3

PATENTS HELD BY BLERIOT (L) and BAUDOT (FBM)

1911
Procedure and mechanisms to remedy engine breakdowns being used in aerial navigation, and to those engines being used for the control of aeroplane propulsion
423.883 26th February 1910 V8
Improvements to compound engines, and notably to internal combustion engines
423.884 26th February 1910 V8

1913
Improvements to tachometers with an active centrifugal system
457.937 15th May 1913 XII3

PATENTS HELD BY LOUIS BLERIOT LTD

1906
Acetylene generator applicable in particular to automobile lamps
362.392 13th January 1906 V3

1911
Improvements to electromagnets and similar machines
432.972 4th August 1911 XII5

1913
Improvements to electromagnets and similar machines
452.153 10th December 1912 XII5
Improvements to electrical contacts with a liquid element, as well as electrical items with contacts
456.251 2nd April 1913 XII6
Mechanism for fixing bulbs in the reflectors of electric lamps for automobiles and other applications
459.094 11th June 1913 XII8
Improvements to sirens and similar machines
459.570 23rd June 1913 XII2

1914
Improvements to a machine where liquid is distributed to another substance, notably to acetylene generators where water falls onto the carbide
464.408 4th November 1913 XV3
Improvements to contact breakers on certain regulators for electromagnetic machines
474.593 24th June 1914 XII5

1915
Improvements to "internal combustion enginesdynamo/magneto ignition", notably for automobiles
477.941 16th September 1914 XII5
2nd addition n° 20.031 10th April 1915

1917
Improvements to fixed induction magnetos
482.922 20th September 1916 XII5
1st addition n° 20.398 2nd January 1917

Improvements to lighting dynamos on automobiles having a starter motor
483.217 19th October 1916 XII5

Power take off point
484.553 20th February 1917 XII6

Mechanism of hand controlled advance and retard of internal combustion engines
484.554 20th February 1917 V8

Portable power take off point for high tension magneto distributor
485.628 26th May 1917 XII5

Improvements to power generator, notably where the brush contact is not external
485.939 20th November 1916 XII5

Improvements to ignition systems for internal combustion engines
486.175 2nd February 1917 V8

1918

Improvements to electro magnets
487.448 7th November 1917 XII5

Improvements to variable current supply regulator, to allow supply to machines needing constant power
487.449 7th November 1917 XII6

Improvements to heat exchangers, notably radiators for internal combustion engines
487.477 7th November 1917 V8

Improvements to current regulators notably for dynamos or installations needing constant current
487.483 8th November 1917 XII6

Improvements to the means of turning in a specified sense, a control shaft, whatever the sense of rotation of its drive shaft
487.484 8th November 1917 V3

Improvements to regulators
489.428 7th November 1917 XII6

Improvements to springs, and in particular to leaf springs used in contact breakers
489.687 12th April 1918 V8

Speed reducing mechanism to allow the starting of internal combustion engines by means of an auxiliary engine
489.984 14th May 1917 V8

Improvements to a transmission between an axle on a railway track and a machine, notably a dynamo being turned by the rotation of the axle
490.003 17th January 1918 III4

1919

Improvements to electric regulator
491.103 31st July 1918 XII6

Improvements to the controls of machines or systems having a certain startup inertia, and equipped with starter motors, notably the controls of similar machines or systems fitted with a propeller
491.145 10th April 1916 VI4

Improvements to fixed induction ignition magnetos on internal combustion engines
492.424 9th October 1916 XII5

Improvements to the systems of internal combustion engine starter motors, in particular those of automobiles
493.763 12th December 1918 V8

Improvements to the systems of internal combustion engine starter motors, in particular those of automobiles
493.764 12th December 1918 V8

Improvements for automatic stop or inversion of an electric motor under the action of variation of tension, of intensity, or of power
493.797 13th December 1918 XII5

Improvements to electric installation contacts
494.131 26th August 1918 XII6

Improvements to relays
494.132 27th August 1918 XII6

Improvements to electromagnets
494.134 28th August 1918 XII5

Improvements to ignition systems for internal combustion engines
494.255 28th December 1918 V8

Improvements to fixed induction magnetos placed outside the rotating parts
494.481 24th March 1917 XII5

Method of fixing rubber shock absorber
494.756 4th May 1917 VI4

Improvements to clutches
495.488 4th February 1919 V3

Improvements to electrical lamps for automobiles
495.489 4th February 1919 XII8

Improvements to electric heating
495.567 5th February 1919 XV2

Improvements to starting of internal combustion engines with the aid of an electric motor
495.597 7th February 1919 V8

Improvements to magnetos
495.665 11th February 1919 XII5

Improvements to radiators notably those for internal combustion engines for aircraft
495.757 27th October 1917 VI4

Improvements to acetylene generators
496.257 26th February 1919 XV3

Improvements to clutches
498.186 27th June 1918 V3

1920

Improvements to regulation of electric machines
1st addition n° 21.227/491.103 20th February 1919 XII6
2nd addition n° 21.230/491.103 24th February 1919 XII6

Improvements to "internal combustion enginedynamo/magneto ignition", notably those for automobiles
500.952 13th February 1919 V8

Improvements to regulation systems for electric installations, notably for electro magnets type "compensated"
501.294 28th December 1918 XII6

Improvements to electric installations having a contracompound dynamo, destined to supply one or several circuits and to charge accumulators
509.310 31st January 1920 XII5

Improvements to speed changers
516.168 31st May 1920 V3

1921

Improvements to electric installations having several regulators with contacts in series
518.562 23rd November 1917 XII6

Improvements to clutches
521.588 30th July 1920 V3

Improvements to electromagnets and similar apparatus
521.589 30 July 1920 XII5

Improvements to regulators to be fitted to electrical installations whose supply circuit tension is not constant, to allow them to supply notably incandescent lamps which function with constant tension
522.063 3rd November 1914 XII6

Improvements to electrical installations containing an accumulator and current generator without constant potential, even though limited power
534.016 2nd September 1914 XII5

Improvements to installations comprising of electromagnetic machines in which the intensity is subject to variations
534.017 29th September 1914 XII5

Improvements to electrical resistances notably for those used to compensate certain phenomena
534.023 20th July 1916 XII6

1922

Improvements to electrical installations containing an accumulator and current generator without constant potential, even though limited power
535.265 2nd September 1914 XII5

Improvements to electrical machines with compound windings notably dynamos
535.266 14th January 1915 XII5

Improvements to dynamos
535.686 27th December 1920 XII5

Improvements to electrical machines carrying magnetising windings, notably regulators whose principle component is an electromagnet
538.362 8th February 1916 XII6

Improvements to suspension systems having one or several hooks, and a control allowing the liberation at a specific moment, of an object suspended to the hook or any hook of the system
541.684 24th February 1921 V6

Cupboard with several compartments
549.224 22nd March 1922 IX4

Antiglare mechanism for automobile lamps
552.379 31st May 1922 XVI

1924

Perfected electric light for automobiles
571.535 6th October 1923 XII8

Mechanism to set the position of head lamps of automobiles
571.536 6th October 1923 XII8

1925

Perfected electric light for automobiles
1st addition n° 29.442/571535
27th September 1924 XII8

PATENTS HELD BY IGLESIS AND BLERIOT Ltd

1922

Improvements in the construction of dynamos for automobiles
548.227 4th March 1922 XII5

Improvements in the control of lighting dynamos and ignition dynamos in automobiles
548.228 4th March 1922 XII5

1923

Security mechanism for electric lighting for vehicles

560.715 5th January 1923 XII8

1924

Improvements to threebrush dynamos
570.368 30th August 1923 XII5

Improvements to brush holder
578.862 19th March 1924 XII6

Security mechanism for electric lighting for vehicles
1st addition n° 27.832/560.715 6th June 1923 XII8

1925

Improvement to lighting dynamos and starting dynamos for automobiles
588.500 4th November 1924 XII5

PATENTS HELD BY BLERIOT AERONAUTIQUE

1924

Improvements to parts to be curved over at least their length, notably to aircraft wing ribs
569.446 4th August 1923 VI4

Improvements to combat aircraft of the type "monoplane aeroplane"
570.492 3rd September 1923 VI4

Improvements to wing surfaces (wings, control surfaces, fins, blades etc) with modifiable action
575.402 8th December 1923 VI4

Improvements to the elements which make up a composite beam, of aerial locomotion machines, notably to aeroplane wings
577.136 14th February 1924 VI4

Improvements to twostroke internal combustion engines, with sleeve and compressor, notably to those for aerial locomotion machines
579.329 27th March 1924 V8

Improvements to transmission of force by servo motors, notably systems of control surfaces and balancing of aircraft
582.680 12th June 1924 VI4

Improvements to mechanisms to give an impulse of rotation to a machine shaft, notably a starter for engines, particularly internal combustion engines for aircraft
583.852 19th July 1924 V8

1926

Improvements to machines of locomotion comprising of suspension surfaces of stabilization and direction, notably those of aerial locomotion
604.102 2nd October 1925 VI4

Improvements to a mechanism of two shafts, whose axes meet, and a lever allowing the rotation of these shafts a certain quantity, either separately or together
604.820 16th October 1925 V3

Improvements to internally sprung wheels, notably those for undercarriages of machines of aerial locomotion
601.462 28th March 1926 VI4

ORGANISATION OF THE DESIGN OFFICE AND OF THE

TECHNICAL DOCUMENTATION (Text of April 1929)

OBJECTIVES

Constitution of pre-projects and projects for new aircraft.

Establishing calculations and drawings necessary for the execution of test elements and the build of prototype machines.

Updating of the basic design after the prototype build.

Establishing the drawings in view of production orders and conforming to current regulations.

Establishing of bills of materials and miscellaneous instructions.

Reproduction of technical documents and despatch to internal and external services.

Classification and conservation of all factory documentation.

NECESSITY OF A NEW ORGANISATION

In order to realise the objectives mentioned above, it was indispensible to proceed to a new organisation of the Design Office and Technical Documentation for the following reasons:

1 - Within the life of the factory, as within the whole of aviation, the design services are taking up a place much more important than ever.

2 - The designs themselves, instead of being based on machines of form and dimension similar to existing types, are now based on new forms, new build procedures and on machines of higher weight.

3 - The general conception of new machines being handed to a larger number of engineers: it was indispensible to build an organisation for the attribution of personnel according to the needs of each service and the urgency of the work undertaken, and to adopt, whenever possible, a common method, as much to take into account the capacities of the workshops, as to insure the liaison between internal and external services.

4 - Up until now, the creation of a new machine meant the immediate build of a static test fuselage, the practical testing being less in-depth than it is now; not only for the reasons mentioned above, but also because we are bringing in more and more new materials and special assembly procedures, it is important to build up a precise documentation of all the testing in a way to benefit all the engineers, and to hasten, by this procedure, the building of new designs.

5 - Up until now, when we made a study machine, the design office limited itself to producing only the drawings indispensible for the build of the prototype in the workshops, without foreseeing the possible production of the machine. The modifications introduced during the build were not always followed, nor those made during the flight tests. The result is, that each time we needed to start the production of a machine, even in a small quantity, all the drawings had to be re-done.

6 - Outside of the drawings and documents which are indispensible to the rational life of the factory, and which are needed to be established with a view to producing these machines, the technical and commercial follow up, the build up of exchange parts, the Government services demand more and more often a detailed documentation, even on the prototype machines. This policy of Government services can only be amplified with the current theory of de-centralisation, and the possible placing of orders with third-party builders even with the first series.

7 - Other than the necessity to take rational methods to establish new machines, it is equally important to file correctly all the documentation concerning past machines, which has not always been done in a satisfactory fashion. It will always be useful, for the future, to be able to refer easily to the experiences of the past.

8 - The work of the Design Office and Technical Documentation is the departure point of all activity of the factory. All that we neglect of the essential at this departure point, has the gravest repercussions in lost time and money in all the services. As an example, the simple fact of not having a precise bill of materials when we re-produce a new machine, stops a rapid supply and the start up of the build. These operations, which determine the build delay and the unit price, can only then happen gradually with the constitution of a new documentation, instead of being done following a rational plan.

NEW ORGANISATION

Outside the above considerations, the new organisation has been established taking into account the diversity of the Engineers charged with the creation of new machines, and their personal methods. As a consequence, as in the past, the design draughtsmen will receive their technical instructions directly from the Design Engineers, within the framework of the orders received from management by the Head of the Design Office and Technical Documentation.

The Engineer, head of this service, works directly for the management of the factory. He is charged with giving the Design Engineers the material means that he has available (and to develop these means) but he is the assistant to none of them, and he must spread his personnel according to the degrees of urgency given by management. All the personnel of this office, outside of the Design Engineers, are under his orders. He will propose himself appointments, bonuses, salaries, holidays etc. ... and is responsible only to the Management for the measures that he believes he must take to insure the best running of his service.

The Chief Design Office Engineer is supported in these different tasks by three Heads of Group, each group reporting in a general manner to the three principle missions of the office:

- Designs – Production – Documentation

The group "Designs" is charged with the carrying out of pre-projects, the design drawings and the updating of the prototype drawings, after the work carried out in the workshops and eventually the updating at the aerodrome. The Head of Group will be in constant liaison with the workshops, to participate as much as possible in the completing of the study machines, and to organise the progress of the design drawings in the order of the workshop's needs.

The group "Production" is charged particularly with the constitution, as the prototype build progresses, of the documentation allowing the reproduction of the machine and in establishing this documentation, conform, on one side with official regulations and current technical conditions, and on the other side with the build methods particular to the company. The Head of Group will bring eventually, *with the agreement of the Design Engineers,* the modification necessary to take into account the existing tooling, the ease of machining and supply, in a word, to improve the unit price. He will establish the technical notices and the documentations concerning the interchangeability of spare parts. He follows and determines as necessary, the modifications to be carried out on the machines, either during their build, or during their utilisation.

The Head of Group "Documentation" is charged with the following services:

- Establishment of transparencies - Establishment of the bills of materials
- Producing blueprints or miscellaneous prints
- Despatching designs or documents to internal or external services
- Archives

The personnel of the Design Office and Technical Documentation is totally spread within the three groups indicated, but each Head of Group is responsible for the correct running and the discipline, even for the personnel who are not directly placed under his orders. Further, following the necessities of the work, the Head of Office can move, without this move being a promotion or demotion, the personnel from one group to another. Each Head of Group will daily submit to Head of Office his appreciation concerning the personnel for whom he will be accountable in the distribution of production bonuses and eventually in propositions of increases of salary.

Messrs Bouly, Paulin and Ferrand, are named respectively, Head of Group "Production", "Design" and "Documentation"

Without going into detail of all the operations to be carried out by the Heads of Group of the design office, we give here a few indications in order to be precise about, on one hand the relationship between themselves, and on the other hand their relations with the Design Engineers and with the Heads of the other services of the factory.

When a design study means that the intervention of the design office must take place, Management will pass a note to the Head of Design Office, specifying if this study should, or should not, give rise to:

- the establishing of a complete set of study drawings

- the establishing of a production documentation, and eventually, to which point the documentation should be progressed. Even if it only concerns a pre-study which will not give rise to the establishing of a project, this pre-study must be handed over to the group "Documentation" who must always keep an up to date "General Study Repertory".

This Repertory will be made up of an album composed of the transparencies (or their prints) giving, for complete machines, the three-view plans, and for special designs either the diagrams, or the assembled drawings and a general history. This Repertory is in the process of being revised for the principle past designs.

If the study gives rise to the establishing of a complete project (type CEDANA), the Head of Group "Designs", places at the disposition of the Design Engineer, the personnel he has available for establishing the general drawings, calculations, and diagrams constituting the dossier. He will personally follow this work. The pre-project dossier, as it is definitively established, must be handed over to the service "Documentation" who must then include all additions or modifications, in such a manner that one can always follow the trace of the evolution of a project.

When the design gives rise to establishing of drawings for the making of test elements, the same process will be followed by the Head of Group "Designs". He must ensure that a qualified draughtsman, whoever the Design Engineer should be, follows though the tests of the construction elements and eventually the static tests. This draughtsman must make a detailed report of each test with supporting diagrams. This report must be established on transparencies in a standard format, and must be handed over to the service "Documentation" who will make an album of all of these reports. This album will be available to all the Engineer Designers who can eventually request a copy of the sheets which interest them. When this study gives rise to the establishing of a set of drawings for the building of a prototype in the workshops, the Head of Group "Designs" will proceed in the same manner as above for the allocation of personnel. In all cases, the Engineer Designer will give his instructions directly to the design draughtsman; he will be, according to needs, helped by one or several detailing draughtsmen. The Head of Group follows the progress of the design drawings and, being in liaison with the workshops, will give priority to the documents corresponding to the progress of the build, his principal mission consisting of establishing a set of prototype drawings, and to give priority of the build in the workshops according to order of urgency. The study drawings, at the time of their first despatch to the workshops, carry only therefore, the strict minimum necessary for the manufacture. The service "Documentation" in order to conserve the complete history, must always keep a copy of this first set of drawings. As the manufacture of the detailed pieces is verified on assembly, the Head of Group "Designs" must carry out an update of the corresponding design drawings, and from them make the "prototype set". This, which will therefore conform to the machine built in the workshops, will be the one which will be presented by the Head of Workshop to the control of the Service Technique, at the same time as the assemblies to be controlled. It will carry a bill of materials of the parts with designation of the material necessary for each part. It will carry a maximum number of references for part numbers, and in all cases for the assemblies of parts ordered generally for spares.

In this manner, the Group "Documentation" will be able to establish, as early as the constitution of the prototype, the bill of materials of the parts and the bill of materials of supply. These bills of materials must be complete when the machine leaves for the airfield. In order for this documentation to be complete, as a large number of parts are not drawn, the Head of Workshop must inform the group "Documentation" every day of the list of parts or items which he will supply or manufacture, without drawing. In this manner, we will be able to see later, for the manufacture of the production drawings, if certain parts which were not drawn for the prototype, will have to be drawn for production.

As the build of the prototype progresses, the Head of Group "Designs", at the same time as a verification of the set of drawings, will ensure the noting of the estimates of weight.

In order to ensure that the update of the prototype set of drawings continues in a precise manner during the tests at the airfield, the management at the airfield must make a detailed report of all modifications made either at Buc, or at Villacoublay, even if it is only details.

Even if the establishing of production documentation is not decided during the manufacture of a prototype, the Head of Group "Production" must follow the manufacture of the prototypes. He must ensure, for the delivery of the prototype by the factory, the establishing of a temporary technical notice, and take into account all the elements which will later be necessary for him to establish a complete documentation.

If the design within the company gives rise to the establishing of production documentation, the Head of Group "Production" must start straight from the beginning of the manufacture of the prototype, to establish his documentation. To this end, as soon as each drawing of assembly or detail has been verified for manufacture or installation, he must re-work it to ensure conformity with current regulations, and with the best economic conditions for manufacture. To this effect he will maintain liaison with the Head of Central Services, and eventually with the Heads of Workshops. When there is production manufacturing, he will ensure the carrying out of necessary additions to documentation and eventually the modifications to the existing documents.

During the time that the study drawings are being made, prototype sets, production sets, the Head of Group "Documentation" ensures the availability of all of the prints necessary, and their despatch. He will file all the original documents, and establish a repertory which allows them to be found in the right place. Outside the establishment of the bills of materials and the inscription of the references of the parts, drawings etc. ... he assures the establishing of modification sheets for the Service Technique, and eventually for the sub-contractors. He is charged also with the filing of all of the archives of the company.

As a consequence:

1 - All design drawings before printing and being sent to the workshops, must carry the signature of the Head of Group "Designs" and of the Engineer Designer of the type in question. When the Head of Group "Documentation" receives for printing and despatch, a drawing which does not carry these two signatures, he must inform the Head of Office.

2 - All drawings for the production set must also carry, before printing and despatch, the signature of the Head of Group "Production" and the Engineer Designer. The same remark as above for the study drawings.

All claims or requests of the internal services from the factory addressed to the Design Office, must pass via the Head of Office or the Heads of Group, but never to the draughtsman (except special orders).

Index

Table of Aircraft

INDEX OF AIRCRAFT DESIGNED AND BUILT BY BLERIOT AERONAUTIQUE AND COVERED IN THIS BOOK

From 1922 onwards, Blériot and SPAD machines were designated by a numbering system explained in the corresponding chapters, without any chronological order.

ABBREVIATIONS :
Engines : AN = Anzani AT = Antoinette B = Blackburne BL = Blériot FA = Farman G = Gnome GR = Gnome & Rhône
HS = Hispano-Suiza Lo = Lorraine LR = Le Rhône Pa = Panhard RE = Renault RR = Rolls Royce Sal = Salmson
Wings : M = Monoplane 2M = Double monoplane B = Biplane S = Sesquiplane T = Triplane

Blériot

Type	Engine	Horse power per engine	Wing	Year	Quantity built	Comments	Page
I	1 BL	100	M	1900	1	Ornithopter	18
II	glider		S	1905	1	Glider on floats, with Voisin	19
III	1 AT	25	B	1906	1	Seaplane with Voisin	20
IV	2 AT	25	B	1906	1	Seaplane with Voisin	21
IV bis	2 AT	25	B	1906	1	N° IV fitted with wheels	22
V	1 AT	25	M	1907	1	Canard	23
VI, VI bis	1 AT	25	2 M	1907	1	Libellule	25
VII	1 AT	50	M	1907	1	Low wing, then shoulder wing, first triangulated undercarriage	27
VIII, VIII bis and VIII ter	1 AT	50	M	1908	1	Fuselage fully covered	29
IX	1 AT	50	M	1908	1	Triangular fuselage	33,35
X	1 AT	50	B	1908	1	Pusher propeller	33,35
XI	various			1909/1913	900	Sixteen different models, including the XIbis, the XI-2, the XI-2bis and the XI-3	33, 40 to 57, 73 to 89, 103 to 110
XI bis	1 AN	various	M	1910			81
XI-2	1 G	80-100	M	1911/1913		Tandem two-seat Land and Seaplane	84-86
XI-2 bis	1 G	50-70	M	1910		Side-by-side two-seater	85
XI-3	1 G	100	M	1911		Military Tandem three-seater	87
XI BG	various engines	60-100	M	1914	100	XI Parasol, called Blériot-Gouin.	90, 110
XII	various 1 ENV 1 AN 1 G Omega	35-60 60 40 50	M M M M	1909 1909 1909 1910	1 2 1 1	Pilot seated under wing. White Eagle. Flying Dutchman	39, 41, 42 68 58-61 68
XIII	1 G Omega	100	M	1910	1	Four-seat Aérobus	91
XIV	1 G Omega	50	M	1910	2	Side-by-side two-seater	92
XV	1 G double Omega	100	M	1910	0	Face-to-face two-seater	92
XX	1 G Omega	50	M	1911	1	Two-seater with semi-flexible wing	93
XXI	1 G Gamma	70	M	1911	12	Side-by-side two-seater	93
XXI Hydro	1 G Lambda	80	M	1913	2	Floatplane	94
XXII	1 G Lambda	80	M	1911	1	Side-by-side two-seater	94
XXIII	1 G double Omega	100	M	1911	3	Racing machine	94
XXIV	1 G	100-140	M	1911/1912	1	Five-seat Limousine	94
XXV	1 G Omega	50	M	1911	1	Canard for the Navy	95

Type	Engine	Horse power per engine	Wing	Year	Quantity built	Comments	Page
XXVI	1 G		T	1911	1	Canard Triplane	96
XXVII	1 G	50- 70	M	1911	2	Single-seat racer	96
XXVIII	1 AN 3 A 2	30	M	1911	1	XI Populaire	97
XXVIII	1 G Gamma	70	M	1913	0	Two-seat version of XI Populaire	97
XXIX	1 G Gamma	70	M	1912	0	Military special	97
XXIX bis	1 G Gamma	70	M	1912	0	Variant of XXIX	97
XXX	1 AN	80	M	1912	0	Four-seater	97
XXXII	1		M	1912	0	Automatic stabilisation of controls	97
XXXIII	1 G	70-80	M	1912	1	Canard Bleu, side-by-side two-seater.	98
XXXVI	1 G Lambda	80	M	1912	1	*La Torpille*, Armoured side-by-side Two-seater	98
XXXVI bis	1 G Lambda	80	M	1912	1	XXXVI with standard undercarriage	99
XXXVII	1 G	80- 100	M	1913	1	Rear engined side-by-side two-seater	99
XXXIX	1 G Lambda	80	M	1913	1	Armour plated with shell fuselage	99
XXXIX bis (?)	1 G double Lambda	160	M	1914	2	Armoured monoplane, one called La Vache,.	100, 109
XL	1 G Lambda	80	B	1913	1	Designed by SIT in Italy	100
XLII	1 G Lambda	80	M	1913	1	Two-seat observation Canard	101
XLIII	1 G Lambda	80	M	1913	1	Armoured monocoque for observation	102
XLIV	1 G Lambda	80	M	1913	1	Single-seat observation	102
XLV	1 AN	60	M	1914	1	Single-seat observation, mid-engine	102
XLVI	1 G Lambda	80	M	1914	0	Single-seater	102
LIII	2 LR	80	B	1915	1	Twin-engined bomber	111
LX (?)	4 AN 10 A4	100	B	1916	1	Four-engined bomber	111
LXV	1 AN	200	T	1915	0	Bomber project	112
LXVII	4 G 9 B2	100	B	1916	1	Bomber	112
LXXI	4 HS 8 Bc	200	B	1916	1	Long range bomber	114
LXXI H	4 HS 8 Bc	220	B	1916	0	Small seaplane project	114
73	4 HS 8 Fb	300	B	1918	1	Three-man night bomber	115
74	4 HS 8 Fb	300	B	1919	1	26 passenger Mammouth	127
75	4 HS 8 Fb	300	B	1920	1	Aérobus variant of 74	127
76	4 HS 8 Fb	300	B	1920	0	Bomber with swept back wings	128
77	4 HS 8 Fb	300	M	1920	0	Twin-fuselage bomber	128
100	5 HS 8 Fb	300	M	1922	0	Transport amphibian	129
101	2 HS 8 Ab	180	M	1923	1	Fighter amphibian	129
102	1 B 6	18	M	1922	2	Avionette, ex ANEC 1	129
103	4 HS 8 Fb	300	B	1923	0	Enlarged military Bl 115	135
105	4 HS 8 Fb	300	B	1924	1	Experimental transport, ambulance with Re engine	130
106	1 RE 12 Jb	450-480	M	1922	1	Transport ambulance	130
107 M	2 Lo 12 Da	370	M	1922	1	Multi-crew combat	143
108	1 Lo 12 Da	370	M	1922	0	Three-seat maritime observation.	130
110	1 HS 12	600-500	M	1930	1	Joseph Le Brix, record machine	155
111-1	1 HS 6 Mbr	250	M	1929	1	Four-seat transport	151
111-2	1 Lo 7 Me	230	M	1929	1	Modified 111-1	152
111-3	1 GR 9 Ady	420	M	1930	1	More powerful version of 111-2	152
111-4	1 HS 12 Jb	400	M	1930	1	111-1 with retractable undercarriage	152
111-5	1 HS or GR	500- 670	M	1932	1	Sagittaire	153
111-6	1 GR 14 Kdrs	725	M	1934	1	111-5 with biconvex wing profile	153
113	4 RE 8 Fg	230	B	1925	0	155 for night bombing	136
115 and 115 bis	4 HS 8 Ac /b	180	B	1923/1924	6	Eight-passenger transport, one ex-135	131-135
117M	2 Lo 12 Db	400	M	1924	1	Combat multi-crew derived from the 107	143
118	2 HS 8 Ab	180	M	1925	1	Two-seat marine aircraft	129
123	2 GR 9 Ac	420	B	1926	0	Night bomber version of 165	137
125-0	2 HS 12 Hbr	500	M	1930	1	Twin-fuselage transport	137

Index: Table of Aircraft

Type	Engine	Horse power per engine	Wing	Year	Quantity built	Comments	Page
125-1	2 HS 12 Hbr	500	M	1930	0	Seaplane version of 125-0	137
127-1M	2 HS 12 Gb	500	M	1926	1	Combat multi-crew	143
127-2M	2 HS 12 Hb	550	M	1928	42	Combat multi-crew	144
127-3M	2 HS 12 Gb	500	M	1928	1	Combat multi-crew	147
127-4M	2 HS 12 Hb	550	M	1929	1	Ex 127-2 n° 22 with new undercarriage	146
127-5M	2 Lo 12 Hd	600	M	1929	0	Combat multi crew	147
128	2 GR 9 Ac	420	M	1929	0	127-2 on floats for Yugoslavia	147
133	4 Sal 9 Ab	230	B	1924	0	Bomber version of 135	135
135	4 Sal 9 Ab	230	B	1924	1	Ex 115 bis	134
137 M	2 HS or Sal	500	M	1930	2	Combat multi-crew	147
155	4 RE 8 Fg	230	B	1925	2	Seventeen passenger transport	135
165	2 GR 9 Ab	420	B	1926	2	Sixteen passenger transport	136
175	2 RE 12 Ja	450	B	1928	1	Ex 165	137
185	2 HS	500	M	1930	0	Flying test stand	147
195-1	4 HS 6 Mb	250	M	1927	0	Postal flying boat for North Atlantic derived from 127	149
195-2	2 HS 6 Mb	250	M	1929	1	Postal aircraft	149
195-3	4 HS 6 Mb	250	M	1929	1	Flying boat version of 195-2	150
195-4	4 GR 5 Ba	230	M	1930	1	Re-engined version of 195-3	150
195-5	4 HS 6 Mbr	250	M	1929	0	Four-engine commercial version	150
195-6	4 GR 5 Ba	230	M	1931	1	Ex 195-4 land version	150
227	2 GR 14 Kcs	725	M	1932	0	Night bomber	147
230	1 HS 12 Nb	650	M	1931	0	Night bomber version of 110	160
250	4 HS		M	1930	0	Twin-fuselage transport amphibian	142
250A	4 HS		M	1930	0	Transatlantic version of 250	142
260	1 HS 18 Sbr	1000	M	1931	0	Transport, derived from 110	160
270	4 HS 18 Sb	1000	M	1931	0	Aerial Cruiser	151
280	4 HS 12 Xbr	500	M	1932	0	Transport flying boat	170
290	1 SAL 9 Ab	230	S	1931	1	Three-seat touring amphibian	162
291	1 Lo 7 Me	240	S	1930	0	290 re-engined	162
292	1 GR 7 Kdrs	300	S	1930	0	291 re-engined	162
330	1 HS 18 Sl	1000	M	1931	0	Eighteen passenger transport, derived from 111	154
350	3 HS	1200-800	M	1933	0	Transatlantic transport	140
370	2 HS 18 R	1500	M	1934	0	Twin-fuselage bomber	140
390	4 HS 18 Sb	1000	M	1930	0	Postal flying boat	163
430	1 HS 12 Ybrs	860	M	1931	0	Long range bomber derived from 111	154
509	4 FA 9 Eb	220	M	1929	0	First pre-project of the 5190	163
2222	2 Lo 12 Ed	450	B	1926	0	Twin-fuselage transport amphibian	142
5190	4 HS 12 Nbr	650	M	1933	1	Transatlantic postal flying boat *Santos Dumont*	163
5193	4 HS 12 Nbr	650	M	1935	0	Mediterranean transport, derived from 5190	169
5194	4 HS 12 Nbr	650	M	1935	0	Troop transport, derived from 5190	169
BZ 1 and BZ 3	4 HS 12 Hbr	550	M	1929	0	Transport project, cabin transformable into "life boat" in the event of a forced landing on water.	142
BZ 2	4 HS 12 Nbr	650	M	1931	0	Second pre-project of the 5190	163
BZ 4	1 HS 12 Nbr	650	M	1929	0	Postal version of the 110	160
BZ 5	1 HS 12 Nbr	650	M	1929	0	Reconnaissance version of the 110	160
CITA 1 and 2	1 Sal 7 Ac or 9 Ac	95 or 120	M	1929/1930	0	Two-seat aircraft and float version	170
CITA 3 and 4	1 Sal 9 Ac	120	M	1930	0	Three-seater transport and float version	170
CITA 5	1 Sal 7 Aq-03	150	M	1930	0	Transport amphibian, derived from 290	170

ANEC

Type	Engine	Horse power per engine	Wing	Year	Quantity built	Comments	Page
ANEC I, II and IV	various engines	16-80	M / B	1922/1926	5	Single and two-seat tourer	172
ANEC III	1 RR	375	B	1922	3	Passenger or freight transport	173
Sky Sign Carrier	3 Siddley Puma	265	B	1924/1925	0	Four passenger folding-wing transport	173

SPAD

Type	Engine	Horse power per engine	Wing	Year	Quantity built	Comments	Page
SPAD A1	1 LR 9c	80	B	1915	1	Two-seat fighter	176
SPAD A2	1 LR 9j	120	B	1915	1	Two-seat fighter	177
SPAD A3	1 LR 9j	120	B	1915	1	Two-seat fighter	177
SPAD A4	1 LR 9c	80	B	1916	23	Two-seat fighter	177
SPAD A5	1 Re 12 Fa	220	B	1916	1	Three-seat fighter	177
SPAD B	1		B	1915	1	Two-seat fighter	178
SPAD C	See SPAD A5		B				
SPAD D	1 Pa	200	B	1915	1	Two-seat bomber	178
SPAD E	2 Re 12 Fa	220	B	1915	1	Three-seat bomber	178
SPAD F	1		B	1915	0	Two-seat fighter	178
SPAD G	1 Cl 9B	130	B	1915	1	Two-seat fighter	178
SPAD H or V	1 HS 8A	140	B	1915	1	Single-seat fighter	178
SPAD I and J	1 G		B	1915	0	Single-seat fighter	178
SPAD VII	1 HS 8	140-200	B	1916	3820	Single-seat fighter	179
SPAD VIII	1 HS 8Ac	180	B	1916	0	Artillery two-seater	180
SPAD IX	1 HS 8 Ca	200	B	1916	1	Single-seat fighter	180
SPAD X	1 HS 8 Ac	180	B	1916	1	Seaplane fighter, future XIV	180
SPAD XI	1 HS 8 Ac	220	B	1918	600	Observation two-seater	181
SPAD XII	1 HS 8 Bec	220	B	1917	300	Single-seat fighter	182
SPAD XIII	1 HS 8 B	200-220	B	1917	8472	Single-seat fighter	182
SPAD XIII bis	1 HS 8 F	300	B	1918	1	Single-seat fighter	184
SPAD XIV	1 HS 8 Bc	220	B	1917	39	Seaplane fighter	184
SPAD XV	1 G	160	B	1917	1	Single-seat fighter	184
SPAD XV-1 to XV-4	1 G	160	B	1917	1	Single-seat fighter	184
SPAD XV-5	1 LR	80	B	1919	2	Single-seat sport	184
SPAD XVI and XVI bis	1 Lo 8 B	240-275	B	1918	657	Observation two-seater	185
SPAD XVII	1 HS 8 F	300	B	1918	20	Single-seat fighter	185
SPAD XVIII	1 HS 8 F	300	B	1918	1	Armoured single-seat fighter	185
SPAD XIX	1 HS 8 F	300	B	1918	0	Two-seat fighter	186
SPAD XX C.1, C.2	1 HS 8 F	300	B	1918/1921	100	Two-seat fighter	186
SPAD XX bis	1 HS 8 Fb	300	B	1921	1	Two-seat fighter	187
SPAD 20 bis-1 to -4	1 HS 8 Fb	300	B	1919	4	Racing single-seater	187
SPAD 20 bis-5	1 HS 8 Fb	300	B	1919	2	Racing single-seater	187
SPAD 20 bis-6	1 HS 8 Fe	330	B	1919	1	Racing single-seater	187
SPAD XXI	1 HS 8 Fb	300	B	1919	2	Single-seat fighter	188
SPAD XXII	1 HS 8 Fb	300	B	1919	1	Single-seat fighter	188
SPAD XXIII	1 Sal RA 9	240	B	1918	0	Two-seat fighter	188
SPAD XXIV	1 HS 8 Bec	220	B	1918	1	Single-seat fighter	188
SPAD 25	1 LR 9c	80	B	1919	1	Long range single-seat record machine	189
SPAD 26 and 26 bis	1 HS 8 Fc	340	B	1919	1	Racing seaplane	189
SPAD 27	1 HS 8 Fa	275	B	1919	1	Transport Berline, derived from XX	190
SPAD 28 and 28 bis	1 HS 8 Fb	300	B	1919	2	Modified SPAD 20	191

Type	Engine	Horse power per engine	Wing	Year	Quantity built	Comments	Page
SPAD 29	1 LR 9c	80	B	1919	2	Two-seat trainer	191
SPAD 30 and 30 bis	1 AN, 1 LR	45-80	B	1920	1	Single-seat tourer	192
SPAD 31 and 31 bis	1 HS 8 Fb	300	B	1920	1	Racing then fighter seaplane	192
SPAD 33 and 33 bis	1 Sal	250-300	B	1920	40	Transport Berline	193
SPAD 34-1	1 LR 9c	80	B	1919	1	Two-seat trainer	195
SPAD 34-2	1 LR 9c	80	B	1919	150	Two-seat trainer	195
SPAD 34-3	1 LR 9c	80	B	1923	1	Mobile leading edge	195
SPAD 34 bis	1 Cl 9 B	130	B	1919	1	Modified SPAD 34	195
SPAD 35	1 HS 8 Ab	180	B	1920	0	Variant of SPAD XX	195
SPAD 36 P2	1 HS 8 Fbr	300	B	1923	1	Reconnaissance two-seater	196
SPAD 37	1 HS 8 Fg	275	B	1920	1	Three passenger transport	196
SPAD 38	1 LR 9c	80	B	1920	2	Navy fighter	196
SPAD 39	1 HS 8 Fg	275	B	1921	1	SPAD Marine	197
SPAD 40	1 Lo 12 Da	370	B	1922	1	Reconnaissance two-seater	197
SPAD 41 and 41 bis	1 HS 8 Fb	300	B	1922	1	Single-seat fighter	197
SPAD 42	1 HS 8 A	180	B	1923	19	Tandem two-seater	198
SPAD 43	1 Cl 9	130	B	1920	0	Variant of SPAD 34	198
SPAD 44	1 HS 8 Fb	300	B	1920	0	Variant of SPAD 20 bis-5	198
SPAD 45	4 HS 8 Fg	275	B	1923	1	Transport, became Blériot 105	199
SPAD 46	1 Lo 12 Da	370	B	1921	38	Derived from the SPAD 33	200
SPAD 47	1 Sal A Z9	250	B	1921	1	Variant of the SPAD 33 bis	194
SPAD 48	1 Lo 8 Bd	275	B	1921	1	Modified SPAD 33	194
SPAD 49	1 RR Eagle VII	350	B	1921	0	Variant of the SPAD 33	194
SPAD 50	1 HS 8 F	300	B	1921	5	Modified variant of the SPAD 33	194
SPAD 51	1 GR 9 Aa	380	B	1924	1	Single-seat fighter	201
SPAD 51-2	1 GR 9 Ab	420	B	1924	1	Single-seat fighter	201
SPAD 51-3	1 GR 9 Aa	380	B	1926	1	Single-seat fighter	201
SPAD 51-4	1 GR 9 c	600	B	1928	3	Single-seat fighter	201
SPAD 52	1 LR 9 Jb	120	B	1924	2	Derived from the SPAD 29	191
SPAD 53	1 Cl 9 Bc	110	B	1920	4	Derived from the SPAD 34	202
SPAD 54-1	1 LR	80	B	1922	26	Derived from the SPAD 53	202
SPAD 54-2 and SPAD 54-2 bis	1 AN then 1 LR	90 then 80	B	1924	9	Modified SPAD 54-1 and 54-2	202
SPAD 54-3 or 54 bis	1 Sal 9 Ac	120	B	1926	1	Banner towing	202
SPAD 54-5	1	80-120	B	1928	1	SPAD 54-5 "All engines"	202
SPAD 56	1 GR 9 Aa	380	B	1923	1	Transport Berline	203
SPAD 56-2	1 GR 9 Ab	420	B	1925	1	Transport Berline	203
SPAD 56-3	1 GR 9 Ab	420	B	1926	6	Transport Berline	203
SPAD 56-6	1 GR 9 Ab	420	B	1927	2	Banner towing	204
SPAD 58	1 Lo 12 Eb	450	B	1922	1	Single-seat racer	204
SPAD 60	1 GR 9 Ab	420	B	1926	3	Two-seat fighter	205
SPAD 61-1 and 61-2	1 Lo 12 Ew	450	B	1923	382	Single-seat fighter of which 381 production SPAD 61-2	205
SPAD 61 bis	1 Lo 12 Eb	450	B	1923	1	Modified SPAD 61-2	206
SPAD 61-3	1 Lo 12 Ew	450	B	1925	1	Single-seat fighter	206
SPAD 61-4	1 Lo 12 Ee	480	B	1925	1	Single-seat fighter	206
SPAD 61-5	1 HS 12 Gb	450	B	1925	3	Single-seat fighter	206
SPAD 61-6	1 Lo 12	450	B	1925	1	Single-seat racer	207
SPAD 61-7	1 Lo 12 Eb	480	B	1926	1	Single-seat record holder	207
SPAD 61-8	1 HS 12 Hb	500	B	1926	1	Modified SPAD 61-5	207
SPAD 61-9	1 Lo 17 Ma	230	B	1929	1	Modified SPAD 61-6	207
SPAD 61 ses	1 Lo 12 Ew	450	B	1926	1	Single-seat fighter	207
SPAD 62	1 HS 8 A	180	B	1923	1	Two-seat trainer	208
SPAD 64	1 LR 9	80	B	1923	1	Lightened SPAD 54	208

Type	Engine	Horse power per engine	Wing	Year	Quantity built	Comments	Page
SPAD 66	1 Lo 12 Da	370	B	1924	34	Modified SPAD 46	200
SPAD 70	1 Lo 12 Eb	450	B	1927	1	Two-seat fighter	208
SPAD 71	1 HS 8 Fb	300	B	1923	1	Derived from SPAD XX	208
SPAD 72	1 HS 8 A	80	B	1923	1	Two-seat trainer	209
SPAD 76	1		B	1923	0	Transport Berline	209
SPAD 81 and 81-1	1 HS 8 F	300	B	1923/1924	81	Single-seat fighter of which 80 SPAD 81-1	209
SPAD 81-2	1 HS 8 F	300	B	1924	1	Modified SPAD 81	210
SPAD 81-3	1 HS 8 F	300	B	1924	1	Modified SPAD 81-1	210
SPAD 81-4	1 HS 8 F	300	B	1924	1	Modified SPAD 81-1	210
SPAD 81 bis	1 HS 8 F	300	B	1923	1	High speed single-seat tourer	210
SPAD 82	1 HS 8 Ad	180	B	1926	1	Banner towing	210
SPAD 86	1 Lo 12 Ew	450	B	1925	1	Modified SPAD 46	200
SPAD 86 bis	1	?	M	1925	0	Transport Berline project	211
SPAD 91	1 HS 12 Hb	500	B	1927	4	Single-seat fighter	211
SPAD 91-1 and 91-2	1 HS 12 Hb	500	B	1927/1928	2	Single-seat fighter	211
SPAD 91-3	1 GR 9 As	420	B	1930	1	Modified SPAD 91-2	212
SPAD 91-4 and 91-7	1 HS 12 Ab	450	B	1930	1	Modified SPAD 91 and 91-6	212
SPAD 91-5	1 GR 9 Ae	420	B	1931	1	Modified SPAD 91-2	212
SPAD 91-6	1 HS 12 Hb	500	B	1930	1	Modified SPAD 91	212
SPAD 91-8	1 HS 12 Xbr	500	B	1931	1	Modified SPAD 91-7	212
SPAD 91-9	1 HS 12 Xcrs	500	B	1932	1	Modified 91-8	212
SPAD 92-0	1 HS 8 A	180	B	1928	15	Single-seat trainer	213
SPAD 92-1	1 Sal 9 Ne	175	B	1928	1	Single-seat aerobatic	213
SPAD 116	1 Re 12 Ja	450	B	1926	1	Modified SPAD 66	200
SPAD 126	1 HS 12 A	450	B	1929	1	Modified SPAD 46	200
SPAD 210	1	230	B	1929	0	Single-seat fighter	214
SPAD 251	1 GR Ab	420	B	1925	1	Variant of SPAD 51-4	201
SPAD 310	1	230	M	1929	0	Single-seat fighter	214
SPAD 510	1 HS 12 Xbrs	690	B	1933	80	Single-seat fighter	214
SPAD 510 J 2	1 GR 9 Kers	600	B	1934	0	Single-seat fighter	216
SPAD 510 J 3	1 GR 14 Drs	760	B	1934	0	Single-seat fighter	216
SPAD 511	1 Lo 12 Hars	600	B	1933	0	Single-seat fighter	216
SPAD 540	1 Sal 7 Ac	95	M	1930	1	Two-seat trainer	216
SPAD 541	1 Sal 9 Ac	135	M	1930	1	Modified SPAD 540	216
SPAD 542	1 Sal 7 Aq	135	M	1930	1	Modified SPAD 541	216
SPAD 610	1 HS 12 Xbrs	690	B	1935	0	Seaplane fighter	216
SPAD 710	1 HS 12 Ycrs	860	B	1937	1	Seaplane fighter	217
SPAD 922	1 HS 12 Hb	500	B	1927	8	SPAD 92 modified to two-seater	213
SPAD 922 V	1 HS 12 Hb	500	B	1927	1	SPAD 92 modified to butterfly tail	213
MARTINET	1 Régnier	200	M	1935	1	Caudron-Renault, modified for racing	217

Blériot-Blanchard

Type	Engine	Horse power per engine	Wing	Year	Quantity built	Comments	Page
HB 3	2 HS 8 Fd Marine	260	B	1922	26	Patrol seaplane	218-219
HB 3 quad	4 HS 8 A	180	B	1923	1	Four engine version of HB 3	218-219
HB 3 T 2	2 HS 8 Fd	300	B	1923	1	Commercial version of HB 3	218-219
HB C 1	1 GR Jupiter	380-550	B	1923	2	Fighter and racing seaplanes	219-220

Type	Engine	Horse power per engine	Wing	Year	Quantity built	Comments	Page
HB 3 T	2 HS 8 Fd Marine	260	B	1925	1	Transformation to traction engines of HB 3	220

Blériot-Guillemin

Type	Engine	Horse power per engine	Wing	Year	Quantity built	Comments	Page
JG 10	1 Re 4 Pb	95	M	1931	1	Two-seat tourer	221
JG 40	1 Sal or Lo	120	M	1930	2	Overseas medical	220
IG 41 and 42	1 Lo 5 Pc	120	M	1932	1	Overseas medical	221
JG 43	1 Sal 9 Nd	175	M	1936	5	Overseas medical	221

Alicia and Louis Blériot at Dover in 1929, at the 20th Anniversary of the Crossing of the Channel.